FLYING KIWIS

For the best OE 'souvenirs'

Liam, Eoin, Jack and Alice
Cara, Nadav, Eitan and Maya
Charlotte and Louisa
Anna and Iain

This is your history

FLYING KIWIS

A History of the OE

Jude Wilson

Otago University Press

Published by Otago University Press
PO Box 56 / Level 1, 398 Cumberland Street
Dunedin, New Zealand
F: 64 3 479 8385
E: university.press@otago.ac.nz
W: www.otago.ac.nz/press

First published 2014

Published with the assistance of the Ministry for Culture & Heritage

ISBN 978-1-877578-26-7
A catalogue record for this book is available from the National Library of New Zealand.

Publisher: Rachel Scott
Editor: Wendy Harrex
Design/layout: Fiona Moffat
Index: Diane Lowther

Front cover: Buzzy Bee representation is used under licence from Lion Rock Licensing Limited www.buzzybeetv.com

Printed in New Zealand by Wickliffe (NZ) Ltd, Dunedin

CONTENTS

PREFACE

IN 1979 I LEFT NEW ZEALAND to go overseas. I was 22 years old and, courtesy of a Scottish grandfather, had the right to live and work indefinitely in Britain. After working for six months in Australia, I flew to Britain. I spent three days in London – playing on what seemed like a giant Monopoly board – before hitchhiking to Scotland to meet my grandfather's family. They were also *my* family, of course, but it didn't take long to discover that we were worlds apart. My ancestors might have been Scottish, but I most certainly was not; I came from a very different culture.

Despite a geographical separation of 12,000 miles (we didn't think in kilometres then), I had expected some social and cultural similarities: we spoke the same language and I was even related to some of these people by blood. But they had such different ideas from mine. My new-found second cousins, who were my own age, could not believe that I had travelled alone, so far away from home. They asked how it was that my parents had 'let' me go; I wondered what it had to do with my parents. They assumed that my parents had paid for me to travel; I pondered the sheer absurdity of such an occurrence. They kept talking about my 'trip'; I was not on a mere trip, I had 'gone overseas'. I had no ticket home and very little money, but I did know two other New Zealanders in London.

What the cousins struggled most to understand was that I was doing something quite normal for people in my country: to go overseas for a few years, to work in London, to travel around and see the famous sights of Europe, was a perfectly reasonable thing to do. The few comments people made when I left New Zealand were rather banal: my mother reminded me to eat my vegetables; my father recommended some London pubs and told me which places he had liked when he travelled in Europe the previous year. Most of my friends were simply jealous; many were saving money to go themselves. My only motivation for leaving was to 'see the world': by doing this in the company of other New Zealanders, and in a particularly New Zealand way, I was just one among many thousands of my generation doing what, a few years after my departure, became popularly known as 'overseas experience' or 'the OE'.

I returned to New Zealand to live in 2000, after two decades away. My homeland had changed in that time and so had I.

Although I had been home for many holidays, I had never had to engage with life here as an adult. Coming home was challenging – I was a forty-something who didn't know how eftpos worked, had few friends, had never owned a car, had no dentist or doctor; even my medical records (apparently) belonged to the British government. I had no idea who anyone in the gossip magazines, the news or New Zealand society was. I found it strange to have to pay for the doctor and for bank fees. These issues are common for migrants to a new country, of course, but I was 'home'.

I decided that a return to study would be a good way to ease myself back into New Zealand life; several years later, I found myself searching for a suitable thesis topic. Social science methodology books suggested the best place to start research was from 'where one already was'. The OE was a perfect topic. I had spent most of my adult life overseas on an OE. When I returned home, there happened to be a surge of media and cultural interest in the OE. With the notable exception of the academic community, everyone was on the bandwagon.

The OE was then alternately lauded and maligned. In its favour, it gave young New Zealanders valuable work, travel and life experience, which – so long as they returned – benefited our society. It was a 'rite of passage' that became our cultural 'right' when its very existence was threatened by tightening immigration rules in Britain. Less positively, this continual (and continuing)

The author a long way from home, 1982.

exodus of educated New Zealanders was held responsible for a significant 'brain drain'. Detractors bemoaned the less than savoury OE practices (of New Zealanders 'misbehaving' overseas) regularly reported in local media. Those who had been on OE in earlier decades questioned the motives of the new generation of OE travellers, for whom going away to improve one's career or to make money was not in the true spirit of the OE.

I already knew a lot about the OE as I had lived it for 20 years. During those years I worked with many New Zealanders in London and had a window into their OEs.

The experience of each new cohort changed in response to new opportunities (and the disappearance of others), but some aspects appeared timeless. In New Zealand, these qualities were manifest in a commonly reiterated, but very stereotypical, description of a classic OE. By examining in my thesis the OE experience, and the ways it changed over time, I set out to test the accuracy of this stereotype.

The stereotype of the classic OE is a condensed version of thousands and is – in many ways – as much a part of the OE as are the myriad individual experiences from which an OE history is garnered. The core feature – that despite being an 'overseas' experience, it is all about being a New Zealander – lies at its heart. Using the stereotype also enables us to manage the magnitude and mess of the OE: more than six decades, many thousands of people, years of individual experiences, all over the world; we know it is a stereotype, but we don't care.

As befits the topic, the material for this book has been collected over a number of years, from many sources and locations. It draws primarily on the recorded oral accounts of several hundred travellers, representing all decades of the OE. I never defined the OE when searching for these story-tellers – if they thought what they had done was an OE, it was. Most talked as much *about* the OE – reflecting, in particular, on what it was – as they did about their own experiences. The significance of their OE in these people's lives was irrefutable and most recalled a phenomenal amount of detail.

Many of these travellers – particularly those from the earlier decades – brought out their treasured travel diaries, along with letters and postcards sent home, to check details. They had pictorial evidence in photographs as well as other memorabilia in the form of tickets, brochures and souvenirs. As the illustrations throughout this book attest, photographic images of an OE (whether recorded on Super 8, or in slide, film or digital media) almost always reflect something of the era in which it occurred: people's hair and clothing styles, their accessories (such as spectacles and luggage) or something in the background (types of cars or other forms of transport, building styles, shop fronts, tourist sites and so on) provide clues and date-stamp any single OE. The repetition of subject matter throughout the decades illustrates the enduring nature of some aspects of the OE.

These personal accounts are supported by published travel memoirs and other literature, travel guidebooks, and by the ephemera of popular culture that illustrates (and underpinned) the travel and social mores experienced by different generations and population cohorts. While this history of the OE comes from the life stories of those who went, and also seeks to tell the story of the phenomenon that is the OE, it does not discuss in detail the social, economic and political contexts of the OE in New Zealand and Britain. Others more qualified than I may do that. As the reader will see, in many ways during the last six decades British society has simply provided a stage backdrop for the OE story.

As a social phenomenon the OE is rather unusual as it happens in a place that is not the society to which it belongs. The home of the travellers might be New Zealand, but the home of the OE has been, undoubtedly, London (it may be changing now). It is there that much of the material evidence of the OE can be found. In London during the 2000s I interviewed people involved, both voluntarily and professionally, with the OE population there, searched the archives of expatriate newspapers and magazines, and attended OE events (as a researcher, rather than the traveller I had once been). In New Zealand, the internet proved invaluable for my research, as both a repository of current OE material, and as a tool to follow myriad 'leads' to OE material and people. While the internet is an integral part of the twenty-first century OE in its own right, as an historical record it is somewhat ephemeral.

The characters of an OE history are the people who went; the plot is what they did. To use the analogy of film or theatre, the OE has, over the years, had a cast and crew of thousands and obviously there are many thousands of individual stories I have not heard. By necessity, those I was privy to have been amalgamated in order to tell this story. The most I can hope for is that any reader who has done an OE will recognise some part of their experience in this book – perhaps in something they did, wanted to do or someone else they know did. If there is something vital to the OE story that I have missed, I apologise. And of course, any factual errors are mine.

JUDE WILSON
Lincoln, September 2013

ACKNOWLEDGEMENTS

THANK YOU to the Ministry for Culture and Heritage for giving me a History Award and to Lincoln University for logistical support. I am indebted to Stefanie Rixecker for 'creating' my position as Writer in Residence, and to both Tracy Berno and Mike Mackay for their constructive criticism and support over numerous cups of coffee. Special thanks to David Hollander for scanning images for this book. Special thanks also to Otago University Press for their editorial and design skill in producing a book that is better than I ever imagined.

The OE trail led me down some convoluted paths, and on more than one occasion I found myself unexpectedly back where I had started. I have been overwhelmed by the magnanimity with which complete strangers responded to my (seemingly) endless questions and requests for images; I would love to meet you all one day and thank you in person. Altogether, an extraordinary number of people have contributed to this book; while space precludes acknowledging contributions personally, please be assured that I have not forgotten any of you.

Every effort was made to find the appropriate copyright holder for images: acknowledgment of copyright permission and, where appropriate, the source of images is provided in the text. Thanks to all those businesses who gave me permission to use their advertising material. Special thanks to Chris Slane and Jonathan Drapes for the use of their cartoons: they not only made telling the story easier, but are a vital part of it.

Thank you to all those people who donated their photographs and mementos: to preserve your anonymity and dignity, your images are not credited individually in the text. Some images and materials are my own: the rest came from Beverley Barnes, Reina Booth, John and Jenny Bradshaw, Douglas Broughton, Polly Burrowes, Gillian Buttle, Graeme Campbell, Esther Cardwell, Ron Chambers, Ian Collins, Judi and Leigh Hancock, Julia Mackay, Mike Mackay, Jocelyn Papprill, John Pickering, Tracey Shields, Ian and Gill Sutherland, Nicky Taylor, Geoff Wilson, Liz Wright and Liz Young.

Finally, and most important, I thank all the OE travellers whose stories I have purloined – for your time, and for sharing your experiences so candidly. I have changed most of your names, but you should be able to find yourself in this book.

PART I
FOUNDATIONS

Chapter One
THE OVERSEAS EXPERIENCE

FLYING KIWIS is divided into parts that loosely follow the chronological order of an OE experience (leaving home, being on OE, returning home) and the ways the experience has changed over time. The OE has its 'Foundations' (Part 1) in our colonial past, and began as a travel experience undertaken by relatively few in the middle decades of the twentieth century. By the millennium, the OE was both named and popularised as 'The Big OE' (Part 2), and had become a travel experience undertaken by thousands. This change has both contributed to – and is evidenced by – the OE's status as 'A Cultural Icon' (Part 3) in New Zealand.

Over the last six decades, from the 1950s into the 2000s, many thousands of young New Zealanders have departed on their 'OE', or overseas experience. While the term 'OE' is now attached to myriad forms of travel experience – short trips overseas, rugby sabbaticals and even bird migrations – it was originally coined to describe extended working holidays, usually in Europe. The term is unique to New Zealand; as Bronwyn Sell wrote in her guide to the OE, 'There is probably no country in which the letters O and E resonate as strongly as they do in New Zealand.'[1] In its purest form, it is elevated to become the 'Big OE': while 'big' alludes to size (the period of time one is away from home, the breadth of the experience, the distance travelled) it also signifies the OE's importance back home.

This significance is visible in popular culture and 'OE' has become part of everyday language. Departure on an OE has long been both socially and culturally acceptable, and is openly promoted as a worthy undertaking; returning to New Zealand, one is accorded merit for having completed an OE. It is seen as a kind of cultural 'rite of passage' that allows young people temporary escape from the geographical isolation and small society of their home country, and an opportunity to test themselves in the wider world.

Defining the OE

Despite wide acceptance of the term 'OE', it has no clear and absolute definition. Dictionaries of New Zealand English and compendiums of slang explain the acronym, but impart limited detail on what overseas experience might involve. Examples include: 'the period spent abroad by many young New Zealanders after completing their formal education'; 'the fledgling Kiwi's mandatory trip to Europe'; and 'Overseas

The OE 'rite of passage'.
Chris Slane

Experience which young Kiwis get, often on a working holiday'. The online encyclopaedia Wikipedia defines OE as 'a New Zealand term for extended working holidays', with London the 'default' OE destination.

The OE existed before it was named; those who set off from New Zealand in the 1950s, 1960s and 1970s now recognise what they did as an OE. Back then, it was described as 'going Home', as a 'working holiday', or as the more generic 'overseas trip'. Some simply 'went overseas'. The first use of the term 'OE' is attributed to Tom Scott in the mid-1970s, but exactly when the OE as a name was universally adopted is difficult to establish.[2] It was common by the early 1980s: it was used in an article on working holidays published in the *Christchurch Star* in 1983, and between 1982 and 1984 Chris Slane's OE cartoons were published in London in *New Zealand News UK*.

Most people would agree that the typical OE is a two- to three-year working holiday, during which young New Zealanders usually live and work in London and travel extensively in Europe. Add work in a pub, life in a shared flat in Earls Court with 15 other Kiwis, a VW van tour around Europe, plus trips to Oktoberfest and to the Running of the Bulls at Pamplona, and you get a commonly employed, but rather stereotypical and dated (circa 1980s) description of what constitutes the OE. At its heart, this description contains two key elements: first, that while work is involved it is not the primary focus, and second, that the OE experience has come to be underpinned by its own traditions. These traditions include where, and with whom, one might live while away from New Zealand, and where and how one might travel.

OE guide for New Zealanders, London guide for Australians.
1st Contact Group

The OE stereotype condenses what would be a long and complicated story into something easily and quickly understood by others. Many people use it as a measure of their own experiences: they may have done an OE, but 'not a very good one', they may describe their experiences as being 'pretty stereotypical really', or as 'not stereotypical', and so on. Further, the accuracy of the OE stereotype does not really matter, as most people recognise it for what it is. In many ways, the stereotype itself is a part of the OE; talking to people who have been on an OE generates a curious mix of fact and fiction, as they intertwine what they 'actually' did with what they 'should', or 'could', have done.

From a cultural perspective, it is significant that this particular travel experience has a name; young Australians, who do the same thing, have no name for it. The term OE is more than just an acronym: it has been elevated to 'word' status in New Zealand speech. Linguistically, to name something both validates its existence and signifies its importance, most strikingly demonstrated by the fact that it is possible to describe an 'OE (overseas experience) experience'.

In many ways, acronyms perform similar functions to stereotypes; they are useful, both as a means of compacting time and effort, and as a form of jargon through which a sense of community among insiders (and often distance from outsiders) is created. The acronym converts a transient combination of words – overseas experience – into something more permanent. A kind of verbal monument is created around the idea of the OE. The term becomes instantly recognisable as shorthand for a specific type of travel experience, one that can be practised only by New Zealanders, its form, purpose and value dictated by our own particular set of geographical and cultural circumstances.

Above all else, the OE is a travel experience driven by curiosity about the world outside New Zealand, a world which, as a result of our colonial history, traditionally centred on London and Europe. In its early years, the distance and the cost of travel necessitated staying away for several years. This, in turn, necessitated working while overseas. The OE was not economic migration, as work was undertaken to support oneself and to pay for travel, rather than to earn money to send home, further one's career, or secure substantial financial gain (although this sometimes happened serendipitously).

In my research, I often found it easier to list criteria that do *not* make an OE. 'Overseas', for example, is not just anywhere outside New Zealand: the general consensus is that Australia is not far enough away (in physical or cultural terms). Going overseas specifically to study, or in search of international recognition in the arts, is not normally considered an OE. Essentially, the underlying motives driving the OE are both more vague and more all-encompassing than those of the many other waves of in-

and out-bound population migrations – of explorers, adventurers, colonists, students, soldiers, artists, expatriate workers, families and tourists – which have characterised New Zealand history. Two key factors differentiate the OE from many other types of migration: the first is its *ordinariness* (these travellers simply go because they can), and the second is that these young people always leave with the intention of *returning home* to New Zealand. One day.

The flying Kiwi

Geographical remoteness is often posited as a key driver of the New Zealander's need to travel. Our country *is* remote from most of the world's major land masses. To fly to our nearest neighbour, Australia, takes about three and a half hours; in the same time, one can fly from London to Athens or Helsinki; in fact, most European capital cities can be reached from London well within this flight time. Consider how much more remote New Zealand must have seemed when travel took weeks or months, rather than hours and days. As John Mulgan wrote in 1947:

New Zealanders, a young people but already with a place in history, are often wanderers and restless and unhappy men. They come from the most beautiful country in the world, but it is a small country and very remote. After a while this isolation oppresses them and they go abroad. They roam the world looking not for adventure but for satisfaction … Those that do not go abroad and do not travel are afflicted with the same sad restlessness. They are all the time wanting to set out across the wide seas that surround them in order to find the rest of the world.[3]

The national identity of New Zealanders is closely linked to travel, in part because of this geographical remoteness, but also as a result of our cultural history as both a Polynesian and a colonised nation. New Zealand has been populated by people with a history of mobility. There is a popular perception that we are among the most travelled people in the world. Some evidence for this exists: in 2006, New Zealanders recorded one overseas trip per 2.2 head of population, compared to one in 4.2 for Australians, one in 7.3 in Japan and one in 7.6 in the United States.[4]

In 1961, C.K. Stead wrote that isolation from experience was not just a matter of geographical isolation, but a combination of 'remoteness and insignificance' that New Zealand's writers felt.[5] Geographical isolation and departure have been recurring themes in local literature and poetry. Lines such as these penned by Charles Brasch in 1948 in 'The Islands' appear frequently:

Remindingly beside the quays the white
Ships lie smoking; and from their haunted bay
The godwits vanish towards another summer.
Everywhere in light and calm the murmuring
Shadow of departure; distance looks our way;
And none knows where he will lie down at
night.[6]

The 'problem' of the flightless kiwi.

Copyright New Zealand Post Ltd, 1997 & 2008. Reproduced courtesy New Zealand Post Ltd

Numerous accounts in early travel literature liken the flight of human 'Kiwis' to bird migrations. Brasch's godwit analogy is often employed to describe our migration overseas: Margaret Clark used it as the title for her anthology of returning New Zealanders, *Godwits Return* (1992);[7] the first chapter in Susan Graham's 1963 travel guide/memoir *The Tender Traveller: A New Zealander abroad* was entitled 'Not Kiwis but Godwits' and began:

We New Zealanders are compulsive travellers. We love our islands but we have to leave them. The flightless kiwi, rooted like a timid stick-in-the-mud to his forest floor, seems an inappropriate emblem for such a migratory people. Surely we are more like the godwits, in whom the seasonal call of the sea and the air throbs like a recurrent pulse. To us, as to the migratory birds, the call of an ancient homeland, far way across vast oceans of time and distance, proves irresistible to each in his generation.[8]

Flying with the help of a Buzzy Bee.

North & South magazine

A recent newspaper article interestingly described bird migration in human terms, reporting that 'adolescent gannets are rarely seen in New Zealand because they typically embark on their own two-year big OE to Australia before returning home for the rest of their twenty-year lifespan'.[9]

The mobile 'flightless' kiwi appeared on a 1997 postage stamp, with a kiwi flying off on the back of another local icon, the Buzzy Bee. The stamp was part of a series entitled 'Cartoonists', offering interpretations of the theme 'Kiwis taking on the world'.[10] The OE also featured as the 'O' entry in a 2008 stamp series offering 'a "T is for Tiki" tour through a veritable A to Z of New Zealand culture, history, heritage and downright Kiwiana'.

In New Zealand, the term OE is both commonplace and ubiquitous, appearing regularly in the media and across an array of cultural forms. It is used in advertising and has been the topic of magazine features, novels and plays; it also appears in poetry and song lyrics. The OE sits comfortably alongside other Kiwiana icons, such as the Buzzy Bee, the kiwi (bird), the koru, the silver fern, the All Blacks, the haka, the bach, L&P and barbecues. Many of these cultural symbols are referenced by New Zealanders when they travel, often with elevated importance as they seek a tangible connection with home. A clever appropriation of the 'flying' Kiwi was a monthly comedy show held in London in the 2000s, entitled *Four Kiwis Walk into a Bar*.

The frequent use of the OE in advertising reinforces just how accepted it is. In a practical sense, having an easily recognisable stereotype and a 'name' is crucial. Reports about young Australians on their OE equivalents refer rather laboriously to 'young Australians on their year away' – terminology difficult to translate into advertising idiom. Perhaps understandably, banks, along with credit card and telecommunications companies, are inordinately fond of the OE in their advertising campaigns. The financial implications of the annual departure of thousands of young people from these shores is not lost on that other great financial institution, the Inland Revenue Department, and the OE's incorporation into tax policy is clear evidence of its institutionalisation in New Zealand society.

Often, advertisements featuring the OE reinforce London as a primary destination. The city is routinely portrayed as cold, wet and challenging; in comparison, New Zealand is a warm, sunny and easy place. For example, the supporting imagery in a Vogel's bread 'Homesick Kiwi' advertisement illustrated some of the difficulties of London life – small cramped flats, dealing with British immigration officials – for the benefit of local viewers. The struggle to survive in such conditions satisfies a core value of the OE.

The OE features in a wide range of literary and visual media in New Zealand: in plays, television documentaries and reality shows, a feature-length movie, a number of short films, histories, memoirs, novels and short stories. The news media run frequent stories about, and references to, the OE and a multitude of internet pages offer information and advice, provide links to a variety of services that facilitate the OE, or tell stories of individual OEs through blogs.

Poster for the show *Four Kiwis Walk into a Bar*...
Jarred Christmas

ADVERTISING also reinforces the notion that ideally the OE should occur within a certain stage of the life cycle. A Westpac bank advertising campaign in 2004 focused on 'Starting something new?' The possible options – framed within a crossword puzzle – included flatting, graduating, owning a car, studying, travel, job and OE. In another advertisement, this time from 2008, four friends were shown moving through life – they left school, went to university, went on OE, returned to New Zealand and settled down – each phase made easier with the help of a hair regrowth product.

Westpac

OE in our culture: the play, the novel, the guidebook and the stories.
Court Theatre and Random House

THE GENERATIONAL CHANGES in the OE were captured perfectly by Rachel Helyer Donaldson in a 2004 *Listener* article:

In 1969: *Young Kiwis hand in notice at Earls Court pub to spend summer tripping around Europe in a Bedford van. More adventurous types take the Hippie Trail via Iran and Afghanistan to Nepal. Shots of the Taj Mahal caught on Super 8 for home movie. Postcards of the Eiffel Tower sent back to Mum and Dad, who have never crossed Cook Strait.*

In 2004: *New Zealanders in London take a couple of days out from their current IT contract for a city break in Reykjavik. Post digital holiday snaps on homepage. Text a message to the folks, currently doing a fly-drive across the US. Agree to go on a tour with partner's parents to Berlin and Moscow when they come over in the summer. With a bit of luck they might even pay.*[11]

The classic OE

The picture of the OE that is presented in advertisements and New Zealand media and culture frequently plays on nostalgia, depicting OEs that are not only stereotypical, but also outdated. The long boat trip to the UK has been forgotten, but the 'classic' OE still includes (among other things) work in a London pub and an extended summer of travel around Europe in a 'clapped-out' Transit van. In reality, the twenty-first-century OE experience is more likely to involve a job similar to that worked at home, with travel limited to a series of weekend trips to European capitals. More significantly, the twenty-first-century OE will not necessarily even be in Europe.

It is, of course, unrealistic to expect that a 1960s OE would be the same as one undertaken in the 2000s. However, the common threads running through the examples above (and through most stories I gathered) – and the story of the OE itself – are the importance of London, the focus on travel, and the ongoing connection between those who are on OE and those left at home.

During my research, I found that each OE occurred within its own political, social and economic context, varying across time and in different locations. Travel destinations were chosen according to their physical or political accessibility, or according to popularity or fashion. Employment opportunities were dependent on the overall state of the British economy, the degree of competition from others in

The classic OE.
Grant Lahood

the employment market and on what types of jobs were around. Where, and how, the OE was 'lived' also differed, as the areas of London with affordable rental housing changed over time, and new social venues and events emerged and evolved. Some people ventured beyond London for work, to other parts of the UK, to Europe or elsewhere overseas, their choices guided by what their friends and acquaintances were doing, and by what visas were available to them. Again, social mores dictated people's expectations and the parameters of acceptable behaviour at any given time. And each traveller also brought their own individual characteristics, circumstances, interests and agendas to their OE.

A nation of travellers

OE travel is founded on the connections generated by exploration and curiosity, trade and settlement between two of the earth's most distant points: Britain and its antipodes. While a wealth of published impressions and experiences of early travellers *to* New Zealand exists in archives, stories by people travelling *from* New Zealand are less common. Yet, even in the early days of settlement, the population movement was never one way.

Traditionally, New Zealanders have taken advantage of available outbound transport: numerous Māori worked and travelled on whaling ships going to Europe and Britain in the early 1800s, and many people travelled on returning migrant ships during the late 1800s and early 1900s. After World War II, the development of aircraft technology and, in particular, the advent of jet services enabled ever-increasing numbers of people to leave home to see the world. These practices, and the journeys undertaken by soldiers who participated in two world wars and several military campaigns, set a precedent for travel which the postwar generations of young OE travellers followed. Weaving throughout these travel stories is the tale of a changing relationship between New Zealand and Britain, and corresponding shifts in perceptions of national identity.

Many Māori travelled the world in the early days of European settlement. The first Māori known to have visited England was Te Mahanga (Moehanga) in 1806, who accompanied John Savage (a military surgeon with a royal commission) when he returned to England on the whaling vessel the *Ferret*. Although 'somewhat cast down by the size and grandeur of London'[12] when he first arrived, Te Mahanga enjoyed life in London, and stayed long enough to gain valuable skills. Arguably, his was the first New Zealand OE; he went, quite simply, because he wanted to 'see the world'. Te Mahanga was reported to be sorry when it came time to go home, but, as John Savage recorded:

I reminded him of his riches, and the man of consequence he would become upon his return to his own country – of his power to entertain all his friends by a recital of the wonders he had seen, and the knowledge he had acquired.

... I have no doubt if he remains in New Zealand (after his return), that he will remember his visit to Europe with peculiar satisfaction for the remainder of his life.[13]

The day before Te Mahanga left on his return journey to New Zealand, two other Māori, Teina and Maki, arrived at Portsmouth on the *Alexander*. Teina fell ill and died not long after arriving, but Maki stayed for some months in London. While there, he kept himself profitably employed as a carpenter, but was eventually kidnapped and sold to work without pay on another ship.[14]

A journey that had a significant impact on subsequent New Zealand history was made in 1820, when the missionary Thomas Kendall took the northern chiefs Hongi Hika and Waikato to England on a whaling ship, the *New Zealander*. During the months they spent in England, they worked on a Māori grammar and investigated British manufacturing and military organisation.[15] Returning through Sydney, Hongi acquired arms that were subsequently used against other tribes in what became known as the musket wars.

In 1859, 60 years after Te Mahanga's visit to Britain, Wiremu Toetoe and Hemara Te Rerehau made a notable trip to Europe. They enlisted as seamen and sailed for Trieste on the *Novara*. According to one account of their journey, Toetoe had 'long cherished a desire to see foreign lands and races'.[16] The two men remained in Europe for nine months, during which they visited cathedrals, palaces and museums, worked in the imperial printery of the Habsburgs and met a number of European rulers, including Queen Victoria. Te Rerehau kept a journal of their trip, one of the earliest overseas travel accounts written in Māori.[17]

Between these and other longer journeys, significant numbers of Māori travelled to Australia and elsewhere, many employed as crew on whaling vessels. Some accounts suggest that, because they came from the warmer North Island, many early Māori travellers found the climate of the British Isles too cold. Australia, with its warmer climate and proximity to New Zealand, was more attractive.[18]

Māori left on these early travels with an adventurous spirit: the time it would take to reach their destination was uncertain, and they did not know how they would return. The *Alexander*, on which Teina and Maki sailed, endured a three-month dockyard stop in Brazil before waiting for a further three months at St Helena for a convoy that would protect it from French warships. The *Ferret*, with Te Mahanga on board, also spent months in passage, rounding Cape Horn to arrive in St Helena in February 1806, and eventually docking at London in April 1806. Toetoe and Te Rerehau's 1859 journey from Auckland to Trieste took seven months. Hongi Hika and Waikato left New Zealand on a whaler and caught a lift home on the *Speke*, a convict ship bound for Australia. Driven by curiosity (although through necessity forced to work some of the time), travellers like Te Mahanga, Toetoe, Hongi Hika and Waikato were the true forerunners of the OE travellers of the second half of the twentieth century.

The New Zealanders

Curiosity about the world is repeatedly cited as the reason why New Zealanders travel. However, deciding what denotes the nation and its citizens has historically been less straightforward. In the 1800s, a 'New Zealander' was a Māori; other people living in New Zealand called themselves 'settlers'.[19] At the end of the nineteenth century, when New Zealand decided against union with Australia, significant consideration was given to how the Māori population might be treated if such a union went ahead. Some Europeans in New Zealand saw their identity as New Zealanders growing out of Māori tradition: recognition that Māori were an important point of distinction within the population led to use of the terms 'Maoriland' and 'Maorilanders' in the late 1800s and early 1900s.[20] When the New Zealand Native Rugby Team toured Britain in 1888–89, 16 years before the first All Black Tour in 1905, the 'natives' in the team were not exclusively Māori; New Zealand-born Pākehā also qualified as 'native'.[21]

While it has been suggested that international experience in the form of rugby tours of Britain and two world wars activated a sense of New Zealand national identity,[22] differentiation between Māori and non-Māori actually tended to continue. For example, the 1888–89 rugby tour was the forerunner of regular international tours, from 1910 onwards, by Māori rugby teams. In World War I, some Māori resisted the idea of fighting for king and country, particularly in Waikato. However, a 439-strong Māori contingent was part of the New Zealand Expeditionary Force's troops training in Egypt in 1915,[23] and in 1916 the politician Maui Pomare claimed that the union of Māori and Pākehā as New Zealanders was confirmed when 'their blood co-mingled in the trenches of Gallipoli'.[24] According to some accounts, it wasn't until World War II that there was full acceptance by both Māori and Pākehā of their shared identity as New Zealanders. While the Maori Battalion formed a separate unit in the armed forces sent to the war, there was mutual pride in the battalion's reputation.

The wars helped New Zealanders to define themselves, primarily in relation to others. During World War I they came up with a variety of names for themselves, including 'Enzedders', 'Diggers'(after gum and gold diggers) and 'Fernleaves'.[25] New Zealanders are thought to have first been called / called themselves 'Kiwis' in the later stages of that war; the name had become a common label for all New Zealanders by World War II.[26]

National identity was slower to develop at home, especially for European settlers for whom continuing dependence on Britain served to accentuate loneliness and isolation. This was despite prime ministers of the late nineteenth century, such as Julius Vogel and Richard Seddon, being 'nothing if not self-confident and bombastic on behalf of New Zealand interests'. Denis McLean writes that in the early years of the twentieth century, 'New Zealanders revelled in projecting a good image of themselves in London, but had more difficulty in coming to terms with who and what they were at home.'[27]

Although New Zealand's colonial history is similar to that of Australia, the relationship between each country and the colonial power has differed.[28] New Zealand was considered to be a potential 'Britain of the south', in part because its early settlement coincided with the growing power of the British Empire, in part because its economy was almost totally dependent on Britain, in part because it was the last of Britain's colonies to be settled, and in part because its temperate climate and fertile land encouraged the idea that New Zealand might become a new version of Britain. As a result, the country had closer cultural ties with Britain and less anti-'Pom' feeling than Australia, although these have also been attributed to its having fewer Irish immigrants, and colonists who were not convicts.[29]

The Enzedders Rest was a pictorial record of the work of the YMCA on active service, published in 1919.

George S. Richardson Album Collection, Auckland War Memorial Museum

New Zealanders in Britain

Despite the expectation that their country would be a mirror image of Britain, European New Zealanders suffered from a kind of 'cultural cringe' well into the twentieth century, based on the principle that things done or achieved overseas were better than those at home.[30] Some writers suggest that this cultural cringe lasted longer for New Zealanders than Australians, delaying the emergence of a confident national identity.[31] For aspiring writers and artists, journeys 'Home' (to Britain) were a necessity. Many artists took repeated trips away and engaged in considerable soul-searching before deciding to live permanently overseas. Writer Katherine Mansfield, for example, left for the *last* time in 1908. Similarly, painter Frances Hodgkins left permanently in 1913.

Michael King suggests that many intellectuals, such as Ernest Rutherford and Ronald Syme, left because there was no institutional or collegial setting within which they could realise their full potential. This applied to departing artists and writers as well; they also lacked an appreciative audience at home.[32] However, when author Frank Sargeson left New Zealand in 1927, King says he 'felt like a European in New Zealand; he left London a year later feeling like a New Zealander in Europe'.[33]

These travellers were increasingly born in New Zealand and unfamiliar with Britain. In 1929, the New Zealand High Commissioner in London published a handbook – *For New Zealand Visitors to London* – that had been 'prepared with the object of providing, in concise form, information and advice on most matters of interest to our visitors'.[36] The establishment in the 1920s of organisations such as the New Zealand Society, *New Zealand News* and the London New Zealand Rugby Club, also indicates a growing New Zealand population either resident in, or visiting, Britain.

A trip 'Home' (with a capital 'H') to Britain was an aspiration for many New Zealanders between the wars. Journalist Ian Donnelly travelled on the *Bendigo* in 1934 (see box) and published an account of the months he spent in London.[37] In his book *The Joyous Pilgrimage: A record of months that realised a dream,* he gives 'A New Zealander's Impressions of "Home"', describing London and the English scene, as well as his meetings with many people famous in politics and literature. Donnelly admits that London, with its cultural and intellectual facilities and stimulation, was the city in which he would most like to live. However, he acknowledges that remaining there was not an option for him, because to 'extract full flavour from London life would cost more than one could earn'. He also recognises that, as a visitor in London, he was accepted in ways that would not continue if he were to take up residence.

THE COST of travel suggests that most New Zealanders travelling in the 1920s and 1930s were privileged. One 1930s travel account begins: 'If the average New Zealander were asked how much a trip to England and the Continent would cost him I fancy he would name a sum ranging from £500 to £1000.'[34] The author and his wife travelled to England from Invercargill, spent three weeks in London, purchased a car and motored through England, Scotland and Wales, then embarked on a three-week tour of the Continent. The total expenses for their trip amounted to £396, less than £200 per person. They attributed the comparatively low cost of their tour to the introduction of one-class and tourist-class fares on ships – their return fares of £205 included rail fares from Dunedin to Lyttelton, passage on the *Monowai* from Lyttelton to Sydney via Wellington, an outward journey on the *Bendigo*, and return on the *Mongolia*. However, this fare was not as cheap as one might think: £396 in 1934 equated to $45,000 in 2013; the £205 boat fares alone cost $23,394.[35]

NEW ZEALAND GOVERNMENT OFFICES.

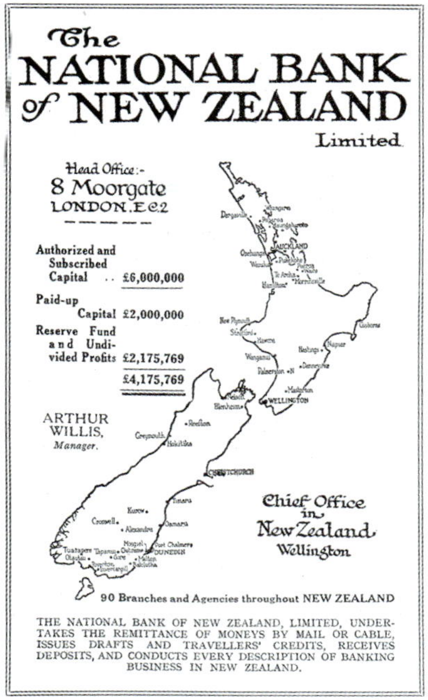

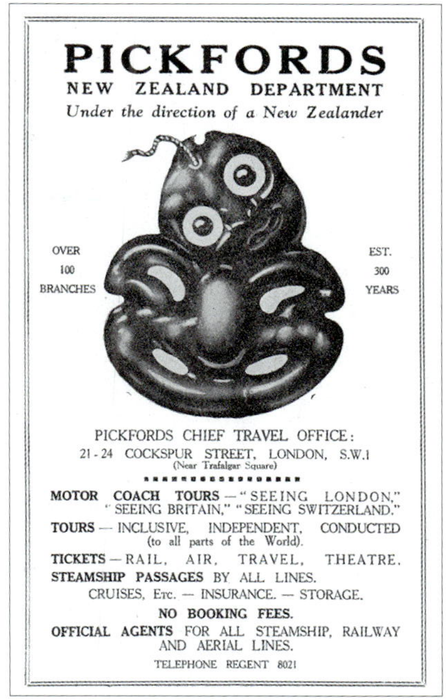

From *For New Zealand Visitors to London*, 1929, published by the New Zealand Government Offices.

Ministry of Foreign Affairs and Trade

His experiences prompt reflection on some characteristics of national identity:

If a colonial comes to London properly humbled by the immensity of what he finds about him, his visit will be profitable … But he must not be arrogant … Australians on the whole, are rather less successful than New Zealanders in England because of their gawky 'I'm telling you' attitude. If Australia's national growth is compared with physical growth, one can say that it is at the stage when the voice is breaking. Some Australians are inclined to foist their new, uncertainly deep tones on ears not particularly anxious to hear them. New Zealanders, on the other hand, are quiet, rather like country boys come to town, and trembling to hear brave tales from the lips of miraculous uncles.[38]

Colonial ties

In an era of expensive travel, going to war was the only way most people could gain a form of overseas experience, albeit horrific; servicemen and women represented the largest group of New Zealand travellers to depart in the first half of the twentieth century. The rush to volunteer in 1914 reflected the patriotic (towards Britain) mood of the time. New Zealand forces were sent first to the Middle East and then to Turkey, as part of the now infamous British campaign to secure the Dardanelles. They went ashore at Gallipoli on 25 April 1915, capturing the strategic point of Chunuk Bair, but after nine months were forced to withdraw. A total of 2721 men, about a quarter of the New Zealanders who landed on the peninsula, were killed, with a further 4752 wounded. Because of the sacrifices both nations made at Gallipoli, the Anzac legacy is important in Australia and New Zealand and many historians attribute the birth of a sense of national identity in both nations to these events.[39]

At the outbreak of World War II, Prime Minister Savage confirmed New Zealand's loyalty to Britain with the words 'Where she goes, we go; where she stands, we stand.' In 1939, on the day voluntary enlistment opened, 5419 New Zealanders stepped forward. Altogether, about 140,000 New Zealand men and women fought overseas during the course of the war. There were 11,625 fatal casualties and, according to postwar calculations, New Zealand's ratio of killed per million of population (at 6684) was the highest in the Commonwealth (with Britain at 5123 and Australia 3232).[42] Large numbers were also taken prisoner, peaking at 8086 in March 1943. Most were captured in Greece, Crete and Northern Africa.[43]

In terms of OE history, the enduring legacy of the world wars was undoubtedly the interest in travel they generated. A number of personal war accounts support this. For example, in *The Soldier Tourist* Joe Brewer writes that – having visited 10 countries and travelled on 10 ships – he could be regarded as a tourist.[44] Some ex-soldiers returned after the war to the places where they had fought. *Kiwi at Large* records a two-year trip made by Errol Allison in the 1950s: he set off from New Zealand to satisfy a life-long curiosity about fabulous cities such as Babylon, Isfahan and Troy, but also to return to the places where he had fought in the war and trace the people he had met in Egypt, Italy and prison camp. It was 10 years before he returned permanently to New Zealand. His return journey, in which he also visited his 'other home' – Crete – for the third time, is told in *Kiwi Vagabond*.[45]

TOWARDS THE END of World War I, two brothers from Blenheim – Gerald and Norman Nairn – decided that they wished to stay on in the Middle East and applied for demobilisation in Egypt. They wanted to operate a transport service in Palestine, Syria and the Lebanon, which they eventually expanded to pioneer the 650-mile desert route from Beirut to Baghdad. The Nairn Bus service to Baghdad began in 1923. In 1950 the brothers handed over the company's shares to their employees, and the cross-desert service continued until 1956, when Iraqi customs imposed stiff customs guarantees that forced the firm to cancel its Damascus–Baghdad service.[40] New Zealander Louise Sutherland enquired about crossing the desert to Baghdad on her cycle tour of the world in 1952, but was unable to get permission from the oil companies that controlled the routes; in her account of her journey she made reference to the Nairn tourist buses operating on one of these routes.[41]

Rainer Fuchs

Another book tells the story of a New Zealand soldier who returned with his wife 18 years after the war to the Italian village that sheltered him as an escaped prisoner; to repay his gratitude to the women of the village, he offered to pay for the installation of a village water pipe.[46]

Many of these accounts contemplate the nature of the New Zealander and the angst of colonial connection. Perhaps the most famous was that of John Mulgan, who studied at Oxford in the early 1930s and stayed on to work in Britain, subsequently fighting in the British army in World War II. In *Report on Experience,* he reflects:

Close ties bound the New Zealanders to England. If the form that clothed these ties was sentiment and tradition, their content and reality was economic dependence and the fact that we were a small country with no nationality of our own. New Zealanders are not given to abstract thinking nor to the formulation of principles. They have never questioned the unity that joins them to England. This same unity has taken them overseas twice in the last generation to correct the errors of someone else's foreign policy. The kind of loyalty that New Zealanders possess is stupid, irrational, and, in some melancholy way, satisfying to the heart. It has the texture of family relationships that can be full of internal bitterness but united against the outside world, that can be relied upon beyond ordinary friendship in times of sickness and death.[47]

IT IS DEBATABLE how strong colonial ties actually were for many young travellers. Often, even their parents did not understand their reasons for going: Carol, who left on OE in 1964, recalled that her father couldn't understand why she kept travelling, as 'for him the world began and ended in Canterbury'. Mary Dudson's mother could not understand why her daughter wanted to go off to foreign places with no job and no place to stay, and supplied the subtitle of Mary's book *Oamaru to Europe: 'What do you want to go there for?'*

Oamaru to Europe: 'What do you want to go there for?'
Daniela Bagozzi and Mary Dudson

However, he goes on to note that New Zealanders were 'growing up' and becoming more able to 'speak objectively of our parents'.

Despite strengthening ideas of national identity and a loosening of ties to Britain post World War II, New Zealanders' relationship with Britain remained intimate. A sense of going 'Home' to Britain lingered, in part because, even as late as the 1950s, children were still being taught British-based subjects at school. English was New Zealand's only official language, and a general knowledge of British culture and history was expected.[48] Many of those who went on their OE in the 1950s spoke of 'returning Home' despite being third- or fourth-generation New Zealanders. Visiting 'Home' in Britain was a cultural contradiction for others;

they were more interested in England – and London in particular – than in the genuine home areas that their ancestors may have come from.[49]

However, mid-century immigration played a part in boosting the numbers of later OE travellers and in maintaining the idea of 'Home'. Between the two world wars, a significant influx of migrants from Britain arrived in New Zealand. These included 13,000 ex-British servicemen and their families, 1400 young men who were to work on farms, and women on their way to marry New Zealand ex-soldiers. World War II effectively closed the door, the notable exception being British children escaping the German air raids, but immediately after the war New Zealand accepted refugees from a number of countries in war-torn Europe. Between 1947 and 1975 an assisted migration scheme brought 77,000 migrants, mainly from Britain and Holland, with preference being given to the young (those aged 20–35, extended to 45 in 1950). The children of these migrants grew up with stories of a 'Home' that was on the other side of the world. It is not surprising, then, that from the 1960s they were to be found among the growing numbers of OE travellers.

Drifting apart or cast adrift?

Despite the popularity of the British royal family in the 1950s, demonstrated most memorably during the royal tour of 1953, most accounts agree that the generation travelling to Britain in the 1960s and 1970s had less attachment to Britain and continental Europe than previous travellers and that the cultural relationship was a colonial connection inherited from parents.[51] Peter Calder describes taking his New Zealand-born mother to see her roots in 'the old country' in 2002, because 'Like many of her generation, she had always regarded herself fundamentally as an Englishwoman, marooned on a distant shore.'[52] Having himself been raised in the 1950s as an 'Englishman abroad', for Peter the journey was one in which he discovered he was actually a New Zealander.

New Zealanders were increasingly visiting non-European parts of the world from the 1960s. They found that the word 'British' on their official passports had

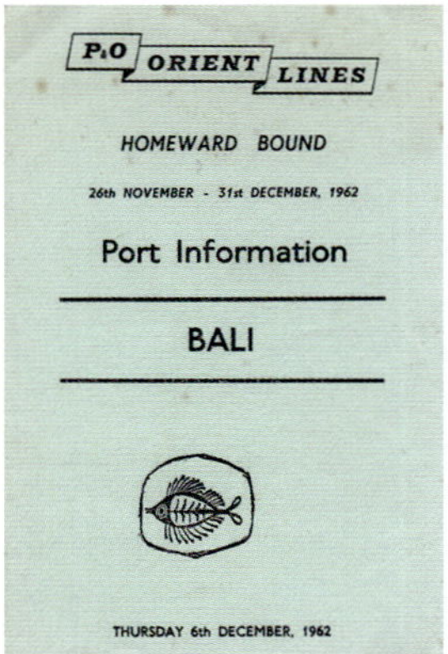

Top: The passenger boats taking New Zealanders to Britain were referred to as 'home boats', with the dates posted on shipping schedules for 'outward' (to New Zealand) and 'homeward' (to Britain) journeys.

Middle: Until 1964, the cover of New Zealand passports had the word 'British' in large type, with 'New Zealand' in smaller type at the bottom.

Left: In 1960 a young New Zealand dentist, Russell Sutherland, went to Norway on a two-year working holiday: *Land of the Bog-Cotton* is an account of his time there. A Norwegian he met on the ship commented that he would find it tough to find work, and asked if he was English. Russell replied, 'I'm British, if that's a help.'[50]
(London: Hodder & Stoughton, 1960)

become a provocative word, uncomfortable for those travelling in parts of Asia and Africa: in 1964 the word was removed. The bearer's status was unchanged, as British subject and New Zealand citizen. According to a New Zealand government spokesperson, 'New Zealand will drop the word British with no pleasure. But changes in the world today are such that we find it best to have just the country's name on the cover … however British that country may be.'[53]

For most of New Zealand's history, the relationship between Britain and New Zealand had been one of patronage, with New Zealand relying on Britain as a market for trade and as an ally in the wider world. During World War II, New Zealand came to recognise that Britain was unable to defend the country militarily. According to Robert Patman, the British defeat at Singapore in 1942 influenced New Zealand's decision to join the Anzus Treaty in 1952. Britain's military limitations were further exposed by the Suez crisis of 1956 and the decision to withdraw its navy from stations 'east of Suez' in 1968.[54] In 1973 Britain's entry into the European Economic Community (EEC) brought about the greatest change to the relationship between New Zealand and its 'mother country'.

For those embarking on OE travel, the most significant aspect of this change was the introduction of new British immigration rules in 1972. Before then, Commonwealth citizens enjoyed more privileges in Britain than European nationals: they were permitted to vote, stand for parliament, enter the armed services, were free from any kind of supervision in employment, and did not have to register with the police.[55] The main objection to the new rules was that Britain's 'kith and kin' in Canada, Australia and New Zealand would lose their advantage.[56] New Zealand newspapers accused Britain of 'swapping old Commonwealth citizens for the people of Europe' under the new regulations.[57] A former Governor-General of New Zealand, Lord Ballantrae, in his maiden speech at the House of Lords, reminded his audience of a number of things for which Britain should be grateful to New Zealand: support in the war, the imposition of voluntary rationing in New Zealand during the war to help feed Britain, the number of New Zealanders prominent in British life, and the absence of restrictions on British people wishing to visit New Zealand.[58]

However, the changing relationship between New Zealand and Britain was accompanied by an emerging cultural independence on the part of New Zealanders. By the late 1960s a more local focus was developing in New Zealand newspapers, magazines and radio, and an increasing number of books sold in New Zealand were published here, rather than in Britain. It has been suggested that this was part of an intellectual shift repositioning New Zealand in the Pacific, with a corresponding world view centred on Wellington instead of London.[59] On the other hand, some claim that the cultural cringe associated with being a New Zealander continued well into the 1970s and was only slowly weakened by rising national confidence, increasingly cheap and quick air travel and improved mass communications, which enabled artists to live in New Zealand and work internationally. Others debate whether a residual cultural cringe continues to exist in business and other sectors, where the 'overseas expert' is frequently paraded and endowed with great authority. And while the exodus of artists and writers halted, many scientists and scholars continued to feel compelled to leave New Zealand, 'opting for the enlarged platform of opportunities offered by countries with bigger populations and more substantial resources'.[60]

The 1970s saw the publication of several collections describing the experiences and achievements of expatriate New Zealanders. The ironic slogan 'World famous in New Zealand', used to advertise the softdrink L&P, is based on the notion that fame can only really be achieved overseas. To be included in *More Famous New Zealanders* (1972), for example, people had to have been 'born in New Zealand but have achieved fame beyond these shores'.[62] The 25 people selected included doctors, writers, sportspeople, musicians, politicians, scientists and soldiers. Likewise, the 14 subjects of *The Fly Away People* (1971), collectively introduced as 'New Zealanders at ease with themselves', had achieved in a wide range of fields, all overseas.[63] Most of the subjects of these two accounts departed from their home country in the first half of the twentieth century, and most never returned to New Zealand to live.

HISTORIAN Keith Sinclair commented on cultural cringe in his book entitled *Distance Looks Our Way: The effects of remoteness on New Zealand* (1961):

'Whim Wham' has found a wonderful symbol for one New Zealand attitude in his term 'Overseasia'. Our norm, he finds, is what is done overseas. New Zealanders not only judge by what is done in 'Overseasia' but, I may add, they suffer from it. It is one of our endemic diseases – 'overseizure'. We are probably the most travelled people in the world – we have to go so far to get anywhere. And at every gathering you may, as in West Africa, listen to the 'Been-tos' – those who have 'been to' London or New York or Sydney. We are not supposed – at least until very recently – to have our own 'culture'. A cultured New Zealander is often taken to be one who has travelled.[61]

New Zealand as home

In contrast, *Godwits Return* (published in 1992) presented stories of New Zealanders who returned, most of them having left New Zealand to study, often with government assistance, in Britain and Europe during the 1950s, 1960s and 1970s.[64] For example, Sir Paul Reeves (later Governor-General of New Zealand) studied at Oxford with the support of a Sir Apirana Ngata Memorial Scholarship. John Mulgan's son Richard, also at Oxford in the early 1960s, recalled that his social life centred, at least initially, on old Auckland friends; he also had introductions to a number of New Zealand expatriates settled in Oxford. Artist John Drawbridge received a National Art Gallery travelling scholarship to study at the Central School of Arts and Crafts in London in the 1950s, and theatre director Sunny Amey had a New Zealand government bursary to study with the English Stage Company at the Royal Court Theatre in London. Malvina Major trained at the London Opera Centre in the mid-1960s and Patricia Rianne left to train at the Royal Ballet School in London in 1962, returning to New Zealand 26 years later. Opera singer Christopher Doig recalled that in the early 1970s the 'normal thing for young New Zealand singers to do was to go to London'; wanting to be different, he went to Vienna. While leaving New Zealand was still a career prerequisite for many of this generation, it no longer led to permanent exile.

Financial constraints meant that few could take advantage of travel opportunities while they were away. Some of those who featured in the *Godwits Return* actually left on an OE. Photographer Robin Morrison was 'young and unencumbered and lived a wondrously free existence' in mid-1960s London.[65] His travel included working on a fishing trawler off the coast of Cornwall and hitchhiking around Europe. Eventually he married another New Zealander on OE and started working as a photographer; his first trip with his wife Dinah was three months in the Greek Isles. On a previous trip to Britain, Sunny Amey spent time in London working as a supply teacher; having arrived with £20 and no return fare, it took her more than three years to save the money to return home.

While language continues to steer New Zealand postgraduate students towards English-speaking countries, a gradual shift in the last decades of the twentieth century saw more students attracted to the United States, rather than to Britain. Historian Tom Brooking attributes this change to the availability of funding and the appeal of American institutions, with their greater enthusiasm and energy and more outward-looking attitudes.[66] Clergyman John Bluck left New Zealand in 1967 for university in Boston, acknowledging he was attracted because 'America's novelty value and cultural disapproval rating gave me enough reasons to go and see for myself. For this was a time when you made decisions by doing the opposite of what you were supposed to do.'[67]

While those who left on scholarships or for training in the second half of the twentieth century were more likely to return

JAN left New Zealand in 1967 with her husband, two young children and sewing machine. Her husband Don was an army dentist doing postgraduate study in oral surgery, training unavailable in New Zealand at the time. They flew to London on an air force Hercules and took up residence in a rental house previously occupied by other New Zealanders. Many of their friends in London were expatriate New Zealanders; they frequented New Zealand House, banked at one of the New Zealand banks in London, and travelled extensively in Britain and Europe, going in a camper van for their longest trip. While they felt different from those on OE because they were a family, they also felt different from the English people they met. Their trip was a very special event in their lives and Jan felt very privileged to have had the opportunity.

to New Zealand, many found careers and opportunities overseas were hard to resist. The contributors to *Godwits Return* wrote 'with pain about the dilemmas of being an expatriate'. Sir Paul Reeves, in 'Issues of Identity', for example, wrote: 'There is a sense in which it is easier to stay away from New Zealand and feel bad about it than to return home and deal with it.'[68] Many of the chapter titles in *Godwits Return* – 'Home and Back Again', 'A Sense of Wholeheartedness', 'To Have Both Hemispheres', 'The Circle is Complete' – reflect this dilemma about belonging and the location of 'home'. When Dinah Morrison became pregnant, she and Robin decided to return home because they wanted their child to be 'New Zealand-born and to enjoy a New Zealand childhood'.[69] Richard Mulgan also married a New Zealander and returned because the couple 'didn't want to deprive their children of the chance to be New Zealanders'.[70]

Stories of leaving home only to discover one's national identity are a recurring theme in our literature, particularly for Pākehā New Zealanders.[71] As long ago as 1905, feminist reformer and novelist Edith Searle Grossmann published *The Growth of a Colonial Sentiment* in which she wrote: 'The New Zealander who at last visits the old country of his childish dreams finds himself almost a foreigner. He has become an alien in the land of his forefathers, but in compensation he is no longer an exile in the land of his birth.'[72] A similar sentiment was expressed 80 years later by Janet Frame in her autobiography, when she wrote of going overseas as a means of 'examining not the place of arrival but the place of departure'.[73]

An OE history

What identifies an OE is its emphasis on curiosity and pleasure. Usually there is no purpose other than a simple desire to see and experience the world. According to these criteria, the earliest and only valid OE travellers from the past were Māori who went to Europe in the 1800s. The New Zealanders who travelled later – to wars, for education and to seek professional experience and international recognition – set an example for the ordinary travellers who followed, but theirs was not a true OE.

By the second half of the 1970s, the large birth cohort produced by the baby boom was passing through the most migratory-prone phase of its life span.[74] To go on an OE was not a particularly difficult undertaking, given the history of connection to Britain, and a high standard of living that made travel overseas affordable. As David McGill suggests:

Many baby boomers knew they were heading overseas. There was always work to come back to. But we hadn't just shrugged off adult suffocation to impose it back on ourselves. The world was our oyster. London was the pearl. All we needed was the price of a ticket there. No worries about getting back. If you ran out of money, get a job … We were naïve but very confident and physically tip top. Britain and Europe, here we come![75]

In 1978 cartoonist Tom Scott entitled his 'saga of a New Zealand family abroad', *Overseizure*.[76] His book served both as a 'timely aid for those who had yet to pursue the dream of overseas experience' and as 'an antidote for those who had already suffered OE, and, from time to time, are laid low by nostalgia' – not that different from how Te Mahanga felt when he had to leave England in 1806.

An OE history is needed for a number of reasons. The OE encapsulates many of the core features most admired in New Zealand society. As a travel practice, it provides a means to explore, examine and develop our sense of national identity and confidence on the global stage. Returning OE travellers bring back work and life experience, new partners, new ideas and expectations, all of which have helped to shape the New Zealand economy and society. Also, New Zealanders on OE have contributed both economically and culturally in Britain and worldwide. Finally, the OE is important as a phenomenon in its own right. It is a travel practice that has endured for more than six decades, with its own icons and traditions. It has been directly responsible for the establishment and longevity of a number of prominent global travel companies. Those early travel companies catering to the youthful OE population travelling in Europe in the 1970s and 1980s provided templates for the companies serving the multitudes of backpacker travellers wandering the world today. The New Zealand tourism industry is peopled by former travellers who cut their own travel teeth – through interest, experience or entrepreneurial epiphanies – while on OE.

The cover of Tom Scott's *Overseizure*, published in 1978.
Penguin NZ (Whitcoulls Publishing)

Any individual OE history lies (and ultimately dies) with the person who went. With the early practitioners now well into their eighties, we are in danger of losing our collective memory and record of the establishment years of the OE. We do not even know who most of these travellers were; anecdotal accounts suggest that they were more likely to come from wealthier families, be better educated and Pākehā. While the OE has become more egalitarian over time, the reality was that at any time Māori men and women could be found in London (and elsewhere overseas). We also have no idea how many New Zealanders have been on OEs. Our colonial past is reflected in messy definitions of citizenship and immigration rights, and the resulting poor records challenge anyone wishing to count an OE population that is already difficult to define clearly.

New Zealand's historical records of the OE are tentative at best, as it defies most attempts at categorisation. Immigration data, for example, record the annual departures of New Zealanders, but it is difficult to separate OE travellers from other travellers. Most accounts of migration have focused on people arriving, rather than those leaving. Likewise, historical data and records relating to tourism are primarily focused on travel to, or within, New Zealand, not away from it. In the social record, the OE most often features in the considerable body of literature addressing and reflecting on national identity. Yet even these discussions are usually limited to the Pākehā population, and to those famous enough to have their opinions sought and

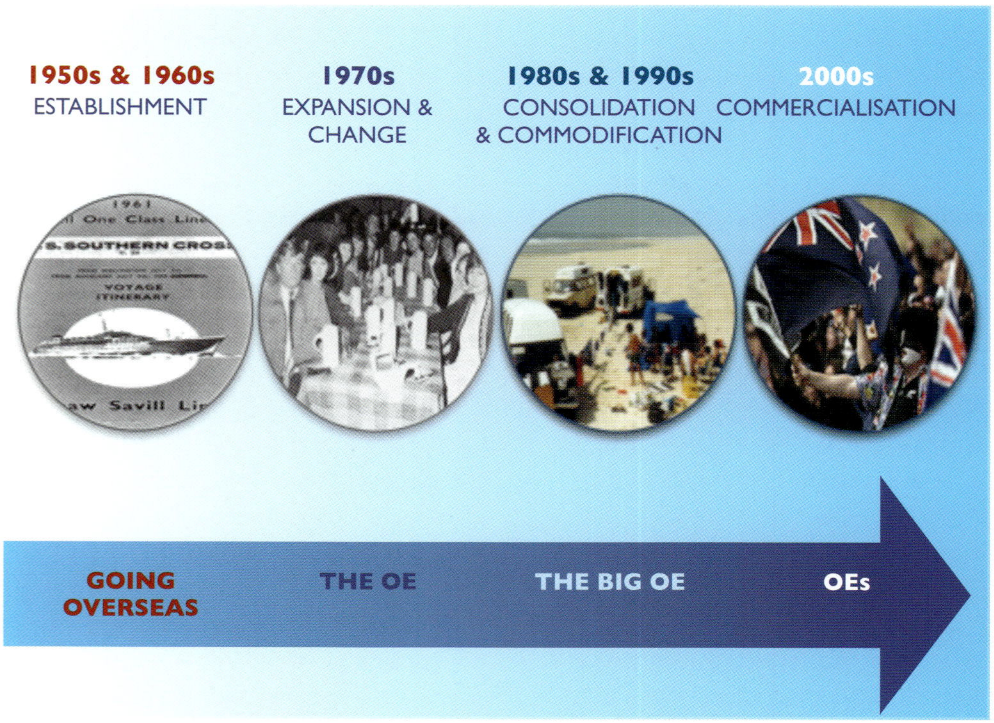

The six decades of the OE.

published; the stories of ordinary New Zealanders 'finding themselves' on their overseas adventures simply do not feature.

Given the stereotypical, or classic, OE based in London, it is in that city that much evidence of the OE can be found. Over the decades, expatriate publications and a support network of shops, travel companies, social and sporting clubs, events and venues have grown up around the OE. The nature of the material available is a reflection of the OE itself. The early decades feature in a few formal histories and club records (although not all specifically relating to the OE population). From the late 1970s, the burgeoning number of expatriate publications in London was evidence of a huge growth in OE numbers; their articles and advertisements provide records of OE life. They also reflect the growing commercialisation of the OE. With the growth of the internet in about 2000, hard-copy publications were at first supplemented by and then (in many cases) replaced by web-based offerings. While offering easy access to a wealth of material, internet sources simply do not have the same durability as the historical records of the past.

Flying Kiwis is more than a record of New Zealanders travelling and of how this travel changed over time. It is also the story of the OE phenomenon: from its establishment in the 1950s and 1960s; to its expansion and change in the 1970s and consolidation and commodification in the 1980s and 1990s; and finally to its commercialisation in the 2000s, and its survival into the following decades of the new millennium. The book describes six decades of economic, political, social, cultural and technological change. It is a story of change at different scales – in individual lives, in New Zealand, and globally – and of changes in the interactions between these. Viewing the OE through a wide temporal lens illuminates the changing relationship between New Zealand and her colonial parent; it also shows that the OE itself has evolved from being a cultural response to become an entity in its own right.

Chapter Two

LEAVING HOME

When I was a young boy
I wanted to sail around the world
That's the life for me, living on the sea
Spirit of a sailor, circumnavigates the globe
The lust of a pioneer, will acknowledge no frontier
I remember you by, thunderclap in the sky
Lightning flash, tempers flare,
'round the horn if you dare ...

'Six Months in a Leaky Boat', lyrics by Tim Finn.

THE NUMBER of New Zealanders going overseas increased dramatically from the 1950s. Assisted migration brought many British immigrants to New Zealand, and the returning migrant ships conveniently provided transport out. Postwar economic growth, cheaper fares and social change all served to swell the numbers leaving. While parents and grandparents might talk of these young people going 'Home', for this generation home was very definitely New Zealand. They were leaving home, not going there.

Many young travellers recognised they were taking opportunities that their parents had missed. Some people recalled parents being proud of them for leaving, in a kind of 'my daughter's in England' way. The opening dedication in a travel account from the 1960s reads:

For our parents ... who, like so many parents of young adults in the 1950s and 1960s, never had the chance to travel themselves, but proudly waved off their sons and daughters on overseas adventures.[1]

The overland trip across Europe and Asia in 1961 that the authors describe was a unique adventure for a young New Zealand couple, *and* for their family back home: all of their letters, postcards and tape recordings were saved. Thirty-five years later, the couple retraced their original journey in the same Volkswagen Beetle, which had been kept in the family.

Social freedom

Those who travelled between the 1950s and 1970s were a relatively privileged minority. International travel was a luxury item, available only to those who could afford both the money and the time required, critical factors given New Zealand's distant location. For the most part, these early OE travellers remembered their parents being happy to let them go. As one said: 'I think they were keen for us to have this experience – and – out of sight, out of mind, fingers crossed, that it was all going to be all right.' Permission to go (from one's parents) was more readily granted if one had family (however distant) in Britain to go *to*.

Early travellers such as Reina, who left New Zealand in 1950, found themselves setting a precedent: post-OE she returned to her old job and, 'because I came back and talked about it, two of the other girls in the office went the next year – my friend blames me for the OE.' The number of New Zealand residents or citizens departing annually either permanently or on a long-term basis reached over 10,000 for the first time in 1959. From then, it climbed steadily throughout the 1960s. Although it is impossible to know how many of these people were going on OEs and who they were, most accounts suggest

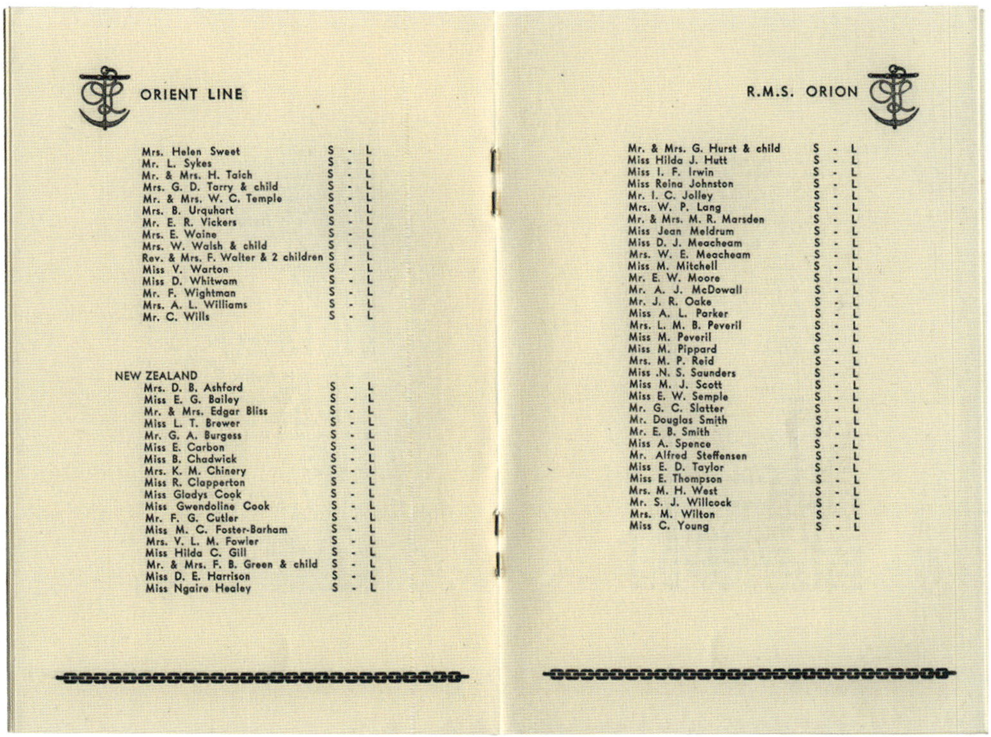

ORIENT LINE

Mrs. Helen Sweet S - L
Mr. L. Sykes S - L
Mr. & Mrs. H. Taich S - L
Mrs. G. D. Tarry & child S - L
Mr. & Mrs. W. C. Temple S - L
Mrs. B. Urquhart S - L
Mr. E. R. Vickers S - L
Mrs. E. Waine S - L
Mrs. W. Walsh & child S - L
Rev. & Mrs. F. Walter & 2 children S - L
Miss V. Warton S - L
Miss D. Whitwam S - L
Mr. F. Wightman S - L
Mrs. A. L. Williams S - L
Mr. C. Wills S - L

NEW ZEALAND
Mrs. D. B. Ashford S - L
Miss E. G. Bailey S - L
Mr. & Mrs. Edgar Bliss S - L
Miss L. T. Brewer S - L
Mr. G. A. Burgess S - L
Miss E. Carbon S - L
Miss B. Chadwick S - L
Mrs. K. M. Chinery S - L
Miss R. Clapperton S - L
Miss Gladys Cook S - L
Miss Gwendoline Cook S - L
Mr. F. G. Cutler S - L
Miss M. C. Foster-Barham S - L
Mrs. V. L. M. Fowler S - L
Miss Hilda C. Gill S - L
Mr. & Mrs. F. B. Green & child S - L
Miss D. E. Harrison S - L
Miss Ngaire Healey S - L

R.M.S. ORION

Mr. & Mrs. G. Hurst & child S - L
Miss Hilda J. Hutt S - L
Miss I. F. Irwin S - L
Miss Reina Johnston S - L
Mr. I. C. Jolley S - L
Mrs. W. P. Lang S - L
Mr. & Mrs. M. R. Marsden S - L
Miss Jean Meldrum S - L
Miss D. J. Meacheam S - L
Mrs. W. E. Meacheam S - L
Miss M. Mitchell S - L
Mr. E. W. Moore S - L
Mr. A. J. McDowall S - L
Mr. J. R. Oake S - L
Miss A. L. Parker S - L
Mrs. L. M. B. Peveril S - L
Miss M. Peveril S - L
Miss M. Pippard S - L
Mrs. M. P. Reid S - L
Miss N. S. Saunders S - L
Miss M. J. Scott S - L
Miss E. W. Semple S - L
Mr. G. C. Slatter S - L
Mr. Douglas Smith S - L
Mr. E. B. Smith S - L
Miss A. Spence S - L
Mr. Alfred Steffensen S - L
Miss E. D. Taylor S - L
Miss E. Thompson S - L
Mrs. M. H. West S - L
Mr. S. J. Willcock S - L
Mrs. M. Wilton S - L
Miss C. Young S - L

RMS *Orion* Passenger List: a lot of 'Misses', 1950.

that more females than males were departing in these early decades. Men were expected to establish their careers and purchase either a house or a section – with a plan to build a house – before they married. To go overseas on a working holiday, taking casual jobs, would be irresponsible.

Social change, in particular, contributed to increasing numbers of young women travelling. At this time women were not expected to have careers as such – they worked in offices, factories or shops, hospitals and schools, often only until they married. Nurses in the 1960s received on-the-job training for which they were paid; when they qualified, they often had savings. New Zealand nurses were highly regarded in Britain and many women took up nursing in order to travel. Few women went to university: in 1966, only 4.5 per cent of men and 8.6 per cent of women had tertiary qualifications, compared with 19.5 per cent of men and 22.9 per cent of women in 1996. (Changes in professional training methods – for example, nurses studying for an academic degree in order to qualify – are partially responsible for these increases.)

Travel offered young women an escape from 1960s New Zealand society, which was

Nineteen-fifties hitchhikers (right) and trip announcement in a local newspaper.

Miss Iris Irwin, Galway street, sailed from Wellington on Friday for Sydney where she will join the Orion to sail for England on July 8. Miss Irwin will spend an extended holiday in England and on the Continent.

Before leaving on a tour of Britain and the Continent, Miss Reina Johnston was entertained by the staff of Orr, MacLean and Fougere, Public Accountants, and received gifts with the good wishes of the firm, staff and clients. Miss Johnston will leave Sydney for London by the Orion, on the eighth of this month.

GENERALLY in the 1950s and 1960s, men had greater social freedom than women, both in New Zealand and overseas. For example, Reina was given the choice of a party or money when she turned 21: 'I said I wanted the money and wanted to go to England – then Dad said I couldn't go on my own – but this girl I didn't know very well said she would go with me.' They eventually left New Zealand in 1950 and Reina (aged 23 by then) used the home of an aunt in Scotland as a base from which to work and travel during the next two years. The two girls purchased backpacks when they arrived in Britain and travelled extensively, mostly by hitchhiking. Reina could not recall how much she told her parents about what they were doing. When they went on a tour of the Continent in 1951, one of the families on tour had a son who was able to escort them to nightclubs and other places to which otherwise, as single females, they would have been unable to go.

still fairly repressive. For example, leaving home before marriage (unless studying out of town) tended to be frowned upon as it reflected badly both on one's own reputation and on one's family. A 1973 guidebook, *Down Under in Europe*, comments that mixed flatting was popular in London, but less popular with parents back home in the Antipodes. The authors recommended that one 'did not write home and tell one's family that they were living in a mixed flat'. In New Zealand, mixed flatting was not widely accepted until the late 1970s.

The same guidebook reported that 'on most voyages from the Antipodes the girls tend to outnumber the men by something like five to one. The odds are often higher. For a man it can be like finding yourself locked in a harem.'[2] Male and female passengers did not share cabins on the passenger ships unless they were married, although this was due more to social expectation than an actual rule. The European camping tours that proliferated throughout the 1960s were also heavily patronised by females.

These early female OE travellers recalled their pre-OE innocence. Usually they had not yet left home, except perhaps to live in a nurses' home while they trained. They had been exposed to television for only a few years. They grew up on a meat and three vegetables diet, with minimal exposure to 'foreign' delicacies such as pasta. Many had never been across Cook Strait, let alone out of New Zealand. They had never flown in an aeroplane or travelled by ship. For some, the OE was exciting simply because they left on passenger ships. Often, these travellers were overwhelmed by the size and pace of Sydney, the first stop on their OE journey.

For many OE travellers today – unwilling to spend precious financial resources before finding a job and somewhere to live in London – the OE does not begin until they step off the plane at Heathrow. In contrast, early OE travellers had the excitement of the long journey to Britain and Europe by ship. In 1806 it took Te Mahanga seven months to sail from New Zealand to Europe. The standard trip by sailing ship was three months. From the 1880s, the advent of steamships reduced the journey to about six weeks. After the devastation of World War II, new fleets of cargo and passenger ships were built; by the 1960s, when most new ships were diesel-powered, boat speeds had increased from 17 to 21 knots, cutting a week off the six-week journey. Two ships of the Italian Lloyd Triestino Line – the *Galileo Galilei* (1961) and the *Gugliemo Marconi* (1963) – further reduced the journey to just 23 days.

'Fresh off the boat'

Assisted migration schemes were available from July 1947; during the next 30 years, more than 100,000 people moved to New Zealand and more than a million British subjects to Australia. The ships serving this migration also served OE travellers, carrying both cargo and passengers on their return trips. The history of their services is complex: shipping companies changed hands, merged, won and lost migrant transport contracts; individual ships were sold, refitted and had their names changed; and the routes they took also changed, due to the political events that caused the relatively brief closure of the Suez Canal in the 1950s and its lengthier, seven-year closure from June 1967.

Passenger ships changed drastically in the 1950s and 1960s, with the construction of purpose-built passenger liners like Shaw Savill's *Southern Cross* (1955) and *Northern Star* (1962). The *Southern Cross* offered one class of passage to 1160 passengers. About the same time, the New Zealand Shipping Company built Rangi-class liners such as the *Rangitoto* (1949), the *Rangitane* (1950) and the *Ruahine* (1951). Two older ships, the *Rangitiki* (1929) and the *Rangitata* (1929) were also still in service until they were replaced by a retired Cunard passenger-cargo liner the *Parthia* (1948), which was renamed the *Remuera* (1962). In 1965 *New Zealand News* in London published a comparison of 19 passenger liners on the UK–New Zealand run. The largest were the *Canberra* (1961), *Oriana* (1960) and *Arcadia* (1954) of the P&O-Orient Line, all three carrying about a third of their passengers in first class. Another P&O-Orient Line ship, the *Orcades* (1954), began operations as a two-class ship; a refit in 1964 converted her accommodation to one class.

The three ships of the Greek Chandris Line – the *Patris* (1959), the *Ellinis* (1963) and the *Australis* (1965) – were one-class only. Originally launched as the *Bloemfontein Castle*, as part of the Union Castle Line of South Africa, the *Patris* was renamed by Chandris in 1959 and operated via the Suez Canal to Fremantle, Melbourne and Sydney, carrying Greek migrants. While the canal was closed, the route to Australia was via Cape Town. The Chandris Line offered cheaper tickets than those on the ships of established companies such as P&O-Orient, Shaw Savill and the New Zealand Shipping Company.

The *Ellinis* started the Chandris 'around-the-world' service in 1963, with outbound sailings to Australia via the Suez Canal (and later South Africa) and return via the Panama Canal. The maiden voyage of the *Australis* (previously the *America* of the United States Line) in 1965 also went from Piraeus to Sydney and returned to Southampton via the Pacific and the Caribbean. After this, her regular route, until its closure, was via the Suez Canal from Southampton to Australia (and sometimes New Zealand).

The Italian Sitmar Line had been awarded the lucrative contract taking British migrants to Australia in 1958; throughout the 1960s its ships – the *Fairsky* (1958), *Castel Felice* (1952), *Fairstar* (1964) and *Fairsea* (1949) – were a common sight in Australia and New Zealand. According to Auckland Port records, the *Fairsea* visited Auckland 26 times between 18 February 1957 and 20 October 1968, the *Fairsky* visited 57 times between 30 December 1961 and 18 May 1977, and the *Castel Felice* visited 37 times between 28 March 1961 and 6 July 1970. Another Italian shipping company, the Cogedar Line, operated a Genoa to Australia and New Zealand service with the *Aurelia* (1954) and the *Flavia* (1961) throughout the 1960s. The *Aurelia* visited Auckland 10 times between 12 January 1965 and 3 February 1968.

Forced out of the Dutch East Indies route by Indonesian independence, the Dutch Mail fleet provided a round-the-world passenger service between Holland and Southampton from 1959, using three ships: the *Johan van Oldenbarnevelt* (1929), the *Willem Ruys* (1947), and the *Oranje* (1938). From 1966, the latter two of these were operated on a service from Europe to Australia and New Zealand as the *Achille Lauro* (1965) and the *Angelina Lauro* (1965) respectively, by Flotta Lauro – yet another Italian shipping company. The outbound route to Australia and New Zealand was via the Suez Canal and homeward via the Panama Canal. Prior to 1966, Flotta Lauro Lines occasionally brought the *Sydney* (1950) to New Zealand.

Auckland and Wellington were the main ports of call in New Zealand, with a limited number of sailings departing from Lyttelton. The number of sea passengers to and from New Zealand generally increased throughout the 1950s and 1960s, peaking at 97,800 in 1967. Departure records for 1967 from the two main passenger ports show 28,250 people leaving from Auckland and 14,257 from Wellington. The number of those leaving from Wellington by sea had been in decline since 1959 and fell dramatically after 1967: from 10,435 in 1969 to 4016 in 1972,

The *Ruahine* and *Southern Cross* leaving Wellington together.
Dominion Post Collection, Alexander Turnbull Library (EP-Transport-Ships-Ruahine-01)

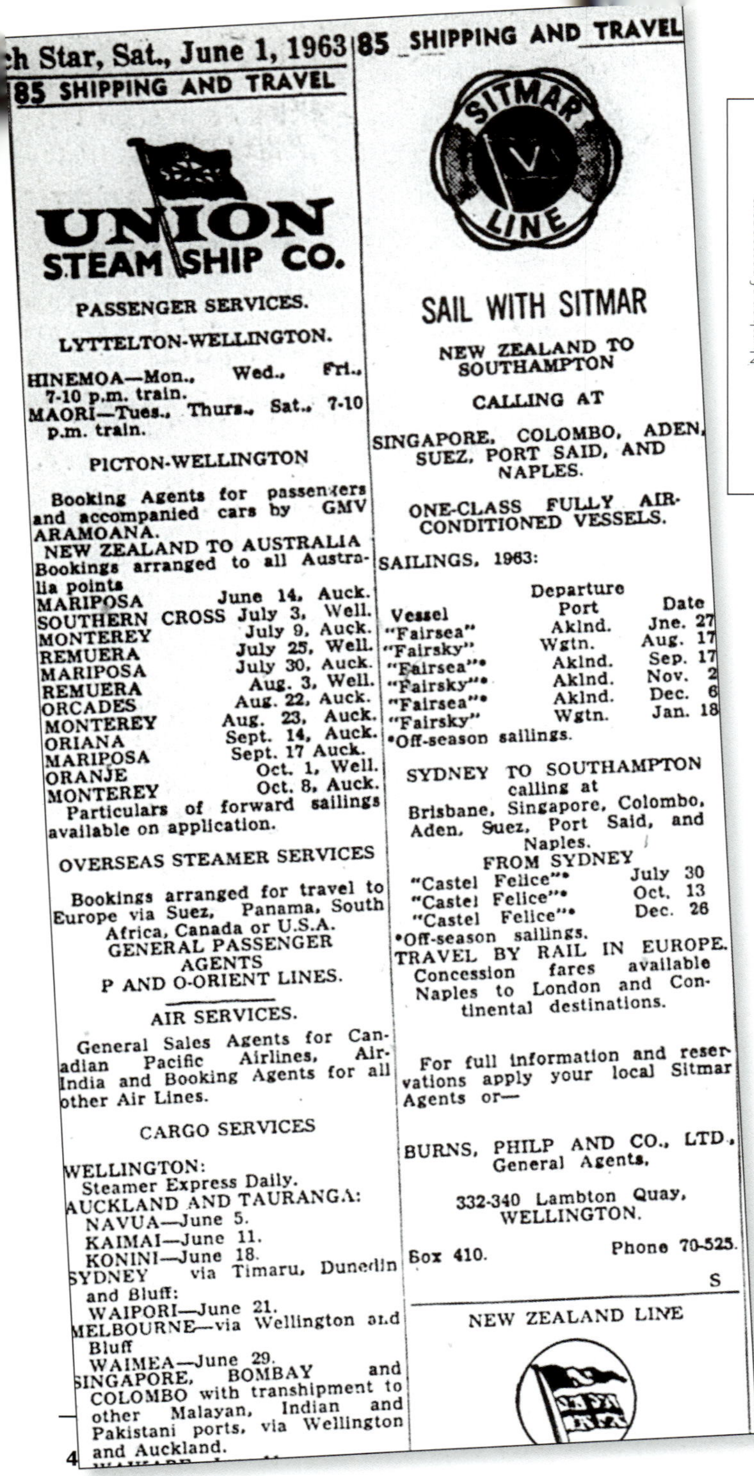

...ch Star, Sat., June 1, 1963 | 85 SHIPPING AND TRAVEL

85 SHIPPING AND TRAVEL

UNION STEAM SHIP CO.

PASSENGER SERVICES.

LYTTELTON-WELLINGTON.

HINEMOA—Mon., Wed., Fri., 7-10 p.m. train.
MAORI—Tues., Thurs., Sat., 7-10 p.m. train.

PICTON-WELLINGTON

Booking Agents for passengers and accompanied cars by GMV ARAMOANA.

NEW ZEALAND TO AUSTRALIA

Bookings arranged to all Australia points

MARIPOSA	June 14.	Auck.
SOUTHERN CROSS	July 3.	Well.
MONTEREY	July 9.	Auck.
REMUERA	July 25.	Well.
MARIPOSA	July 30.	Auck.
REMUERA	Aug. 3.	Well.
ORCADES	Aug. 22.	Auck.
MONTEREY	Aug. 23.	Auck.
ORIANA	Sept. 14.	Auck.
MARIPOSA	Sept. 17	Auck.
ORANJE	Oct. 1.	Well.
MONTEREY	Oct. 8.	Auck.

Particulars of forward sailings available on application.

OVERSEAS STEAMER SERVICES

Bookings arranged for travel to Europe via Suez, Panama, South Africa, Canada or U.S.A.
GENERAL PASSENGER AGENTS
P AND O-ORIENT LINES.

AIR SERVICES.

General Sales Agents for Canadian Pacific Airlines, Air-India and Booking Agents for all other Air Lines.

CARGO SERVICES

WELLINGTON:
Steamer Express Daily.
AUCKLAND AND TAURANGA:
NAVUA—June 5.
KAIMAI—June 11.
KONINI—June 18.
SYDNEY via Timaru, Dunedin and Bluff:
WAIPORI—June 21.
MELBOURNE—via Wellington and Bluff
WAIMEA—June 29.
SINGAPORE, BOMBAY and COLOMBO with transhipment to other Malayan, Indian and Pakistani ports, via Wellington and Auckland.

SITMAR LINE

SAIL WITH SITMAR

NEW ZEALAND TO SOUTHAMPTON

CALLING AT

SINGAPORE, COLOMBO, ADEN, SUEZ, PORT SAID, AND NAPLES.

ONE-CLASS FULLY AIR-CONDITIONED VESSELS.

SAILINGS, 1963:

Vessel	Departure Port	Date
"Fairsea"	Aklnd.	Jne. 27
"Fairsky"	Wgtn.	Aug. 17
"Fairsea"*	Aklnd.	Sep. 17
"Fairsky"*	Aklnd.	Nov. 2
"Fairsea"*	Aklnd.	Dec. 6
"Fairsky"	Wgtn.	Jan. 18

*Off-season sailings.

SYDNEY TO SOUTHAMPTON calling at
Brisbane, Singapore, Colombo, Aden, Suez, Port Said, and Naples.

FROM SYDNEY

"Castel Felice"*	July 30
"Castel Felice"*	Oct. 13
"Castel Felice"*	Dec. 26

*Off-season sailings.

TRAVEL BY RAIL IN EUROPE.

Concession fares available Naples to London and Continental destinations.

For full information and reservations apply your local Sitmar Agents or—

BURNS, PHILP AND CO., LTD., General Agents,

332-340 Lambton Quay, WELLINGTON.

Box 410. Phone 70-525.

S

NEW ZEALAND LINE

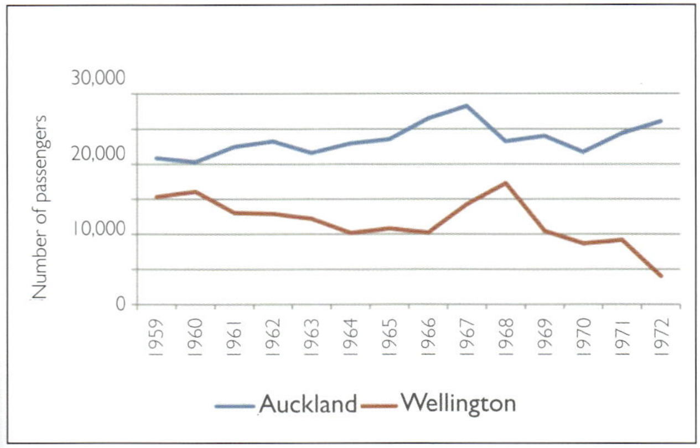

Figure 2.1 Passengers departing by sea.

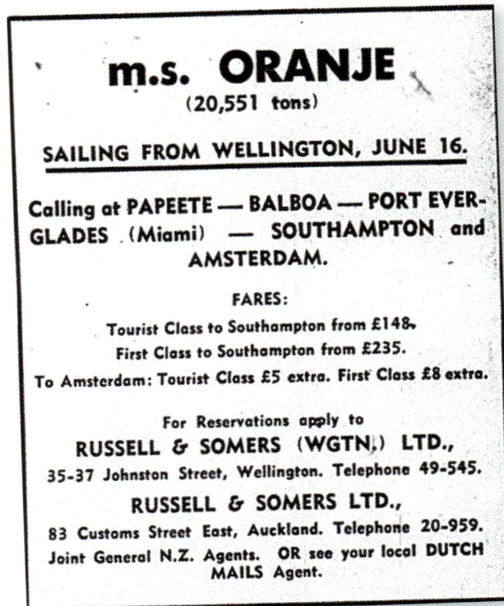

m.s. ORANJE
(20,551 tons)

SAILING FROM WELLINGTON, JUNE 16.

Calling at PAPEETE — BALBOA — PORT EVERGLADES (Miami) — SOUTHAMPTON and AMSTERDAM.

FARES:

Tourist Class to Southampton from £148.
First Class to Southampton from £235.
To Amsterdam: Tourist Class £5 extra. First Class £8 extra.

For Reservations apply to
RUSSELL & SOMERS (WGTN.) LTD.,
35-37 Johnston Street, Wellington. Telephone 49-545.
RUSSELL & SOMERS LTD.,
83 Customs Street East, Auckland. Telephone 20-959.
Joint General N.Z. Agents. OR see your local DUTCH MAILS Agent.

MS *Oranje* departure notice, 1962.
Christchurch Star

Shipping listings, 1963. *Christchurch Star*

whereas Auckland held its own for longer, perhaps as a counterbalance (Figure 2 1).

Most of the travel advertising in *New Zealand News* between 1950 and 1970 was for passenger shipping, targeting potential immigrants (who would often be transporting household goods), as well as those returning from OEs. By contrast, travel advertising in New Zealand newspapers focused on the new airline routes to Europe and, in particular, on the speed and comfort jet aircraft could offer. Shipping advertisements were less common, although the shipping companies or their agents published sailing dates, and occasionally routes and fares, in the classified section.

For example, the Shipping and Travel classifieds in the *Christchurch Star* in February 1970 carried an advertisement for several 'special calls to Lyttelton' by the *Northern Star* and the *Southern Cross* in April and October 1971. Sailing dates for passenger ships were usually publicised well in advance; a listing published in February 1967 (the peak year for sea passengers) showed 63 departures for the rest of that year and a further 24 in 1968. Among the 1967 sailings were five by the *Angelina Lauro*; four each by the *Achille Lauro*, the *Castel Felice*, the *Fairsea*, the *Northern Star* and the *Australis*; while the *Southern Cross* and the *Ellinis* each departed New Zealand three times.

Some of those departing on OE in the 1960s travelled to Australia, where the wages were higher, and worked for several months before moving on to Britain. Passengers who sailed on ships to European ports such as Genoa, Naples and Athens were able to purchase concession rail fares to London. Chandris Lines advertised rail tickets that allowed up to two months' travel between Athens and London. Passengers travelling through the Panama Canal sometimes disembarked in Miami, travelled around the United States, and resumed their ship journey from New York.

Choice of ship was determined by the timeliness of its departure, the price of tickets and, less often, the routes taken. Some travellers recalled choosing ships that

Figure 2.2 Planned departures for October 1967.

1967 (Oct)	**Ship**	**Route**	**Departing**
6th	*Oronsay* (P&O-Orient)	via Suez	Auckland
15th	*Castel Felice* (Sitmar Lines)	via Suez	Auckland
19th	*Southern Cross* (Shaw Savill)	via Panama	Wellington & Auckland
20th	*Australis* (Chandris)	via Panama	Auckland
22nd	*Angelino Lauro* (Flotta Lauro)	via Suez	Wellington
23rd	*Fairsky* (Sitmar Lines)	via Panama	Wellington
24th	*Aurelia* (Cogedar Line)	via Suez	Auckland
27th	*Gothic* (Shaw Savill)	via Suez	Not given*
28th	*Orcades* (P&O-Orient)	via Panama	Auckland

* Auckland Port records show that the *Gothic* called at a number of smaller ports around New Zealand before departing for Britain.

The Farmers' PASSENGER SHIPPING VACANCY GUIDE

Ship	Date	Route	Destination	Vacancies
Canberra	Mar. 1 (S.)	Suez	U.K.	Most types
Castel Felice	Apr. 22 (A.)	Panama	U.K.	Most types
Fairsky	May 6 (W.)	Suez	U.K.	Odd berths
Marconi	May 31 (S.)	Suez	Genoa	All types
Fairsea	June 2 (A.)	U.S.A.-Panama	U.K.	Most types
Northern Star	June 3 (W.)	Panama	U.K.	Odd berths
Orsova	June 7 (A.)	N. America, Far E., Suez	U.K.	Most tourist
Oriana	June 25 (A.)	Panama	U.K.	Am. 1st, lim
Rangitane	June 30	Panama	U.K.	Limited
Southern Cross	July 15 (W.)	S. Africa	U.K.	Most types
Gothic	July 22	Panama	U.K.	Available
*Fairsea	Aug. 24 (A.)	Suez	U.K.	Most types
*Northern Star	Aug. 30 (W.)	Panama	U.K.	Limited
*Himalaya	Sep. 30 (A.)	Suez	U.K. & F.	Most types
*Rangitoto	Oct. 6	Panama	U.K.	Ample avail

*Off seasons sailings. (A.) Auckland, (W.) Wellington, (S.) Sydney, (F.) Flushing.

BOOK NOW AT

The Farmers' TRAVEL BUREAU

CHRISTCHURCH, RANGIORA, LEESTON.

Vacancy guide, 1965. *Christchurch Star*

Type of Cabin	Off-season	On-season
Private facilities	£134 ($5023)	£159 ($5960)
2 berth	£128 ($4798)	£153 ($5735)
4 berth	£116 ($4348)	£141 ($5285)
6 berth	£108 ($4048)	£133 ($4985)
8 berth	£103 ($3861)	£128 ($4798)

Figure 2.3 Fares to Southampton on the *Ellinis* in 1965 (the 2013 ticket values in brackets).[3]

A SAMPLE of some other fares (with 2013 values in brackets):

1951: £67.10s ($4042) for one-way fare in a six-berth cabin on the *Rangitiki* (32-day journey via Panama and Curacao)

1956: £120 ($5719) for one-way fare on the *Southern Cross*

1961: £137.10s ($5787) for return tourist-class passage on the *Arcadia*

1962: £235 ($9576) for first class, £148 ($6032) for tourist class to Southampton on the *Oranje*

1962: £89 ($3627) for fare to Britain on the Sitmar Line

1966: £143 ($5189) for off-season tourist-class fare, Wellington to Southampton, on the Flotta Lauro Line

1970: $342 ($5084) fare to Britain on the Chandris Line's *Australis*

1973: $337 ($3905) for one-way passage to Britain on the *Northern Star*

were going out and back on different routes because they wanted to go 'right around the world'. Tickets were booked up to two years in advance; the shipping companies would fill in the passenger's name in pencil, changing it to ink when a deposit had been paid. The balance was due two months before departure. Occasionally travel agents published a vacancy guide with details of the number and types of berths remaining on upcoming departures. Although many ships were one class only, they offered a choice of cabins. The *Ellinis*, for example, had two-, four-, six- and eight-berth cabins (Figure 2.3). More expensive cabins came with private facilities. For all types of accommodation there were also off-season fares available.

While these fares appear expensive when converted to more recent values, they were still cheaper than flying. For example, in 1960 the travel agent Dalgety & Co. offered both 'aloft' and 'afloat' options: off-season (up to December) single sea fares from £85 ($3628) and the new BOAC economy single airfare at £253 ($10,798). By 2013 standards, even the sea fare was a substantial amount of money and people still remembered 40 years later what they paid. Most people had to save long and hard for their ticket money. Many still have their original tickets.

LYNETTE still has her trip book with details of her fares (and a record of what she bought in each port). In 1962 she paid £30 ($1223) for a one-way passage to Sydney on the *Southern Cross* and £100 ($4076) for her one-way, off-season passage in a second-class, four-berth cabin on the *Orcades* from Sydney to Britain. A friend she made on the ship, with whom she is still in contact, paid slightly less for her ticket as her cabin was a deck lower. Their five-week 'variety cruise' went via Melbourne, Adelaide, Fremantle, Bali, Singapore, Bombay, Aden, Suez, Port Said, Naples, Marseille and Gibraltar, arriving at Tilbury on 31 December. Their fares also secured five weeks' room and board.

The shipboard experience

Generally, Italian and Greek shipping companies offered the cheapest fares but the downside to these was less comfort on board ship, the quality of the food, a limited number of ports visited and the need to purchase forward travel to Britain if one's final port was in Italy or Greece.

Down Under in Europe compared food and accommodation on those shipping lines still sailing in 1973. On Chandris Line ships, food was 'more Greek' on the *Patris,* with the rest offering Greek-style plain roast beef and Yorkshire pud; accommodation on the lower decks was a bit 'rabbit-warrenish'. Food on the Sitmar Lines was British as interpreted by Italians, with crowded accommodation on the bottom decks. The Shaw Savill ships served adequate food. The P&O-Orient Line had good service, entertainment and food, but was not recommended for the budget traveller. While the younger passengers would happily go on the cheaper ships, their parents were often a little fussier, insisting

THE PRICE PAID for the fare did not always reflect how much fun one had on the ship journey. Diane recalled her experiences on the *Northern Star* in 1973:

It was exciting sailing out of Wellington – without a backward glance – but then two days later we berthed in Auckland which was a bit of an anti-climax. I think it was the Italian shipping lines that had more fun. We had these pasty faced British stewards, either in their dotage or very young and pimply and we had a lot of disillusioned English folk returning home and it [the ship] was dirty, the band had jumped ship in Australia ....

Carol remembered having 'loads of fun' on the *Remuera* in 1964 because it was smaller than the P&O ships: with only one class, passengers had free run of the entire ship. Also, at least half the 200 passengers were under 35 years of age. However, after calls en route through the Pacific and Caribbean, Carol was disappointed to arrive at the industrial and dirty-looking Tilbury dock in London.

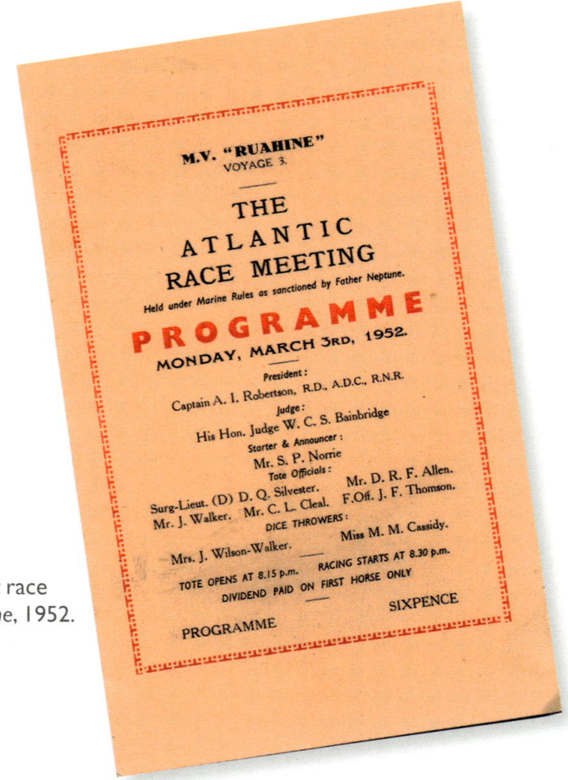
M.V. "RUAHINE"
VOYAGE 3.

THE
ATLANTIC
RACE MEETING
Held under Marine Rules as sanctioned by Father Neptune.

PROGRAMME
MONDAY, MARCH 3RD, 1952.

President:
Captain A. I. Robertson, R.D., A.D.C., R.N.R.
Judge:
His Hon. Judge W. C. S. Bainbridge
Starter & Announcer:
Mr. S. P. Norrie
Tote Officials:
Surg-Lieut. (D) D. Q. Silvester. Mr. D. R. F. Allen.
Mr. J. Walker. Mr. C. L. Cleal. F.Off. J. F. Thomson.
DICE THROWERS:
Mrs. J. Wilson-Walker. Miss M. M. Cassidy.

TOTE OPENS AT 8.15 p.m. RACING STARTS AT 8.30 p.m.
DIVIDEND PAID ON FIRST HORSE ONLY

PROGRAMME SIXPENCE

Shipboard entertainments: race card, MV *Ruahine*, 1952.

IN 1968, Donna's excitement started even before leaving New Zealand: *I went by boat – the ferry from Lyttelton to Wellington and the day after left on the* Ellinis. *It was a very rough sailing to Wellington – the day after the* Wahine *sank – but there were all these people needing to get to Wellington for other ships. We went through Panama. It was a Greek ship – the boat trip was absolutely wonderful – we had loads and loads of fun – turned night into day, and we would have been quite happy when we got to grey Southampton to have said – well we've had a wonderful time let's go home now. The boat took about three and a half weeks – it was quite a quick trip because it didn't really stop – the more expensive P&O liners went all up the coast of America and down to Mexico, but ours went straight through. Most of the passengers were young people – it was more the thing for girls, even engaged girls, to have this good time. There seemed to be more Australian males so the boat must have come from Australia.*

they sail on the 'English' ships of the P&O-Orient and Shaw Savill lines, or with the New Zealand Shipping Company.

Life on board ship was an adventure in itself, with meals served formally in the dining rooms: eating out was uncommon in 1960s New Zealand. Many younger passengers found it rather glamorous to eat Italian-style food, compared with what they were used to at home. If the weather was good, one could lie by the pool or play deck sports; there was a ceremony for crossing the equator, dancing every night, fancy dress parties, movies and so on. Sports were important on all the ships; the *Southern Cross* and *Northern Star,* in particular, were known for their extensive sports decks. The on-board cricket 'test' matches between Australians, New Zealanders and South Africans were 'full-on' events.

Most of the stories featured in Nigel McCarter's book *The Big OE* are from travellers who left New Zealand by ship. Often the voyages were memorable for the wrong reasons. On one mid-1960s *Ruahine* sailing the ship broke down twice, once in the Pacific and again in the Atlantic, and was threatened by Cuban gunboats in the Straits of Florida. In another account, from a 1976 *Galileo Galilei* sailing, older passengers were dissatisfied with the standard of accommodation, food and organisation on board, while the younger women were continually pestered by the crew. The ship's planned stop at Acapulco, cut short because it had stopped to rescue

Shipboard entertainments, clockwise from top left: Neptune ceremony, 1950s; Neptune ceremony, 1970s; on-board sports: RMS *Orion*, 1950s; Shaw Savill Line, 1970s; and talent quest on the RHMS *Ellinis*, 1960s.

LYNETTE found that returning to New Zealand by ship was quite different from the trip to Europe, when she sailed on the *Northern Star* in 1964:

Going over we were all young people – we went via South Africa [on the way back] and it was a lot of older people – you would just get friendly with people and they would all get off – so you broke that group. Going over we were all in a group from the beginning and were there for the five weeks. On the way back when we hit Australia all the Aussies got off and a whole lot more got on who were starting their trip – they were all starting off excited and eager.

an injured seaman from an oil tanker, led to a mutiny by some passengers.

Enjoyment of individual sailings could also be dependent on the weather encountered during the voyage. Patricia described her six-week passage on the *Southern Cross* in 1965 as 'interminable': passengers were stuck inside the whole time because it was the end of the hurricane season and the weather was 'horrible': they couldn't even go outside and swim. Her six-berth cabin in the bowels of the ship was so cramped that only two people could get dressed at the same time.

By the 1970s, some of the ships were showing their age; when Penny and her husband sailed on the *Australis* in 1971 it was 'a creaky old thing that shuddered all the way to England'. Bob has a photograph of himself and his girlfriend with two other young women at dinner on the first night of their journey to Singapore on the *Patris* in 1973; one of the women was subsequently so sea sick that they never saw her again.

Stories of the *Southern Cross* – referred to by some as the 'Suffering Cross' – have generated numerous posts on the Ships Nostalgia online reunion board.[4] For one 1970 *Southern Cross* crew member, departure was marred by the fact that 'most of the "Belfast contingent" of the deck department were in various states of intoxication, thus causing extra work for the rest of us'. During the trip there were three deaths: a crew member 'disappeared' one night, a passenger died of a heart attack, and there was one other death of which they could not recall the circumstances. The crew member was attacked while sleeping; the person responsible was apparently unaware the next day of what he had done due to being high on various 'substances'. Another post recalled sailors' gossip: 'Tales I heard [about the *Southern Cross*] – 1959–62 – included a claim that she once sailed from Oz with over 1000 female passengers under 25. I was told that with seven passenger decks, there was an unwritten rule about on which deck [the] deck officers and cadets socialised, so that they did not encounter each other in difficult situations.'

According to a former Shaw Savill employee, ships' engineers would 'spot' young women, inviting them to party in the engineers' quarters. All the single females on board were usually allocated cabins in one area – known as 'fluff alley' on all the ships. While he questioned the 'over 1000 female passengers' claim (the *Southern Cross* carried about 1180 passengers), he recalled a *Northern Star* Auckland-to-Sydney sailing, with 1400 people on board, where the ratio was six to one, female to male. There was a rape in the cinema lounge, the only really bad incident he could remember: 'Today there would be harassment claims, but back then it was different.'

'Now is the Hour'

Ships returning to New Zealand were usually fully booked with migrants, making it more difficult for OE travellers to get a berth home: 'return passages guaranteed' was a feature in many 1950s travel advertisements. However, from the mid-1960s it became more common to leave by ship and return by air; by the late 1960s, some shipping companies advertised an 'air/sea interchange', with concessions on return airfares. Chandris Lines took over the government contract to transport British migrants to Australia in 1970 but the numbers travelling by ship were declining; by 1976, the *Australis* was the last liner sailing regularly between England and Australia.

Air passengers increased at a much faster rate than passengers by sea in the 1950s. While passenger liners remained in service until the mid-1970s, competition from airlines had a growing impact. In November 1961 *New Zealand News* reported that the halfway mark for air versus sea travel to and from New Zealand was reached in 1956–57; by 1960–61, 63 per cent of passengers were carried by air. By 1970, 90 per cent of international travellers to and from New Zealand went by air. To combat the decline in sea passengers, Shaw Savill offered special 'youth fares' in 1973 for those aged under 26, and 'wayport fares' that enabled passengers to join or leave sailings at ports en route. The youth fare of $402 ($4658) competed with a special one-way economy class Pan Am airfare of $420 ($4867). In another effort to support shipping lines, travel companies offered passenger services to Britain that split the journey between the competing transport modes. In 1972 the *Patris* operated between Fremantle and Singapore, taking advantage of the cheap airfares available from Singapore to Europe. The fare for travel by ship to

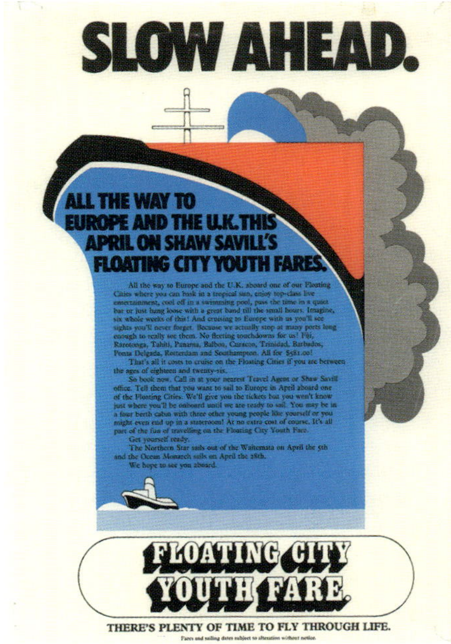

Above: In 1972 Shaw Savill offered a cruise/jet service via Los Angeles with the *Ocean Monarch*; the $385 ($4799) fare (for a four-berth inside cabin) included the sea voyage via Rarotonga (where the vessel was at anchorage for only three hours) and Tahiti (a 23-hour stop), three days in Los Angeles, and a charter flight on to London Gatwick.
Ian Read (Shaw Savill)

Above left: Passengers purchasing youth fares did not know which type of cabin they would be in until sailing time.
Ian Read (Shaw Savill)

JUDI left Australia in May 1980 on the *Kota Bali* in the company of several hundred young Australians and New Zealanders en route to London. Her ticket cost AUS$1025 ($3930 in 2013 value)[5] for a one-way passage (flying Brisbane to Perth, seven days on the ship, several days' stopover in Singapore and a flight to London via Bangkok). The ship satisfied some of her expectations of a cruise ship – it was painted white and had a swimming pool – but it also had a cargo of live sheep on the lower decks, which passengers could smell if the wind was blowing from the wrong direction. The cabins were very cramped. The young people didn't care, though, as alcohol was available at duty-free prices (a can of beer cost 25 cents) and they were there to have a good time. The highlight of the trip was the party to celebrate crossing the equator.

Life on the *Kota Bali*.

Singapore and an onward flight to either Athens or London was advertised in October 1973 as $373 ($4322 in 2013 value).

The New Zealand Shipping Company pulled out of the passenger business in 1968, Flotta Lauro lines withdrew its service in 1972, and Shaw Savill followed in 1975. The Sitmar Line's *Fairstar* departed Southampton for Sydney and Auckland, via Cape Town, for the last time in November 1974, the *Marconi* from Australia in 1974, and the *Galileo* in 1976. The last passenger ship on the New Zealand and Australia service, the *Australis*, departed Southampton on its final voyage to Australia in 1977, after which it was laid up in Timaru before being sold to American Cruise Lines in 1978. Since 17 January 1966 the *Australis* had visited Auckland 79 times. In 1979, after a major refurbishment, it was renamed *America*, and operated briefly as a cruise ship out of the United States before being sold again, this time back to Chandris Lines, renamed the *Italis* and used for Mediterranean cruises. It eventually ended its life in 1988, run aground near Piraeus (in order to stop it sinking), as the *Alferdoss*.

Many ships from the UK–New Zealand service went on to serve as passenger ferries and cruise liners. By the mid-1970s, for example, P&O-Orient had ceased line voyages between Australia, New Zealand and Britain, but was still running shorter cruises out of New Zealand and Australian ports with some of its passenger liners.

Crowds line the wharf and streamers fly from the ship in *Southern Cross* departures of 1955 (above)and the 1970s (left).

Dominion Post Collection, Alexander Turnbull Library (EP-Transport-Ships-Southern Cross-01); Ian Read (Shaw Savill)

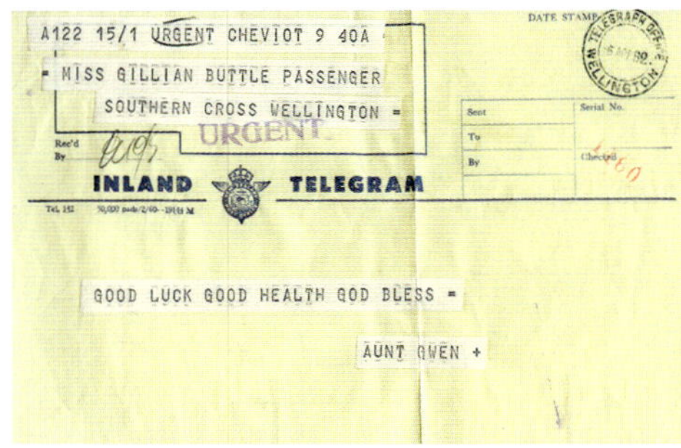
A122 15/1 URGENT CHEVIOT 9 40A
MISS GILLIAN BUTTLE PASSENGER
SOUTHERN CROSS WELLINGTON
URGENT
INLAND TELEGRAM
GOOD LUCK GOOD HEALTH GOD BLESS
AUNT GWEN

People also sent farewell telegrams to the ship.

The last vestiges of the journey by ship to Britain lived on into the early 1980s, with the continuation of sea/air tickets offering a seven-day sea passage from Fremantle to Singapore, followed by a flight to London.

The end of the passenger shipping services between Australasia and Europe signalled the end of an era. It also meant the end of an important ritual of farewell on New Zealand wharves: crowds gathered on the wharf, streamers thrown from the decks to friends and family below, and bands playing 'Now is the Hour'. Lynette remembered this being very emotional:

People went knowing they might not see their families again – I still can't bear to hear 'Now is the Hour'. I wanted to get off that boat. Mum had bought a hat for the occasion and it blew away – she didn't even notice.

Visitor passes were available to those seeing passengers off. Often they would come on board with a flagon of beer for a farewell drink; the ship's bar did not open until it left port. The crew would then have to try and get the visitors off before the ship sailed.

Family and friends who could not be at the wharf often sent farewell telegrams to the ship. Going by sea gave a sense of distance to be travelled that was missing from air travel. Those who sailed one way and returned by air often commented on the anticlimax of the relatively quick return flight.

Jet lag

While the 1960s was the peak decade for passenger shipping, it was also a decade in which air travel changed significantly. Airfares and travelling times fell as changing aircraft technology and the introduction of jet services made travel to and from New Zealand both faster and easier. Reduced journey times were a feature of airline advertisements in the 1950s and 1960s: in 1959 Pan Am offered a JET Polar Service, with Jet Clippers cutting the polar flight time from the west coast of the United States to London almost in half (to only eight hours), while the 1960 TEAL Electra service from Auckland to Sydney took only 3 hours 50 minutes. Qantas slashed the flight time on its Sydney–London route from 48 hours to only 27.[6] In the words of one 1963 advertisement: 'Air travel is so exciting … Modern luxury air travel that leaps whole countries between meals and telescopes seasons into days is thrilling.'[7]

TEAL (Tasman Empire Airways Limited) was New Zealand's international carrier and began services to Australia in 1940, expanding throughout the Pacific in the 1950s. Flying-boats were replaced by DC6 aircraft in 1954; a final flight over the Coral Route brought the last Solent flying-boat home to Auckland in September 1960. Increases in international flights brought new airport construction: Wellington's Rongotai airport opened in 1959 and Christchurch International Airport in February 1960. Auckland, with its greater population, had always been home to New Zealand's main international airport, which was located at Whenuapai until the opening of Mangere Airport in 1965.

Throughout the 1950s and 1960s a growing range of flight options was available from TEAL, as well as from other international airlines. By 1964 several airlines operated flights to and from New Zealand: Pan-American World Airways (Auckland to America via Fiji, American Samoa, Canton Island[8] and Honolulu); Canadian Pacific Airlines (a fortnightly return service between Auckland and Vancouver via Fiji, Canton Island and Honolulu); and BOAC (British Overseas

Airways Corporation) (Auckland to London twice a week via the Middle East). Qantas Empire Airways began trans-Tasman operations in October 1961, initially providing three services to every seven operated by TEAL. By January 1962 TEAL reached a record 33 weekly return services across the Tasman.

TEAL became Air New Zealand in April 1965. Its first non-stop flight (on a DC8) from Los Angeles to Auckland arrived in July 1965. December 1965 brought the inaugural DC8 Auckland–Los Angeles service, via Nadi and Honolulu. Auckland–Hong Kong and Auckland–Singapore flights were added in 1966. An Air New Zealand office opened in London in 1967. By January 1972 there were six Auckland–Los Angeles flights each week. In January 1974 Air New Zealand completed an aircraft interchange agreement whereby an Auckland–Los Angeles Air New Zealand service connected with a Los Angeles–London British Airways flight. Both services were operated by Air New Zealand-owned DC10 aircraft.

In 1982 Air New Zealand began its own twice-weekly B747 service to Britain, flying Auckland–Papeete–Los Angeles–London and return. April 1984 saw the first non-stop B747 flight from Auckland to Los Angeles, as part of a weekly one-stop service to London. At that time, the northbound journey took 24 hours: the fastest flight from New Zealand to Britain.

Year	**Airline**	**Return Fare*** Auckland–London	**Single Fare*** Auckland–London
1950	Canadian Pacific	£502.4.0d ($33,414)	£279 ($18,563)
1955	Qantas		£244 ($11,926)
1960	BOAC	£455.9.0d ($19,438)	£253 ($10,798)
1964	Canadian Pacific		£253 ($9821)
1967	KLM Royal Dutch Airlines		$506 ($8531)
1969	Air India	$632.30 ($9889)	
1973	Pan Am	$714.70 ($8218)	$420 ($4867)
1981	Air New Zealand	$1780 ($7099)	$1140 ($4547)

Figure 2.4 Selected airfares 1950–81 (2013 values in brackets).

*The prices for both return and single fares were advertised in newspapers; the single fares (no return fares were published) are for single economy and come from a bi-annual travel information booklet published by the Union Line/Union Steam Ship Company of New Zealand. The airlines listed above are indicative only, all the airlines operating at the time offered tickets at exactly the same price.

Falling prices and more choice

Airline competition, along with technological change and increasing passenger numbers, slowly reduced the price of travel to and from New Zealand. Passenger figures for the 1950s and early 1960s – as recorded by the airlines – show that TEAL carried 22,579 international passengers in 1950, 43,575 in 1955, 84,130 in 1960 and 108,891 in 1963 (almost a 500 per cent increase). Pan Am passenger numbers almost trebled in the same period (from 2233 in 1954, to 6272 in 1963). Combined figures for later years show that international air passengers increased from 277,913 in the year to March 1965, to 553,557 in the 1970 calendar year, and

BE IT KNOWN TO ALL MEN…

That in this Modern Age of Scientific Achievement in the Conquest of Nature and by the Co-ordination of Mechanical Invention and Human Service in the Transportation of Peoples over the Lands and Seas of the World

JAMES WILSON

HAS CROSSED

THE LINE OF THE EQUATOR

(Where the transition from South to North and North to South is achieved in an instant and in the Demesne of Uranus, Polus Boreus and Polus Austrinus are equi-distant.)

IN THE PROUD CARE OF

AIR NEW ZEALAND

THE FIVE STAR JETLINE

THIS CROSSING OF THE EQUATOR LINE WAS ACHIEVED IN AN AIR NEW ZEALAND JETLINER

IN FLIGHT BETWEEN SYDNEY

AND HONG KONG ON THE 5 DAY OF MAY 1971

CAPTAIN

In witness whereof this certificate has been signed by the Master of an AIR NEW ZEALAND Jetliner on the day and year above-mentioned.

In 1971 passengers flying from New Zealand to Britain received certificates commemorating their crossing of the International Date Line and the equator signed by their Air New Zealand captain.

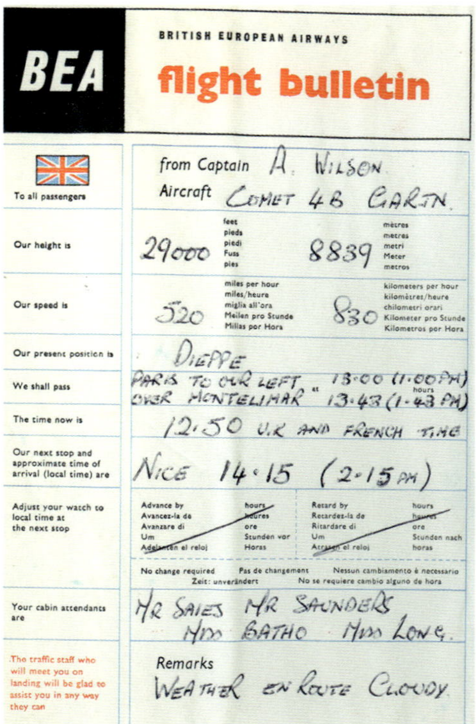

BEA

BRITISH EUROPEAN AIRWAYS

flight bulletin

To all passengers	from Captain A. WILSON Aircraft COMET 4B G-ARJN
Our height is	29000 feet / pieds / piedi / Fuss / pies — 8839 mètres / metres / metri / Meter / metros
Our speed is	520 miles per hour / miles/heure / miglia all'ora / Meilen pro Stunde / Millas por Hora — 830 kilometers per hour / kilomètres/heure / chilometri orari / Kilometer pro Stunde / Kilometros por Hora
Our present position is	DIEPPE
We shall pass	PARIS TO OUR LEFT at 13.00 (1.00 PM) hours OVER MONTELIMAR 13.43 (1.43 PM)
The time now is	12.50 U.K AND FRENCH TIME
Our next stop and approximate time of arrival (local time) are	NICE 14.15 (2.15 PM)
Adjust your watch to local time at the next stop	Advance by / Avancez-la de / Avanzare di / Um / Adelanten el reloj — hours / heures / ore / Stunden vor / Horas Retard by / Retardez-la de / Ritardare di / Um / Atrasen el reloj — hours / heures / ore / Stunden nach / horas No change required / Pas de changement / Zeit: unverändert / Nessun cambiamento è necessario / No se requiere cambio alguno de hora
Your cabin attendants are	MR SALES MR SAUNDERS MISS BATHO MISS LONG
The traffic staff who will meet you on landing will be glad to assist you in any way they can	Remarks WEATHER EN ROUTE CLOUDY

Passengers on European flights in the 1960s received a printed 'Flight Bulletin', with information on the type of aircraft, the flight, crew details and weather en route.

1,415,000 (another 500 per cent increase) in 1978.

Airline advertising rarely included fares, although the types of aircraft were listed. The 1955 BOAC 'fleet' consisted of Stratocruisers, Constellations, Argonauts and Hermes; in 1964, Canadian Pacific operated DC8s, Bristols, Britannias and DC8Bs; in 1967, KLM Royal Dutch Airlines advertised DC8s, Lockheed Electras, Viscounts and Convair 880s. Normally fares were calculated for each individual passenger on a mileage basis, with a certain number of miles allowed for a journey. If the mileage was exceeded (because of extra stops or side trips), the fare increased in proportion to the number of excess miles travelled.

Although prices were falling, air travel from 1950 to the early 1970s remained the domain of the wealthy. Flying was treated as a special and memorable experience for passengers. An *Advice for Your Flight* booklet published in 1972 by Air New Zealand provided comprehensive information for the intending traveller, including a list of approximate clothing weights (to assist with packing within the baggage limits). It suggested including 'sunglasses for wear in-flight as well as on the ground' in one's cabin bag. Smoking was 'normally' permitted on board except during take-off and landing. According to *Down Under in Europe* the following year, meals were provided on flights, although only first-class passengers were entitled to free drinks; the book also advised passengers to take magazines or paperbacks on board in case they missed out on the airline's available reading material.

Several ticket options introduced during the 1960s and 1970s greatly benefited New Zealanders wishing to fly. First were 'Round-the-World' tickets, introduced to assist Commonwealth migration by heavily reducing fares between Britain, Australia and New Zealand. These long-distance flights were much cheaper for New Zealanders and Australians than for passengers who wanted to depart from Rome or San Francisco.[9] While they allowed for 'flexible and elastic travel', however, they did not extend beyond a narrow corridor of stopovers. Those travellers wishing to venture off the usual flight paths faced a large increase in ticket price. Youth (for those under 26) and one-way economy fares were also introduced in the early 1970s. These were especially significant in relation to the OE: many chose to fly on these fares rather than go by ship. However, New Zealanders often had to fly to Australia to pick up such fares.

In 1979 a new cheap fare between Auckland and London was awaiting government approval; at the time, apart from currency-related changes, Auckland–London fares had not changed since 1975. The new fare package promised to be cheaper than the current return fare of $1284 ($6949 in 2013 value), although 'New Zealand's devaluation and fuel price rises had destroyed earlier hopes of an ultra-low return fare.'[10] This new fare package introduced seasonal prices for air travel.

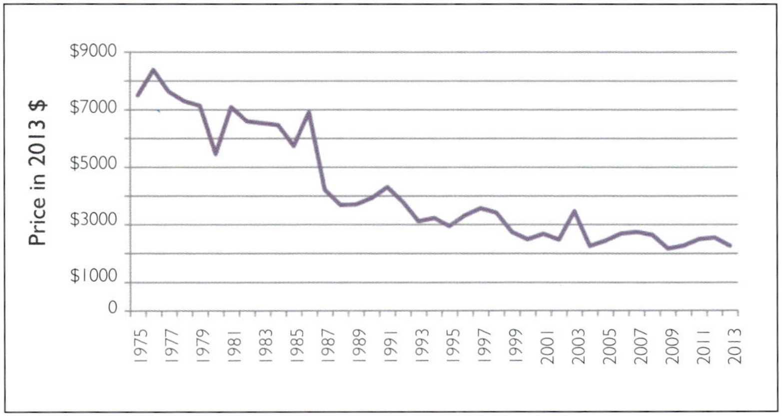

Figure 2.5 Return ticket price New Zealand–London, 1975–2013.

While the reduction in airfares slowed considerably from the 1970s, they continued to fall in real terms. Figure 2.5 shows the cheapest advertised return New Zealand–London flight each February since 1975 (adjusted to 2013 prices). The greatest fall in price (in 1986–87) was due to increased competition, facilitated by a liberalised external aviation policy for New Zealand announced in 1985, which resulted in an expansion of available international air services.

Other calculations also reveal dramatic falls in airfares over the OE decades. According to data shown in *Flightpaths*, for example, the average weeks' earnings required to fly from Sydney to London fell from just over 90 in 1950 to 32 in 1960, 14 in 1970, six in 1980, under four in 1990, and just over two weeks in 2000.[11] Similar data featured in the Air New Zealand history,

Exotic stops en route for sea travellers: Egypt, 1960s; Colombo, 1950s.

Conquering Isolation, demonstrate the number of working days required to pay for Auckland–Wellington and Auckland–Sydney fares between 1940 to 1990.[12]

Declining prices helped to facilitate travel and, in effect, reduced the distance between New Zealand and Britain. Bigger planes brought economies of scale to a different level. From the mid-1970s, flying became the only option available to those going on OE (unless one went overland). Gone was the five- or six-week holiday en route afforded by sea travel. Time became more important; those going on OE could leave a job in New Zealand, organise a job in London, and be there within a week. Air passengers preferred to make only brief stopovers, if they stopped at all, on their way to Britain. The stopovers also changed: Colombo, Bombay, Aden, Suez and Gibraltar or Panama, Balboa and Curacao gave way to flight connection hubs and refuelling stops more familiar to today's travellers – Singapore, Bangkok and Los Angeles.

Overland on the Hippie Trail

It was possible, of course, to travel most of the way from New Zealand to Europe overland, although this was usually an option taken by more experienced travellers returning to New Zealand. The travel account referred to at the start of this chapter, *For Love and a Beetle*, described one such journey. In another account from the early 1960s, entitled *Four Kiwis and a Falcon*, David Harford described a two-year 'drive' around the world in the company of three other New Zealanders. After shipping their vehicle to Singapore, they drove across Asia, through the Middle East to Europe, crossed the Atlantic on the *Canberra,* travelled around the United States and through Central America, then shipped their car and flew themselves over the Darien Gap between Panama and Columbia, before driving around South America. They (and the Falcon) eventually returned to New Zealand from Lima, Peru, on the *Amalric* (1960), a Shaw Savill & Albion Company freighter. The four Kiwis had driven 94,000 miles through 50 countries in 21 months, at a cost of £930 each (equal to around $39,000 in 2013).

New Zealanders travelling overland were part of a travel phenomenon practised by a new breed of tourists, the youth travellers of the 1960s and 1970s. The classic overland trip – the 'Hippie Trail' – followed a route from London to Nepal, usually finishing in Freak Street in Kathmandu. Many early accounts of travel on the Hippie Trail focused on the counter-culture aspects of the hippie lifestyle and its associated drug culture. In *The Great Railway Bazaar*, for example, Paul Theroux reported meeting many young 'drop-outs' travelling.[13] The growing popularity of the Hippie Trail during the 1970s brought increasing commercialisation, with the publication of dedicated guidebooks and the advent of organised tours.

The 1970 *BIT Travel Guide*[14] was the earliest practical guide to the route and consisted of 'a half dozen or so duplicated foolscap sheets stapled together with one staple and no cover'. By early 1975, updated with contributions from travellers, it had grown to over 200 pages (although it was still missing a cover and held together with one staple). In Australia, publication of the *Student Guide to Asia* in 1972 (with updated editions throughout the 1970s) illustrated the interest in overland travel – and in Asia – by young travellers.[15] In 1975 the Wellington Overland Club published a *Travel Handbook* which outlined transport options, gave advice on vehicle purchase and necessary equipment, and described types of accommodation available, the documentation required and probable costs. Climate, political situations and road conditions likely to be encountered in Africa, Asia, Australia, Europe, Japan, South Korea, the United States, Canada, South America and Trans Siberia were also described. The guide was only 98 pages long, leaving rather a lot of detail for travellers to discover for themselves.

Most guidebooks from the 1970s are long forgotten and out of print today; older editions of the few publications that have survived are difficult to find as new editions supplant previous ones in libraries and bookshops. Occasionally old editions appear in the bins at library sell-offs, in secondhand bookshops or, increasingly, on internet book sale and auction sites. The style of writing and the language used in these early guides are curiously dated. For example, in *The*

Four Kiwis and a Falcon.
Penguin NZ (Whitcombe & Tombs)

Overland on the Hippie Trail with Asian Greyhound (Swagman Tours) Ltd in 1975.
Derek Amey, www.overland.biz

Overlander's Handbook (published in 1976) Mary Gage advised:

If you have room, take one really square outfit to wear at frontiers, which will help you through quickly. Never mind if you don't like this get-up; you can wear it out in Singapore and Malaysia, where hippies are persona-non-grata, and long haired travellers are given forty-eight hours to get a haircut or get out.[16]

In addition to the haircut rule, Singapore in the 1970s also strictly enforced laws against hitchhiking. The *Student Guide to Asia* included a full page of 'helpful hints' with respect to long hair and quoted the Singapore Foreign Minister of the time saying that 'long hair was an essential ingredient of hippie style' and this lifestyle could destroy Singapore because hippism was 'a new version of the opium of the people. It is the kind of opium war an enemy would launch for the successful conquest of a country. Hippism is not mumps. It is cancer.'[17]

Perhaps the most enduring legacy of the Hippie Trail is the Lonely Planet Company. The first Lonely Planet guide, *Across Asia on the Cheap*, published in 1973, described the overland route taken by Tony and Maureen Wheeler from London to Sydney. The countries they visited and the tourists who visit them are today vastly different from those they described: Nepal, for example, was so renowned as 'a hippie haven that people hardly realise that it has so much to offer'; Afghanistan was 'a marvellous, crazy country'; and the Iranian government, 'in an effort to attract even our type of tourists', had opened a number of excellent government campsites. One and a half pages (of a total of 94) in the book are devoted to drugs, with the 'best' places to find each type of drug described in detail. Under the heading 'Dope' the guide notes, 'If that's what you want then you are going to the right places! Some people seem to use the overland route as an excuse for a long term high.'[18]

Overland companies were shuttling backwards and forwards across Asia like city buses by the mid-1970s.[19] Some of the more successful included Transit Travel, Autotours, Sundowners, Penn Overland and Top Deck. Many of these companies had begun their operations running European camping tours out of London for the expatriate Australasian market. Asian Greyhound, for example, started in 1958 as Swagman Tours, based in Earls Court. Overland tours offered return passage for young Australian and New Zealand travellers and were often advertised alongside shipping and airline options. A 1968 *Penn: European and overland tours* brochure, for example, advertised tours in conjunction with Qantas, Cathay Pacific, Shaw Savill and Lloyd Triestino. Throughout the 1970s, overland companies also advertised in New Zealand newspapers: Penn Overland in 1973, Sundowners in 1979, Top Deck in 1980.

Top Deck ran converted double-decker London buses all over Europe and out to Delhi. Its first overland trip on the Hippie

Trail, in 1975, was described in the book *Top Deck Daze*: by way of preparation, the driver attended another overland company's promotional sales evenings to find out about the route. Fortunately, one passenger on the trip 'had in-depth knowledge of history and current affairs which greatly added to our understanding of, and interest in, the countries visited'.[20]

The prices of these tours varied enormously, depending on the speed of travel and the types of accommodation used along the way. An 11-week Asian Greyhound trip to Kathmandu in 1974 cost £160 (£1368 in 2011 value).[21] In 1976, a 72-day Penn Tours budget bus trip from Kathmandu to London, sleeping in youth hostels or cheap hotels, cost US$828.75 ($3406 in 2013 value).[22] Overland companies used a variety of vehicles, ranging from converted fire trucks to luxury coaches. One passenger recalled being driven to Dover in a near-new luxury coach before transferring to a Budget Bus (which had no MOT for the UK) – which they then had to push-start – not an auspicious beginning to a long trip. Other companies operated buses to India for as little as US$150 ($616 in 2013 value). The infamous non-stop 'Magic Buses' travelled from Amsterdam to India in four days, carrying mainly hippie travellers who wanted to get to India as quickly as possible; the fare could be as little as US$45 ($185 in 2013 value). Next cheapest was Budget Bus: in 1977, London to Delhi cost £80 (£408 in 2011 value).

Overland on the Hippie Trail with Asian Greyhound (Swagman Tours) Ltd in 1975.

OVERLAND TRAVEL was not for everyone. Diane – on her OE in the mid-1970s – saw Asia (as a destination) and overland travel (as a style) as more suited to couples than to single women, or for those who were 'braver and more practical' than she was. Heather and a girlfriend travelled overland in 1976 using a TrailFinders Asian Rover Pass, a booklet of pre-paid vouchers that could be exchanged along the way for local bus and train tickets. She wanted to be a little more 'freelance' than taking a tour but, because of her age (she was only 19), preferred to be semi-organised and have the security of pre-paying at least some of the trip. In Iran and Afghanistan, Heather and her friend met mainly Australians and New Zealanders, as well as a few Europeans and Britons, and the occasional South African. They found places like Pakistan, India and Kabul were used to dealing with tourists: those travelling picked up the same information and ended up gathering in the same places, usually in big cities. In Delhi, they met up with a busload of people who had come through from London on an organised tour where things had gone 'haywire': the bus had broken down, the driver had hepatitis and so on. From Delhi, they travelled with some of the abandoned bus passengers on local transport to Nepal.

TrailFinders' *Asian Rover Handbook.*
Mike Gooley, TrailFinders

The world at their feet

In 1973 *Down Under in Europe* described (and critiqued) the different ways of travelling the overland Asia route: best was by private vehicle, provided one was well equipped and prepared for anything; hitchhiking was risky and uncomfortable; and rail travel was cheap and still 'adventuresome'. The simplest way to travel was by bus tour, although this option was much more expensive. However, the guide pointed out that since the closure of the Suez Canal, when ships had ceased regular services to the area, it had become more difficult for New Zealanders and Australians to get to India, to the start of the route.

According to a forum posting on an overland travel website,[23] TrailFinders sold thousands of Asian Rover tickets in the 1970s; travel from London to Delhi on the tickets cost about £50 (around £540 in 2011 value). So many of these tickets were sold to Australians and New Zealanders that TrailFinders eventually started to provide cheap air tickets for passengers to fly from Delhi or Kathmandu to Australia and New Zealand.

For those travelling further into Asia or Australia, or travelling west from Australia and New Zealand to Europe, the 'Trail' extended into other Asian countries. The Vietnam War ruled out several other destinations to these early travellers; *Across Asia on the Cheap* reported that 'due to the continuing effects of the American charade in South East Asia travel to other

South East Asian countries is difficult, not recommended or impossible.'[24] The *Student Guide to Asia* (which covered 24 countries) did not include Vietnam, and although Cambodia was included readers were advised that travel beyond the capital Phnom Penh was not safe. Ron, travelling in 1977, did not stop in Thailand for long, because it was a 'rest and relaxation' destination for American servicemen stationed in Indochina, rather than a 'backpacker' hangout. Others remembered Bangkok being the primary destination, rather than rest of the country. According to *Across Asia on the Cheap*, Thailand was a poor second to other Southeast Asian countries in terms of its food, and little English was spoken outside the capital city; the northern city of Chiang Mai was noted only for the contrast it offered to Bangkok.

In the 1970s, Bali was a more popular stop for the overland travellers than Thailand. Some passenger ships also stopped in Bali, although Bali today would be barely recognisable to these early travellers. Lynette's memory, from a stop there on the *Orcades* in 1962, was of a 'fabulous place – there wasn't even a wharf – they sent boats out for us. The next stop, in Bombay in India, was the biggest culture shock for me.' Another ship passenger recalled Bali as 'absolute heaven', with the women all topless; she remembered trading make-up for souvenirs. Hazel passed through Bali overland in 1978 when 'Bali had one tar-sealed road in Denpasar – from the airport to the Bali Beach Hotel – there was no electricity in Kuta and you had to walk through the paddy fields to get to the beach.'

It was also possible to travel overland through Africa, as a number of 'safari' overland tours operated from Cape Town to Nairobi and from Nairobi to London. The most economical way to travel this route was to take a ship to Cape Town, travel overland to Nairobi and then fly to London. Both air and ship connections could be used to facilitate overland travel in the Americas.

ONE OF THE MOST ADVENTUROUS overland travel stories undertaken by a New Zealander must surely be Louise Sutherland's round-the-world bicycle trip in the early 1950s. In her account of the trip, *I Follow the Wind*, she wrote:

After all, I thought to myself as I cycled, I HAD left home to see the world. There was £40 in my pocket. My entire savings since I had arrived in England nine months before. [Louise was a nurse.] My time was entirely my own. All that was left to be done was to collect my passport from London and leave a few belongings with some friends.[25]

Her trip took her through Europe and to the Middle East, where she worked for a few months in Nazareth, Amman and Beirut. After taking a train and bus through Iraq to Basra (Iran was closed at the time), she caught a ship to Bombay. One of the officers on the ship told her that it was the fourth trip running that they had Kiwis on board; on the previous trip, a young Māori couple were going home overland, travelling on a motorbike.

After hearing that her father in New Zealand had taken ill, Louise took a passage home to New Zealand from India on the *Wairemu*. After a year in New Zealand she set off again, this time on the *Oronsay* to Vancouver, before cycling across Canada to New York, from where she sailed on the *Queen Mary* back to London.

The overland stories in Nigel McCarter's *The Big OE* anthology are primarily those of people returning home. One couple drove from London to Delhi in 1962 in a classic car, following the Marco Polo trail. Another New Zealand couple 'set off home' in 1966, via Iraq, Iran and Afghanistan. With rather bad timing they 'arrived in Iraq from Jordan just after the 1966 coup that brought the Baathists, and eventually Saddam Hussein, to power'. In another story, a keen surfer took his surfboard with him on his OE in 1965. He surfed in Colombo and Aden en route to Europe; when he arrived in England, he lived in Brighton, in order to surf. He eventually set out for South Africa driving a converted van with surfboards on the roof, but only got as far as Libya. Yet another New Zealand couple drove by van from London to India in 1972 and took a ferry to Singapore from Madras, before flying to New Zealand.[26]

Trouble on the Hippie Trail

While some destinations and types of travel fluctuated in availability and popularity as a result of changes in available transportation, the fate of others was determined by political events. The late 1970s was a period of political instability in Asia and the Middle East, as the Soviet Union invaded Afghanistan and the Shah of Iran was deposed by an Islamic revolution. One casualty of this was the closing of the Hippie Trail. Some travellers – like Hazel, who was travelling overland to Britain with her husband in 1978 and got as far as Delhi – were, quite simply, stopped in their tracks: '[We] struck a problem because Khomeini was in Iran and Pan Am wouldn't fly there and Bhutto had just been assassinated in Pakistan and the Russians had just invaded Afghanistan – so the only flight we could get was Iraqi Airways, via Baghdad to Istanbul.'

It was a difficult time for companies still running overland tours through Asia. For Top Deck, overland trips were 'becoming a continual source of almost insurmountable operational problems': motors blowing up in obscure locations, drivers coming down with serious illnesses or getting arrested, border closures, wars, invasions and revolutions added up to a tour operator's nightmare.[27] Lew Pulbrook was leaving Tehran on the last Top Deck bus (a double-decker named 'Bollocks') when the revolution started in Iran in 1978. He recalled seeing some horrible sights as he drove 27 hours non-stop from Tehran to the eastern Turkey border near Lake Van, with 22 passengers on board. In 2008 his tour group held a 30-year reunion in Australia, with some New Zealanders flying in for the event.

Running overland trips had never been easy. Sometimes passengers, rather than external factors, were the cause of problems, as one Swagman Tours driver recalled:

Most drivers did a round trip of 17,000 miles (25,000 km) in about five–six months. The life was hard, constant bouts of stomach problems and having to keep a group of travellers amused and safe took its toll. Not all travellers were in it for the right reasons, there were the 'get rich quick by smuggling dope crowd', the 'rip off other travellers type', and many who were 'so far off their heads that they weren't safe out on their own'.[28]

Asian Greyhound went broke in the mid-1970s, stranding a driver with a broken-down bus and a load of passengers in Afghanistan. The driver managed to fix the bus and eventually made it to Kathmandu, where he took the bus in lieu of wages and started the Anglo Australian Comfortable Coach Company with a fellow driver.[29] Penn Overland finished in the early 1980s when a brand new coach, worth £60,000 (uninsured) was smashed up by Iranians; the passengers escaped but the bus never made it out of Iran.

In 1978 an article appeared in the New Zealand *Consumer* magazine describing the experience of a young New Zealand woman who, having booked and paid for an overland trip through her travel agent in Dunedin, arrived in Kathmandu to find no bus waiting. After two weeks in Kathmandu, she made her own way to London (at considerable additional expense) to find the company – Asian Greyhound Swagman Overland Tours – had closed its doors. When her father pursued the matter with the New Zealand travel agent with whom she had booked the trip, he was told that the responsibility for compensation lay with the tour company itself. He persisted and eventually she received some compensation from the bankrupt company, with the balance repaid by the New Zealand travel agent.[30]

Overland travel, while still feasible today, is a little more difficult than it was in the 1960s and 1970s; one Australian traveller's account of his return to Sydney overland in the 1990s was entitled *The Wrong Way Home* in recognition of this. Although it is possible to obtain visas for Iran, conflicts in Iraq, Afghanistan and parts of Pakistan continue to make the route difficult for the current generation of independent travellers. Top Deck operated overland tours, with altered routes, until 1997. Sundowners still runs a number of overland tours through Central Asia and along the Silk Road (although the people involved have no connection with the older company of the same name). In September 2007 a new bus service, Oz-Bus, started between London and Sydney; this trip, marketed as following the route of the Hippie Trail, travels from Turkey to Nepal through Iran, Pakistan and India. In 2012 the itinerary for this Sydney–London 'overland' route included Darwin–Bali, Java–Singapore, Bangkok–Kathmandu and India–Tehran flights.

Chapter Three

THE EARLY OE TRAVELLERS

MOST EARLY OE TRAVELLERS headed for London. For many, landing in Britain signalled the end of a fabulous holiday. Those arriving by ship berthed either at Tilbury Docks, 40 kilometres below London Bridge on the Thames, or on the south coast at Southampton. From Tilbury, passengers travelled by bus or train into the city. From Southampton, passengers could catch boat trains, which departed for Waterloo Station in central London from platforms housed within the Ocean Terminal; tickets were sold on board for these. Those arriving by air at Heathrow took a bus to Hounslow and then the tube into London; Heathrow Central underground station (now Heathrow Terminals 1, 2, 3) did not open until 1977.

For young New Zealanders, Southampton and London were disappointing after such ports as Panama, Curacao, Colombo and

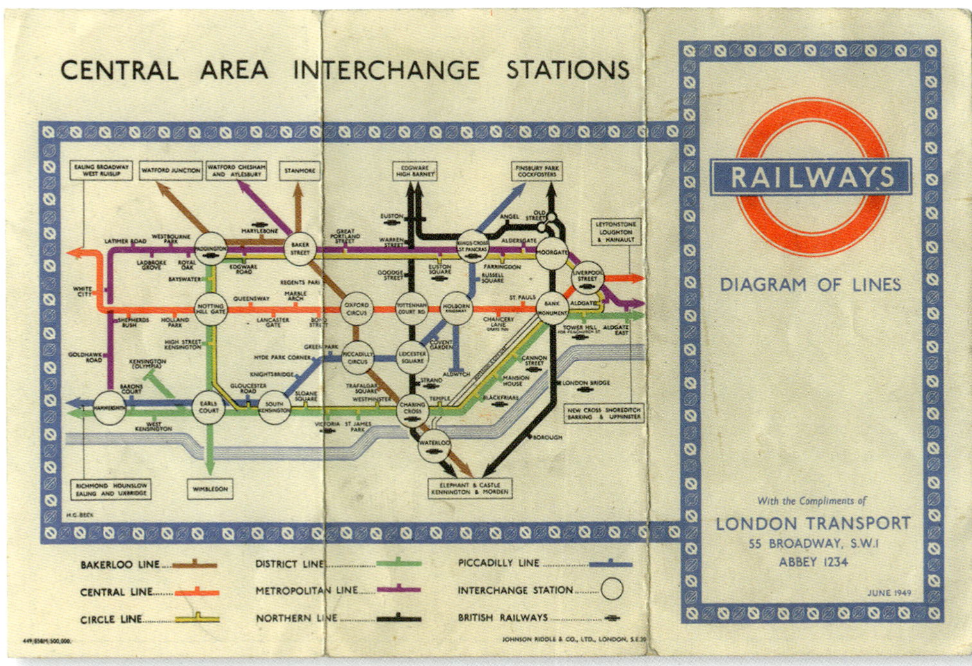

London Transport map, 1949.
London Transport Museum

Aden. On arrival, they were overwhelmed by the sheer number of people in London, appalled by the highly visible air pollution, and often (since they had taken advantage of off-season fares from New Zealand) their misery was compounded by its being midwinter. London was dirty, cold, grey and it wasn't home. It was also different: some people remembered feeling like country bumpkins when they arrived in the sixties, the era of the Beatles, Mary Quant, Twiggy and Carnaby Street.

Having relatives or friends to stay with was a bonus for some young travellers, as it gave a little time in which to get used to the crowds and transport systems before going it alone. However, the long sea voyage also introduced them to other adventurous souls and many subsequently flatted or travelled with people with whom they had shared cabins, dining tables, or shore excursions en route to Britain. Lifelong friendships evolved, with people still in contact more than 40 years later.

The Overseas Visitors Club (OVC)

Travel agents in New Zealand usually recommended the Overseas Visitors Club (OVC) for those who, needing commercial accommodation in central London, were unable to pay for 'good' hotels. Established by two South Africans and an Australian in 1954,[1] the club had its original premises at 3 Templeton Place, Earls Court, and expanded into nearby properties as it grew. Initially, it operated in conjunction with the Union Castle Line ships sailing between South Africa and Britain, offering young colonials one week's accommodation on top of their ship passage. By the mid-1960s, the business had grown to include Chandris and several other shipping lines. Bed and breakfast accommodation was cheap, costing between 15/- and 25/- ($30 and $50 in 2013 value) in 1963. In 1965, a sea fare from New Zealand to Southampton, with transfers to London and one week's accommodation at the OVC, cost £160 ($5997 in 2013 value). Many of those who stayed at the club recalled it being 'just the sort of thing you did', in the same way that going by ship was the 'appropriate way to head off'.

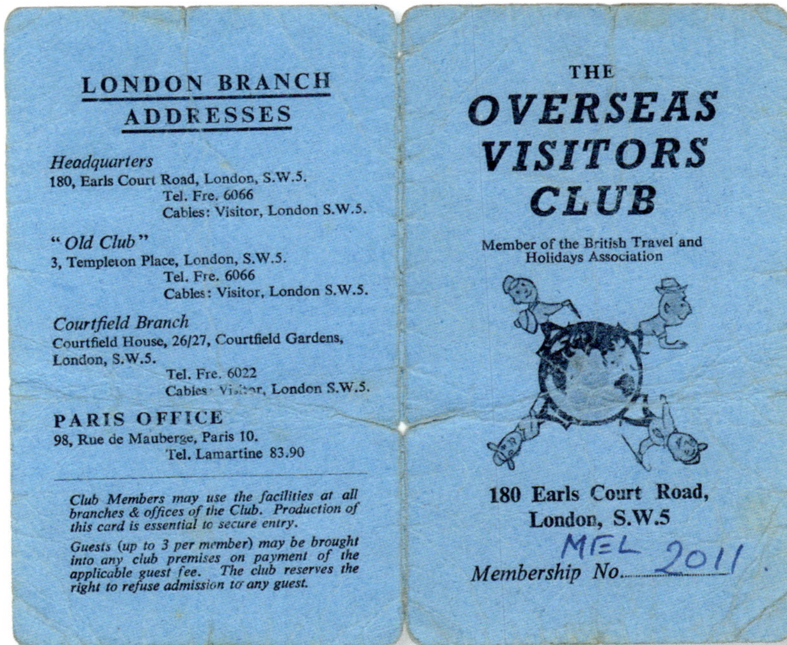

Overseas Visitors Club membership card. The club also published *The Globetrotter* magazine.

John Dickinson

In New Zealand, advertisements for the Overseas Visitors Club usually appeared in the classifieds, with the shipping listings, and occasionally in the main body of newspapers.
Christchurch Star

NEW ZEALAND travellers gave the Overseas Visitors Club mixed reviews.

In 1961, Ian and Gill arrived in Southampton on the *Fairsky* and took the bus up to London and the OVC. They stayed only a few nights because 'it was miserable, all very South African'.

In 1962, Mary and two friends had joined the OVC before leaving home. When they arrived on the *Orcades*, their luggage was sent to the club from Tilbury, but a snowstorm prevented them getting there until the following day. Their rooms were at the top of a building with a sloping attic roof and so cold they had to use newspapers to keep the heat in the beds. They were not supposed to cook in the rooms, but they had a tiny gas cooker and bought a saucepan and can-opener. Mary remembered some good features: 'lovely breakfasts and evening meals where they served things like Scottish salmon' (then unavailable in New Zealand). She also recalled London – and especially the OVC – being socially 'looser' than home.

Another traveller, Donna, remembered the club from 1968:

We arrived in Southampton and we had already joined up with the Overseas Visitors Club – it was painted as being 'home away from home' – well, that was a load of cobblers – their coffee was dearer than anyone else's and they met you with a snarl rather than a smile – it was a flophouse to go to, and you got out of it very quickly.

In its heyday, the OVC provided accommodation (it comprised five hotels), five restaurants and seven bars, a nightclub, an employment agency, a *post restante* office, a theatre booking desk and a travel agency (Trafalgar Tours). There was also a noticeboard on which travellers posted advertisements for cars, travel companions, jobs and flatmates. It was here, and at New Zealand House, that John Anderson posted flyers offering the 12-week, 15-country tour of Europe that started the Contiki company. Many other travel companies also advertised at the OVC.

The OVC catered specifically to the needs of young people on working holidays, with a free flat-finding service, a free employment service, baggage storage and access to medical and dental care. The club also hosted performances by New Zealand singers – such as Prince Tui Teka and the Maori Volcanics – which attracted many New Zealanders living in London.

The OVC played an important role in the history of 'colonial' London and was partially if not wholly responsible for Earls Court becoming known as 'Kangaroo Valley' in the 1960s. It was a magnet not only for young expatriate travellers, but also for the numerous employment agencies, travel companies and other support services that sprang up to cater to them. Other clubs opened in London before the end of the 1960s, although at least one of these – the Downunder Club in Fulham – was eventually annexed by the

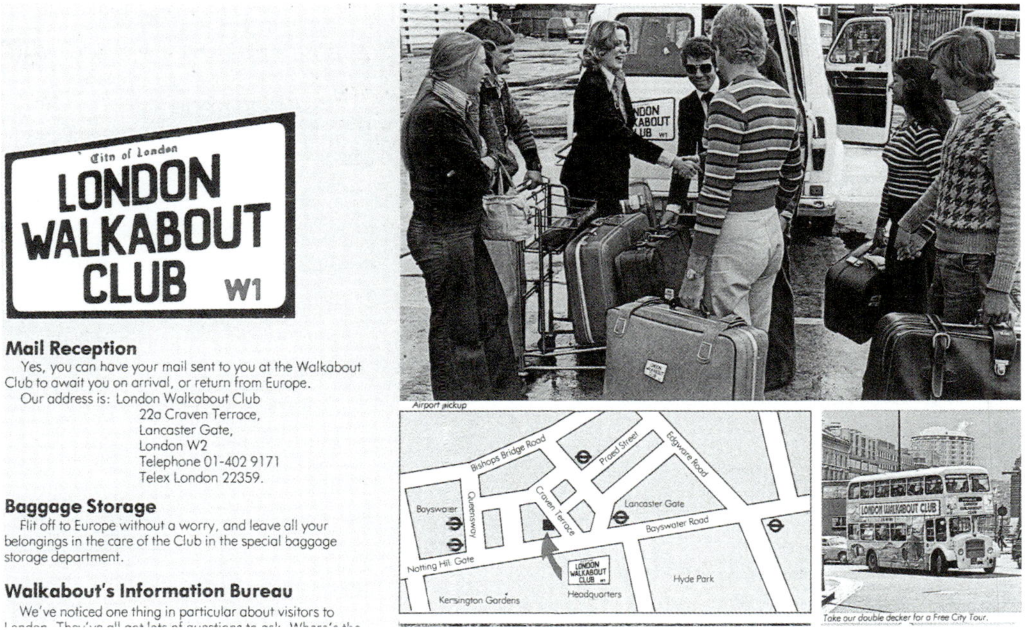

At their Lancaster Gate premises, the Walkabout Club also collected travellers' mail, stored baggage, hosted social events and published a regular club newsletter.

Alexander Turnbull Library (Eph-B-TOURISM-External-1980)

OVC. The OVC closed in 1973 when, as a result of their country's expulsion from the Commonwealth, young South Africans were forced to leave London.

After the demise of the OVC, a host of other clubs continued the tradition. The 1978 edition of *Downunder in Europe* listed three clubs designed to meet the needs of young New Zealand travellers in London: Walkabout Club, Adventure International and Trend Travel. This last was established in 1970 by a New Zealander aiming to help young New Zealanders and Australians find accommodation and employment and, supposedly, 'help them to mix rather than stick together'.

The London Walkabout Club began in 1973 and was initially associated with Autotours (a camping tour company). Through a deal with Chandris Lines, a representative of the club was on each sailing from New Zealand and Australia, with exclusive rights to sell Autotours camping trips. With three-quarters of the 2000 passengers on each sailing at that time consisting of singles under the age of 35, the 'rep' would arrive at Southampton with 700–800 recruits. Club membership included pick-up from the airport or the docks, accommodation in a choice of over 500 beds in centrally located London hotels, access to a register of available flats, a free city tour of London, and the services of an employment agency.

New Zealand House and *New Zealand News*

New Zealand appointed a government agent to represent it in London in 1860; the office was raised in status when the first high commissioner was appointed in 1905. In November 1927, in the Foreword to the first edition of *New Zealand News*, High Commissioner Sir Christopher Parr expressed pleasure that there would be 'a print which can tell them [New Zealanders settled in London and New Zealand visitors] about the activities of New Zealand House'.[2] According to the author of *Travelling Light*, in 1934,

New Zealand House is rendering splendid service to all Maorilanders who find themselves in England. Everything possible is done to make you feel at home. No request seems too trivial or too exacting to the courteous members of the staff. It admirably combines the functions of a club, an inquiry agency, a library, a tourist bureau, and a publicity office.[3]

A Welcome to Britain, a handbook published by New Zealand House in the 1960s.
Ministry of Foreign Affairs and Trade, Alexander Turnbull Library (Eph-A-TOURISM-External-1968)

New Zealand House occupied premises in The Strand from March 1916 until May 1963, when the high commission moved into purpose-built premises in the Haymarket. In *The Tender Traveller* (written in 1963, when the new building was under way), Susan Graham described:

Mr Trevor Campbell, genial public relations officer and good friend to all visitors, kindly arranged for me to go to the top of the then

Views from the Roof Terrace

unfinished building, and Mr William Cox, the planning engineer, gallantly escorted me up in a temporary lift suspended down an outside wall and then by narrow-runged ladders right up to the flat roof for a sky-high view of London. And oh, what a view it is![4]

New Zealand House became a landmark, a focal point, for expatriate New Zealanders in London. In the 1960s its public relations department distributed *A Welcome to Britain*, describing the high commission's work and giving practical information and advice and hints for travellers. Visitors could read New Zealand newspapers and cast their votes in New Zealand elections. A visitors' book was maintained until the mid-1990s, when it was given over to the *New Zealand News UK* office. From its very first issue in 1927, the *News* published a 'Callers at New Zealand House' list based on this book. The New Zealand Women's Association (established in 1930) hosted morning teas and luncheons at

The view from the New Zealand House penthouse was subsequently famed. Views from the Roof Terrace in 1968 (far left) and 2004. Sadly, both penthouse and viewing platform are no longer accessible to the public, due to security concerns and because the premises are often rented out for private functions.

From *A Welcome to Britain*, 1960s. Ministry of Foreign Affairs and Trade; Alexander Turnbull Library (Eph-A-TOURISM-External-1968)

New Zealand House. Mail could be directed to and collected from New Zealand House. A 1976 *New Zealand News* article reported that with London still 'Mecca' for many young New Zealanders, new faces appeared at New Zealand House every week in search of letters from home or the hope of seeing a friend. For younger visitors, a noticeboard displayed advertisements for jobs, flats, travel companies and travel companions. By 1978, New Zealand House had dispensed with this noticeboard and replaced it with a less useful newsletter. However, the close relationship between the high commission and *New Zealand News* meant that as services provided by one declined, the other filled the gap.

New Zealand News was founded by New Zealanders Angus and Hilda Harrop in 1927, with the aid of a grant from the high commission. The foreword of the first edition suggested that the time had come for the country to have 'its own identity and express its own especial spirit'. The opening editorial, titled 'Twelve Thousand Reasons', commented:

It was once said that there were twelve hundred reasons why New Zealand should not join the Commonwealth of Australia. The

Travel information for visitors to Britain and Europe was always a feature of *New Zealand News*: an advertisement for 'George Lunn's Tours' appeared on the front page of its first edition.

New Zealand News UK

The New Zealand News

No. 1. November 29, 1927. LONDON. FORTNIGHTLY, 5s. per annum.

TWELVE THOUSAND REASONS.

The need of a New Zealand newspaper in London has been felt for a very long time and the support which the present enterprise has already received shows that New Zealanders in this country are very anxious to have a publication devoted to the Dominion's affairs. All the other Dominions have newspapers, and some of the Crown Colonies as well.

It was once said that there were twelve hundred reasons why New Zealand should not join the Commonwealth of Australia. The reasons were the twelve hundred miles of sea which separated the two countries. It may be argued with equal force that there are twelve thousand reasons why New Zealanders should have their own newspaper at this end of the world. Separated as they are by 12,000 miles of sea from their home country, they want all the news they can get in a form as easily readable as possible.

The first aim of the "New Zealand News" will be to give a summary of the cabled and mailed news from the Dominion and to express, quite independently of any party, the New Zealand point of view upon affairs of the moment. There is no doubt that an entirely independent expression of New Zealand's voice will receive a sympathetic hearing from the Press and public of Great Britain. New Zealand, colonised by the finest band of settlers which ever left these shores, owes a debt of gratitude to the Mother Country that she can never repay, and the "New Zealand News" will do all in its power to strengthen the good relations between the two countries.

The paper will try to give New Zealand visitors to this country useful information of every possible kind. There will be descriptions of historic places in London and how to get to them, and of visits to different parts of the country. Hints on shopping places and restaurants will be supplied to newcomers applying for information. One or two plays which should be seen will be described in each issue, and coming events likely to interest New Zealanders will be mentioned. Brief accounts of concerts by New Zealand artists will be given and books about New Zealand or by New Zealanders will be reviewed whenever possible.

To do all these things at the very low subscription rate, an immediate response from subscribers is required, so that the number of pages may be increased. The last census showed that there were over 7,000 New Zealand-born people in this country. There should therefore be no difficulty in securing a rapid extension of the paper. New Zealanders are invited to consider the "New Zealand News" as completely at their service, to write to it on any topics of interest, to send suggestions for improving the paper, and to forward addresses of any New Zealanders who they think may not have received it.

London has had New Zealand papers twice before—in the days of colonisation and in the days of war. Both these papers will be described in the "New Zealand News." We shall be well content if the third New Zealand paper is as useful in its generation as the first two.

A FOREWORD.

By the Hon. C. J. Parr, K.C.M.G.

High Commissioner for New Zealand.

The inauguration of a London journal of New Zealand news is, I think, all to the good. If, as I gather, the object of the new fortnightly is to give New Zealand a distinct and independent voice in London, we shall welcome it whole-heartedly. At present, there is no publication which is distinctly and exclusively of a New Zealand character. There is, therefore, ample room for the paper.

Hundreds of New Zealand people settled in London, many of them in business and others retired, will be glad to get a synopsis of New Zealand news from a reliable source. Our visitors from New Zealand too, who numbered last year over 2,000 persons, will be pleased to have a print which can tell them about the activities of New Zealand House, about the movements of their friends, and which will give them in tabloid form the latest news from New Zealand itself.

New Zealand has sufficiently grown to have its own point of view about things. Your journal will discharge a valuable function if it expresses this point of view with force and accuracy. The time has come when New Zealand should have its own identity and express its own especial spirit. I welcome the arrival of your paper and wish it all the success it deserves.

C. J. Parr.

The regulations governing the trout fishing at Taupo, which were gazetted recently, record several innovations, all of which are likely to meet with the approval of anglers. Formerly fishing was prohibited from 9 p.m. until 4 a.m. Now the prohibition extends only from 12 p.m. until 4 a.m. Licences confer a free right-of-way over the land opened by their possession except over such parts which are let as camping sites under permits, but, as in the case of licences issued for other parts of New Zealand, do not give the right of entry to lands not covered by the proclamations. Fresh-water crayfish, worms, creeper, and matai grub are prohibited baits.

An innovation which the majority of fishermen will welcome is the restriction of the bag to fifteen trout in one day. Formerly the limit was twenty-five.

reasons were the twelve hundred miles of sea which separated the two countries. It may be argued with equal force that there are twelve thousand reasons why New Zealanders should have their own newspaper at this end of the world. Separated as they are by 12,000 miles of sea from their home country, they want all the news they can get in a form as easily readable as possible.[5]

Published fortnightly, the paper provided news from home for New Zealanders living in Britain and information on New Zealand for intending migrants; for its first 50 years it was available only on subscription. As migration to New Zealand slowed and the number of young New Zealanders in London increased, the paper published more practical information on life in London. In 1965 a classified section was added, with travel, employment and accommodation advertisements. About the same time, feature articles covered practical topics such as the regulations surrounding car importation into New Zealand, travel options and tips for seeing the Continent, London sights, and working and living in Paris.

The newspaper added *UK* to its title in the mid-1970s and from November 1977 was circulated for free in Greater London areas where New Zealanders congregated. At the same time it became a weekly publication. In 1978 it opened an office in the Royal Opera Arcade behind New Zealand House, where a 'Marketplace' service operated for New Zealanders looking for flats, jobs or cars, and searching for friends. A noticeboard replaced the one previously maintained by New Zealand House.

In 1981 *New Zealand News UK* started its own MAILBAG service.
New Zealand News UK

OE work in London and elsewhere

In the 1950s and early 1960s there were few restrictions on the type or amount of work OE travellers could do in Britain. The 'lucky' ones with British parents were automatically allocated a work permit. Other New Zealanders could freely enter Britain on visitors' permits, work for up to two years, and then apply for a work permit for a longer stay. *New Zealand News* reported in 1965 that approximately 15,000 Australians, Canadians and New Zealanders whose visitor passes had expired and who had not obtained work permits were evading immigration officials in Britain.

Most young travellers expected to and succeeded in finding jobs similar to those they had done in New Zealand. Often it was simply a matter of looking up contacts given to them by their employers at home; in

IAN (on OE in 1961–63 with his wife) found businesses in London were sometimes wary of employing Australians and New Zealanders. He had worked for Kodak in New Zealand and had contacts in London, but struggled when at each interview he was asked if he was staying on through the summer. Unable to lie, he eventually took a less-qualified job in a camera shop, but only because those interviewing him had not asked about his summer plans. His wife Gill found laboratory work similar to what she had done in New Zealand but after a summer of travelling could not find another job in the same field. She decided not to work for the rest of their time in Britain.

some cases, a direct transfer to the London office of the company was possible. Some accountancy firms, for example, encouraged their young staff to gain international experience, organising transfers for them, although there was no guarantee they could return to their original job.

While some employers were wary of employing holiday-prone colonials, others took a more positive view of the working holidaymaker. An early travel guide, *Teach Yourself Travelling Abroad* (1957), recommended solid qualifications as the basis for successful travel and seeing the world without a large bank balance, giving the following example:

I know four New Zealand girls who came over to this country several months ago. They were acquainted with each other in New Zealand, and became friendly when they found they were all united by one purpose: they wanted to travel, and they intended to start by coming to England. They saved their fares, and at last set off. One, a kindergarten teacher, obtained a job here as a supply teacher in a primary school at once; another had no difficulty in getting taken on for the seasonal rush at Christmas, at a big London store; the other two have secretarial jobs. It is the general experience of girls and men who do this kind of travelling-by-earning that employers admire their enterprise, and are sometimes willing to give them extra time off at week-ends so that they can see as much as possible of the surrounding country.[6]

Most New Zealand women going on OE had worked as nurses, teachers or secretaries at home: all of which were in demand in London. Nurses were particularly popular and able to find work through specialist nursing agencies. Agency work was well paid and many jobs were live-in, which suited the itinerant New Zealanders.

The number of specialist employment agencies advertising in *New Zealand News* increased throughout the 1960s and early 1970s. Many were run by Australians and New Zealanders, which they claimed meant they understood the problems travellers on working holidays might have. Young job-seekers were put at ease, encountering their compatriots when they applied to agencies for work.

A *Weekly News* (in New Zealand) article in 1962 reported that many London employment agencies were inserting

LYNETTE, a trained Karitane nurse, arrived in Britain on New Year's Eve 1962. She tried various jobs when first in London – washing dishes, working at car fairs and exhibitions at Earls Court Exhibition Centre, picking daffodils on the Scilly Isles – but eventually went back to nannying because it gave her a warm place to live. The winter of 1962–63 in England and Wales was the coldest on record since 1740, with much of England under snow from Boxing Day 1962 until early March 1963. Lynette worked as a nanny/nursery nurse for a millionaire family for the rest of her stay in Britain; each time she went touring, friends filled in for her. Generally, New Zealanders had a very good work ethic and reputation; many people on OE were able to do as Lynette did, travelling for weeks or months and returning each time to the same job.

advertisements in local newspapers. One agency had even appointed an Auckland representative, a New Zealand woman who had worked in London and was familiar with conditions there. The agency hoped to interest more young women in taking summer jobs in London. The benefit they could offer was jobs awaiting travellers on arrival in London. A later advertisement, published in 1971, offered all types of office work as well as help with accommodation if required. The good reputation of New Zealand employees in London was also noted:

At one time, London employers distrusted Commonwealth girls who worked only a few weeks before taking off on trips. Now, New Zealanders, in particular, enjoy a high reputation because of their politeness, punctuality and consideration. For instance, the basic courtesy on the employee's part of 'phoning when too ill to go to work, is quite novel to some employers.[7]

Economic conditions affected what work was available. A New Zealand company director with business dealings in London warned that 1976 could be a particularly bad year for young New Zealanders on working holidays:

In past years, he said, it had been possible to arrive with little money, find work and accommodation and, in one way or another, get by. However, with the rapidly declining economic situation in England and Europe generally, he said it was critically unwise for parents to allow this sort of thing to continue unless their offspring were adequately prepared for what lay in store for them. Mr Fisher said girls who had general office experience and no particular skills found it difficult to quickly secure employment, although well-qualified shorthand typists did not have this problem. There were some unskilled labouring jobs available for men, he said, but he had doubts about how long that would continue.[8]

Other concerns raised by Mr Fisher were the low wages – barely enough to cover lodgings, food and fares – earned by unskilled workers, especially females. Even young lawyers, unable to find employment in their

THE STEADY STREAM of New Zealanders arriving in London often meant that jobs were simply passed from one New Zealander to another. For example, Penny became pregnant while on OE with her husband and (needing the security and comfort of the warm home it offered) took a job as a carer; her husband was to do some limited janitorial maintenance work while continuing in his accountancy job. Penny took over the job from someone they had met on the ship to Britain. The woman they worked for always employed New Zealanders.

In one account in *The Big OE*, a New Zealander met an Australian in a bar one night and took over his job as a maintenance carpenter for a London hotel, as the Australian was about to go travelling. A similar thing happened to Bob and his girlfriend in 1974: when collecting their mail at New Zealand House, they bumped into some friends from home who were just leaving a job in a Kent pub, which Bob and his girlfriend took over. The publican was an ex-army officer who had served with New Zealanders during the war and always employed Kiwis.

profession, were forced to take less-skilled jobs.

Hotel and bar work was popular: the jobs were easy to get and relatively recession-proof, previous skills and training were not usually required, and many pubs also provided accommodation. By the 1970s, employers were used to dealing with people who would work for only a few months. In the earlier years of the OE, however, pub jobs were perceived as more suitable for men, while work as a chambermaid was more 'appropriate' for females. The 1973 guide *Down Under in Europe* advised female travellers not to write home and tell their parents that they intended 'becoming a barmaid (topless or otherwise)'. From the early 1970s, specialist pub job agencies were established in London. The Cathy Coyne Agency – which opened in 1971 and was still operating in the 2000s – regularly had a line of job-seekers stretching down the stairs from its central London office during the 1970s.

The establishment of a wide range of employment agencies was part of the growing network of London-based support services catering to an expatriate New Zealand population, and helped to cement London as *the* OE destination. The city was an appealing base for those on working holidays: work was plentiful and London jobs usually paid more than those in the provinces. Pub agencies such as Cathy Coyne always had jobs outside London on their books, but found it difficult to get people to go there. Those who did take work outside London were often keen to avoid their fellow colonials and the expatriate lifestyle in the big city, and gave the potential loss of earnings little consideration. Some travellers saw the OE as a good opportunity to temporarily change their occupation, trying novel jobs or just taking a break from the nine-to-five jobs they were used to in New Zealand. Even mundane jobs like working as nannies, au pairs or carers could offer encounters with lifestyles beyond the experience of ordinary New Zealanders. In contrast, office workers usually found themselves surrounded by British co-workers, who rarely invited them home or to socialise.

Moving outside London opened up many more employment possibilities. Job

MOST OF THOSE on OE throughout the 1960s and 1970s did not expect to earn a lot of money. Work was a means of basic support, with any surplus saved for travel. Sometimes money was made unexpectedly: in the mid-1970s Heather found a job with a cleaning company and soon became one of the bosses, making much more than she hoped for. Her only aim had been to get a job so that she could travel; although the cleaning job felt like normal work (that she could have done anywhere), her attitude was still different: 'If your job didn't fit in with your holidays, then you would quit your job.'

listings in *New Zealand News UK* during 1975 included work on ships, a position as a Karitane nurse working for a New Zealand mother, mother helps, and general farm staff including lambing help. New Zealanders had a good reputation as farm workers, although the work available was often seasonal, such as lambing and shearing.

Scotland was popular for all types of work. Bob was travelling around Scotland in the mid-1970s and called in to see a friend of his brother, who asked if he wanted a job. The position was as a logistics manager with a helicopter company that spread fertiliser on farms and forestry blocks and Bob knew nothing about helicopters, but he was taken on. One of his responsibilities was to hire staff; although the job was based in Dumfries, Bob had a standing advertisement at both New Zealand House and Australia House in London, preferring to employ Antipodeans because they were prepared to work seven days a week, were young and fit, and many were farmers' sons. The company also worked in Northern Ireland, where workers received an extra 50 pence a day danger money.

Other travellers worked on the Continent, often in the hospitality industry or as tour guides and crew with the numerous camping tours patronised by their fellow expatriates. In 1970 *New Zealand News* reported that young New Zealanders on working holidays in Denmark were having difficulties because of changes in the law: they had been able to apply for work permits on arrival in Denmark, but a new law required them to secure these prior to arrival. Large numbers of New Zealanders were going to the British embassy in Copenhagen for help but, as the numbers increased, sympathy was beginning to wear thin. This story was reported by the Southern Cross Club in Copenhagen, an expatriate support club for Antipodeans living in Denmark that still exists today.

Agricultural work was available in both Britain and Europe through farm exchange programmes; one working holiday option popular during the 1970s was kibbutz work in Israel. Although it did not pay very well, it combined work and travel and could be organised through agencies in London. Grape picking in France was also popular; according to Camp Agricole International, it offered a 'unique opportunity', a 'rewarding experience' and an 'opportunity to get to know French rural life'. The agency advised 'drinking in moderation' during the season. Although the grape harvest lasted only about three weeks, the work paid well: FFr28 per day's work (equivalent to about $87 in 2013 value), with free board and lodging.

Working in countries other than Britain often meant working illegally, although even before the opening up of Europe those with access to a British passport had more options. The New Zealanders whose travel stories were recorded in *The Big OE* worked in countries as diverse as Iceland, France, Libya and Saudi Arabia. Some countries were easier than others with regard to casual or

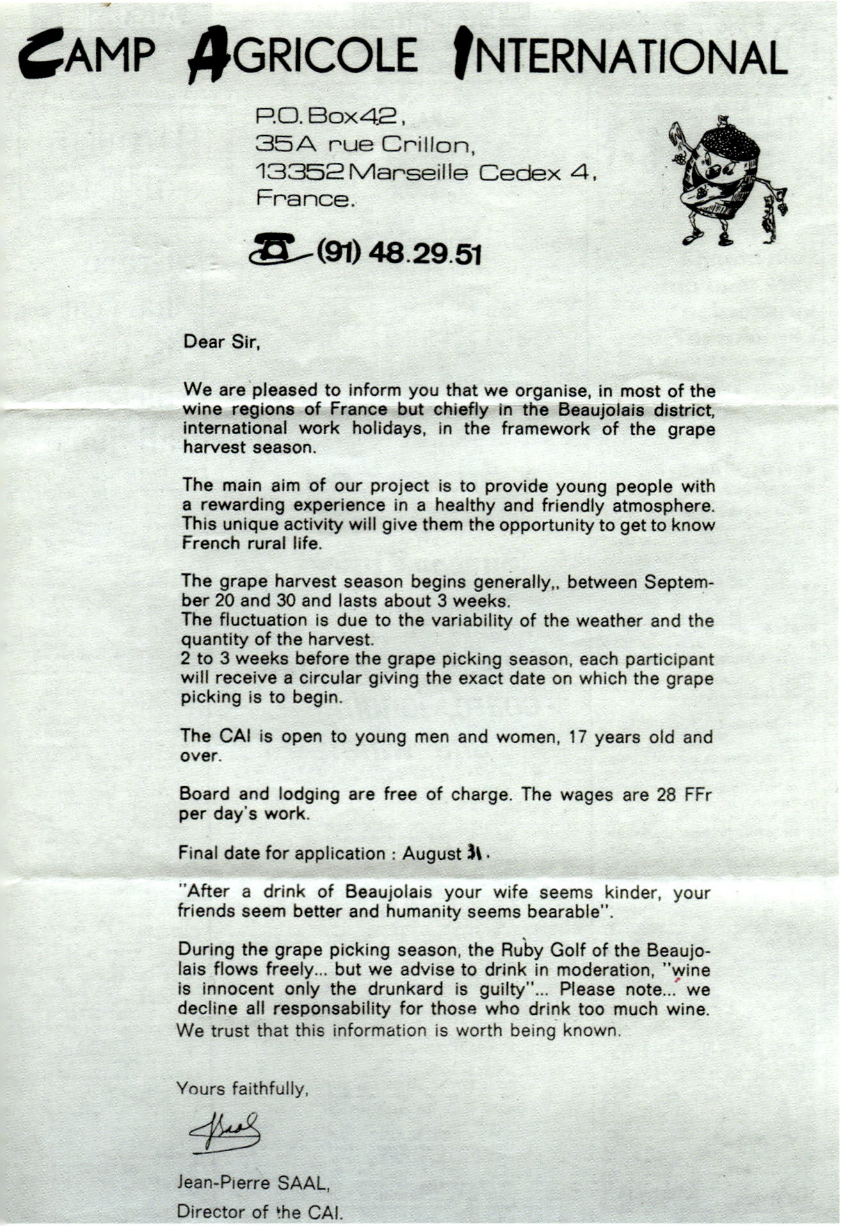

CAMP AGRICOLE INTERNATIONAL

P.O. Box 42,
35A rue Crillon,
13352 Marseille Cedex 4,
France.

(91) 48.29.51

Dear Sir,

We are pleased to inform you that we organise, in most of the wine regions of France but chiefly in the Beaujolais district, international work holidays, in the framework of the grape harvest season.

The main aim of our project is to provide young people with a rewarding experience in a healthy and friendly atmosphere. This unique activity will give them the opportunity to get to know French rural life.

The grape harvest season begins generally,, between September 20 and 30 and lasts about 3 weeks.
The fluctuation is due to the variability of the weather and the quantity of the harvest.
2 to 3 weeks before the grape picking season, each participant will receive a circular giving the exact date on which the grape picking is to begin.

The CAI is open to young men and women, 17 years old and over.

Board and lodging are free of charge. The wages are 28 FFr per day's work.

Final date for application : August 31.

"After a drink of Beaujolais your wife seems kinder, your friends seem better and humanity seems bearable".

During the grape picking season, the Ruby Golf of the Beaujolais flows freely... but we advise to drink in moderation, "wine is innocent only the drunkard is guilty"... Please note... we decline all responsability for those who drink too much wine.
We trust that this information is worth being known.

Yours faithfully,

Jean-Pierre SAAL,
Director of the CAI.

Information about grape-picking work in France.

'under the table' working opportunities. The biggest drawback was that such jobs were usually at the low-skill and low-pay end of the spectrum. However, such work offered insights into the culture of countries in a way that tourist travel could not match.

An expatriate population

The early decades of the OE saw the introduction of numerous services catering specifically to the needs of young New Zealanders in London. Employment and accommodation agencies took care of mundane work and housing requirements. Travel companies offered interesting holiday and leisure options. Storage companies provided useful practical services: those who did not have relatives in Britain needed somewhere to leave their belongings when they went travelling for long periods; others stored items they didn't need on a daily basis, trying to live minimally. Lynette, for example, stored a trunk to which she added any souvenirs purchased on her travels; at the start of each season, she returned to the trunk to change her wardrobe for more suitable clothing.

Many early OE travellers lived in Earls Court which, as well as being the home of the OVC, had an abundance of cheap flats and bedsits. Living standards were often well below what people were accustomed to back in New Zealand. Central heating became increasingly desirable from the late 1970s. Flats were slightly better equipped than bedsits, although *Down Under in*

Europe pointed out they rarely had washing machines or clotheslines as people used local launderettes. Proximity to the tube was important – the closer one lived to central London (where many jobs were), the more expensive accommodation became. By the mid-1970s, when rental property in Earls Court became more expensive, the colonials were moving further west.

In 1956, when Louise Sutherland arrived in London at the end of her round-the-world cycle trip, she was interviewed by a newspaper reporter who was a New Zealander. He took her back to the flat he shared in Soho with another Kiwi, Pat Andrew. Louise was searching for a flat at the time and solved her accommodation problem by marrying Pat. In his account of their early life together, Pat described the London flat:

Louise and I have lived in flat 3 since the day of our marriage. It is not a very big one. Merely consisting of a small kitchen (including bath), a narrow sitting room-cum-spare bedroom-cum-art studio-cum-dining room-cum-carpenter's workroom-cum-anything, and a tiny box like bedroom. It is not very big; but for all its inconveniences we wouldn't exchange our KIWI KORNER, as we call it for the largest, plushiest apartment in Mayfair![9]

Regrettably, the newspaper did not have space for the full story of Louise's cycle trip.

The support of other New Zealanders made London easier to cope with. While many people tried to avoid Earls Court or had jobs where they mixed with English people, they usually lived and socialised with other Antipodeans. Extensive social networks could form simply as a result of each person in a flat having their own New Zealand friends. Flats were often overcrowded with broke Antipodeans, with temporary visitors charged a nightly rate for 'dossing' down. Those with live-in jobs were sometimes able to sneak their friends in to stay with them temporarily.

Even OE travellers who made a conscious effort to avoid 'Kangaroo Valley', as it became known for its predominance of Australians, usually ended up there at least once or twice. Donna avoided the place for months but eventually went there to meet a friend; she found it lived up to her expectations: 'It was exactly the life we had left behind

MARY lived with a friend in an Earls Court bedsit in 1962. If they wanted a bath, they got up at 4.30 in the morning and shared the water, taking turns for first bath. Penny recalled that she and her girlfriend were the only ones who ever used the bath in their bedsit. They also put money in a meter to make the heater and stove work. Ian and Gill remembered going for dinner at a Shepherds Bush flat where the bath was kept under the table; on bath nights the table was lifted off and the flatmates took turns to bathe.

– which we'd thoroughly enjoyed here [in New Zealand] but we hadn't gone all the way there for that. It was just pubs with lots of Kiwis and Australians getting absolutely plastered. A lot of people only ever made it as far as Kangaroo Valley.'

Others attempted to avoid New Zealanders in London altogether, usually with mixed success. Of course one could avoid London completely; the downside was that then one missed out on the many cultural and social opportunities the city offered. As David McGill noted, for young people in the 1960s '[London] was where it was at.'[10]

Young New Zealanders on the steps of a Chelsea flat, 1960s.

Susan Graham also extolled the attractions of London life in *The Tender Traveller*:

It is simply wonderful, when you are young and ambitious and the world is still an unopened oyster, to work in London, to be a cog, no matter how small, in that mighty machine. For that matter, there is no better way to get to know any city than to work in it, to travel in its trains and buses, to shop for food, to keep house, even if it is in a bed-sitter.[11]

Often, social circles were determined by the type of job one had. Those working in secretarial or in professional jobs tended to have more English friends than those working as nannies or in unskilled jobs. Having a live-in job or travelling while married were both seen as socially restrictive. Even in the early decades of the OE, social behaviour was defined along a continuum, with the party-focused, expatriate Antipodean lifestyle at one extreme and a more ordinary and culturally integrated lifestyle at the other. Most people knew where they fitted, and why; personal circumstances often determined how one behaved.

Most young travellers were aware that as 'colonials' they occupied a special place in the British class structure. *Down Under in Europe* explained:

It is essential to realise that anyone from anywhere other than England is a 'wog' in the Englishman's eyes. He might not actually call you a wog to your face but he will call you a 'colonial' with a patronising smile. All the protesting you can muster regarding your homeland's long independence and non-colonial status will not alter this tag. The patronising smile that goes with it stems from the Englishman's firm knowledge that colonials have no class or background.[12]

Readers were also warned of the erroneous preconceptions held by the English about Australia and New Zealand: that they were one and the same country, all farms were big sheep stations, the climate everywhere in both countries was good enough to enjoy pineapples and bikinis year round, and every New Zealand male was, if not an All Black, at least a first-rate rugby player. The guide advised playing on these notions rather than dispelling them, in order to remain an unknown quantity.

Of course, back home was different and it was special. A shop at New Zealand House sold New Zealand products to those who needed a 'home' fix. It was also possible for family in New Zealand to send food parcels directly to London. *Down Under in Europe* suggested getting a lamb or half calf carcass sent from home to one's local London butcher, who would then, at a reasonable cost, keep the meat in cold storage and supply pieces as required. Intimating that the meat came from your own station/farm at home was recommended as a useful piece of one-upmanship when entertaining the English. However, caution was advised when it came to serving Australian and New Zealand wine – unless you got hold of some 'really good stuff', apparently no one would be impressed.

As the expatriate New Zealand population in London became increasingly heterogeneous, many of its longstanding social clubs – such as the New Zealand Society and the New Zealand Women's

IAN AND GILL worked in London for three years in the early 1960s. They felt that as a couple they did not mix with as many people as did others they knew. Also, they led an ordinary life – Ian took an interest in British politics, they travelled on the tube every day – but they drew the line at having children while there. Neverthess, they found their life in London differed from that of their workmates as 'on the weekends we just toured London – work would always ask me where we had been in the weekend and they would never have been [to those places] – they just lived in their little area of London'.

Lynette was also on her OE in the early 1960s and 'didn't go wild and party like a lot did' because she was living in. Heather took her first OE in the mid-1970s and had a mixture of friends; she recalled always trying to have at least one English person in their flat. (It helped that she had a brother in London who was married to an Englishwoman.) In contrast, Susan remembered her OE in 1974 being 'totally irresponsible – we didn't have a lot of money, but what we did have we spent on booze. We certainly socialised with the Australians and a few Canadians, but never any English people.'

ISOBEL'S FAMILY sent her a Canterbury frozen meat parcel once a month: it arrived in a box and she and her flatmates would go to East London to pick it up. She recalled this being the only time they ate meat; otherwise, their mid-week evening meal would normally be a couple of slices of cheese on toast. She also remembered the luncheon vouchers she received at work being very important. *Down Under in Europe* explained the luncheon voucher system:

As an office worker you will meet the system of luncheon vouchers. These are quite substantial, because of the English habit of eating the main meal in the middle of the day, and starving colonials have been known to save the vouchers up to cash in on one gigantic meal. They are redeemable at numerous eateries.[13]

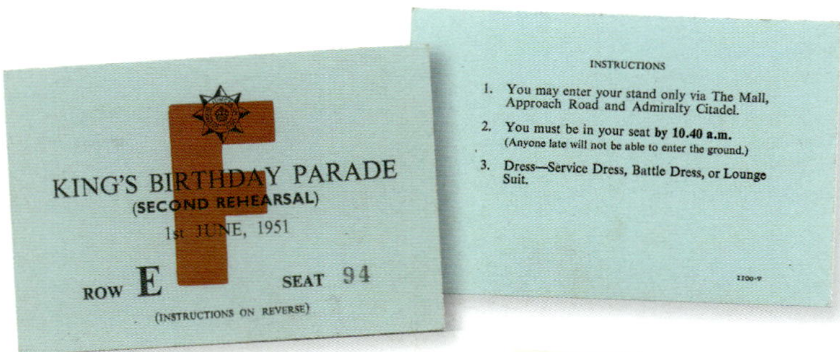

London life included the celebration of royal events and supporting the All Blacks.

Association – were unsuited to the needs of young new expatriates. Several sporting clubs and a notable new club – the London Maori Club – emerged in the 1960s. Started by a small group of New Zealanders living in London at the time, the Maori Club's aim was to provide an environment in which people could teach, learn and participate in Māori culture. Renamed the Ngati Ranana Maori Club in 1971, the group is still going strong.

Sports could be enjoyed either as a spectator or as a participant. Iconic annual events such as Wimbledon, the Badminton Horse Trials, the British Grand Prix, and soccer and rugby internationals at Wembley or Twickenham were popular with New Zealanders. For some sporting and social events, New Zealanders had special colonial privileges – they could apply for tickets to the Royal Enclosure at Ascot and to the Royal Garden Party through New Zealand House. In 1963 an advertisement for the following winter's All Black games appeared in *New Zealand News*: New Zealand passport holders could enter a ballot for tickets.

Participation in sport was very male oriented, with cricket and rugby being the only real options readily available. While local clubs welcomed New Zealand players, there were several expatriate New Zealand sports clubs in London. The oldest of these, the London New Zealand Rugby Football Club (RFC), was first established in 1926 but the depression and war intervened. The club was re-established in 1962.[14] The London New Zealand Cricket Club began in 1951.[15]

These clubs also provided opportunities for social interaction. The London New Zealand RFC was affiliated with the Aorangi Sports and Social Club, which leased grounds next to the Wimbledon tennis courts from 1967 until 1981, when the All England Club expanded.[16] The London New Zealand RFC website explains:

The mid to late 70s were the real heydays. Instead of heading to the usual Antipodean drinking establishments it wasn't uncommon for 100s, even up to 2000, to flock to the Aorangi Club rooms for social functions, hangis, discos and BBQs. In 1978 the club even had the All Blacks visit.

A FASCINATING account of an early OE can be found in the letters home written by Mary Dudson, a New Zealand teacher on her OE in the early 1950s, published as *Oamaru to Europe*.[17] Mary was a keen sports fan: in 1951 she wrote to New Zealand House seeking tickets for the 'Springboks and Internationals' games in the coming rugby season; she described in detail the day's play at a Lord's test match between England and South Africa. She also wrote of meeting many people she knew at New Zealand House in The Strand in 1952: 'The "boys" and I moved across the road to "N.Z. corner", a bit of the Tivoli Pub set aside for NZedders as they always seem to gather there.'[18]

Over time, a number of pubs became established as informal Antipodean drinking venues. The Prince of Teck in Earls Court was a popular haunt, along with the Bunch of Grapes in Knightsbridge, the Denmark in Kensington and the Golden Lion in Fulham Broadway. *Down Under in Europe* recommended an occasional visit to any of the pubs in Earls Court if one wanted (or needed) to hear familiar voices and accents. In the 1970s, some of these pubs were guaranteed popularity with the Antipodean expatriates simply because they sold imported Australian beer, a rarity at the time. According to the author of *Top Deck Daze*, the Sunday lunchtime strip show was the main drawcard of the Golden Lion.

Because wages were usually low and London was an expensive city in which to live, many OE travellers recalled being on such limited budgets that they rarely socialised at all. Instead, they saved hard to travel and enjoyed London in other ways: spending all the money they earned on cheap concert and theatre tickets, rather than on drinking and socialising.

They found there was still much in London that could be enjoyed either cheaply or for free; just being in London was a big part of their overseas 'travel' experience. Donna remembered being careful with the money she earned on her OE from 1968 to 1971, but she still endeavoured to take full advantage of what London had to offer, like taking in at least one performance a week. As she noted, 'I did not, at the time, expect to ever get back – nobody foresaw the ease of world travel.'

The early travellers

Britain and Europe were still rebuilding after World War II when the earliest of the OE travellers arrived in London; some recalled having to get a ration card. The

A sample of entertainment on offer in London in the 1960s.

Enjoying London's famous sites, 1950s.

war had led to increased interest in travel; throughout the 1950s, standards of living rose sharply in Britain, as they did in New Zealand. Increased private car ownership, the introduction of paid holidays, the development of package tours, along with transport developments and road improvements, all contributed to a growing demand for travel. The package tours became cheaper, more flexible and catered to increasingly diverse, but often specialist, markets. One of the first companies catering expressly to the youth market was Industrial Recreation Services (IRS), which operated a 21-day 'Young Commonwealth Special' tour of the Continent in 1958. The IRS had its office in the OVC; in 1958 it changed its name to Trafalgar Tours and is part of the same company that owns Contiki today.

Travel in Britain was very popular with early travellers. New Zealanders were familiar with British history and literature; while they found themselves automatically immersed in history in London, they also visited famous British literary and historic sites and cultural events. Some OE travellers were like Lynette; when she left New Zealand, all she wanted to do was to go to England because at school all the books she read were English, they sang English songs, and England was the 'mother country'. It was only when she arrived in England and found that everybody she met was planning trips to the Continent, that she decided to stay longer and travel.

REINA left New Zealand on her OE in 1950; she wanted to see something of Britain, Ireland and Europe, and to meet the unknown Irish relatives who had sent her money every Christmas. She worked in Scotland, living with an aunt, and travelled as often as she could afford in the two years she was away. As no practical guidebooks were available at the time (although she and her girlfriend did have the Youth Hostel book and map), they relied on other travellers they met – many of whom were Australians and New Zealanders – for information. In Ireland, because her relatives disapproved of girls hitchhiking, she used public transport.

There are similar stories in Mary Dudson's letters home. During the two years she was away, as often as she could afford it, she travelled extensively around Britain, visited relatives in Ireland and made a number of trips to the Continent. While she travelled independently, on one occasion she spent almost two hours at Thomas Cook and Sons making decisions about routes to take and organising the required train tickets and accommodation in youth hostels.[19]

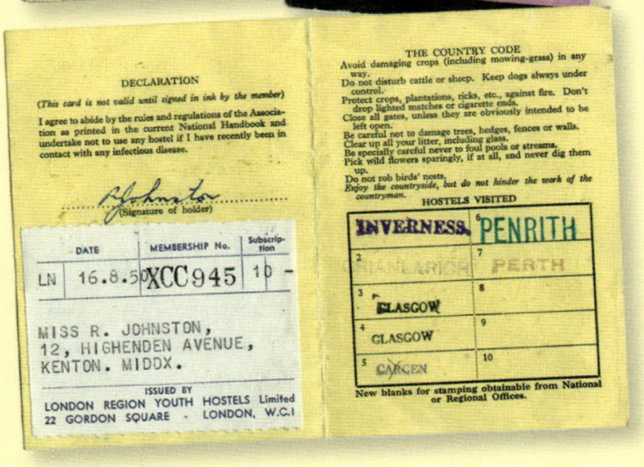

DECLARATION

(This card is not valid until signed in ink by the member)

I agree to abide by the rules and regulations of the Association as printed in the current National Handbook and undertake not to use any hostel if I have recently been in contact with any infectious disease.

R Johnston (Signature of holder)

	DATE	MEMBERSHIP No.	Subscription
LN	16.8.50	XCC945	10 -

MISS R. JOHNSTON,
12, HIGHENDEN AVENUE,
KENTON. MIDDX.

ISSUED BY
LONDON REGION YOUTH HOSTELS Limited
22 GORDON SQUARE - LONDON, W.C.1

THE COUNTRY CODE

Avoid damaging crops (including mowing-grass) in any way.
Do not disturb cattle or sheep. Keep dogs always under control.
Protect crops, plantations, ricks, etc., against fire. Don't drop lighted matches or cigarette ends.
Close all gates, unless they are obviously intended to be left open.
Be careful not to damage trees, hedges, fences or walls.
Clear up all your litter, including glass.
Be specially careful never to foul pools or streams.
Pick wild flowers sparingly, if at all, and never dig them up.
Do not rob birds' nests.
Enjoy the countryside, but do not hinder the work of the countryman.

HOSTELS VISITED

1 INVERNESS	6 PENRITH
2 CRIANLARICH	7 PERTH
3 GLASGOW	8
4 GLASGOW	9
5 CARGEN	10

New blanks for stamping obtainable from National or Regional Offices.

Travel was cheap, especially if one was prepared to hitchhike and stay in youth hostels.

Above and below: In 1951 Reina and her friend went on a 15-day 'luxury' coach tour of the Continent; the other passengers were a mixture of ages, with few other young people.

An article by the Paris correspondent of *New Zealand News* in 1965 outlined what was on offer: 'any New Zealander – be they penniless student or opulent sheep-farmer – could feel completely at ease travelling on the Continent'.[20] The travel options suggested in the articles were differentiated by cost, and included hitchhiking, conducted tours, private car, rail and bus. Students were advised to hitchhike and stay in youth hostels, although in some countries it was illegal to hitchhike and/or youth hostels officially discouraged hitchhikers. In contrast, conducted tours were expensive but well-informed tour guides ensured the tourist could 'finish' Europe knowing much more than other travellers. The overriding theme in 'Travelling on the Continent' was value for money, and the article concluded:

And when you want a drink in the afternoon, take a leaf out of the book of James Bond and look at the clientele before you enter. Even in the most posh areas there has to be a café catering for chauffeurs and servants. Being a typical New Zealander, that will probably be the café for your pocket.[21]

The literary and historic attractions of Britain.

Independent travel held most appeal for young – and budget-conscious – New Zealanders. Each form of transport had its own advantages and disadvantages and most also involved a particular accommodation option. Cars could be leased, hired or purchased, the latter being an advantage if the vehicle was to be taken back to New Zealand. The most convenient accommodation for those travelling by car was camping, and most European campsites were an improvement on those found in New Zealand at the time. Travel by bus could be an adventure, as a greater command of local language was required. Also, the price of bus travel varied considerably between countries. Rail travel provided a good way to meet locals, with concession travel rates available to tourists in many countries and cheap bunks to sleep in on most night trains.

Few commercial guidebooks were available, but travel information was available from other sources: motoring and camping organisations published information leaflets; the Youth Hostel Association published its own guide and map to hostels; national tourist offices for each country provided information on campsites, hotels and roads, as well as relevant travel and customs regulations. As increasing numbers of young people began to travel independently, there was a corresponding increase in demand for more practical and youth-oriented travel guidebooks, with information on transport, accommodation and travellers' services, rather than just descriptions of historic sites.

Throughout the 1960s and 1970s the only guides catering to youth travellers were from series such as *Let's Go* – published by Harvard Student Agencies – which had a strong American focus. While few New Zealand travellers had heard of or used *Let's Go*, its publishing figures demonstrate the growth in youth travel in the 1960s: *Let's Go Europe* grew from 64 pages and 6500 copies in 1961 to 321 pages and 65,000 copies in 1968. Only in the early 1980s did the *Penguin Guide to Europe* introduce a special section aimed at those who were travelling around Europe from a British starting point rather than an American one. Guides such as *Down Under in Europe*, with information on working and living in London, were much better suited to the needs of the OE population, although this guide was not published until 1973. Prior to this, word-of-mouth and the informal noticeboards at New Zealand House and the OVC were invaluable.

Ian and Gill's Goggomobil at Pont du Gard (near Avignon).

IAN AND GILL were typical independent travellers. In 1962 they bought a second-hand Goggomobil for £210 (£3676 in 2011), made a New Zealand sticker to attach to the number plate of the car, and set off on a four-month tour of Europe. They used British AA touring information as a guide and picked up local kits from BP petrol stations along the way. They tended to take a similar route to other travellers – mostly Australians and New Zealanders – and would meet up with the same people at different stops along the way. Because they were camping, they were self-catering; learning how to shop in the different countries was a memorable part of their trip.

Van tours and rail passes

Travel by van in Europe became popular with young Antipodean travellers in the 1960s. Those seeking travel companions or wanting to buy and sell vans advertised in *New Zealand News* and on the noticeboards at New Zealand House and the OVC. These ads often appeared alongside those for commercial camping tours. In London, a series of informal van markets evolved, with the vans parked at weekends and their owners often 'camping out' until a sale was made. This was not always popular with local authorities, and every few years the 'market' was forced to move. For example, an article in the London magazine *LAM* reported in 1978 that councils, police and traffic wardens wanted to shut down the Australia House 'used van sale yard' forever that summer.

Over subsequent decades, the van tour evolved to become one of the key components of the classic OE trips, often undertaken for that reason alone. Its popularity in the earlier decades had a lot to do with its appeal to these oddly confident – but relatively innocent and inexperienced – New Zealanders and their 'she'll be right' attitude. Most van stories involved some sort of travel disaster or adversity, often related to money. Isobel, for example, recalled having little money left for the second and third months of a three-month van trip in 1966: to save what money they had, she and her friends resorted to stopping at the side of the road and stealing food from fields. By not buying food, she had enough money to buy herself leather boots in Italy.

By the end of the 1960s a number of articles published in *New Zealand News* suggested that travelling New Zealanders were not always popular on the Continent. For example, a former Napier woman, resident in Copenhagen, had at first welcomed any New Zealand travellers she encountered, but became increasingly wary of inviting them to her home. Once, when a minibus driven by New Zealand nurses attracted her attention, she allowed them to cut costs by camping in her back yard: 'I was sorry afterwards. They had no self-control. They emptied my larder, slopped around in my bathroom, and days after they'd gone – after I suggested they should move on – I was still cleaning up litter around the place.'[22]

According to the same report, the types of young New Zealanders abroad in 1970 included the bore, the unenlightened, the whiner, the horse and the odd-ball. The bore was uninterested in his surroundings, preferring instead to tell everyone he met about New Zealand. The unenlightened was convinced he was correct – for example, that the Eiffel Tower sits by the Rhine – and could never be persuaded otherwise. The whiner complained – the sugar was not as

CAROL and her friends bought a Combi van for their European travels in the mid-1960s, as it was the common thing to do; while in Europe they were in the company of many other van travellers who were Australians or New Zealanders, whereas 'the British tended to congregate in the south of France where they could get their fish and chips and they just lay on the beach and got sunburnt'. Penny and her husband bought a van in 1971 from other travellers, and sold it on to New Zealanders. She recalled that 'it was pretty rusty and would never have got an MOT, but it did go on another trip' when they sold it. They had New Zealand stickers on it, using 'Kiwi Polish' ones they had brought from New Zealand, as they couldn't get plain 'Kiwi' ones.

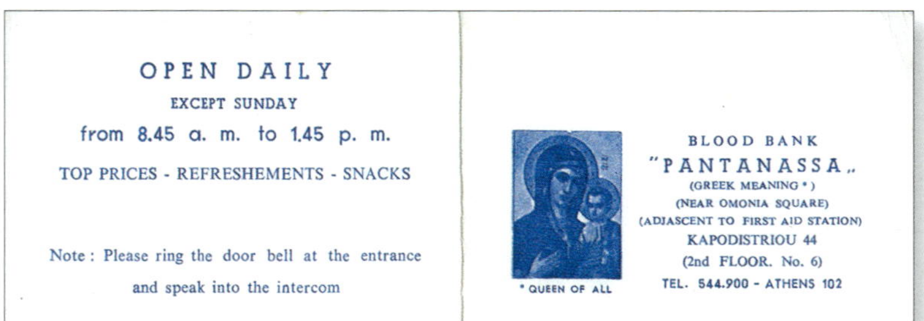

Some travellers resorted to selling their blood to a Greek blood bank as a way of picking up more money, as well as getting some free food and drinks, while travelling in Europe.

sweet as in New Zealand, the people could not understand his accent, the doors of trains closed too quickly. The horse was a heavy plodding, poorly dressed female who appeared to have trudged the distance to Europe. The odd-ball was personified by the New Zealander who ended up in a Swedish prison after being found standing in knee-deep snow, wearing shorts, and peering through trees at a military missile site.

Rail travel offered an independent travel experience without the stress associated with unexpected vehicle maintenance costs, and was facilitated by the introduction of flexible rail passes permitting cheap travel across the rail networks of Europe. The Eurail Pass was created in 1959, when the post-World War II mass tourism market was in its early stages of development. Initially for pre-paid first-class travel across 13 countries of Europe, a youth version of the Eurail pass was eventually added that offered second-class travel to passengers under the age of 26. In 1975 the Student Railpass, available to those under 26, cost about US$200 for two months of second-class travel. Eurail was not, and still is not, available to travellers resident in Europe. The original 13-country pass was available only in the Americas, indicating the growth in travel by young Americans during this time.[23]

This European restriction did not apply to the rail passes sold by Inter Rail, although passengers were required to pay 50 per cent of their fares when travelling on the issuing rail network. When Inter Rail began in 1972, it was restricted to people up to 21 years of age. In 1976 the age limit was increased to 23, and in 1979 to 26 years.[24] In addition to these multi-country passes, a range of individual country rail passes were available. The 'Britrail Pass', for example, allowed unlimited travel for one, two or three weeks on either first- or second-class trains; a special youth fare for travellers aged under 22 was available in the mid-1970s.

IN THE LATE 1960s Donna and three New Zealand girlfriends found that their own countrymen could not always be trusted: 'We bought a van off another Kiwi – we thought, "He's a Kiwi, he'll treat us well" – what a laugh! At the first petrol stop the chap at the garage said, "It's not petrol you want, it's oil," and that was what we had to do – fill it up with oil at every petrol station. But we set off knowing we had bought this lemon. When we got to Barcelona the big end went, and the engine had to be completely stripped down and rebuilt. We stayed for a few days in Barcelona getting the van fixed, but we didn't even take any notice of the architecture, as we were so worried about the van – we were really worried about the cost of it.' The van repairs meant that two of the group ran out of money in Rome: 'We got to a camping ground south of Rome and set up there and had to have a summit meeting – although it wasn't nearly as polite as that – and say well, "This is where we get off" (we had enough money to get back to London by train), but this all came as a surprise to the others who were well funded – we hadn't really talked much about money.'

The camping tour

Not everyone was prepared to travel independently, however, and in the 1960s and 1970s dozens of cheap tour operators set up business in London to cater to the 'colonial' market. Many had offices in Earls Court. Names like Contiki, Protea, Autotours, Transit, Metric Tours, Pacesetters, Penn, Tan Travel, Vikings, Continental Camping Tours, Atrek, Sundowners and Top Deck will no doubt evoke fond memories for hundreds of New Zealand travellers. Few of these companies survived beyond the early 1980s and records are difficult to find; the notable exceptions are Contiki and Top Deck, both companies with published histories and both still operating.

Top Deck began in 1973, when a young Australian bought a double-decker bus and sold seats on it for a tour from Morocco to London. As with Contiki, the company was ambitious and grew rapidly, with tour tickets often sold before the tour vehicle had been purchased. According to the *Top Deck Story*, Earls Court in the late 1960s and 1970s 'was an unbelievable time. You only had to leave the back doors of a Transit open for five minutes and you'd return to find half a dozen people in the back waiting to leave for Europe.'[25] Throughout 1974 and 1975 Top Deck expanded to cover numerous European routes, with many trips timed to coincide with either the Running of the Bulls at Pamplona, or the Munich Oktoberfest. By 1976, Top Deck had a fleet of seven buses and had carried more than 50,000 passengers. The company continued to expand; it ran a six-month tour to Australia in 1977, offered ski trips to Andorra in 1978 and Russia–Scandinavia tours from 1979.

Down Under in Europe advised that only those wary of travelling alone, or with no one to team up with, should consider taking a camping tour: 'We stress this as last resort travel. There is little doubt that independent travel, though often frustrating, is more rewarding. But if you don't feel like coping alone, do take one of these tours.'[26] However, the guide did suggest that this form of travel should not be overlooked for travel to Moscow or beyond Europe; bureaucratic difficulties associated with travel behind the Iron Curtain meant that the tours to Russia and Eastern Europe became popular, attracting even those who normally travelled independently.

Travellers also received a diploma for visiting North Cape.

MARY and her girlfriend used rail passes to travel around Scandinavia after travelling by coastal steamer up the coast of Norway, from Bergen to Kirkenes (on the Russian border) and back to Trondheim. She recalled hearing about this trip from other travellers and that it was the 'thing to do'. She still has her guidebook from the ship, the *Polaris*, with a special page that was stamped with the date and time the ship crossed the Arctic Circle: 14.6.63 at 0740 hrs. From Trondheim they hitchhiked with suitcases to Oslo. They had no plan for how they would get back to Britain (it was a case of how much money they had left), but they did have rail passes and knew they could sleep on trains, so were not worried about accommodation.

European camping tours were a far cry from the air-conditioned all-comfort coach tours of Europe: they were designed for a young clientele (usually under-30s); travel was usually in mini-vans; and, while the tour companies provided camping equipment, passengers contributed to a food kitty and meals were cooked by tour members on a roster system. Their main advantage, of course, was that they were cheap. The crews on these tours were usually male, while most, if not all, of the passengers were female.

One of the biggest operators in Europe during the 1960s was Transit. Like many other tour companies, Transit offered both European and longer overland tours. Often companies began with a single European trip, then expanded their operations to a range of European tour options, and finally extended beyond Europe to cover the overland routes to Asia and Africa.

Many of these companies were started by New Zealand, Australian and South African travellers who, having gained some experience with other companies and at travel clubs like the OVC and the Walkabout Club, branched out on their own. According to the author of *Top Deck Daze*, companies could be differentiated according to whether they sought commercial success or were motivated purely by a sense of adventure. Those established by the colonials usually occupied the latter position. A sense of adventure did not guarantee commercial survival, however. Some camping tour companies were run by 'fly-by-night' operators, with the company itself badly managed and/or not protected by surety bonds in case of commercial failure.

Often companies in better financial shape would bail out those that were struggling. Atrek was started in 1971 by Mervyn Hanna, a New Zealander from Christchurch. The company used Ford Transit vans similar to those used by Contiki. Many of the company's early crew were New Zealanders or Australians, but by the time the company went broke in 1975 there were only two crew left. The founder had borrowed money from Top Deck, which took over Atrek's buses, camping equipment and crew.

CONTIKI, now one of the world's biggest coach tour operators, was started in London in 1962 by New Zealander John Anderson. He presented himself as a travel guide and took bookings and deposits for a tour of Europe, using the deposit money to buy the van to be used for the tour. Until that first tour, he had never driven on the right-hand side of the road and he had no real idea of where he was going (although he did take a road map and a Fodor's guide with him). After this first tour in 1962, Contiki ran more European tours and by 1964 John had enough passengers to take two vehicles on each tour. The company introduced ski trips to Europe in 1965 and tours of the Middle East and Israel in 1966. During the European winters, Anderson ran summer tours in New Zealand. On his own way back to England by passenger ship, he had a captive audience and would sell all the seats on the next season's European tours. By 1971, Contiki had 50 minibuses travelling in Europe alone.[27] Contiki actually started out as 'Tiki Tours' until an injunction by the Government Tourist Bureau (which had a company with the same name) forced a name change. The new name combined continental (con) with 'tiki', the Māori good luck charm.

Protea, whose office was directly opposite the OVC, was one of the first of the 1960s camping tour companies. A camping tour 'the Protea way' meant barren campsites and lending a hand with the cooking – on the plus side, the European tourist sites were considerably less busy than they are today. By today's standards, these 'shoestring' travellers were also rather well dressed.

The *Overland Club Travel Handbook* published in New Zealand recommended checking that the camping tour company one chose was a member of either ACTO. (Association of Camping Tour Operators) or ABTA (Association of British Travel Agents) so that, if the tour company did go bankrupt, the traveller would either have money refunded or be offered an alternative tour with a member company. Advertising in 1976, both Contiki and Transit declared that they were bonded members of ACTO.

By the mid-1970s the quality of tours was improving. The colonial tour companies catered almost exclusively to their own expatriate populations. Contiki tours to Rome almost always included a visit to the Olympic Stadium where Peter Snell and Murray Halberg won gold medals in 1960. There were also specialist tours that went only to sporting events or to festivals like Oktoberfest.

Often there were significant price differences (and associated quality issues) between the camping tour companies. Susan went on a six-week European tour with Vikings Travel in 1975; most of the emphasis on the tour was on drinking and the bus was prone to breaking down, but the company did look after its passengers. She also remembered there being a lot of Australian staff. At the time, Contiki was the 'big' company, but she couldn't afford to travel with them. Loyalty to a familiar company could also influence subsequent selections. Susan's first trip – a 10-day Ireland tour to see the All Blacks – had been with Vikings. That tour introduced her to a number of other travellers with whom she subsequently socialised, lived and travelled.

The great unknown

What stands out in accounts of early travellers is the extent to which OE was an adventure into the great unknown. New Zealand was very isolated and, without today's electronic media, few of these young travellers had much previous awareness or knowledge of the world they were going to see apart from what they had learned in school.

Almost 50 years later, many still recall the novelty of eating Brussels sprouts, encountering bats, or – if they were from

In 1976 Transit offered 'Transit's Young Europe', a special 'under 30s' hotel tour, as well as more traditional camping tours.
Derek Amey, www.indiaoverland.biz

Even if the timing of a tour did not coincide with Oktoberfest, a visit to a German beer hall was always popular.

A COMMON CAMPING TOUR CATASTROPHE was passengers stranded on tour, although trouble occasionally occurred before a tour even began. In 1963, the night before Mary's camping tour was due to leave – with a company called Tan Travel – the company went 'bottoms-up'. The travellers were lucky, however, as they were rescued by another company (possibly Contiki) but, instead of travelling to Yugoslavia and Greece in two smaller vans, they ended up touring Western Europe in a 22-seater Bedford bus. Only five or six of the 22 passengers were male, and there were six New Zealanders on board; the others passengers were all Australians and South Africans. The driver and co-driver were also South African; because of widespread antipathy towards South African politics and in particular the policy of apartheid, their presence caused problems at every border the tour crossed. The six-week tour cost £108 (£1856 in 2011 value), including evening meals (which passengers cooked) and the promise of pension accommodation (rather than camping) if the weather was too bad. This upgrade happened only once. The tour was unguided as such: the driver usually dropped passengers off in the middle of each town square and told them to 'walk it'. Mary recalled buying her own guidebook for each place.

THE FIRST two-month camping trip Lynette went on (with Autotours in 1963) was advertised on the noticeboard at the OVC and cost £100 for eight weeks, plus a £12 food kitty (she was earning £8 a week in a live-in job). They stayed in camping grounds, with six people to a tent. One of the tour stops was the Munich Oktoberfest. The passengers were mainly colonials: South Africans, Australians, Canadians and New Zealanders. When she joined the tour in Earls Court, the first fellow passenger she saw was a nurse she had trained with in Invercargill. The same thing happened to Patricia in 1965: she arrived in Earls Court to join her tour to Scandinavia and the Soviet Union and found she had trained at Christchurch hospital with the two girls behind her. Carol was in a Leningrad camping ground with her tour in 1965 when they heard people singing rugby songs; they followed the sound and found a group of nurses from Christchurch. They hadn't even known the other tour group was at the camping ground, and they never saw them again.

the South Island – seeing oranges growing on trees for the first time. Singapore was a shock to some, because there were few Chinese in New Zealand at the time; others recalled meeting homosexuals and Jewish people for the first time. While Susan fondly recalled the little pension where she stayed in the Greek Islands, she also recalled that before leaving New Zealand she had never even heard of a pension. Passing through Amsterdam in 1963, Mary encountered the drug scene for the first time, although she did not personally partake: her most daring effort was a cigarillo. Patricia and her friend were surprised by Jerusalem when they first arrived there; with 'good religious upbringings' in New Zealand, and being familiar with biblical pictures, they expected 'flat-roofed houses, with palm trees and camels in a hot desert setting'. The reality was somewhat different.

Looking through early travel guides, one gets a sense of a Europe (and world) very different from that encountered today. According to the 1973 edition of *Down Under in Europe*, in France hitchhikers under the age of 21 had to carry a letter of authority from a parent or guardian, stating that they had permission to hitchhike. There were also potential traps for unwary drivers: in some countries it was illegal to clean your car on a Sunday or religious holiday, and in the Soviet Union it was illegal to have a dirty car. In many European cities it was an offence to sound your car horn, but in Italy and Spain, it was required when overtaking.

Cultural misunderstanding on the part of locals could also get travellers into trouble:

Girls who don't intend to make their travels a sex tour of the Continent should realise that Europeans can't imagine that any un-chaperoned girl isn't leaping from bed to bed. When some dark-eyed Latin offers to show you the sights you can be fairly sure he isn't leading you into a grove of temples for cultural purposes.[28]

The logistics of travel were also very different for early OE travellers, especially with regard to visas and currency regulations. Passengers on ship stopovers were covered by a group passenger visa, and entry into Britain was relatively open for New Zealanders. Once in Europe, however, visas were required for travel to Iron Curtain countries. When Reina toured Europe in 1951, she needed Belgian, German and Italian visas. According to the receipts she still has, her visas cost £3.4s.9d (equivalent to about £83 in 2011).[29] Her 15-day tour – to the Rhine, Black Forest, Tyrol, Dolomites, and the French and Italian rivieras – cost £57.15s.0d (approximately £1488 in 2011). In 1957, holders of some dominion and colonial passports required visas for Metropolitan France. By the 1970s New Zealanders did not need visas for most of the EEC countries, although visas to visit Portugal were required. Those wishing to drive in Europe needed to have an international driver's licence; for some European countries, pre-purchased petrol coupons were necessary. In 1965 petrol concessions were available to tourists travelling in Italy and Yugoslavia. Some European countries required proof of smallpox or cholera vaccination. Prior to 1979, when the World Health Organisation announced the disease eradicated, smallpox vaccinations were compulsory for all international travellers from New Zealand.[30]

Currency regulations were strict in most countries in the postwar decades. For example, in 1952 Mary Dudson wrote home that she was unable to go to Italy in September as hoped because she had to wait until her next £50 allowance for travel started in October. As it happened, she 'wangled' the money, because the friend she was going with wanted to do only a short trip and was able to give her spare money to Mary when they arrived in Rome.[31]

Reserve Bank permission was required to take money out of New Zealand. In 1968

DONNA recalled arriving in Southampton in 1968:
The first thing my friend and I did – we were just so depressed at getting off the ship – and the weather was ghastly so we got on the ferry and went to Belgium. Then we got on a bus and went into Paris – straight into the Paris riots in May 1968 – looking for adventure. We were rather innocent, but then everyone was – even our parents. So we got to Paris and these riots were going on – we only had very dim ideas about the whole reason for the things, but it all looked like good fun and we were staying in a pension right in the middle of it, so we thought we might as well join in – we went marching and were quite affronted to see another Kiwi there in an anorak and Kiwi badges up his sleeves.

the 'pleasure travel' rate was $14 per day for the first 14 days spent overseas on land and $12 a day thereafter; for time spent on board ship, $6 per day was permitted. This allowance had to fall within an overall limit of $1400 per trip, provided the person had no allocation of funds in the previous three years.[32] Susan Graham suggested three ways to calculate how much money to take:

... what seasoned travellers tell you is an absolute minimum, usually about £10 per day; what the Reserve Bank will allow you to take, which for the average traveller is much less than that; and what you can afford to spend anyway, which in my case was less still.[33]

Most of those going on OE were in the same category as Susan Graham and these regulations did not affect them significantly. Moreover, they planned to work when they arrived in Britain. While some purchased a return ticket (or had the return fare with them), these were often either cashed in or spent; they then had to save up or borrow money from their parents in order to get home. In March 1977 a report in *New Zealand News UK* described a 'fly now/pay later' scheme that had been running for a year; it was started by a travel agent to help destitute New Zealanders stuck in London and desperate to go home.

Many New Zealand banks had London branches to which money could be transferred; in 1968 these included the Bank of New Zealand, National Bank of New Zealand, Australia and New Zealand Bank Ltd, Bank of New South Wales and Commercial Bank of Australia. Usually OE travellers transferred most of their money to an English bank and took travellers' cheques for spending en route to Britain. Sterling was used on board many of the shipping lines; Chandris Line ships accepted sterling, Australian dollars and Greek drachmas. Money could also be accessed by letter of credit, but only within the limits of the daily allowance. According to a 1968 Chandris Lines passenger information sheet, New Zealand currency regulations required that passengers obtained a Certificate of Export – covering overseas bank notes, travellers' cheques, letters of credit, drafts and so on – from their bank.

By 1973 New Zealanders were able to take up to $4000 out of the country without Reserve Bank approval. The 1973 edition of *Down Under in Europe* advised:

The London branches of your home banks are a friendly bunch who will take on many tasks for you – from forwarding mail to getting theatre tickets. And don't forget that, if need be, you can see your bank manager. He mightn't give you any money, but he will probably give you some sound advice.[34]

This advice clearly depicts a different era, when it was special to travel.

These were the years when both passengers and those seeing them off dressed up for the occasion. Travel advice and help were always at hand, but often from sources that would be unlikely today. In *The Tender Traveller*, Susan Graham recommended:

If you should find yourself flying into a strange city where you have no ideas on accommodation at all, try asking one of the hostesses or pilots where they stay. The chances are they will recommend a very good little place which is sure to be clean, central and reasonable, with good food and some English spoken.[35]

The author of *Wake up in Europe,* a 1959 travel guide for Australians and New Zealanders in Europe, persuaded the hostess from his KLM flight to show him around her home city.

The biggest difference most of these travellers recall was their isolation from home and family. Once one left New Zealand the only communication was by mail or, very occasionally, by telephone. Letter writing was often prolific. Mary used to write home twice a week and her parents rang her on the *Orcades* for Christmas Day (on ship-to-shore radio). Her boyfriend also rang; the call was a 'four-minute cry'. She had left this romance to do the trip in 1962 and recalled that 'he was letting me do it but he didn't want to go'. She was away for just over a year but 'he didn't want to stay the distance' and left her heartbroken.

Mail for passengers on board ship could be forwarded to shipping company agents at each port of call; a list of postage dates was published with the relevant addresses. A 'telegraphic' address for the shipping

MANY of the New Zealanders on OE in the 1960s and 1970s have travelled since and appreciate their earlier travel. Gill and Ian fondly recalled their 1962 Europe trip:

A lot of people did continental trips but they did not include Spain. We have been back to Spain in the years since, but it was so different then – now it is just another EU country. We were lucky to have travelled at that time – at the Alhambra in Spain there were only about five other people – when we went back years later there were thousands. Similarly, at the Sistine Chapel in Rome there were only three or four others. We were also able to see things that are no longer open – like the Lascaux Caves (which closed in 1963) in France.

Portraits of a much emptier Rome in the 1960s.

company was also available. As Lynette recalled, 'The great thing on the ship – when it got into port – was not to go off sightseeing, but to get your mail.' Airlines in the early 1970s also provided mail facilities; a 1972 Air New Zealand *Advice for your Flight* booklet advised that passengers could have mail sent to them care of the airline, and that letters written in flight could be given to the crew for mailing (this service was complimentary for first-class passengers).

Once in London, mail could be sent care of clubs like the OVC or to New Zealand House. The 1968 handbook *A Welcome to Britain*, published by New Zealand House, advised that their mail collection service (mail could be held or redirected) covered the first year of a stay in Britain and that most banks also provided mail facilities for their customers. The camping tour companies issued a list of dates and addresses for mail pick-ups for travel around Europe.

HEATHER recalled it being a big emotional event to call home on the phone, even in 1975. On her OE in 1968, Donna remembered, 'If the phone ever rang, and it did once, you knew it was something very serious – that must have been dreadful for these parents.' She reflected, 'We were quite reckless in that we thought nothing could ever happen to us – at the time we thought we were completely invincible and Teflon coated.' Patricia, who lived for a year in the Middle East, found it difficult to write home: 'How do you write about something that was so different?' She also recalled ***not*** telling her parents that she had been hitchhiking through France.

Postcards were very popular, both to send home and to keep as mementos. Many early OE travellers still have trip photo albums and scrapbooks in which they collected postcards, photographs, tickets and other travel ephemera. In the late 1970s Hazel and her husband sent regular postcards and letters home from their OE travels. They numbered all of their letters – their parents then knew if one was missing. They kept a diary for the first part of their trip but tired of writing it up after a while, deciding that the letters were just as good as a record. Hazel still has them all.

As international telephone calls were very expensive in the decades of the 1950s to 1970s, it was common practice to write first to arrange a time to call. For some, it was years before they heard their family's voices again; often, when they returned to New Zealand and heard them speak, they thought their accents sounded dreadful. In 1970, if one wished to make a telephone call to New Zealand at Christmas, limited line availability meant that the call had to be booked in advance:

Christmas telephone calls to New Zealand from London have been fully booked this year by hundreds of New Zealanders and relatives in England. A spokesman for the Post Office said this week that bookings for international calls to New Zealand closed on November 23 and most had been taken well before that date.[36]

PART II

THE BIG OE

Chapter Four
THE BIG OE

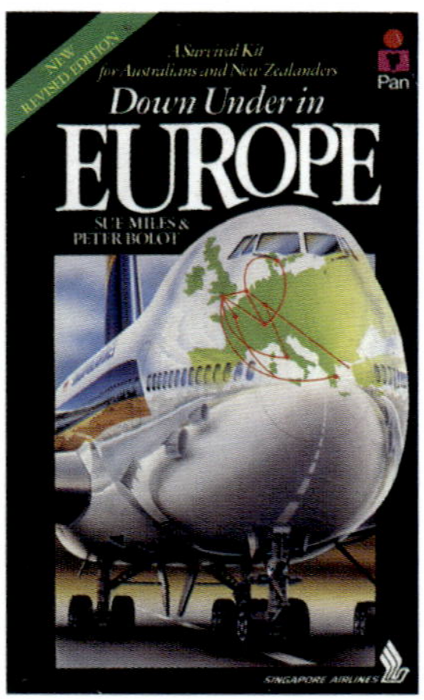

Down Under in Europe: the front covers of the 1973 and 1978 editions.
Pan Macmillan

THE 1970S WERE PIVOTAL in OE history. That is when the method of departure from New Zealand changed, as the jet plane took over from the long ship voyage. Britain entered the EEC and the imposition of immigration regulations on New Zealanders signified a shift in what had been an easy and familiar relationship. New labels entered the traveller lexicon: New Zealanders no longer departed for 'Britain', they departed for 'the UK'; once there, they were Australasian and Antipodean, and (increasingly) became 'Kiwis'. Importantly, it was in the 1970s that New Zealanders (and not Australians) started departing on their OE rather than 'going overseas'.

The 1970s was the decade in which the baby-boomer generation reached travelling age: there was an explosion in the numbers departing New Zealand. Many of these were the children of postwar migrants from Britain and had UK connections already. When they arrived in London, these young travellers found that the casual welcome and support previously offered by fellow New Zealanders was increasingly replaced by commercial services.

The early OE travellers of the 1950s and 1960s had prepared the foundations for those in subsequent decades who departed on an increasingly well-worn path. Exemplifying the shifts under way, for Australians and New Zealanders using *Down Under in Europe,* the guidebook to 'London & thereabouts' had a homespun look about it in 1973; by 1978, it was more professional looking and had Singapore Airlines sponsorship. Over the next three decades the OE was to grow and to evolve, becoming 'The Big OE' by the 1990s. This chapter describes how that travel template evolved.

Entry to Britain

If the OE were likened to a human being, the 1950s were its childhood years, it was a teenager in the 1960s, reached early adulthood in the 1970s and has matured in the decades since. Taking this analogy further, we could say that economic, social and technological changes in New Zealand and globally all contributed to the birth of the OE in the 1950s. Its lifeline – or perhaps oxygen supply – was, and remains, the colonial connection between New Zealand and Britain. The legacy of this connection was some shared history and heritage, a common language, similar education and qualification systems and, most important, the institutional or regulatory access that enables New Zealanders to live and to work in Britain. Access to some kind of 'working holiday permit' was, and remains, fundamental to the OE. Over the decades, the conditions attached to the permit determined what work people did and for how long, and thus the very shape of their OEs.

During the first two decades of the OE, New Zealanders were able to travel, work and live in Britain for as long as they liked. This situation continues today for those born there, or with at least one British-born parent, but since the Working Holiday Permit and the Grandparent Entry Visa (now known as the Ancestry Visa) were introduced in the 1970s, all other New Zealanders have faced limitations on both conditions of entry and length of stay.

Since the 1970s, as can be seen in the table overleaf, a number of apparently minor changes in visa regulations have been significant in determining the overall length and shape of the OE experience. Usually the New Zealand public was alerted to these changes by the media, with factual information accompanied by a storm of commentary and opinion pieces. Most of the changes were instituted as part of Britain's broader immigration reforms; reaction in New Zealand was normally one of affront and indignation. The common theme – the likely impact of an increasingly legislated OE – was that young New Zealanders were being deprived of their historical and cultural 'right' to work in Britain. Occurring when Britain entered the EEC, the imposition of visa regulations was another sign of her abandonment of New Zealand.

There is an important difference between the two visas introduced in the 1970s: those entering the UK on Ancestry Visas have never been subject to restrictions as to the type or amount of work they do; in contrast, the working holiday regulations do not (usually) permit full-time professional employment or a continuation of one's career; permit-holders are restricted to either part-time work, or to full-time work for short periods, within the total visa period. The reality was that the new rules introduced in 1971 initially had little impact on most OE travellers. As the authors of *Down Under in Europe* put it, 'You can now work and waffle your way around the United Kingdom for about five years before the authorities consider you might be a permanent fixture, and insist that you leave.'[1]

In 1981 the introduction of a two-year time restriction on the working holiday generated considerable media response in New Zealand, with most articles highlighting the contribution to the British economy made by working holidaymakers. It was argued that half a million New Zealanders and Australians arrived in London each year, each bringing with them on average $4600. They worked only six weeks per person per year, primarily doing work not wanted by other people: 'They extend their stay by filling occasional and casual employment often in menial roles well below their

Passport documentation of Grandparent Entry and Working Holidaymaker visas.

Date	Working holiday/OE regulations	Notes
Pre-1962	Unrestricted access for New Zealanders	Those wishing to work permanently required to get freely available entry certificates or work vouchers
1962 Commonwealth Immigrants Act		Entry criteria for Commonwealth citizens tightened, but no change to the rights of New Zealanders
1968 Review of this act	Passports usually stamped for 6–12 month period, but extension of stay possible (up to 2 years)	Immigration acts did not apply to those born in Britain or holding British passports
1971 Immigration Act	Working holidaymakers could enter on a visitor's visa and undertake either temporary work or work that was secondary to their holiday; 5-year limit imposed	Grandparent Entry Visa introduced for those with one or more grandparents born in Britain – indefinite entry (with no age restrictions)
1981 British Nationality Act (Enacted 1983)	Working holidays restricted to those aged 17–25, with a maximum stay of 2 years	No change to Grandparent Entry Visas or to the rights of those with parents born in Britain
Late 1980s		Grandparent Entry Visa reduced to 4 years (although this could be extended)
1993	Two-year working holiday time limit changed to run continuously from date of entry	Previously, time spent out of Britain could be added on
1994	Working holidaymaker clearance required prior to arrival in Britain, age limit extended to 27	
Late 1990s	'Valid from' date added to working holiday visa	Had previously been valid for 6 months from date of issue
2002 Immigration Policy Review (Took effect 2003)	Working holiday visa upper age limit extended to 30; all existing work restrictions lifted; after one year could switch to work permit employment provided applicant qualified	
2005 Immigration Policy Review	Extended age limit remained; only one year of work allowed within 2-year stay; still possible to apply for work permit employment	
Mid-2000s		Time limit on Grandparent Entry Visa extended to 5 years, renewable and offered avenue to settlement in Britain after 5 years
2006		Plans announced to scrap Working Holidaymaker Scheme
2008	Working Holidaymaker Scheme replaced by Youth Mobility Scheme for those aged 18–30; allowed to work in any lawful job for full 2 years	Not allowed to have previously held a working holiday visa

capabilities, but are willing and happy to extend their stay in this manner.'[2]

Again, it is difficult to judge how closely the rules were followed, and what impact they actually had on OE travellers. An article in the *Christchurch Star* commented on the newly imposed age restriction of 25 years (which replaced the rather vague 'young' people in the regulations):

One way for young New Zealanders to get around the age restriction and travel to the United Kingdom is to apply for a visitor's permit which expires at the end of six months. On its expiry travellers could spend a week in France or anywhere on the Continent and they [sic] apply for another visitor's permit. Working on a visitor's permit is illegal but the chances of being prosecuted are said to be slim.[3]

The change that had the most impact came in 1993, when the two-year working holiday permit was altered so that it was no longer possible to add time out of the UK on to the total length of one's stay. In 1994 it became compulsory to have working holidaymaker clearance in one's passport before arrival in the UK. Several years later the regulations were changed again: a 'valid from' date (at which the two years permitted would begin) had to be specified on application for a permit. According to a representative of the British High Commission in New Zealand, the British authorities implemented these changes to simplify the running of the scheme.

The announcement of another British immigration policy review in 2002 again triggered responses in the New Zealand newspapers. In an article in the *Press*, entitled 'End of the Big OE?', NZPA correspondent in London Diana Dekker noted:

Working holidays to Britain are an institution, which is why the proposed changes made headlines here. As well as the ingrained idea that Britain is still the spiritual home of many New Zealanders, young Kiwis see Britain as a place they can pit themselves against the real world.[4]

As it happened, fears for the demise of the OE were unfounded and the subsequent changes actually favoured both those going on OE and the British economy. Three key changes took effect in August 2003: the upper age limit was extended to 30 years; all existing work restrictions were removed; and, after one year, working holidaymakers could switch to work permit employment provided they qualified for the permit.[5] The head of the British High Commission's consular department in Wellington at the time commented that the OE workforce was 'taking employment, contributing to the tax base, contributing to the skills base, playing their part in the economy and as such they are not a huge problem. The rules changed because we wanted to access those skills – use them as a flexible short-term workforce. We don't want to keep them permanently.'

Demonstrating how difficult it was to achieve an acceptable balance between the

The New Zealand Youth Hostel Association started a petition to 'Save the Big OE' in response to another review of British immigration policy in 2002.
YHA New Zealand

needs of the two countries, some concern was then expressed in New Zealand that these changes would bring about an increase in what was already perceived to be a significant 'brain drain'; one newspaper report suggested that the numbers of those going to the UK on working holiday visas could more than double. In the same report, the general manager of STA Travel was quoted as saying, 'Many young people who put off travel because it interrupted their career, or because they missed the cut off age to obtain a visa, will now be revisiting the idea of working in the UK.'[6]

In 2005, with 'gap-year' travellers arriving in New Zealand in growing numbers, a rule change was made to bring the British working holiday scheme into line with the rules for British citizens coming to work in New Zealand.[7] Work in the UK was again restricted to only one year of the two-year term of the visa. And once again the New Zealand reaction was one of indignation, although as the Minister of Justice noted, 'We're not in a position where we can express outrage … It's disappointing given that it [the scheme] was not abused by New Zealanders.'[8]

In March 2006 the British government announced plans to scrap the Working Holidaymaker scheme altogether, introducing in its place a Youth Mobility scheme. The new visa came into effect late in 2008 and was 'points based', with points being awarded for having a sponsorship certificate from one's home country, for being in the correct age band and for having sufficient funds in the bank. Australians and New Zealanders were exempt from the first of these requirements. Under the new rules, it was also possible to work in any lawful job other than professional sportsperson, doctor in training, or business start-up. In 2012 a quota system restricted the number of places available on this scheme. This quota – of 10,000 places for the 2012 year – illustrated the continuing popularity with New Zealanders of a UK working holiday, particularly in relation to total population (4.5 million). Australia, for example, was allocated 32,500 places (23 million population), and Canada 5000 places (35 million population).

Working outside Britain

While the British regulations were of vital importance in facilitating the OE's mainstream flow, some OE travellers never sought work in Britain. In the earlier decades the work they found, with the possible exception of agricultural jobs, tended to be either very informal or undertaken illegally. Student work exchange schemes and working holiday programmes which offered jobs teaching English were other popular and legal options. The holiday programmes differed from working holiday visa schemes in that the former usually arranged specific work positions while the latter left applicants to find employment. However, the names by which they are referred to – programmes, permits, schemes, visas – are used somewhat interchangeably by OE travellers.

A variety of programmes offered temporary overseas work for students. Camp America is one of a number of organisations offering visas and employment as camp counsellors in American summer camps and has been operating since the late 1960s. New Zealand students wishing to work temporarily in the US have done so under the auspices of the Camp America programme. Another work travel programme, available since 1962, is the International Exchange Program (IEP), operated in later years in association with BUNAC (British Universities North American Club). In 2000 this programme offered Summer Camp USA and Work and Travel Britain options. OE travellers often took the Camp America option at the start of an OE, before moving on to Britain. More recently, Camp America Work Ventures, a sister programme of Camp America, offered a 12-month gap-year option. This is essentially now covered by the US Working Holiday Visa Scheme, which – because it is open only to full-time students or recent graduates – differs slightly from most other working holiday schemes.

In 1979 a New Zealand Student Travel Centre brochure advertised work-exchange programmes for students in America, Canada and Ireland. Globally, a number of work and study programmes are now available (often open only to those who qualify for working holiday visas). The Council on International Educational Exchange (CIEE), established in 1947 as a service to American students, grew significantly throughout the 1980s, globalising both its activities and membership. In 2000 Internship USA and Teach English in China were just two of the work and study programmes it was operating.

There have been many other opportunities for teaching English abroad, particularly in Asian countries, under agreements such as the JET (Japan Exchange and Teaching) programme. This programme, established by the Japanese government, allows New Zealanders under the age of 40 the opportunity to teach English in Japan for up to one year (renewable twice by mutual agreement). Since its inception in 1987, more than 2000 New Zealanders have participated in the programme. In July 2011 there were 226 New Zealanders in Japan on the JET programme. While Japan has a working holiday scheme in place with New Zealand, this programme presented an alternative for those wishing to work there. One advantage was that the programme paid the participants' airfares to and from Japan.

Another option for OE travellers has been working on agricultural programmes such as the International Agricultural Exchange Association (IAEA), which has been operating since 1963. Agricultural (and other work) was also possible on schemes such as the New Zealand/Switzerland Trainee Exchange scheme set up by the Swiss and New Zealand governments in 1984. Under this scheme, similar age restrictions

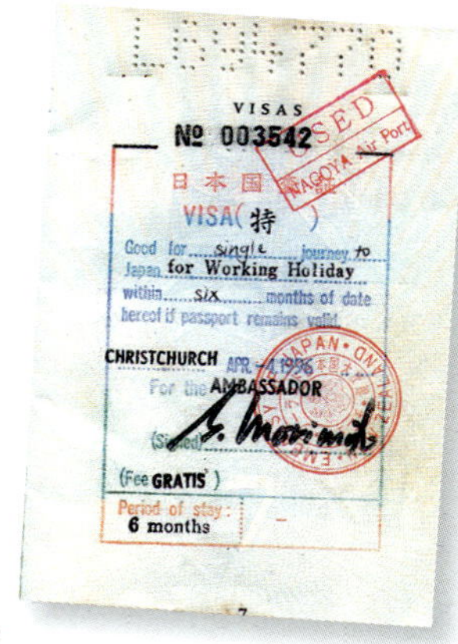

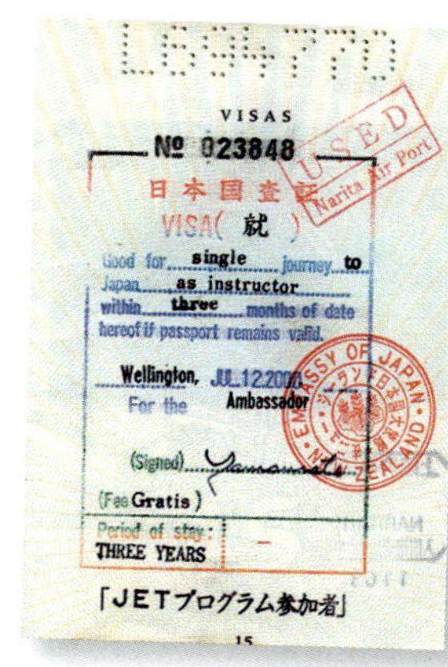

Alternative visas for working in Japan: the Working Holiday and the JET programme.

applied as for working holiday visas, but applicants had to have a working knowledge of German, French or Italian. The problem with a lot of agricultural work – such as the fruit or grape harvests described in Chapter Three – has always been its temporary or seasonal nature; it simply did not pay enough to support the OE traveller. The same applied to volunteer work. For example, the World Wide Opportunities on Organic Farms (WWOOF) organisation, which started in Britain in 1971 as British Working Weekends on Organic Farms, was never very popular with OE travellers as most of them needed at least some financial returns from working.

It was sometimes possible to work in countries where labour shortages facilitated the issue of temporary visas. New Zealand shearers have been able to work an annual shearing season in Britain and other European countries for many years. In the 2000s, special work visas were widely available to teachers, nurses and social workers to fill severe employment shortages in Britain. Some other options available during some decades of the OE have included Icelandic fish factory work and agricultural work on Israeli kibbutzim or moshavim. Work on cruise liners or on expatriate contracts was also possible, as visas were not required.

In the earlier decades of the OE it was possible to work in Europe in hospitality jobs or on skifields without concern about being checked for work permits. In general, working illegally in Europe became increasingly difficult; partly as a result of employment and immigration data being computerised (making it easier to keep tabs on who was working) and partly as a result of increased protectionism and competition for jobs within the European Community. Australasians employed as guides and other road crew for camping tour companies worked almost entirely on the Continent, but their employers were British-based, which meant that they needed British rather than European work permits.

Young people from many countries have been increasingly mobile internationally since the 1980s. In the 1980s and 1990s the New Zealand government established Working Holiday schemes with Japan (July 1985), Canada (January 1994), Malaysia (March 1996), Ireland (May 1996) and France (1999). These were seen to have considerable value in strengthening New

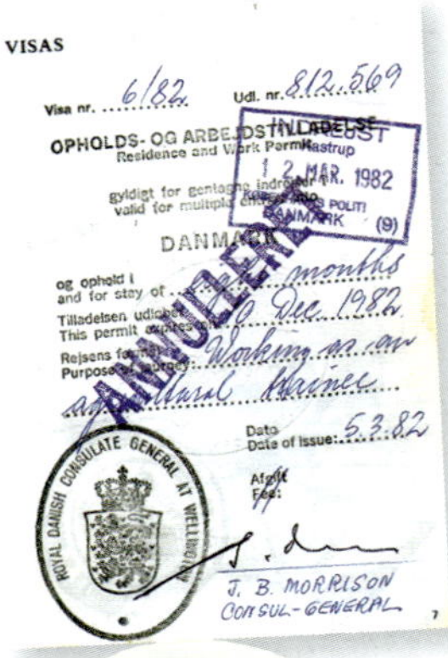

Examples of schemes for agricultural work available in Europe.

Many European countries have a tradition of offering au pair programmes; these remain popular today with younger New Zealanders going on pre-university gap-years.

Zealand's global links. In August 2013 New Zealand had 40 reciprocal Working Holiday schemes (in addition to that with Britain) in place, with countries as diverse as Mexico, Poland, Brazil and Latvia (all added in 2008), Peru, Slovenia and Spain (added in 2010), Turkey and Israel (2011), and Hungary (2012); in October 2012 a working holiday agreement was signed with the Philippines. Altogether, there are schemes in place with 21 European, nine Asian, six Latin American, two North American and two Middle Eastern countries.

About half of the working holiday schemes have annual quotas and half (commonly the longstanding agreements with European countries) offer unlimited places. Most have an age restriction of 18–30 years and, with the exception of Britain, are for a 12-month period. The type of work permitted is commonly restricted to that of a casual or temporary nature. The rules for Thailand, for example, state that a holder must not work for any one employer for more than three months.

Other visas or temporary work programmes reflect the types of work New Zealanders have historically undertaken in particular countries. For example, the website of the French embassy in Wellington in 2012 listed the regulations surrounding working holiday visas and au pair visas, and gave advice for New Zealanders working as crew on private yachts in France. A *Compétences et Talents* permit was also available, allowing visitors to exercise a professional activity related to a specific work project; this permit could be granted to anyone likely to make a significant or lasting contribution to France's economic development or to its academic, scientific, cultural, humanitarian or sporting sectors.

How big is the OE?

Despite its familiarity and supposed popularity, no one knows how many New Zealanders have been on an OE, or how many are on OE at any given time. The characteristics of the OE population are also largely unknown, although the general assumption – based on strong logic but often weak evidence – is that OE travellers were mostly young, middle class, well educated and Pākehā. 'Youth' was determined by working holiday permit regulations overseas and New Zealand's acceptance of its young people going travelling. In the early decades of the OE, the interrelated attributes of being middle class, well educated and Pākehā probably produced the cultural and financial capital required to generate an interest in travel. Māori were also possibly less aware of any direct familial or ancestral connections to Britain.

The task of counting the OE population is complicated by the array of regulations and permits available, the changes in regulations over time, the somewhat fluid definition of the OE and variations in New Zealanders' citizenship rights (and how these are recorded in immigration statistics). New Zealand migration statistics and British population and labour force statistics give some indication of OE numbers, although the classification of 'New Zealanders' varies between New Zealand resident, New Zealand citizen and New Zealand-born. Records of the number of entrance permits issued are either poorly kept, or not readily available; even if they were available, they would not include the thousands of New Zealanders who hold British passports, or those who went on OEs in the pre-permit decades.

In respect of New Zealand migration data, the 'best guess' is that OE travellers are likely to be among those leaving either permanently or long term (measured as 12 months or longer).[9] These data show that the number of New Zealanders emigrating increased progressively from 1945 onward, with the trend intensifying in the 1970s (see Figure 4.1). During the 1970s international travel (and the OE) became more egalitarian, with falling transport costs, increasing economic wealth and social change in New Zealand. As previously noted, the means of transport changed as air travel replaced shipping and overland travel, but the patterns of OE travel were already established. The baby boomers started travelling in earnest in the 1970s, but during subsequent decades the numbers leaving were strongly affected by working holiday regulations and economic circumstances, both overseas and in New Zealand. Increasing OE traveller numbers also changed the nature of OE support in Britain.

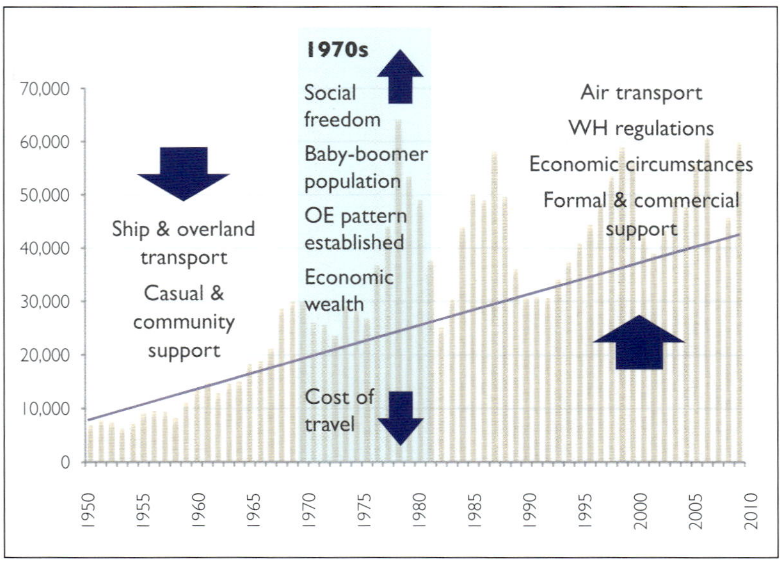

Figure 4.1 Long-term and permanent departures of New Zealand citizens 1950–2010. (WH = Working Holiday).

Australia was the most popular country of next residence for long-term New Zealand citizen departures in all years. The large peaks in departures shown in the graph – in the late 1970s, late 1980s and late 1990s/early 2000s – coincided with economic recession in New Zealand and relatively favourable economic conditions in Australia. The sharpest increase in numbers leaving coincided with the fall in airline ticket prices brought about by New Zealand airline deregulation in 1985.

The problem, of course, is that there is no way of knowing how many of those departing were going on OE. While the large numbers going to Australia are unlikely to be OE travellers, in some years Australia was a popular staging post before OE travellers moved on to other destinations. Working in Australia en route to Britain – an option taken only by some in the 1960s – had become more commonplace by the end of the 1970s. The benefits of a work sojourn in Australia were openly advertised: according to a 1979 Student Travel Centre brochure, for example, wages in Australia were on average 40 per cent higher than in New Zealand. Many potential OE travellers never made it past Australia.

The volatile period of out-migration in the 1970s and 1980s coincided with the adulthood of the baby-boomer population; the oldest of the baby boomers reached their teenage years in the 1960s.[10] Since more babies were born in the second half of the boom (i.e. from 1956), the numbers of those leaving increased from the late 1970s. By 1994, only 37 per cent of long-term departures were in the baby-boomer age groups, compared to 61 per cent in 1981.[11]

The data available for the years since 1979 provides some differentiation according to migrants' citizenship and country of next residence. Figure 4.2 shows the dramatic peaks in migration to Australia from 1979 onward; the numbers departing to Europe, while considerably fewer, followed similar trends until the early 2000s. Migration to Europe was much less volatile, however, representing 13 per cent of total migration in its lowest year (1982) and 28 per cent in its highest (1999).

Britain attracted about 90 per cent of the Europe-bound emigrants every year until the end of the 1990s; a substantial portion

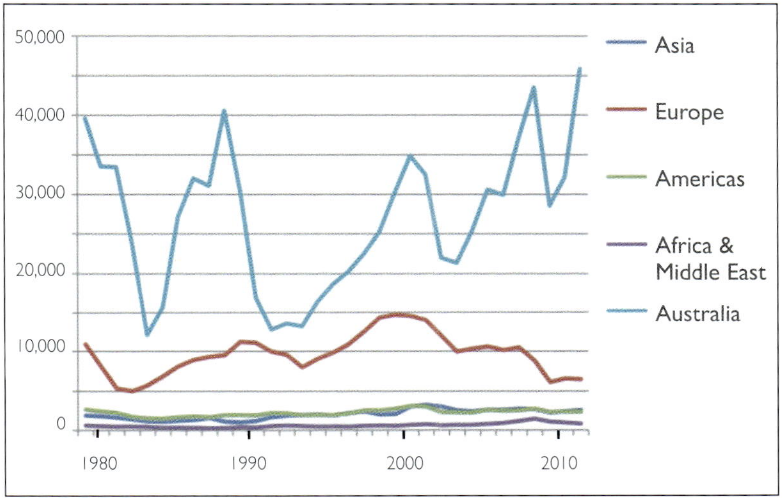

Figure 4.2 Long-term and permanent departures of New Zealand citizens, by region of next residence 1979–2011.

of these were probably OE travellers. From then on the percentage going to Britain slowly declined, falling to below 80 per cent for the first time in 2009. Of the other European countries, the Netherlands, France and Germany were most popular during the 1980s and early 1990s, but were overtaken by Ireland when the Irish Working Holiday scheme started in 1996. The number of New Zealand citizens going to Ireland peaked at 950 in 2002 before slowly declining, most likely as a result of changing economic circumstances in Ireland. An increase in the number of European countries attracting New Zealand citizens during the 2000s was probably associated with the working holiday schemes being put in place. France and Germany, for example, attracted about 4 per cent of the Europe-bound migrants in the late 2000s (up from 1 per cent in 1979).

Migration to other regions was more stable and possibly included more non-OE migrants. Both the Americas and Asia attracted about 4 or 5 per cent of New Zealand emigrants each year. In the Americas, about 90 per cent of New Zealanders were going to either the US or Canada, with the US attracting twice as many New Zealanders as Canada in most years. Many of those going to the US may have been going for educational purposes, however.

The most popular Asian country (in total numbers) was Japan, followed by Singapore, Hong Kong, China, Korea and Taiwan. It is reasonable to assume that many of these emigrants were teaching English, some as part of an OE, others as part of an expatriate work experience. Africa and the Middle East were significantly less popular; the only countries attracting double figures in most years were the United Arab Emirates, Bahrain, Saudi Arabia, South Africa and Israel. Those going to the first three of these were probably expatriate workers, rather than OE travellers.

Identifying the OE population

Overall, as a proportion of the total New Zealand population, the numbers leaving the country long term were never large. Census-year population and migration figures show that in the four census years between 1991 and 2006, the number of 20–29-year-olds departing long term to all destinations represented only 4 or 5 per cent of the total population in that age group. Census-year figures going back to 1981 show that at each census those aged 20–29 years, departing long term or permanently to Britain, represented less than 2 per cent of the New Zealand population in that age group. The cumulative effect of the departing OE population, however, adds significantly to the number of New Zealanders living outside the country at any one time.

The majority of OE travellers have left and still leave New Zealand during their twenties, partly due to working permit regulations, but also because it is socially acceptable to go on an OE at this age. For country of next residence, British figures differentiated by age and gender are available, although not by New Zealand-citizen departures (i.e. the British destination figures include all people departing New Zealand long term). In each of the four-year periods shown in Figure 4.3, between 56 and 69 per cent of long-term departures to Britain were those aged 20–30 years; within this age group, the most common OE age of departure was 20–24 years, although the percentage in this age group decreased with each decade. A combination of changes to the working holiday age limits and social change in New Zealand were responsible for the ageing of the OE population.

The OE has always fitted well into the period of early adulthood between finishing education or training and making career or life commitments (such as starting families), although the conditions surrounding these changed during the OE decades. Between 1966 and 1996 the proportion of New Zealanders with formal qualifications, and the time required to gain those qualifications, increased markedly. Moreover, earlier OE travellers completed their education and/or training with no debt, in contrast to many of those who studied after the introduction of student loans in 1992.

Social expectations also changed over time, affecting the perception of the appropriate age at which one should marry, have children or settle into a career. Hazel, for example, was only 24 when she and her husband returned after three years away in the late 1970s, but they found themselves under pressure – from their families, and even from their doctor – to have children. The ages of first marriage and first child born have changed considerably in New Zealand during the last four decades. The average age of women entering their first marriage rose from 21.7 years to 27.1 years between 1971 and 1996; trends in childbearing age show that by 1986 25–29-year-olds had replaced 20–24-year-olds as the peak childbearing age group. By 2002, the 30–34-year-olds were the peak childbearing age group. The median age of New Zealand women giving birth (to all children) during the year ended December 2002 was 30.1 years, compared with 28.2 years in 1992 and 24.9 years in the early 1970s.[12]

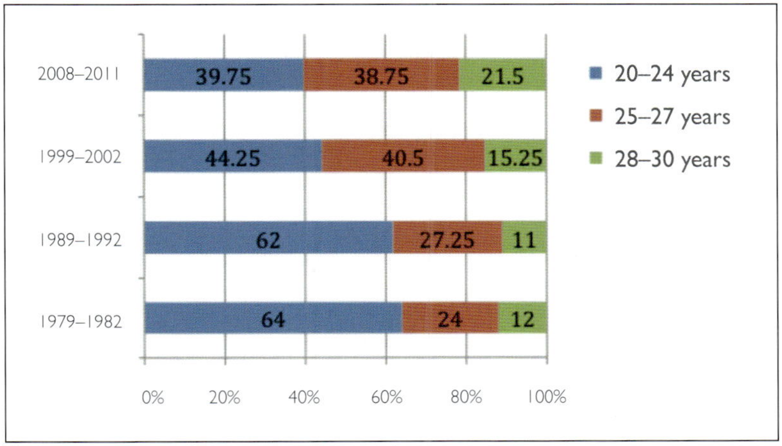

Figure 4.3 Long-term and permanent New Zealand emigrants to Britain aged 20–30, for selected periods since 1979.

In the early decades of the OE, anecdotal evidence and passenger lists on ships indicated that more females than males were going on OE. This trend continued: in the years since 1979 between 5 and 12 per cent more females than males aged 20–30 years have departed from New Zealand long term to the UK as country of next residence.

In the late 1990s and 2000s, a new OE traveller appeared in the statistics as increased numbers of older people (in their late forties, fifties and sixties) departed New Zealand on a long-term basis. Some of this increase was directly related to the ageing of the baby-boomer population cohort, with a significant proportion of that population becoming 'empty-nesters'. With their children off their hands (and often, usefully, based in London) and their own parents still in reasonably good health, the baby boomers were still young enough to

Older people began going on OEs in the late 1990s and 2000s: cover of the *New Zealand Listener*, 19–25 June 2004.
New Zealand Listener

enjoy working and living overseas for a few years. Many of these older OE travellers were taking the opportunity to do the OEs they had missed out on when they were young, having chosen marriage and childrearing in the 1970s. The difference in their OEs was rather eloquently described by one older OE traveller thus: 'The young go to see what life offers, while we were going to see what we had missed.'

Although well documented in the media, this group of OE travellers is even harder to quantify than their younger compatriots. One explanation is that departure statistics are reliant on travellers' self reports of their reasons for leaving New Zealand: for those over the age of 30, and no longer eligible for working holiday visas, declaring an intention to do anything other than take a short-term holiday often invites awkward questions from immigration officials. As a result, the most commonly given reasons are 'holiday' and 'visiting family and friends', rather than working holiday, even when the intention is the latter. While they are too old for working holiday permits, many older OE travellers are eligible for Ancestry Visas or British passports, or have employment skills in demand in Britain.

Because migration figures do not differentiate long-term departures by ethnicity, it is difficult to argue against the supposition that the OE has been primarily a Pākehā practice, although there is certainly evidence of a longstanding Māori visiting history and presence in Britain. As noted earlier, Māori were keen to travel to Britain from the early 1800s, Māori battalions fought in both world wars, Māori sportspeople represented New Zealand internationally, and the London Maori Club was established in 1960. Certainly, the number of Māori cultural and sporting clubs in London increased significantly throughout the 2000s.

In the early 2000s the British High Commission in Wellington noted that the number of second-generation New Zealanders with Asian backgrounds applying for working holiday permits was increasing. This suggests that in the 2000s the OE had become something that all young New Zealanders aspired to do, not just those who had some ancestral connection to a long-forgotten mother country.

New Zealanders in Britain

New Zealand migration figures show that Britain is a popular destination for long-term emigrants, many of whom are likely to be OE travellers. The UK census and other data sources in the UK also give some idea of the number of New Zealanders either resident in, or working in, the UK. Unfortunately, figures on the number of working holiday permits issued each year are not readily available.

The International Labour Organization (ILO) records the number of immigrants arriving in the UK (these data do not include visitors, passengers in transit or students). The five most significant groups by citizenship are reported. In 1992, 10,600 New Zealand citizens arrived in the UK (the third-largest immigrant group by citizenship). The number of New Zealanders arriving remained consistent at about 11,000–12,000 each year until 1997. No figures are available for 1997 or 1998; in 2000 and 2001 New Zealand did not rank in the top five groups (although the numbers may still have been high, as the cut-off figure for the top five was over 15,000).[13]

These figures are based on a range of data (Labour Force Survey, International Passenger Survey and OECD figures) but there is nothing to show how citizenship was counted. The number of New Zealanders holding other passports (especially since this gives them unrestricted entry to work in other countries) and the number who are born outside New Zealand may distort the figures.

Over the years, estimates of the New Zealand population in the UK have come from a variety of sources. One official estimate suggested that there were 30,000 New Zealanders in the UK in 1991.[14] In 2002 the British High Commission in New Zealand put the figure at up to 50,000 in the UK short term, and an unknown number long term. In 2004, according to the New Zealand High Commission in London, there were between 100,000 and 200,000 New Zealanders resident in the UK, with the majority of those in London; this estimate was based on market research carried out by Sky TV. How New Zealanders were defined for these figures is unknown.

The 10-year UK census counts the New Zealand-born population in the UK; this population increased from 41,203 in 1991, to 57,916 in 2001. London was by far the most popular area, with 44.6 per cent of the New Zealand-born British population in 1991 and 47 per cent in 2001. The New Zealand-born population in London was 10,872 in 1981, 18,379 in 1991 and 27,493 in 2001 (increases of 70 and 50 per cent respectively in each census period). Most estimates suggest that there were many more New Zealanders in London than these figures indicate. A New Zealand Treasury paper released in 2004, for example, suggested that of the almost 60,000 New Zealand-born people resident in the UK at the 2001 census, it could be assumed that 50,000 lived in London (making London New Zealand's eleventh-biggest city).[15] In 2001, the second most popular area was Scotland, with 3413 New Zealand-born people (an increase of 50 per cent from 1991). Population figures released in the UK in 2010 reported that there were 70,000 New Zealand-born (or 48,000 if measured by nationality) people resident in the UK.[16]

For a number of reasons, the census offers a poor measure of the OE population. First, the 10-year census is a snapshot only and counts only those who are resident at each census date – many OE travellers arrive and depart the UK in mid-census periods, despite staying for two to three years. Second, counting only New Zealand-born potentially misses out many New Zealanders

POLLY'S EXPERIENCE of not completing the census was quite straightforward: in 1981 she was working at one pub and living in another and, while the second pub was owned by the same company, it was not supposed to have as many 'occupants' as it did. The pub's own staff lived on one floor, six staff from Polly's pub occupied another floor, and the floors above Polly's were rented out. Polly and her workmates were instructed by their boss *not* to complete the census.

present in London. Third, for a variety of reasons, many New Zealanders do not take part in the census. Anecdotally, it has been suggested that this is because they don't consider themselves to be 'proper' residents.

The cost of OE travel

While the cost of OE travel limited who went in the 1950s and 1960s, going on an OE was still a costly undertaking in the 1970s. Britain's entry into the EEC and the international oil crisis brought increasing inflation and unemployment in New Zealand, making it difficult to save the money required. In addition to the air ticket, OE travellers needed travel insurance, a passport, travel equipment (a backpack and sleeping bag) and a visa (in 1997 a grandparent entry visa cost $192, equivalent to $275 in 2013 value; in 2013 the working holiday visa cost $410). Money was also needed for stopovers or travel en route to Britain, for travel in Britain or Europe at the start of the OE, and to cover expenses until work was found.

Organising one's finances also took time. It wasn't until after the New Zealand dollar was floated in 1985 that the foreign exchange market was freed up and travel controls removed. Travellers' cheques and foreign exchange had to be ordered in advance as Reserve Bank permission was still required to take substantial sums out of the country; tickets had to be presented as evidence of intended departure. When the New Zealand dollar devalued by 20 per cent in 1984, as widely expected, intending travellers were unable to buy forward exchange as they were not allowed to purchase foreign currency until seven days before departure.

In 1978, *Down Under in Europe* advised that the British immigration authorities could refuse entry to New Zealanders if they wished, even if an entry certificate was stamped in a passport. The guide recommended having evidence of funds, and not giving the impression of being penniless and planning to stay for years. Initially, the amount required was simply described as 'sufficient funds', rather than any specific figure; over time evidence of funds became a formal requirement for a visa to be issued.

Guidebooks provide a record of how much was considered to be 'sufficient'. In 1990, for example, when working holiday visas were issued on arrival in the UK, applicants had to have either £1000 or a return airfare.[17] From 1994, working holiday visas had to be applied for in New Zealand, with applicants proving that they had enough funds to support themselves in the UK until they found work. The amount required was about £1500, after airfares.[18] By 1997, applicants had to have either £2000, or £1500 and a return airfare.[19] In 2000 the amount required was £1800 after airfares had been paid,[20] while in 2004 working holiday visa applicants had to have funds to support themselves for at least a month and the money for a ticket home.[21] Several guides published that year recommended saving a minimum of about £2000.[22]

The qualifications for entry continued to change. In 2006, applicants were required to show that they had at least the cost of their journey to the UK and enough money for accommodation and living expenses for the first two months. If they had a prearranged job and this job would pay enough to cover accommodation and living expenses, then they needed funds for a minimum of one month. Full bank statements, in the applicant's own name, for the three months prior to visa application were required as evidence. Credit – through credit cards or borrowed funds – was unacceptable. In 2012 maintenance funds of £1600 were required, again with full bank statements as evidence.

The new Youth Mobility Scheme introduced a requirement that all people going to the UK for more than six months had to provide biometric data (fingerprints and digital photographs). Initially, the only location at which biometric data was collected was the British High Commission in Wellington, adding the cost of a separate trip to Wellington to the working holiday permit process. This became a little easier when Immigration New Zealand took over the collection of these data on behalf of the British High Commission, as it had offices in Auckland, Wellington and Christchurch. In early 2012, however, the Christchurch office was closed (as a result of the February 2011 earthquake). While those entering Britain on Ancestry Visas or with British passports did not have to show evidence of funds, they were often grilled by British immigration officials as to how much money they had, whether they had a job and what address were they going to. This was particularly the case when these travellers returned to Britain after travelling in Europe.

Jet-lagged before you start.
Chris Slane

As for seeing the world, a stopover for a few days somewhere en route to Britain was all that many could afford. In the early 2000s it cost $8000–10,000 to get to London with a comfortable safety net, after a week in Asia or a few days in the United States.[23] The advantage of travelling via the US was the more generous luggage allowance, useful for people going away for years rather than weeks or months. The Asian route offered the option of a cheap holiday before having to deal with the stress of finding work and somewhere to live in London. For many, a break was much needed after the busy weeks leading up to OE departure, as flats and houses had to be packed up, belongings stashed in parents' garages, finances sorted and farewells made to family and friends.

London arrivals

By the mid-1970s, given the demise of passenger shipping services and the difficulties of the overland route, most OE travellers flew directly from New Zealand to London. The first few days in the big city were overwhelming for these small-town New Zealanders as they came to terms with the idea of a population more than twice that of their entire country. In 2004 *The Big OE Companion* recommended leaving the serious business stuff – finding a job, finding a flat – for a couple of days in order to get used to London, and spending a few days sightseeing. The author described London as daunting, but also exciting as one encountered 'those Monopoly Board names', the sense of history, the buzz of Soho and so on.

The first few days as a tourist were relatively easy, although a guidebook and a map always helped. In 1973 the authors of *Down Under in Europe* suggested if you hadn't bought a detailed map of London before you arrived you were 'going to be in trouble'. For many, the main concern – both in advance of going and in their first days in London – was getting to grips with the underground railway system. Arriving on a direct flight from New Zealand did not make it any easier. Wendy recalled her experience in 1985:

It was really trial and error when we got there … we got to Heathrow totally knackered and thought, how the hell does this tube work? Where do you get a ticket? How do you get through this barrier? Where the hell are we going? What fun! I suppose

SOME LONDON ARRIVALS were more dramatic than others. In the late 1970s Eric and a friend were travelling overland, on their way to London, when they decided to stop and work somewhere warm. They found jobs picking olives and oranges in Crete, and were intending to stay the whole winter, until the friend got hepatitis. He wasn't keen on the thought of a hospital stay in Crete, so they returned to Athens and flew to London. Eric's first sightseeing trip through London was in an ambulance on the way to the infectious diseases hospital, where his friend was quarantined. Eric's other memory of those events was that his friend ended up being well fed and looked after while he, broke, had to deal with London and searching for a job.

people these days have got maps or a London A–Z *before they even get there – you couldn't get them here [in New Zealand] then.*

Young New Zealanders arriving in London were not entirely alone, however; as the number of Kiwis in London increased, so did the chance of having either friends or siblings to stay with – by the 2000s, they would even be waiting at Heathrow. Even those without close friends or family often had, at the very least, the address of a New Zealand contact. However, the number of New Zealanders arriving from the 1970s into the 1990s put some pressure on the resident population; a 'distant acquaintance' turning up at the door became a popular joke and cartoon subject.

The increasing numbers of New Zealanders also put pressure on many of the organisations that had served their London community. In the 1920s, when New Zealand House published its *Handbook to London for New Zealand Visitors,* and *New Zealand News* was first published, 2000 New Zealanders visited London each year; by 1978, when many of the services of New Zealand House had been passed over to *New Zealand News UK*, there were 70,000. Necessarily, this increase reduced the degree of support these more official sources could provide, and from the 1960s the gap was filled by travel clubs and employment agencies offering practical assistance as well as informal (and usually free) community support to the OE population.

Getting to grips with London Transport.
London Transport Museum

A less-than-friendly London welcome. Chris Slane

New Zealand House remained a focal point for New Zealanders in London, with the Whitcombe and Tombs shop (Whitcoulls from 1973) and the *New Zealand News UK* offices in behind the building. But the 'welcome' provided by New Zealand House gradually diminished from the early 1980s; new arrivals still went there to 'touch base', but the only practical service offered was the room in the basement which displayed New Zealand newspapers. There were also some useful public toilets in the basement, but eventually they were locked. By the 1990s it was impossible to walk through the foyer of New Zealand House: to get to the offices of *New Zealand News UK* in the Royal Opera Arcade (which the newspaper occupied until 2001), one had to exit the building and walk around the outside.

Many longstanding support services and organisations in London no longer suited the New Zealand visitor. The OE population was not the old guard of elite travellers visiting the home country; they were behaving differently. In 1976 *New Zealand News UK* carried pictures of a group of young New Zealanders protesting at Downing Street when their prime minister, Robert Muldoon, visited London: they carried placards against racism and the rugby tour to South Africa and in favour of open immigration to New Zealand. By the early 1980s, few New Zealand banks had branches in London. When the National Bank of New Zealand closed its offices in 1985, the only New Zealand bank still offering retail services in London was the Bank of New Zealand. With a minimum £2000 required to open an account, its services were not tailored towards the impoverished OE population.

Although *New Zealand News UK* was distributed free of charge, it was funded

Too many New Zealanders.
Chris Slane

through advertising. When New Zealand House services were transferred to the *News* during the 1970s, it was one of many signs of the emerging OE market that provided a wealth of commercial opportunities for the entrepreneurial.

OE guides: from books to websites

After getting to grips with the tube, recovering from jet lag and doing some London sightseeing, the next thing on the agenda was to find a job and somewhere to live. To start working life in London, one required a bank account and registration for national insurance and income tax. These involved a considerable amount of organisation. It was relatively easy to open a British bank account through one's New Zealand bank in the 1970s and 1980s. Tighter money-laundering controls made this more difficult; by the mid-1990s it was necessary to use the services of an authorised broker. There was usually a charge for this service, regardless of whether it was done in New Zealand before departure (easier) or in London after arrival. Trying to arrange things in London drew many into a vicious circle: an address was required for a bank account, a bank account was required for a job, and a job was needed to get a flat and an address.

The first OE guidebook – *Down Under in Europe* – was published in 1973. Prior to this, the *Welcome to Britain Guide* distributed by New Zealand House had provided advice on banking, employment, income tax, finding accommodation and visa regulations. *Down Under in Europe* was much more than a travel guide; while it included information on 'The Grand Tour', roughly half of the content was devoted to practical information on how to live and work in London. It was

also written specifically for Australians and New Zealanders. A *New Zealand Herald* review noted that it was 'Crammed with valuable information ... One can no more imagine the young Antipodean heading north without a copy in his rucksack than someone trying to cross the Sahara without a water bottle.'[24]

Several other London-based expatriate publications – through which young travellers could find flats, jobs, travel companies and travel companions, and keep up with news from home – appeared in the 1970s. For the most part, they replaced the noticeboards at New Zealand House and in the travel clubs that had served OE travellers in the 1960s and early 1970s, although *New Zealand News UK* maintained its Marketplace noticeboard throughout the 1980s.

By the late 1970s the patterns of information distribution were well established, but the methods of delivery would change significantly over the ensuing decades. The amount and nature of the information available that was relevant to the OE increased considerably from the 1970s. From the 1980s into the early 1990s the expatriate newspapers and magazines ruled supreme, and many publications continued into the 2000s, but by the mid-1990s they were accompanied by, or had been replaced by, electronic versions.

The publications also went through some significant market repositioning during these 30 years, reflecting changes in the OE itself as access to information about travel became more important. The *Australian Express* was published from 1973; a title change to *Australasian Express* in 1974 broadened its market appeal. *LAM*, another magazine for Australasians in London, began publication in 1977. The *LAM* acronym has stood for a variety of titles: it began as a monthly publication for Australians (*London Australia Magazine*) in December 1977, went weekly in 1978, and in May 1979 became 'London's only Australasian Magazine' when a page of New Zealand news was added. In October 1979, *LAM* became 'London's Australasian Magazine: for Londoners and Australasians'. It changed again in 1988, to become 'London's Australasian Magazine'; at the time it had an average circulation of 50,000. *LAM* was, for many years, a major competitor of what was to become the ubiquitous *TNT Magazine*: the *Australasian Express* re-launched in 1983 as 'The United Kingdom's free travel magazine: incorporating home-line – news and sport from home for all Australian, American, Canadian and New Zealand visitors'.

Many OE travellers arrived in London with only the vaguest of plans to 'travel in Europe'. During the 1980s and 1990s the travel articles, practical travel advice and travel advertising in these publications alerted them to the wide range of destinations and types of travel possible.

The 1990s saw the publication of a number of OE guidebooks in New Zealand, some of which used the 'OE' term in their titles. The first of these – *The Big OE Guide* – was published in 1990 by the New Zealand Youth Hostel Association. Written as a response to the many thousands of questions the YHA received each year from New Zealanders going overseas, the guide advertised a YHA 'OE Starter Kit', which included forms for YHA membership, passport and international driver's licence applications, travel insurance information and discount travel coupons. It also carried an advertisement for *New Zealand News UK* and for *Overseas*, a twice-yearly magazine published by the *News* that had information on jobs, accommodation and travel. *Overseas* was available from travel agents in New Zealand.

In the mid-1990s the first edition of *Live, Work and Play in London and the UK* was published, with separate editions for New Zealanders and Australians. More work-focused guidebooks followed in the late 1990s. In 1999, *Working in London and the UK (plus Ireland, the Netherlands and Malta)* was published by Global Exchange, which specialised in international work opportunities for Australians and New Zealanders. Other titles from the same publisher included *Teaching Overseas for Australians and New Zealanders* and *Japan: A working holiday guide for Australians and New Zealanders*. While the primary focus of these guides was work, they included some general information and advice on how to make the most of life overseas. No travel information was supplied.

The Big OE Guide was updated throughout the 1990s.
YHA, New Zealand

Opposite: Antipodean publications were distributed free in locations around London where New Zealanders were likely to congregate.

British High Commission
44 Hill Street, PO Box 1812, Wellington 1
Phone: 04 924 2889 Fax: 04 924 2822
E-mail: PPAmailbox@fco.gov.uk
Web: http://www.britain.org.nz

presents

The Big OE Evening
CHRISTCHURCH

Date: Tuesday 12 March 2002
Time: 17:00—19:00

The British High Commission organised 'Big OE' evenings from 1997.

A growing focus on work was also evident in London-based publications. *Recruitment UK*, for example, was established in 1999 for New Zealand and Australian professionals seeking British-based employment. The founder had been in London since 1989 and had worked at the New Zealand High Commission in London, been editor of *New Zealand News UK* and president of the New Zealand Society. Her partner was one of the New Zealand owners of Down Under Insurance. *Recruitment UK* was distributed through travel agents, public libraries, universities and other tertiary institutions, and more than 600 schools in New Zealand. The company was purchased by *New Zealand News UK* in 2005 and was still providing employment information via a website in 2012.

More information about the OE was becoming available in New Zealand throughout the 1990s. From 1995, the British Tourist Authority distributed a 'Big OE Pack' with information about working holiday visas and other information travellers needed for a shift to London. From 1997 a series of 'Big OE Evenings' – initially organised by the British High Commission and then by a public relations company on its behalf – were held biannually in Auckland, Wellington and Christchurch. In 2004, the first year the PR company ran the event, about 800 people attended; the peak year was 2008, when more than 1500 people attended the two events.[25] These evenings attracted older OE travellers as well as young people: 9 per cent of the 653 people surveyed at the 2005 evenings, for example, were aged over 45, and over half of those in this age group recorded 'working holiday' as their main reason for travelling.

Each Big OE Evening started with an introductory talk on visa regulations by a representative of the British High Commission, after which attendees were able to browse exhibitors' information stands. Exhibitors at the 2005 Christchurch evening included nine specialist employment agencies, three companies offering general OE support services, three travel company representatives (Contiki, New Zealand Youth Hostel Association and Harvey World Travel), British High Commission staff providing information on visas and passports and the New Zealand Inland Revenue Department advising on tax and student loans. A further two employment agencies had display stands, along with Tourism Ireland, VisitBritain, i-uk (the British Foreign Office website), and *New Zealand News UK*. While most of the employment agencies attending had offices in New Zealand, one employment agency representative had flown from the UK especially for the event.

Dwindling numbers of both attendees and exhibitors brought the Big OE Evenings to an end in 2010. The organiser attributed the decline in travellers to fewer people going on OEs, and increasing use of the internet by those who were going, whereas the decline in the number of exhibitors was a result of many employment agencies relocating their offices to Australia. The frequent changes in the British visa regulations, the increasing complexity of the visa process (with its biometrics requirement), and a 'distancing' by the British High Commission in relation to the Big OE Evenings had not helped.

With no geographical and physical constraints, the internet brought exponential increases in both the amount and accessibility of OE information in the 2000s, although many expatriate publications in London continued to be available in hard copy. By 2002, however, *LAM* had reverted to monthly publication and had become mainstream: *LAM* now stood for 'Living Abroad Magazine'. Its focus was on London life and, in particular, the London social scene; the only sections of the publication with an Australasian focus or flavour were a handful of advertisements for clubs and pubs, as well as the advertisements and articles in the travel section.

By way of contrast, in the mid-2000s *TNT Magazine* still had several pages devoted to New Zealand, Australian and South African news and sport.[26] Its editor described *TNT* as a 'getting started/finding your feet magazine', although readers commonly described it as 'just a register of advertisements'. Many readers also noted that it was not a good source of up-to-date information, as most of its content barely changed from month to month. However, *TNT* had broadened its focus to become the 'must-have guide for independent travellers' – not just Antipodeans. In 2004 its London office employed 75 staff and its readership figures of 400,000–500,000 per week were significant.

More OE, and still strongly London-focused, guides appeared in the early 2000s, some published in association with Antipodean media companies, others by recruitment agencies. Many were available in New Zealand. *New Zealand News UK* published an annual *Directory* with London information; *TNT* published a *Guide to London*. In the 2000s, in addition to its free weekly magazine that was distributed around London every Monday morning and available digitally on its website, the *TNT* group published a mid-week guide for events in London, an annual travel diary, a guide to the UK and Ireland, and an *Offshore Recruitment Directory*, aimed at Antipodeans before they arrived in the UK. Additional travel and OE information was provided on their website. In 2003 BUNAC (Working Adventures Worldwide) published a work and travel handbook for Britain. The recruitment company 1st Contact published an annual *Big OE Guide* throughout the early 2000s, and the financial recruitment firm Joslin Rowe Temporaries (established in 1982 to fill jobs in financial markets) published the *Essential Guide UK* for those going on OE in 2006.

Some of these companies also presented seminars in New Zealand on working overseas. In 2009, for example, 1st Contact presented seminars in Auckland, Wellington and Christchurch; the topics covered included getting started in Britain, life in London, visa regulations, and how to find work before

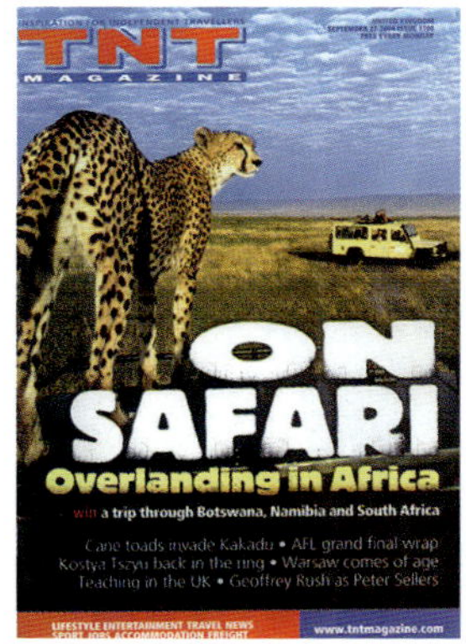

Two Antipodean publications: *TNT Magazine*, and *New Zealand News UK*.

New Zealand News UK, TNT Magazine

arriving in Britain. BUNAC (IEP) and Camp America also regularly present seminars in New Zealand.

The growth of the internet rendered many of the services and information previously provided by the expatriate publications obsolete; while the tradition of expatriate publications remained relatively strong in London, their focus changed. A major change was the access to New Zealand news that the internet gave those on OE. The launch in 2003 of *In London*, an expatriate magazine focusing on life in London rather than reporting news from expatriate homelands, was indicative of a significant change in the needs of OE travellers.

1st CONTACT was started in the mid-1990s by a New Zealander who had gone on his OE in the 1980s. A taxation service company, it expanded to become one of the most prominent London expatriate recruitment companies in the 2000s. One OE guidebook described 1st Contact as 'ubiquitous'; the company advertised extensively in the (also ubiquitous) *TNT*. It also offered a pre-OE service in New Zealand – a *Kickstart London Package* – which included a British bank account, a British Telecom account, mail holding and luggage storage services, as well as an orientation meeting. According to its managing director, Mike Kaye, the package was:

... more taken up by the South Africans than the Aussies or the Kiwis, but I think that reflects the history Australia and New Zealand have with the OE – even though they are more organised and the whole thing is more sanitised and structured [than in the past] they still don't want their hands held too much. To be honest, the package is built around the bank account and, if that wasn't there, we wouldn't even offer the package in Australia or New Zealand.

In London, many community-focused websites sprang up to facilitate expatriate life and print publications began to decline. Some websites were supported by print material. *In London* magazine was published in conjunction with an already established website; a drop in online advertising revenue prompted the creation of the print publication, but that ceased in 2008. The *New Zealand Times* was launched in London in 2005 by Blue Sky Publications, a company that already published the *Australia Times*, the *South Africa Times* and the *Career Times*. By 2006 the *New Zealand Times* had a print run of 12,000, an estimated weekly readership of 42,000, and 3500 email newsletter subscribers. It was distributed across 168 locations in London and 10 outside London. Hard-copy publication ceased in 2009, but the service continued via its website.

Finally, in August 2006 – after 79 years – the print edition of *New Zealand News UK* ceased publication. According to a report in the New Zealand media, 'It is another newspaper that has fallen foul of the internet with the company opting for a daily updated internet site to bring news to the estimated 100,000 New Zealanders in the UK.'[27]

A changing OE

These changes in the way OE material was delivered and in the type of material being delivered were indicative of a changing world and a changing OE. The 1980s were the heyday of OE print material; community support via expatriate websites reached its zenith in the mid-2000s and has declined since. These two peaks indicate significant shifts in the OE from a travel-oriented working holiday from the 1950s to the 1980s, to a much more work-focused one by the 1990s and 2000s. These changes were accompanied by the increasing availability of OE support in both New Zealand and London.

Because OE support was driven, to a large degree, by commercial interests, it is difficult to know to what extent there was a real need for it. The Big OE became 'big' business, often – somewhat ironically – orchestrated by those on OE themselves. Moreover, while the Big OE was presented as needing to be planned carefully and strategically, the reality was that the OE was still an adventure into the unknown, even if the destination was London.

An indication of how the OE changed over time was the publication in 2004 of *The Big OE Companion: A guide for New Zealanders in the UK*, 31 years after *Down Under in Europe* first appeared. Its focus was very much on life in London, with only small sections addressing travel and work. The guidebook recommended the internet as a good place to start one's search for work and provided a number of email and web contacts for employment agencies representing a wide range of industries. According to the author, the book was 'designed to make things easier' because 'Until now, Kiwis have flown into London relatively blind, with random snippets of advice gleaned from friends here and there, and arrive at Heathrow blinking and overwhelmed. We all reinvent the wheel and make the same mistakes.'[28] As the next three chapters show, from the 1980s OE travel episodes became shorter, OE work became more serious, and life in London became a celebration of New Zealand culture, rather than an exploration of other cultures.

In London was aimed at a more 'professional' market than *TNT Magazine*.
Simon Larcey

NEW ZEALAND TIMES
NEWS FOR KIWIS LIVING IN LONDON

Move to us from a Ltd Co provider & get £100 CASH!* 0800 082 0452 www.1stcontact.co.uk 1st Contact

Police and minister deny speed-ticket quota

Police Minister Annette King and Police Commissioner Howard Broad restated after a meeting on Monday that there was no quota policy for speed tickets.

LONDON LIFE
LONDON LIFE
TRAVEL
SPORT

BUYING A HOUSE ? NEED A WORK PERMIT/VISA ?
You are at the right place!
Specialists in Immigration & Property Law
Expert advice by qualified lawyers at no extra cost !
We have the knowledge!
Breytenbachs
www.breytenbachs.com • info@breytenbach.co.uk • 0207 499 3111

The *New Zealand Times* was published in hard copy for three years during the mid-2000s.
NewZealandTimes.co.uk

Chapter Five

THE GRAND TOUR AND BEYOND

EARLY OE TRAVELLERS took a long time to get to Britain and Europe; once there, they wanted to make the most of their time and of the available travel opportunities. They were budget travellers, but they had time to travel slowly. They were young and far from the constraints of home, and they were ready to enjoy themselves. The ideal of early OE travel was that it was undertaken independently and was exploratory in nature, although it shared the desire common to many tourists, to 'spot the landmarks'. Europe was the primary attraction; from a British base, many European destinations were accessible.

Even though they were 'organised', the early commercial camping tours around Europe satisfied these travel prerequisites. Most were several months long, they were casually run and often haphazard in both planning and execution; having to help out with cooking and setting up camp gave travellers the illusion of independence, and the tours were lots of fun. The 'ideal' remained the truly independent van tour, but by the late 1970s camping tours had become such fixtures on the OE agenda that they were unchallenged by all but the most 'hardcore' travellers (who often avoided them only because of the cost). Some camping tours, along with the van tour and a few select destinations and events, were well on their way to achieving iconic status within the OE.

From the late 1970s, OE travel out of London changed significantly, partly in response to shifts in the interests, priorities and opportunities of each successive cohort of travellers, partly because of entry regulations, and partly due to more general changes in travel and tourism. The result was that OE

Spotting the landmarks. Reproduced with the permission of Ashley Smith. Alexander Turnbull Library, New Zealand Cartoon Archive Collection, Paintings and Prints (DX-023-016)

travel became shorter and – by necessity – evolved into a series of more structured travel episodes. For some travellers, by the 2000s the long summer on the Grand Tour of Europe had fragmented into long weekends, short breaks, and single destination holidays when it was possible to take time off work in London, with perhaps a European tour on the way home. The iconic van tour and camping tours were still an option for others, but these, too, changed over time.

The OE travel map

Until the 1980s many OE travellers flew into London and set off almost immediately on a tour of Europe. As a result of changes in the visa regulations, this practice became less common; OE travellers were more likely to start work immediately and travel once their visas ran out. As compensation, there was always London to explore.

OE travel history is complicated by the fact that OE transport and travel styles, destinations and interests changed in response to political, commercial and technological developments. While the focus was on Europe, OE travellers had global aspirations. 'OE Europe' included the Middle East and North Africa. The rest of Africa was seen as easily accessible. The Americas and Asia offered stopovers, overland routes or stand-alone holiday destinations; for those who worked outside the UK, they were also an alternative home base to travel from.

Travel status is commonly associated with the destinations visited: the more remote, exotic or less mainstream the destination, the more meritorious the travel. On the OE, travel kudos often came from one's *style of travel*, rather than destinations per se. In Europe, independent travel was considered best, although the iconic OE travel experiences – which were often 'organised' – also had high status. Deregulation of the air industry in Europe in the early 1990s opened the way for budget airlines; by the 2000s, OE travel status was associated with getting the cheapest fares. Travel to non-European destinations was determined and judged according to a different set of criteria. Organised tours – particularly rougher overland-style expeditions – were always acceptable in Africa, Eastern Europe and the Americas, simply because independent travel was difficult bureaucratically, politically or logistically. Asia was always popular: after the closure of the Hippie Trail, the world's backpackers discovered the easy, cheap and exotic attractions of Southeast Asia.

OE travel changed many New Zealanders' perceptions of the world, both while they were on OE and afterwards. This can be summarised in the OE travel map on the next page, which has three overlapping, but relatively distinct parts. The outer circle represents the destinations visited (rather eloquently referred to as 'the bits in between' by some OE travellers) and means of accessing them between New Zealand and Britain. Some of these travel options no longer exist; others have varied over time in both their availability and popularity.

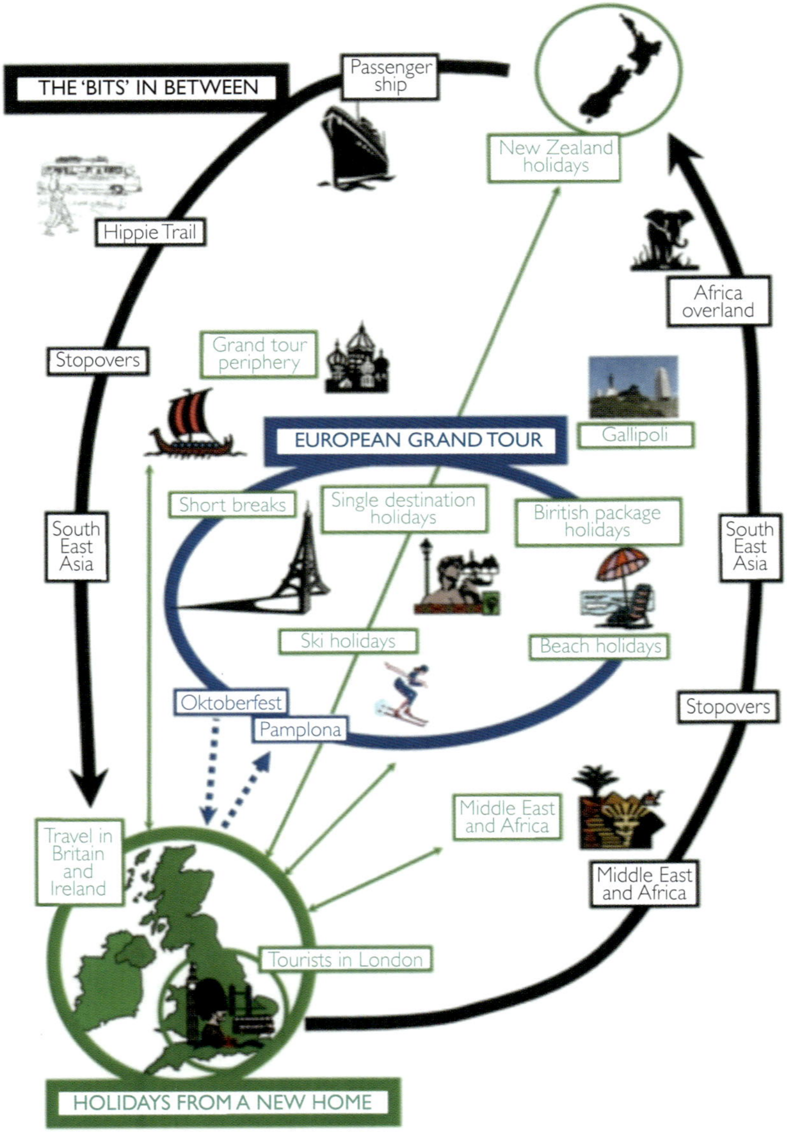

The OE travel map.

The inner circle represents the European Grand Tour, which is tightly defined both geographically (mainland Western Europe) and temporally (July to September). The ultimate destination is of course Britain, which offers a variety of weekend and special interest trips and holidays, including to locations that are geographically and temporally within the Grand Tour. Likewise, travel to the Middle East and Africa can be undertaken on holiday from Britain or as visits on the way to or from Britain.

The travel map also illustrates the range of tourist attractions – historic and iconic tourist sites, wildlife viewing, beach and ski holidays – enjoyed by OE travellers. Europe and North Africa offered a smorgasbord of travel delights; most OE travellers aspired to at least one summer-long Grand Tour of Europe to sample these.

The spread of railways across Europe in the nineteenth century, the simplification of travel by travel agents and the development of a considerable tourism infrastructure benefited the travelling public.[1] By the 1980s many ways of touring Europe were available to OE travellers. Transport options ranged from independent (hitchhiking, cycling, purchasing or hiring a vehicle), to public (buying tickets or using travel passes), and to organised (such as Top Deck or Contiki). The destinations making up the OE Grand Tour were more or less established and, while there were some changes in travel styles, its essence did not change much during subsequent decades.

Van tour

The independent tour by van attained 'classic' OE status during the 1970s. By the end of the decade, it was usually of three or four months' duration and followed a circuit that began in July with the Running of the Bulls in Pamplona, Spain (colloquially referred to as 'Pamps'), and finished in Germany in October at the Munich Oktoberfest (the 'Beerfest'). This route became so established as the 'van tour' that it offered a yardstick against which European travel could be measured. Some people did sections of the tour or shorter trips to the 'markers' at either end: 'Did Pamps one year and the Beerfest a couple of times, but not the tour.' Others recognised that they had their timing slightly wrong: 'We did a Combi trip and did the circuit, but left a month later than usual … but we did end up at the Beerfest.'

POST RENAISSANCE, educational tourism was popular as people travelled to see the great artworks and buildings of Europe. A special licence (freely granted through universities to encourage scholarship) was required to travel abroad; by the seventeenth and eighteenth centuries, such travel had developed into the 'Grand Tour', as young men travelled Europe for up to four years as a kind of finishing school.[5] In a pattern common in tourism history, the early travellers on the Grand Tour were the sons of the aristocracy and the gentry; in time, they were followed by the middle classes.[6] As the social class of travellers changed, so did their motives for travel: educational or cultural enlightenment was replaced by eyewitness observation and recreational and leisure travel.[7] The more recent 'Grand Tour' was quite hedonistic, with many of those on the tour spending their time 'in alehouses, meeting "local ladies" and generally behaving badly'.[8] A review of a television documentary from 2000, which followed a group of New Zealanders on a Top Deck bus tour of Europe, noted remarkable similarities: 'So much to drink, so many hormones and only twenty days and eight countries for it all to slosh around in.'[9]

The publication of several dedicated guidebooks is evidence of the popularity of van travel with New Zealanders and Australians. *Europe: By campervan*, published in 1979 by an Australian company, covered the logistics of van travel, outlined routes, reviewed the different models of van available, gave tips on budgeting and directions to the informal 'van market' (at the time located in The Strand beside Australia House).[2] A later guide, also titled *Europe by campervan*, was published in Australia in 1991.[3] It covered all aspects of van travel, but the opening chapter 'Europe – the Australian Way',[4] along with a subsequent chapter titled 'UK for the long term traveller', signalled a target audience of British-based Australians and New Zealanders.

The independent van tour has featured in New Zealand popular culture. In the play *the big o.e.*, by Alison Quigan and Ross Gumbley, the characters set off by van on their 1970s European tour.[10] The van tour was also celebrated in the 1982 Men at Work song, 'Down Under':

Travelling in a fried-out Combie,
On a hippie trail, head full of zombie.[11]

Grant Lahood's 2003 movie *Kombi Nation* immortalised the modern van tour.[12] This docu-drama followed four actors (playing three female friends and a male who

MANY VANS were given names and were decorated with national flags and other artwork. Often each new 'crew' recorded the year of their tour on the bodywork of the vehicle. For participants, recognition that they were on 'the tour' was important. For example, Hannah did a van tour in 2003, and 'painted a New Zealand flag on the van – we actually did it halfway through the trip – until then it didn't really stand out as a van tour van – it was just a blue van. Luckily we have found some other Kiwis to sell it to.'

Vans at the beach in Spain, 1990s. One has New Zealand markings, the other was called 'Armpit'.

'buys into' their van) as they journey from Pamplona, to Lagos, Barcelona … Tension arises as, along the way, all three girls become 'involved' with their male companion and matters come to a head when the girls discover that he is selling drugs to fund his trip. The movie was filmed on location at real van tour stops, the extras were actual van tourists and the parties were authentic.

The VW 'Combi' was the quintessential van for touring, although it supplied the generic moniker given to any type of van. The vans toured for many years, recycled each year through the London van market. There is an entertaining van market scene in *Kombi Nation* in which the characters devise an elaborate coding system to signal their personal evaluations of the various vans they inspect. At the time, the van market was located near Caledonian Road in Islington; by 2004, it had disappeared, superseded by message boards on the internet. While the advertisements and the medium used to advertise them were contemporary, the vans themselves were far from new or modern: the listings for second-hand vans on the Gumtree[13] website in 2005 included vans from 1973, 1980, 1986 and 1989.

The age of the vans and their owners' temporary residence in the UK made it difficult to get insurance. In response to this, a New Zealand-owned and operated insurance company (Downunder Insurance) started in London in 1992, specialising in 'non-resident' motor and travel insurance for Kiwis travelling to Britain and Europe. Their vehicle policy stipulated that vans must be less than 32 years old; other insurance companies were more restrictive, insuring only vans less than 20 years old.

Many vans suffered mechanical breakdown of some sort. A 1996 *TNT Magazine* survey found that most problems involved electrics and starting systems, but oil leaks, clutch and brake faults and flat tyres also occurred frequently. The survey also reported the following statistics for van tours:

Average miles covered: 8640
Average length of trip: 4.9 months
Average cost of van: GBP£1800
Average spent on repairs: GBP£305
Average age of van: 18 years
Each van spends an average of £1200 on fuel
Van travellers spend an average of £5 each a day on food.[14]

Bought the Combi, ready to go, 1980s.

Afterwards, van tour disaster stories were often the best remembered, or treasured, parts of a trip. For example, Stuart was driving through Turkey in 1988 when he hit a donkey. The services of a local panelbeater were required; while he fixed the van, the travellers stayed with his family for several days. It was the highlight of their trip.

A basic lack of planning and poor budgeting led to other problems on the road. Barry described his van tour: 'I worked the first summer in England and then went around Europe in 1980, which was one of the wettest summers on record in Europe. We had bought a Combi and another mate came over just for the Europe trip but my money only lasted five weeks because we were on the piss all the time. I got the Magic Bus back from Greece – had no money to eat for the three days the bus took.'

Van companions were generally found from among friends or acquaintances, although some advertised (both for spaces in a van and to fill vans). In *Kombi Nation,* the three girls found their male companion through an advertisement; the girls accepted him after agreeing among themselves that he was 'probably OK because he came from Napier!' Occasionally, if things weren't going well, van passengers would swap to another van en route. Some passenger exchanges were made for romantic reasons.

Despite the longstanding traditions of the van tour (the recycling of vans, the fixed routes), it is perceived by many to have changed over time. The New Zealand owners of a London travel agency, who did a van tour in the late 1980s (early in their own OEs) and were still closely involved in OE travel in 2004, described these changes:

[The] van tour has become pretty feral. In its heyday in the 1970s and 1980s there were upwards of 200 vans collected in various European cities; this year there were probably less than 100. Today's travellers are not as adventurous – I know that when we were going out we were going on an adventure – just the fact that we weren't going to be able to contact people – we were going out to sample European culture – possibly not as

SOMETIMES van trouble started before even leaving London. In the mid-1990s, Scott and a friend had planned a van tour for themselves and two other friends (who were flying over from New Zealand for the summer). The London-based Kiwis bought a van on the understanding that the other two would pay their shares when they arrived. They kitted it out, insured it and, a few days before they were due to start their tour, picked up their friends from Heathrow. They went back to their flat and parked the van. The two new arrivals went off to see the sights of London, leaving their gear in the van, as they were planning to sleep in it until they left for Europe a few days later. While they were out, the van was stolen. Luckily their passports and money were with them, but they lost all of their gear and were, understandably, reluctant to pay their quarter shares of the van purchase price. The insurance policy had started only the previous day and the insurance company – suspicious of a van loss so soon after the policy started – paid out only many months later. The four would-be travellers were considerably out of pocket and had no van. They rearranged their travel plans, but had to cut short their summer tour as it was more expensive travelling by train and bus and paying for their accommodation each night.

much as a cultural student – we were going out to drink, but we were going to visit as much as possible as well.

Some of this change can be seen in van tour advertisements. On Gumtree in 2005, the 'enticements' of the van tour were to share a travel experience that offered a combination of freedom, the chance to see the sights and to party (the exact wording was 'party hard' or 'start it off hard in Pamps'). The perceived freedom to travel wherever one wanted was moderated by mention of 'convoys' or of doing the 'round trip thing' in many advertisements. By comparison, the advertisements in *New Zealand News UK* in 1980 were more circumspect.

In 1983 *New Zealand News UK* reported that touring Europe by van was declining in popularity because of soaring petrol costs, the decline in value of the New Zealand dollar and the availability of a wider range of budget-priced camping tours and European rail passes. There may have been a resurgence in van tour popularity in the 1990s, although the figures seem a little inflated. In 1995 the London *Evening Standard* published a double-page van tour feature that began 'Spring heralds the arrival of Aussies and Kiwis in London' and went on: 'Every year they come to our cultured continent to do what has become known as the Grand Combi Tour. But they are not in search of culture. Armed with Vegemite and enough alcohol to float every navy in Europe, they're out to drink, drive and inject drugs.'[15]

In 1996 *TNT Magazine* reported that 15,000 Aussies, Kiwis and South Africans were preparing for a summer-long tour of Europe by campervan, and 'with an average of three occupants per van that meant 5000 vans left these shores [the UK] each summer.'[16]

Some sources suggest that the independent van tour declined in popularity once again in the decade after this renaissance. In 2005, in a newspaper article entitled 'Campervan Kiwis at risk of becoming endangered', a British journalist described his fruitless search around Europe looking for New Zealanders travelling by campervan. The author lamented the decline of the van tour:

The Kiwi inspires us to travel, to think for ourselves and to be free. New Zealanders are, the world over, liked and respected for

2 N.Z. GIRLS, willing to share expenses in van around Europe, leaving late July.—Tel. (collect) Leanne 031-229 7739.

2 N.Z. GIRLS would like to tour Europe in van, either share or purchase one jointly, M/F's.—Please Tel. 584 3060, after 7, or leave message at N.Z. House (C. Martelli).

N.Z. COUPLE, mid 20's, wish to join others with van for travel around Europe. Share expenses, etc.—Ring 886 1049, after 6 p.m., ask for Kevin or Marg.

2 N.Z. GIRLS require lift one-way, Pamplona, leaving 5th July. Share expenses.—Tel. Michelle, work 486 8241; home 360 8409.

ONE or Two Girls want space in a van to travel around Europe. Beg. July or thereabouts. Share expenses. —Please Tel. Sue, 340 5838, evenings and weekends.

New Zealand News UK advertisements in 1980.

SARA (a long-term New Zealand expatriate living in London in 2004) did a Combi tour in her early OE days and, at times, found it embarrassing:
By the time I did the Combi trip it was '91 – so I would have been 28. I was embarrassed by the behaviour of Kiwis and Aussies on their Combi trips. You spent hours on a ferry watching the Kiwis get drunk and throw up all over the deck – with the Greek families sitting there. What is the point of going around Europe if all you are going to do is sit in your Combi and get completely hammered?'

HANNAH and her flatmate Alice compared their 2003 tour to what they knew of their respective mothers' trips in the 1970s:
Hannah: *My mum has classic stories – like she did a van tour and they stayed in places for three weeks at a time and took drugs and that. They left one of their mates in a kibbutz to get married.*
Alice: *It sounds like when my Mum went: back then they had no money and all they did was travel in vans and eat nothing – they had the best time.*
Hannah: *That was the real van tour.*
Alice: *Maybe it was easier to travel like that then because facilities weren't there like today – it is hard to turn down what is there.*

their kind and easy-going manner, sense of adventure and love of life. It isn't broke – so don't fix it. You're only young once. Get a campervan and do your country proud.[17]

The Kiwis the journalist did find were on cheap weekend trips away from their career jobs in London. In the author's opinion, they had been both 'possessed by the English' and 'swallowed by the capitalist machine'.

Several 'dedicated' van tour websites recognised the iconic status of the van tour in the mid-2000s:

Vantour is a European pilgrimage spanning the memories of decades of Antipodean travellers. The route around Europe follows roughly the same path each year although there is no itinery [sic] or organiser – only what has been handed down from one year to the next and plans that are made on the way.[18]

'Roughly the same path' was actually a detailed tour route: after a late-June start in London and a stop in Pamplona, the tour moved to the Algarve in Portugal; here the vans collected in a Lagos campground affectionately known as the 'dustbowl' (where some of *Kombi Nation* was filmed). The vans then travelled to Gibraltar (with many making a side trip to Morocco), before winding their way up the Spanish coast to Barcelona. The next big stop was Rome, before the vans were parked in Athens while their occupants visited the Greek Islands. From here, vans tended to split, with some going up through Eastern Bloc countries and some across to Croatia or back up through Italy. The 'ultimate' destination was Munich and Oktoberfest; the speed of travel and routes taken were determined by how much time and money the travellers had.

Carolyn did a van tour in 2002, over this exact route, adding that *Lonely Planet* was the travellers' 'bible' and that vans travelling in convoy would stay in touch by text messaging. Perhaps it is a misnomer to describe such a tour as being only roughly planned or as having *no* itinerary. The same route was described in a 2012 *TNT* guide to the van tour, which also noted that while buying a van is an option, 'there's always the danger you'll end up with a piece of crap'.[19] Instead, the article recommended Spaceships Rentals and Wicked Campers – companies familiar to New Zealanders – which specialised in van tour rentals.

Opposite: Van tour scenes, 1980s and '90s.

Doing a Contiki

Many of the original camping tour companies faced financial problems in the early 1980s; often their vehicles were unsafe and they had no financial support if things went wrong on tour. Contiki, Top Deck, Autotours, Sundowners and Transit were the only companies that survived into the 1980s; of these, only Contiki and Top Deck were operating in the new millennium (Sundowners no longer runs European tours).[20] Their longevity and continuing prominence in the OE travel market bestowed both Top Deck and Contiki with extraordinary renown and notoriety: 'Doing a Contiki' became a generic term for any type of organised tour. The tours themselves changed slowly from the 'rough and ready' tours of the 1960s and 1970s into more organised, sophisticated and luxurious trips. The first major change was the provision of a cook, rather than passengers having to cook on rotation. Gradually, both accommodation and transport standards also improved.

Many of these tour companies operated – or were associated with – London travel clubs. As noted in Chapter Three, the Walkabout Club began in 1973 in conjunction with Autotours and sold Transit, Contiki and Top Deck tours; Top Deck started the Deckers Club in 1981–82 in the Enterprise Hotel; Drifters Travel operated the Drifters Club from 1983 until early in the 2000s (Drifters Travel was still operating in 2012); and in 1986 Contiki started Farthings Club, which ran for five or six years. Some of these clubs were much like the OVC, offering airport pick-ups, accommodation packages, tours of London, mail services, employment services and social events. Travellers commonly joined a club before leaving New Zealand or Australia. The services of most use were the mail services and accommodation: they offered beds in shared rooms in the years before independent hostels were widespread in London. Other clubs simply offered a bar facility associated with a particular tour company.

Contiki always tried to stand apart from the other camping tour companies: it never had a front office in Earls Court (although it had office space there); instead, its first retail store was in Rathbone Place and its early tours all left from Notting Hill Gate. The turning point for Contiki was in the late 1970s when the company put its first Mercedes bus on the road, giving it a vehicle that was safe and reliable. The company pulled further away from the pack when it erected permanent tent villages at some European stopovers, so that clients did not have to put up tents each night. The volume of passengers it carried enabled Contiki to offer tours with accommodation in chateaus, villas and castles at reasonable rates. While Contiki was more expensive than other camping tour companies, it offered superior value, according to company founder John Anderson.

It was about this time that Contiki added the word 'security' to its advertisements. Contiki continued to upgrade its product, although it was not the only company to do so. A 1980 Autotours brochure advertised that 'unlike some other companies we still believe in small groups rather than crammed coachloads'. It called its smaller coaches 'puddle jumpers'. Autotours also introduced a new concept in camping tours: surprise overnight stops in hotels, chalets, bungalows and lofts. The company added pre-erected cook tents and advertised widely through travel agents in New Zealand in the mid- to late 1980s. Despite having good advance bookings, Autotours went out of business in December 1992, when the company directors decided to voluntarily liquidate after the bank called in their overdraft. The premises of the associated London Walkabout Club were taken over by Drifters.

That left Contiki and Top Deck still in business, although to satisfy changing markets and tourist expectations they had been through numerous metamorphoses over the intervening years. Contiki expanded its tour programmes to include America (1982), Australia (1984), an India to London tour (1986), Egypt (1991), Israel (1993), Africa (1995) and Turkey (1996). The company still offered camping tours, but also ran hotel and 'concept' tours that stayed in luxury or unusual accommodation. In a shift even further into mainstream tourism, it opened a resort on the Greek island of Mykonos in 2004.[21]

Contiki carried more than 250,000 passengers between 1962 and 1989, when it was sold. An article on the company in 2005 reported that 1.6 million people had 'stepped aboard' a Contiki bus since 1962.[22] A new generation of travellers are now taking Contiki tours, however the luxury of Mercedes coaches with reclining seats, televisions and toilets are a far cry from the original Ford Transit vans, just as castles and comfort have largely replaced campgrounds. In the company's 2004–05 brochure, Contiki camping tours were advertised nostalgically as 'the original Contiki classic. Traditional touring combined with a can-do team spirit.' In 2013 Contiki offer the chance to 'Discover loads of Europe like we did back in '62 – the original way to go. Stay on some of Europe's best campsites and you may even get the odd hostel or even hotel upgrade. Eat locally-

TRANSIT, Contiki's biggest competitor, collapsed at the beginning of the European summer season in 1980. Maggie's Transit tour was in Corfu at the time but, given the option of abandoning the tour or continuing (after paying more), they continued on to Istanbul. Maggie and another woman took over the cooking when the tour's cook (who had not been paid and went to work on yachts in Greece) left. Other camping tour companies, like Contiki, helped them out with the occasional meal. When she returned to London, Maggie was offered a job cooking for Sundowners, which she did for two years before it folded at the end of 1982. On a trip in 1981 out of Russia, their coach was involved in a collision with a car in Poland and was burnt out. The passengers were all okay but tragically people in the car were killed. The passengers lost any gear they had in the coach; their suitcases were in lockers that did not burn, although they stank afterwards. After Sundowners folded, Maggie and a driver went over to Autotours, where she worked for another three years; she was the first female courier with Autotours.

sourced produce cooked by our amazing On-road cooks.'

The Top Deck expansion story was similar to Contiki's, and would not have been possible without the thousands of colonial travellers in Europe in the 1970s and 1980s. From its first Moroccan trips in 1973–74, the company expanded throughout Europe and beyond, adding an overland trip to Kathmandu in 1975, and American tours in 1981. The original founders of Top Deck sold the company in 1986 (and went on to establish Flight Centre), although the company continued to be run by Australians and New Zealanders. In 2012 its brochures covered: Summer Europe; Europe Winter; Africa; Anzac; Egypt; European Festivals; Australia, New Zealand and Fiji; and Gap-Year travel.

While camping tours were derided by many simply because they were 'tours', the main criticisms were of the speed at which they travelled – often exaggerated as '17 countries in five days' – and the on-tour behaviour. In 2000 this was documented in a fly-on-the-wall television series produced in New Zealand, *The Big OE,* which followed a group of New Zealanders on a 21-day Top Deck tour of Europe.[23] According to a programme review, the tour was a 'hair-raising mix of sex, drugs and high-spirits'.[24]

The tour companies travelled on similar circuits and would meet each other on a regular basis. In the early 1980s they would sometimes swap passengers if someone on one tour had missed something or wanted to change the schedule they were following. They also played practical jokes on other tours: a Sundowners tour group once put laxatives in the chocolate pudding of the neighbouring Contiki tour; the Contiki passengers eventually retaliated by flour-bombing the Sundowners group at another campsite. Changing safety regulations, and customer expectations and demands, gradually had an impact on such behaviour; customer service became more professional. The behaviour of passengers, however, could still be questionable.

While generally *all* tour companies were criticised, often people made a point of saying which company they had, or had not, travelled with. Price was an important factor

FORMER tour company employees were often defensive about some of the antics that went on. One ex-Contiki employee, for example, agreed that Contiki tours were 'party trips' (with a major party every second night), but argued that people slept it off when they were driving on the motorways, and that 'no one missed the important things like the Eiffel Tower'. Sally did a Contiki tour in 1984 and disagreed:

It was one big long party – we spent most of it drunk. I missed things entirely … I was so hung over – I have felt ashamed of this for years – like Saint Peters Cathedral and the Sistine Chapel because we could not get out of our tent – there were three of us who were that sick.

Craig spent several seasons employed as a driver on camping holidays around Europe in the mid-1990s and described the tours:

It was like see Europe – see 12 countries in 20 days. It was quite cool in some ways, but for a lot of them it was just a big piss trip. You know, the first stop was Calais where you went to the big liquor barn and loaded the bus up to the gunnels with cheap liquor and then every few days you stopped in one of the big supermarkets and stocked up on the grog supplies.

when picking a tour company, but there were also some quite subtle differences between companies. For example, Nicky opted for Top Deck in 1982, saying she 'didn't want to do the Contiki thing because that was naff. Top Deck was a more eclectic mix of people – it was a bit cheaper as well. It was more that Top Deck was not something everyone else did.' The original unique selling point, which contributed to Top Deck's more eclectic image, was its use of converted double-decker buses for transport and accommodation, an advantage it lost through the tightening of transport regulations in Europe.[25]

One of the owners of a London travel company remarked that there was a difference in attitude towards tours, and Contiki in particular, that depended on nationality: 'Aussies love it [the Contiki tour] but you ask any Kiwi [about theirs] and they are embarrassed.' Sometimes the concern was based on perceptions of how others would judge them, rather than personal experience of such tours. Kate, for example, didn't like package tours (and had not done one), reflecting that 'it is probably an identity thing – thinking about it – because I don't want the social stigma of being a bus tripper.' Some destinations and types of trips, as well as individual companies, became more acceptable when judged according to certain criteria. Contiki, for example, had the 'worst' reputation as a company (perhaps because it was prominent in the market), but was a popular and acceptable choice for ski trips.

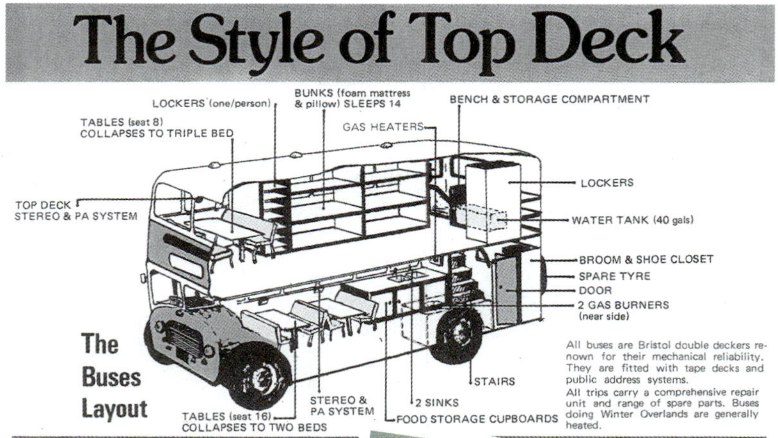

Travel Top Deck style: from 1996, height restrictions meant that no bus over 4 metres could carry passengers in Europe; the 'Deckers' were 4.1 metres.

Right: A Top Deck group dressed in national costume at Volendam in the Netherlands.

'Scandi–Russia' tours became increasingly popular in the late 1970s and 1980s. Scandinavian travel was generally very expensive compared with the rest of Europe, and before the collapse of communism travel in Eastern Europe was bureaucratically very difficult.

Taking a tour was 'almost' acceptable as a first experience of travel, as it boosted confidence and provided an introduction to both the destinations and the mechanics of travelling. Sally and her friend were typical 'novice' travellers:

We did a Contiki trip around Europe – two and a half weeks – it was all booked and paid for before we left New Zealand. I remember at the time thinking it was a kind of tacky thing to do, but it was our first proper big adventure, and we always talked about the fact that if we did this Contiki trip it would give us an idea which countries we wanted to go back and visit and spend more time in, and from that point of view it did have its advantages.

Tours were also seen as being more suited to females, singles, or younger people. Steve was with a girlfriend when he first went away in 1992 and they did a Contiki trip on first arriving in Europe. While it was good fun and boosted his travel confidence, he thought it would have been better to do as a single male. The tours continued to attract more female than male passengers, as in the 1960s and 1970s; this was perceived by some to make jobs as tour guides or drivers more appealing for males. In *Rule No. 5: No sex on the bus*, Brian Thacker 'confessed all' and described numerous instances of crews breaking this code of conduct with passengers. One long-term New Zealand expatriate, whose OE was in the 1990s, recalled, 'I have done my Contiki trip and my Top Deck trip and shagged the bus driver and all that kind of stuff – as you do – and he was from my home town! I didn't know him before, but his mother knew my mother.' For male passengers, on the other hand, as the cartoon opposite shows, the 'Con-a-Kiwi' tour reality did not quite match its advertised delights. However, Contiki and Top Deck tours were responsible for many marriages (and some babies). John Anderson, Contiki's founder, married one of his passengers, as did Bill James, the author of *Top Deck Daze*.

Chris Slane's take on camping tours. Chris Slane

Trains, buses, boats and planes

An extensive European public transport network catered for those wanting more independence than van or camping tours offered. Eurail and Inter Rail youth passes were popular in the early 1980s. Athens was known for its 'bucket shop' student flight deals, and many travellers had fake student cards. Local and long-distance buses were another option.

Train travel offered more flexibility than organised tours, although travellers often visited only the bigger cities, as local trains were slow. Increasing prices and safety concerns affected the popularity of train travel. By the late 1990s, Eurail and Inter Rail passes had been condensed into shorter packages (two or three countries rather than 'all' Europe).[26] Unless one qualified for a Youth Pass, rail passes offered convenience rather than price advantage (rail was an expensive transport option). The increasing age at which New Zealanders were going on OE, and the tendency to leave extensive travel until British visas ran out, meant many were too old to qualify for the

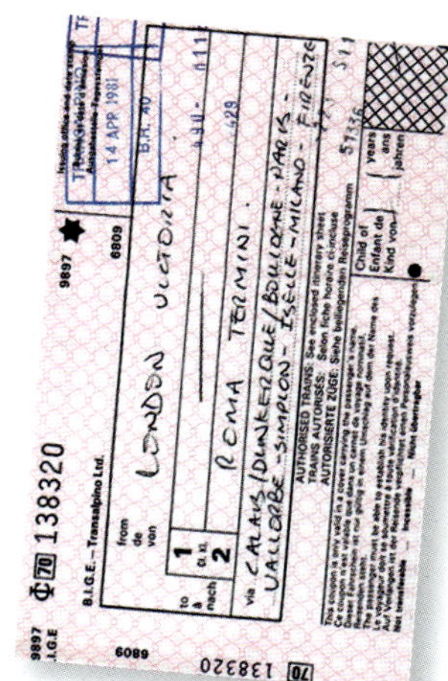

Travellers under 26 could get Transalpino/BIGE tickets, which allowed rail travel for up to two months on fixed international routes.

Ferry travel gave access to the Greek Islands and to Turkey; once in Greece, donkeys and scooters could be used for transport. Using local public transport often involved sleepless nights and long waits.

cheaper options. According to *The Big OE Companion*, however, train travel was still (in 2004) the most comfortable and romantic way of travelling within Europe.

Kate used a rail pass in 1988 and recalled that visiting *just* big cities was fine, as she had never been *anywhere* in Europe before. She found that another advantage of train travel was that one could save money by sleeping on trains:

We would go to the cities for a day and then we would catch the train to some long-distance place so you could sleep on the train overnight and wake up in a new city. You got very good at the 'finesse' aspects of it – travel is an art form really, in that you work out how not to get anyone else in your carriage by hanging out all your dirty socks and making the place look really uncomfortable, so when other people opened the door they would think 'eeh, horrible foreigners'.

In some countries, bus networks were more extensive than rail and bus travel more economical. In the 1980s Amsterdam, Athens and Istanbul were centres for low-priced private bus lines for long-distance routes across Europe and overland to India. Most famous of these was the Magic Bus, which folded late in 1982 but, according to *TNT Magazine*, was rolling again in February 1983. In 1981 the Magic Bus fare from Athens to London was US$56 (a 'student charter' flight was US$150).[27]

Rail travel was very popular with OE travellers during the 1980s.

POLLY took the Magic Bus from Istanbul to Graz in Austria in 1981 (although she managed to stay on the bus until she got to Salzburg without the driver noticing). According to her diary, the ticket cost 3500 Turkish Lira (which was £17.50) and she had to pay another 1000 Turkish Lira (£5) for a Bulgarian visa – passengers who didn't get this visa in advance had to pay US$25 at the border. The 38-hour trip was 'hideous': the drivers changed over while driving; the bus was falling apart, with broken seats and what looked like bullet holes in the windows; the drivers appeared to be smuggling goods into Europe; and the bus spent hours at each Eastern European border post (they drove through Bulgaria and Yugoslavia) while it was taken apart and searched.

London to Athens by bus.
Chris Slane

Very few long-distance bus routes now operate, possibly due to competition from cheap airlines. The Eurolines Company operates Europe's largest regular coach network, incorporating 32 independent coach companies. In 2008 a 'value single' ticket from London to Rome for those under 26 was £73; London to Rome on EasyJet was advertised at £48, and on Ryanair at less than £30. However, Eurolines did offer a number of travel passes that were cheaper than rail passes.

Hop-on hop-off bus services were introduced in the 1990s, promoted as an option occupying the middle ground between organised tours and independent travel. Busabout, established in 1998, was the primary operator in Europe in the 2000s; prior to this, a similar product was offered by Eurobus. On-board guides dispensed travel advice, accommodation could be booked ahead and passengers were dropped off at hostels (although only if they stayed at one preferred by the bus company). The services were promoted as an easy way to meet other backpackers, but there were downsides: a limited set of destinations, and the possibility of being stranded when buses were busy.

In the late 1990s one of the New Zealand founders of Kiwi Experience started Stray Travel in the UK. The company offered a rail-based hop-on hop-off service in Europe and a bus service in Britain and Ireland. Stray did well in Britain, despite the foot-and-mouth outbreak in 2001, but the European operation was dependent on the availability of flexible rail tickets. It lost access to these in 2003, when its supplying rail company was liquidated. The European trips offered by Stray was the most flexible of all the hop-on hop-off services. Travellers were able to take any train they liked, the use of guide services was optional and they offered travellers more options to see local life in Europe than did other hop-on hop-off services.

Busabout offered trips ranging from short 'adventures' to longer 'explorers', with cheaper prices for students. Most of their routes initially began in London, where many of their customers were based, but this changed over time as a result of cheap airfares in Europe. In 2003, for example, most passengers started their Busabout trips in London; in 2006, fewer than 50 per cent did so (the Busabout brochure showed 'feeder' connections from London to the European starting point). In 2006, 75 per cent of Busabout passengers were Australians and New Zealanders. On the Busabout website in 2012, all trips were entirely within mainland Europe, and the mode of operation had also changed in response to passengers' changing demands: originally trips were booked by 'time', but they became destination-based, with an open time limit over the summer months, and trips able to be split into smaller parts. The northern route, taking in iconic European cities – Paris, Munich, Amsterdam and Berlin – was the most popular in 2006. The advent of budget airlines (in that they facilitate this style of trip) was the catalyst for some of these changes, but the company also attributed change to a new generation of travellers who wanted 'some glamour, good meals, no backpacks and … to go clubbing'.

In the 2000s the availability of cheap flights fostered a 'cheap city-break' approach to seeing Europe, and the abandonment of 'connecting the dots'. One long-term expatriate noted that today's OE travellers 'will probably know more European cities, but they won't know much about the countryside, nor have a feel for the difference, say, between Tuscany and Umbria'. In 2004 Tara and James had 'been to

'Andy Podean' gets a cheap flight to the Norwegian town of Haugesund.
Jonathan Drapes

15 countries already' in their first year away, all on weekend breaks to European capitals or major cities. Haydn and his partner did not even care particularly where they went for weekends, but would 'take the cheapest flights on offer – once we went to some little place in Finland we had never heard of and had a great weekend.'

Many OE guides point out the pros and cons of each transport option. Budget airlines, for example, offered great deals and allowed travellers to cover a lot of ground quickly, but they could be costly if one wanted to change plans or travel more spontaneously. Also, budget airlines often used smaller airports located further out of the major cities. The downsides of rail or scheduled bus travel included having to 'figure out schedules for yourself', and finding your own way to your accommodation. Bus services were often limited, and a disadvantage of Eurail passes was that the network did not include Eastern Europe and Britain. On the other hand, both train and bus travel had a big 'pro': the opportunity for travellers to mix with the local population.

Another way to mix with locals was hitchhiking.

Pamplona, Oktoberfest, Gallipoli: OE icons

In 1965 *New Zealand News* published travel articles on Pamplona and Oktoberfest; interestingly, the Pamplona one did not mention the Running of the Bulls festival. In 1978, trips to Pamplona and Oktoberfest were advertised in *LAM*; a travel article in the same magazine in 1979 suggested that Pamplona was popular with young Antipodean travellers because of James Michener's book *The Drifters*. Other sources suggest that Ernest Hemingway's *The Sun Also Rises* (referred to in *The Drifters*) put Pamplona on the map for tourism in general.[28]

Although Pamplona (for Running of the Bulls) and Munich (for Oktoberfest) were an intrinsic part of both van tours and many organised camping tours, they were also popular as standalone trips. In 1978 most trips advertised to the two destinations were for 8–14 days; in 2004, the longest trips were eight or nine days and many packages were for three or four nights only. While cheap flights facilitated these changes, increasing numbers of passengers were wanting to limit the time they needed to take off work. Those involved in the companies running the trips thought that by flying and meeting on site, passengers were missing out on the 'fun of getting there', and the whole trip atmosphere. When travelling by coach from London, the party used to start with some companies selling alcohol en route, supposedly to 'police' their passengers' drinking!

Eight companies offered trips to Oktoberfest in *TNT Magazine* in July 2003, compared to only two in 1980, indicating either a larger market in the 2000s, or more competition within the market. In the early 1980s the tour companies held an annual competition at Oktoberfest to see who had travelled the furthest off their intended itinerary in order to get there. Autotours was the winner one year after driving a tour group from Barcelona; another year a Top Deck tour of Scotland won: the Top Deck passengers even paid the extra money needed to get their bus over the English Channel (and back). In 1982 Top Deck had a record 22 'Deckers' at the opening day of Oktoberfest.[29]

Busabout, Contiki, Top Deck and a number of companies specialising in the festival and short-break market still operate Pamplona and Oktoberfest trips. Many of the specialist companies were founded by, and for, Antipodeans in London. PP Travel, for example, was originally Kozzie Travel (from 'Kiwi-Ozzie') and about 90 per cent of its passengers were from Australia and New Zealand. The business started in 1991, with 'two coach loads of passengers, a handful of tents at Pamplona and three ground crew'; in the 2000s they routinely took over 1000 passengers to Pamplona, and in 2007 took 2850 passengers to Oktoberfest.[30] Another prominent company in the late 1990s and 2000s was Backpacker Co., an existing travel company bought by two New Zealanders in 1999. Renamed First Festival Travel in early 2007, it operates a range of festival trips, as well as longer tours to Turkey; it also sells a variety of hop-on hop-off tours to Britain, Ireland, Europe and Egypt. In 2004 Backpacker Co. took 1600 people to Pamplona.

Three decades of 'Pamps': 1980s, 1990s and 2000s.

Bill James, *TNT Magazine*

According to the travel companies, many OE travellers did not appear to recognise the importance or historical significance of the festivals they were attending. Instead they viewed them as opportunities to party with other drunken Antipodeans. Many long-term expatriates in Britain think that recent OE travellers are geographically and historically ignorant compared to those of their era. In fact, visiting these festivals usually taught travellers some history (even if only the history of their own attendance, as in the cartoon below); many people admitted to finding them more 'interesting' than they expected.

Antipodeans at the Beerfest. Chris Slane

Remembering Oktoberfest. These two cartoons from the early 1980s and mid-2000s show that behaviour has not changed much over two decades.
Chris Slane; Jonathan Drapes

It is perhaps difficult to blame the passengers when trips were and are openly advertised as 'party tours'. For instance, PP Travel were 'Your Party Professionals'. In 2004 First Festival Travel advertised that it 'operated the biggest party tours'. (It is worth noting that in 2012 the company emphasised its 'drive to promote the cultural integrity of each festival'.[31])

Descriptions of these trips ranged in travellers' recollections from 'cheesy' to 'feral', and some people made excuses for going. Craig, for example, admitted going to Oktoberfest several times in the mid-1990s 'but that was with work, so it was all right'. Others blamed friends for persuading them to go. A well-known feature of Oktoberfest is the Hundred Club, colourfully described on a travel website as:

... the disgusting, feral, appalling but legendary Hundred Club (100 Club). It takes place at a free campsite in a Munich park every year on the Friday before Oktoberfest

Enjoying the Beerfest, 1990s. Training could be done in London, as the cartoon shows.

kicks off … If you've heard of the centurion drinking game where participants attempt to down 100 shots of beer in a hundred minutes then you're halfway to understanding the 100 Club. But there's more to it than that! Throw in a few evil judges, hundreds of spectators, pissing, puking, nakedness and some beer bongs packed with things like tuna, olives, vodka, and raw eggs and you've got the 100 Club![32]

The same article suggested that van tours, where 'participants party their way around Europe, drink loads, and basically have a crazy time while cramming in the occasional sight between drinking binges and hangovers' provided 'training that is put to good use when the vans meet up at a free camp and kick off Oktoberfest in fine, feral fashion with the 100 Club'.

Pamplona also involves heavy drinking and can be dangerous for participants who elect to 'run' with the bulls. In 2006 a New Zealander was one of the seven tourists injured there by bulls.[33] A dangerous tradition developed of alcohol-fuelled tourists diving off a Pamplona statue – this featured in *Kombi Nation* – into the arms of the crowd. Most tour companies have tried to dissuade their clients from participating, although tour drivers and leaders also have had a reputation for partying hard. In recent years, La Tomatina and Las Fallas in Spain, and the Venice Carnival, have been added to the European festival calendar.

PP Travel carries many repeat passengers on its Oktoberfest trips; tours to Pamplona and the newest 'iconic' OE destination, Gallipoli, have usually been 'one-offs', trips that OE travellers have to do once. New Zealanders travelling in Turkey in the past visited the battlefields of Gallipoli, but the popularity of this destination has increased over the last 20 years, reflected in growing numbers of London-based travel companies running tours for Anzac Day commemorations. Top Deck ran tours to Gallipoli from 1978, but it wasn't until the late 1990s that passenger numbers increased significantly; a 1989 trip description noted that 'today the peninsula

Despite the varied attitudes towards these trips, thousands of Antipodeans visit Oktoberfest and Pamplona every year, evidenced by the numbers that can be seen in London and back in New Zealand wearing their festival T-shirts.

rests silent and mostly undisturbed except for the occasional busload of visitors.'[34] In 2006, 50 per cent of Top Deck's Gallipoli bookings came from clients resident in London.

Gallipoli 'packages' are often labelled according to military themes. In 2012, for example, Top Deck offered Raid, Patrol, Sortie and Expedition tours; FEZ Travel offered The Digger, The Corporal, The Sergeant, The Major, The Brigadier and The Colonel (with tour length increasing with rank). The Gallipoli segment of these tours offered an interesting blend of 'serious' pilgrimage and 'party' tour. According to On the Go's brochure, the enticements offered by the 'best ANZAC tours you will find' included the Anzac Day dawn service, an exclusive 'on the go' party in Istanbul (with food, a disco and belly dancers), and a Turkish lamb barbecue on Anzac eve. Some have questioned which facet of the experience takes precedence. *The Big OE Companion* recommended maintaining an appropriate sense of decorum and keeping in mind that Gallipoli is not a party. There are usually numerous reports of drunken and inappropriate behaviour.

Immediately after Anzac Day each year editorials, opinion pieces, articles and letters to the editor appear in London expatriate publications and in New Zealand media, questioning the appropriateness of visitors' behaviour at Gallipoli. Many suggest that New Zealanders travelling from London are merely 'ticking off' another destination on an OE list, treating Gallipoli in the same way as Pamplona and Oktoberfest.[35] The tour companies argue that most of those going to Gallipoli are respectful; that it is the Turks who sell the beer; and that many of the problems are caused by the lack of facilities. However, they are scathing about their clients' lack of knowledge about Anzac Day and Gallipoli history. Some of the 'favourites' from clients' regular questions were:

Why is Anzac Day in Gallipoli?
What time is the dawn ceremony?
What day is Anzac Day?
What is the beach like?

Jonathan Drapes' Andy Podean cartoon makes a salient point.
Jonathan Drapes

An estimated 30,000 people attended the 2005 Anzac Day commemorations; the roads and facilities around Gallipoli were clogged with people travelling for what the Turks call 'Anzac Season'.[36] That year, in response to media reports of bad behaviour both before and during the Anzac Day services at Gallipoli, *TNT Magazine* surveyed its readers: of the 233 respondents who had attended services, nearly three-quarters described behaviour the night before as either 'impeccable' (20 per cent) or 'appropriate' (54 per cent). Almost half of the respondents thought their fellow attendees' behaviour was 'impeccable' (40 per cent), while a further 8 per cent thought it was 'appropriate' throughout the services. However, respondents supported an alcohol ban and a cap on numbers permitted to attend.[37]

Prior to the Anzac service at Gallipoli the following year, it was announced that visitors would be required to remove all their own rubbish; also, alcohol and rock music videos were banned.[38] In 2009 the author of Lonely Planet's *Turkey* guide suggested that New Zealanders and Australians stay away from Gallipoli on Anzac Day in order to protect the peninsula from the environmental destruction caused by many thousands of visitors. In 2011 First Festival Travel offered an alternative Anzac experience, with a Western Front tour to Messines, Passchendaele and Ypres in Belgium, and the Somme in France. Top Deck currently offers an Easter tour of the Western Front.

Of the iconic OE traditions, Gallipoli stands out as the one that has significant meaning for New Zealanders. For some, the pilgrimage to Gallipoli teaches them about their own heritage and history; they return to New Zealand with a new respect and appreciation for the meaning of Anzac Day. The huge increase in the numbers attending dawn services and Anzac parades in New Zealand can be credited in part to the OE and the numbers of New Zealanders who have lived in London and 'done' Gallipoli.

The rest of Europe

While many other places in Europe have some historical connection to New Zealand, relatively few have been of interest to OE travellers. There are notable battlefields from both world wars, the birthplace of Abel Tasman (Lutjegast in the Netherlands), the Menton home of Katherine Mansfield, and the Berlin stadium where Jack Lovelock raced to gold in Hitler's Olympics. In Britain, there are the birthplace of Captain James Cook, the grave of writer Robin Hyde in Highgate cemetery, and the 'battlefields' of legendary sporting contests, such as Lord's Cricket Ground or Cardiff Arms Park (now the Millennium Stadium).[39] Of all these, the sporting venues (and events) have most commonly been visited by those on OE; as noted in Chapter Three, the 1960 Rome Olympics stadium was a common stop on early Contiki tours. The Olympic Games themselves – especially those held in Europe – attracted many OE travellers: Munich

1972, Barcelona 1992 and Athens 2004 were all popular. Richard, on his OE in the early 2000s, typified the modern OE traveller:

I have a list of about 25 things that I want to achieve travelling-wise in the next 10 years – Gallipoli, trekking in Nepal and that ... but it is focused on sporting events ... tennis at Wimbledon, a Formula One Grand Prix somewhere – preferably Monaco – a Rugby World Cup, the Hong Kong Sevens ...

From the 1980s, the weekend breaks or package trips to key European events offered by London-based travel companies became increasingly significant forms of OE travel. Many OE travellers have informal 'must-do' lists and companies tried to satisfy these. On its website in 2005, for example, PP Travel advertised that it was:

... the biggest operator to the huge Aussie, Kiwi and South African 'must do' festivals such as Munich's famous Oktoberfest, the Running of the Bulls (San Fermin festival) in Pamplona and Hogmanay (New Year's Eve) in Edinburgh. We also operate supporter tours to the European All Black, Springbok and Wallaby internationals in November as well as other favourites such as ANZAC Day at Gallipoli, the Grand National, Royal Ascot's Ladies Day and long weekend tours to Amsterdam.[40]

OE travel was becoming absorbed by mass tourism. Apart from the rugby internationals that involved their respective national teams, Gallipoli is really the only one of these events that has particular meaning for New Zealanders and Australians. Budget airlines offered a huge range of cheap flights to European destinations. Among the advertisements in a July 2003 *TNT Magazine* were 'long-weekend' European tours to Paris (with a Disneyland option), Amsterdam, Switzerland and Poland; weekend trips to music concerts in Ireland; and festival tours to the Edinburgh Tattoo or Oktoberfest. The same issue featured advertisements for tours to the British Golf Open and the Rugby World Cup (in Australia). All Black games have always been popular with New Zealanders. In August 2004, tours were available to All Black rugby internationals against Italy, France and Wales, to the Belgian Grand Prix, and the US Tennis Open.

Beyond the Grand Tour, and in addition to event travel and short breaks, Scandinavia and Eastern Europe beckoned. While challenging, Eastern Europe was very popular in the 1980s. The opening of Eastern Europe after the fall of communism eased travel restrictions, and Russia remained a heavily 'toured' destination. Many cities in the former Soviet Bloc, such as Prague, Ljubljana, Budapest, Tallinn, Riga and Budapest, also became popular weekend trips, facilitated by the availability of cheap flights and the relaxation of visa requirements. Sailing holidays in Croatia became popular in the 2000s. In 2004, 'established' tour companies such as Top Deck and Contiki were still running Russia

The opening of China to individual travellers in the early 1980s offered a relatively accessible overland route on the Trans-Siberian and Trans-Mongolian rail routes.

ON HER 1982 SUMMER EUROPEAN TRIP Polly got her Yugoslavian and Egyptian visas in London before leaving and her Bulgarian visa in Istanbul. She made a special trip to Dusseldorf in Germany to get a visa for Spain, which wasn't easy since the embassy staff spoke only German and Spanish and the visa forms were in Spanish. Although formal visas were not required for any of the other countries she visited, she collected passport stamps at almost every border she crossed. For others travelling in the 1980s there would be no evidence of a visit to Russia, as the visa was 'removable'; the East Germans also left no record.

tours, alongside newer options such as the Beetroot Bus and the (slightly more independent) Vodka Train. This train offered independent rail travel through Russia and points east to China, with a support network of local tour guides and services at each city stop along the way.

In 1980s Europe some countries required travellers to apply for visas in advance of travel; others issued visas at the border, or did not require visas from some nationalities of travellers. New Zealanders usually required fewer visas than South Africans (and, on occasion, even Australians).

Because visa regulations vary for different nationalities of tourists and because they can change rapidly, few guidebooks include specific information. The YHA's *Big OE Guide* was an exception, perhaps because it was written for New Zealanders. In 1990 New Zealand tourists in Europe still needed visas for Bulgaria, Czechoslovakia, France, East Germany, Hungary, Poland, Portugal (a visa was required but it was free), Romania, USSR and Yugoslavia. In the late 1980s the French government instituted visas for metropolitan France and all of the French territories (such as Tahiti) after a series of terrorist bomb attacks in France. The *Big OE Guide* advised taking a good book, a deck chair and a lot of patience if trying to get a French visa in London. By 1995, visas were no longer required for France, and East Germany and Yugoslavia were no longer countries.

Since 1990, border controls have been progressively eliminated between the European countries under the auspices of the Schengen Agreements (named after the small town of Schengen in Luxembourg, near which they were signed). The Schengen area now covers most of Europe, and New Zealand has visa-free status for all member countries. While this makes travel considerably easier (and cheaper), it also means that passport stamps are less interesting (and prolific) than in the past. Most European border stamps are now identical, except for the initial of the country one is entering or leaving, and a small drawing representing one's mode of transport.

Travelling, or taking a holiday?

From the 1980s most OE travellers differentiated between travelling and taking 'holidays': travelling described multi-destination trips of longer duration; holidays were normally to a single destination (one country or one location) and much shorter. Holidays were perceived to be more relaxing and easier than travelling. As work on the OE became more 'serious', the time available for travel was restricted to annual leave and statutory holidays; serious work necessitated restful holidays.

Christmas offered more free time. OE travellers – a population without the usual family Christmas commitments – presented a receptive market for the tour companies. In the mid-2000s a number of companies

LIKE MANY TRAVELLERS, Nicky had a visa story. She was on a five-week Top Deck tour of Europe in 1982 which left the UK on the first of November. By an unhappy coincidence the visa regulations for a number of European countries changed from that date. Three Brazilian passengers found themselves without the correct visas (and with no time to get them). The tour went ahead with the Brazilians on board, but they had to be smuggled across several border posts in the luggage compartments of the bus. Apparently, European border guards were quite lax about searching tour buses, especially when compared to their equivalents in the Middle East and Asia.

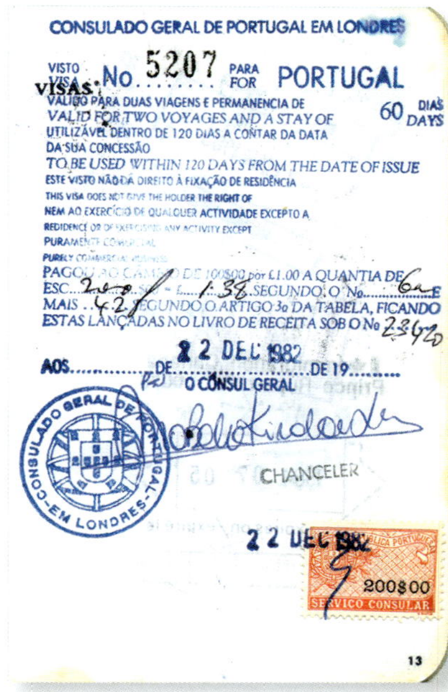

In the 1990s a Portuguese visa was required but was free.

On 1 January 2002 Europe became even more homogeneous when many individual European currencies were replaced by the euro.

Mementos of travel in Greece.

Liz (right) with Mrs Kaliope.

operated special Christmas and New Year tours to Russia; the Beetroot Bus ran the Christmas Cracker 'party trip', while its Christmas and New Year Combo was advertised as the 'double party blow-out'. Christmas trips to Egypt were popular (it was warm), as were special-interest diving trips. Easter was also a popular time for a break and if the dates were right could be combined with an Anzac Day Gallipoli trip.

Earlier OE travellers had spent more time 'hanging out' in places. Allison, for example, 'just lived on a beach in Sicily for a month' in the early 1980s; in 1973 Diane stayed on a Greek island for about six weeks 'just being'. They regretted the way the OE changed later. An OE traveller to Greece in the 2000s was more likely to book a package to the Contiki resort on Mykonos and to holiday in the company of compatriots, with limited interaction with the local Greek population or with tourists of other nationalities.

It is unfair to blame all these changes on the changing demands of OE travellers alone. European tourism became busier and more structured, travel companies identified packages they could offer and OE travellers obligingly responded. One aspect of OE travel that did remain constant, however, was the need for budget accommodation for independent travellers. Where one stayed was linked to the mode of transport used, with most independent travellers staying in youth hostels or camping. Some camping grounds (Camping Seven Hills in Rome, Camping Michelangelo in Florence) were popular with the camping tour companies; others (the Dustbowl in Lagos) were legendary because of van tours. Camping Thalkirchen in Munich attracted all types of travellers, although it banned Australasian vans in 1992.

In the 1980s cheap hotels or family-run pensions were the most affordable accommodation option in southern Europe; owners would wait at bus, train and ferry terminals to capture would-be guests. One's accommodation often became a memorable travel experience. Liz stayed in a family-run pension on the tiny Greek island of Telendos (off Kalymnos) in 1985. The place was ruled by the matriarch of the family, who would yell at her if she went to the toilet in the middle of the night. As the photo shows, Mrs Kaliope (Liz remembers her name 27 years later) was only four feet tall.

In the 1970s and 1980s most European hostels were operated by the YHA, often with strict rules (particularly in Germany). Throughout the 1990s and 2000s scores of independent backpacker hostels opened, many operating in association with tour companies like Busabout. By the 2000s hostel touts worked the trains (particularly in Eastern Europe, where new hostels were opening almost weekly), capturing independent travellers much as the pension owners had done in the past. Private accommodation was still available, but many backpackers preferred hostels for the security offered by advance bookings and the company of other travellers.

During a month-long European trip in 2004 Frances stayed in hostels in Prague and Rome. She found that many backpackers spent the day in bed and surfaced around dinner time to eat, chat and – eventually – get ready to go out clubbing. They came home each morning at about four or five to go to bed … then did it all again the next day. In contrast, she went sightseeing by day and slept at night.

On the whole, although they visited mainstream tourism destinations and conformed to mass youth tourism standards, OE travellers were still doing it *their* way. If they intended to return to New Zealand, they were still faced with the need to see Europe before they went home. Many had bosses and workmates who understood their travel needs. Kelly, who was in London in 2004, for example, recalled her boss being quite flexible about time off: 'He knows what us lot are like with travel and that.' Sandra was called 'backpacker girl' by her British workmates: she took her backpack into work every Friday in order to go away for the weekend.

Some OE travellers who stayed longer eventually went on 'British-style' package holidays to the Canary Islands or to other Spanish holiday islands, such as Ibiza. Ben and his girlfriend on their OEs in the late 1990s 'started doing British package deals – the Canary Islands, Lanzarote, and Tenerife as well – it was a good laugh. Like for Tenerife we paid £160 for both of us for a week – we didn't even know where it was.'

Britain and Ireland

As New Zealand became more culturally independent of Britain, interest in the historical attractions of Britain and Ireland waned. Many OE travellers had family connections there, which meant that travel for them was often social. Many places could be visited on day or easy weekend trips with friends. Travel in Britain and Ireland was more expensive than in Europe and did not feature so much on 'must-do' lists. The result was a less defined set of tourist 'must-sees'. More recent OE travellers commented that they had to *make* themselves see Britain, by planning day or weekend trips at least once a month.

Another change – or perhaps loss. When the official YHA hostels were widely used, hostel stamps were collected to show off to other travellers.

Coronation Street was familiar to many New Zealanders. Chris Slane

British travel was undertaken in a variety of ways. Some had their own vehicles; others hired cars and travelled independently, or used rail passes and other public transport. The common language made it easier to travel independently in Britain and many travellers took risks they would not have taken elsewhere. Kate, a fairly timid traveller in terms of risk-taking, hitchhiked around Ireland with a friend in the late 1980s: 'We hitchhiked in Ireland because that was what you did: you go to Ireland – you hitchhike – it was the job description for [travelling in] Ireland.'

The range of camping tours, packages and styles of travel on offer did not evolve in the same ways as with mainland European travel. OE travellers coping with the visa

Another drawback to travel in Britain, neatly identified by Andy Podean.
Jonathan Drapes

changes of the mid-1990s found that travel had to be fitted into shorter time periods in order not to 'waste' too much of the two-year working holiday allowance in the UK. A plethora of companies offering hop-on hop-off bus services (similar to Busabout in Europe) started up. In 2004 one could tour Ireland on the Shamrocker or Tir na Nog tours; Scotland with Haggis, MacBackpackers or Wild in Scotland; Ireland and Scotland with Celtic Connections; Wales with Dragon Backpacker Tours; and England and Wales with Road Trip. Most of these tours were packaged as trips of three to seven days' duration: 'The Full Monty' tour advertised by Haggis Britain, for example, explored the 'very best of England, Scotland and the Scottish Borders' in seven days, with an option to jump off and discover the Highlands as well. Short breaks to festivals, such as the Edinburgh Tattoo and to Scotland for Hogmanay, were popular events on the annual OE calendar, as were globally famous music festivals, such as Glastonbury.

A wide range of activity holidays was also on offer in Britain, some of which involved activities not customary in New Zealand. Pony trekking in Wales, for example, was popular in the early 1980s, even with people who had never ridden before. Exploring the British countryside on a canal boat was also popular. Kate, a keen tramper in New Zealand, did several long-distance walks in the late 1980s and greatly enjoyed the different scenery. She found the accommodation was also very different: the first of the hundreds of youth hostels in which she stayed was a castle, 'a proper real dinkum castle'.

Travel in Britain was often strongly linked to personal interests and circumstances. On her OE in 1982 Nicky travelled extensively in Britain after initially staying with an uncle outside London. She was knowledgeable about British history and knew what she wanted to see, unlike her travel companion: 'The friend who went with me did so because it was the thing to do – she had no idea of what she wanted to see or do. That was a source of conflict as I had very clear ideas: I wanted to go to Dorset and to Thomas Hardy country. She would just end

The varied attractions of UK and Irish travel.

up tagging along and didn't really enjoy it.' A multitude of interesting places – Oxford, Cambridge, Bath, Stonehenge, Brighton and the Cinque Ports – were accessible as day trips from London. Some saw more of Britain because they worked and lived outside London.

Many went to meet distant relatives or to trace family histories. Figures from the 1997 British Tourist Authority international visitor survey showed that 23 per cent of New Zealand visitors to England also visited Scotland; the high number was attributed to the family links resulting from the numbers of Scottish settlers in New Zealand.

The Middle East and Africa

For OE travellers, the Middle East and North Africa offered 'exotic' locations that were easily accessible from Britain. Morocco was a favoured destination for stand-alone trips or was sometimes incorporated into the Grand Tour. The 1981–82 *Let's Go Europe* included Israel, Turkey and Morocco. Often these places were remembered more clearly than travel in European countries. Emma recalled her 1992 trip to Morocco:

When I was in Gibraltar my friends said, 'Let's go across on the ferry to Morocco and go for an adventure.' That was really exciting … partly I think because I had always had a bit of an inferiority complex about my mother who had done all this amazing, very brave travel and I was much more nervy than her … And so I went with these friends

Chris Slane

to Morocco and even though it was awfully scary I loved it – I remember it so well I think because it was so different and going there was so unexpected.

Egypt, too, was popular with OE travellers. In the 1950s and 1960s there was a sense of connection from World War II, as New Zealand forces had been stationed there. The same applied to Greece, and to Crete in particular; even in the early 1980s OE travellers found themselves especially welcome there, because they were from New Zealand. Turkey was a popular destination long before Anzac Day tour packages were offered. Often overlanders on the Hippie

Trail travelled through Turkey and parts of the Middle East en route from Asia to Europe proper. Political changes and unrest, along with periods of terrorist activity, had a marked effect on the popularity of Egypt and Israel, however. Aaron was typical of many OE travellers of the late 1990s: over a three-year period he took annual holidays in Turkey, Tanzania and Egypt, interspersed with weekend breaks to European capitals and a week of skiing in France each year.

In the early decades of the OE, Israel was popular; Israeli visas were stamped on removable pages to enable entry to other Middle Eastern countries. The same applied to South African visas until the end of apartheid, as many countries took exception to passports displaying them. One way around this was to carry two passports.

Hop-on hop-off bus services started in Turkey (the Fez Bus, the brainchild of a New Zealander) in the late 1990s and in Egypt (the GoBus) during the 2000s; only the Fez Bus was still operating in 2013. In the 2000s Red Sea diving holidays and Christmas trips to Egypt were increasingly popular, despite sporadic terrorist activity in Egypt. Other parts of the Middle East were less visited, although a number of camping and tour companies travelled overland between Cairo and Istanbul. These tours ceased when the border between Israel and Egypt was closed. In the countries slightly further east, such as Iran and Iraq, travel was never easy, and often impossible.

Many New Zealanders travelled independently in the Middle East in the 1970s and 1980s, sometimes with unexpected consequences. Marguerite van Geldermalsen was travelling with a friend in Jordan in 1978, when she met and fell in love with a souvenir-seller at Petra. After a childhood in the Moutere Hills near Nelson, she found herself living like a Bedouin in a 2000-year-old cave, learned Arabic and converted to Islam.[41] *The Scent of Rosewater*, another story from the same era, is by a New Zealander who fell in love with a Persian while on OE in Britain. In the early 1980s she moved to Iran with him.[42]

The idea of travel in Africa was popular across all of the decades of the OE but in the early days political unrest and the difficulties of travel restricted its appeal to the really adventurous. Kenya increased in popularity in the 1980s as a British destination for safari and beach holidays; reasonably priced flights were available to Nairobi. Tanzania experienced similar development as a destination in the 1990s and 2000s. However, it remained challenging to travel independently in these countries; most of the tourist infrastructure was centred on the needs of package-holiday tourists.

Nairobi had always been the hub from which overland routes radiated to points north (to Cairo), northwest (across West Africa, to Morocco and Europe) or south (to South Africa). The routes open for overland travel changed frequently as borders opened and closed in the wake of political and military conflicts. In 1977 the main overland route was through Morocco, Algeria, Niger, Nigeria, Chad or the Cameroons, the Central African Republic, Zaire and then (avoiding Uganda) south of Lake Victoria to Kenya. There were no Cairo–Nairobi trips operating at that time because of war in Ethiopia. Going south, the route went through Tanzania, Zambia and Zimbabwe (then Rhodesia) to South Africa. In 1988 the Nile route through Sudan was impassable because the countryside in the south was entirely controlled by anti-government forces. Prior to Nigeria's land borders opening, travel across the Sahara and through West Africa went via Lake Chad, Cameroon, the Central African Republic and Zaire. Then, because Uganda was still not safe for travel, overland expedition operators cut south around Lake Victoria and through Tanzania to finish in Nairobi.

One of the oldest Africa overland companies was Encounter Overland, which started business in 1962 and closed up shop only in 2001.[43] Other companies operating in Africa in the late 1970s included Overlanders, Exodus and Trans-Africa Expeditions. The 1980s saw a number of new companies, some of which – Kumuka, Dragoman, Economic Expeditions – are still around over 20 years later. Another longstanding company was Guerba, which started in 1988 and was sold to Intrepid in 2008.

It was possible to travel across Africa using public transport and trading trucks or in one's own vehicle, although conditions could be very tough. In 1988 Ross and some Australian friends took a full year to get from London to Nairobi in a Land Rover. They travelled south to Senegal, back north to Niger, then down to Benin where they picked up a New Zealand friend from London. They lived on a beach in Ghana for a month and stopped for long periods in other places. Ross described the freedom to stop and start as being one of the 'beauties' of independent travel, although they were travelling quite 'hard': camping with fly sheets, cooking on fires, and so on. They were also exposed to the whims of local populations and vulnerable to local authorities. The Land Rover found the going tough: they had to rebuild the gearbox nine times. Not many independent travellers were around at the time, but there were a few overland companies. The second day they were in the Sahara, Ross bumped into someone he had been to school with in Australia, who was a tour driver.

According to a 1999 African guidebook, routes through Algeria, Mali and Niger had been closed since late 1996 due to political unrest, limiting the Sahara route to Morocco, Mauritania and Senegal, and then the rest of West Africa. There was also the possibility of Zaire blocking the route through to Nairobi. The Nile route involved either overflying southern Sudan, or travelling from northern Sudan through Eritrea and Ethiopia to Nairobi. From Nairobi south, several options were possible. The most popular was via Tanzania, Malawi and Zambia to Victoria

ANGELA'S WAS A TYPICAL OASIS TRIP, taking seven weeks to travel from Nairobi to Cape Town via Tanzania, Malawi, Zambia, Zimbabwe, Botswana and Namibia. The millennium was celebrated in Cape Town. Twenty-four passengers were on the truck, most of them in their twenties. A handful were British (setting off on the first leg of round-the-world, gap-year trips), and there was a German woman who had been living in London and a South African on her way home after living in London; the rest were Australians and New Zealanders, about half on their way home post-OE and the other half on holiday from London. The trip cost £575 plus £260 kitty; most of the excursions were extra. The extras added up, especially at Victoria Falls, where the group stayed for some days, and where rafting, bungy jumps, microlight flights and sky diving were available. Drinking every night added significantly to the cost: the overland trip resembled a travelling party.

Africa by overland tour.

Falls and onward through Zimbabwe, Botswana or Namibia to South Africa.

Overland trips through Africa, with onward flights from South Africa to Australia and New Zealand, became popular homeward routes post-OE from the mid-1990s. Apartheid in South Africa had come to an end; changed political circumstances brought fewer restrictions and cheaper travel. From information in the first Lonely Planet guide to the region, *Africa on the Cheap* (published in 1977), flights to and from Australia were previously expensive. Only South Africa Airways or Qantas flew that sector, and Qantas was considering stopping its flights because of low returns and political distaste.[44] As an illustration, a ticket from Sydney or Melbourne to Johannesburg in 1977 was A$788; at the 1977 exchange rate of £1=A$1.5731, this equated to £500.[45] An advertisement for Platinum Travel in *TNT Magazine* in 2004 offered a Johannesburg to Sydney flight for £480. The relative value of £500 1977 pounds in 2011, based on the retail price index (RPI), was £2549.[46]

More overland companies started up in the 1990s, taking advantage of this new market. Oasis Overland was started in 1997 by two people with extensive experience working with other overland companies. It was at the no-frills end of the market (in 2005, a 52-day Nairobi to Cape Town overland trip cost £650 plus £295 kitty);[47] at the other extreme, a 63-day trip with Exodus cost £1725 plus £525 kitty. Most overland companies stayed at the same campsites, however, and the main difference was the quality of the camping equipment and food on offer (such as backs on camp chairs and bacon for breakfast). Oasis passengers coveted both. For travellers in South Africa, the Baz Bus (started in 1995 by a South African who had used similar services as a backpacker in Europe) offered a hop-on hop-off service covering the country.

The overland industry has changed its emphasis since 2000; instead of trans-Africa epics taking months, they now run many shorter two, three or four-week trips. These are scheduled so that they can be combined into a longer journey if desired.

The rest of the world

As the OE travel map on p. 126 reveals, the rest of the world consisted of 'the bits in between', destinations visited between New Zealand and Britain. The United States and Canada were often visited en route to Britain, with some taking advantage of summer camp jobs in the US or skifield jobs in Canada. Budget or youth travel in North America was never as organised (or uniform) as in Europe or Africa. Top Deck started American trips in 1983, but these were never as successful as those in Europe. Canada was more 'backpacker friendly', with a hop-on hop-off bus service – the Moose Travel Network – started in 1997 by two Canadians who were inspired by similar companies they had seen operating in Australia and New Zealand. Prior to this service, crossing Canada by train or Greyhound bus was popular.

The Greyhound bus network extended to Canada.

Travel in the United States involved incredibly diverse destinations, travel styles and motives. Some people had friends and relatives to visit; others did a coast-to-coast road trip. It was not cheap to travel in the States; vast distances were involved and, compared to Europe, little infrastructure existed for backpacker or budget travellers (this has slowly improved since the 1980s). Some hostels were open only to foreigners and attracted young Europeans, Brits, and Australasians who were working illegally. Flying was often the cheapest way to get around.

For overland journeys, travellers either bought vehicles (which isolated them from other travellers) or used trains and/or Greyhound buses. Reasonably priced travel passes were available on the Greyhound network, with discounts for students (useful if one had a fake student card) and, in the 1990s, for YHA members (by 2008 Europe was the only part of the world in which the New Zealand YHA offered any travel deals). For solo female travellers, the Greyhound experience could be daunting, as the terminals were usually located in each city's worst downtown area.

The Amtrak rail network was not as extensive as Greyhound, but student discounts applied and in the late 1980s discounted passes were available on production of a foreign passport. Lisa found Amtrak a peculiar travel experience as most of her fellow passengers were Americans excited to be travelling by train for the first time; usually they flew or drove around their own country.

The Caribbean became more accessible to the average British package holidaymaker (and to New Zealanders based in Britain) throughout the 1980s and 1990s. It became possible to buy relatively cheap charter flights to island flight hubs such as Barbados or Trinidad and travel independently around the other islands from there. However, the tourist infrastructure was not set up for independent travellers, since it had previously been an exclusive and expensive destination. Another way getting to and from the Caribbean was to crew yachts across the Atlantic.

Flights to South America were much more expensive than those to the Caribbean, although they were much cheaper from London than from New Zealand. Like Africa, South America was a difficult place in which to travel, with bad roads and some politically 'dangerous' countries. For New Zealanders, communication was also a problem, as English was not widely spoken. Some adventurous Kiwis travelled independently in the early years of the OE: in 1978 Louise Sutherland (who had cycled around the world in the 1950s) biked 4000 kilometres along the TransAmazonica (the east–west route that stretches from the Atlantic Ocean to the Brazilian state of Acre, at the Bolivian and Peruvian border). The road was often little more than a dirt track, and sometimes impassable with mud. On this trip she combined travelling with raising money for medical aid programmes in the areas she rode through. The story of her trip is told in *The Impossible Ride*.[48]

Despite the cost and difficulties, South America has been a popular post-OE destination. A number of South American overland tour companies started in the 1970s, many involving people with experience of camping tour companies in Europe. One of the stories in *The Big OE* describes a five-month trip across South America in 1975, the second undertaken by Encounter Overland. The driver on the trip was a New Zealander; neither he nor his 'co-pilot' had done the trip before, and seven of the 22 passengers dropped out before the end. In 1976 Goway started South American tours with a bus imported from Britain: the La Gran Aventura took 80 days to get from Bogota, through Peru, Chile, Argentina and up to Brazil. The company operated these trips for the next eight years.[49] Inca Tours started in January 1980, with a similar 80-day overland expedition across South America from Cartagena on the Columbian coast to Rio de Janeiro in Brazil. The company was started by Australian Lew Pulbrook, who previously worked for Atrek and drove overland for Top Deck. Inca continued doing overlands until 1990 (having operated through the Falklands War), when its focus changed from adventure-overland tours to hotel-based custom-made tours (still operating in the 2000s). In the 1980s Dragoman started South American overland tours and was still running them in the 2000s. Kumuka and Oasis Overland also do both overland and shorter tours in South America.

The Pacific Northwest (Japan, Korea) offered more affordable destinations in terms of airfares from New Zealand, but once there travel was expensive. Being able to work (for example, teaching English as a second language) helped; those who travelled extensively around Japan did so while based there, with some travel arranged as part of work programmes. Ski trips to Hokkaido and temple touring in Kyoto were popular short holidays, and Korea was a cheap option for weekend and longer breaks from Japan. Other destinations in Asia were also easily accessible from Japan.

From New Zealand, Southeast Asia was conveniently located, relatively close and cheap (compared to Europe) for travel pre- and post-OE. Bali, Singapore and Thailand were popular destinations, the first particularly so with surfers.

New Zealand holidays

People who stayed away on a long OE often returned to New Zealand for holidays. Some felt they saw more of New Zealand then than they would have if they had been permanently resident. Often on holiday for an extended period, they visited old friends all over the country, were relatively wealthy because they had sterling currency, and were in the 'habit' of doing tourist things. Mid-OE travel home became more affordable from the 1980s. In 1982 low-season return flights from London to Auckland were advertised in *New Zealand News UK* for £648; in *TNT Magazine* in 2002, London–Auckland return was advertised for £645 (the relative values of these flights in 2011 were £1876 and £861, respectively). In 2004 the price advertised in *TNT* for a London–Auckland return had fallen even further to £549 (£692 at 2011 value).[50]

Many OE travellers of the 2000s worked in highly skilled jobs and were affluent, although getting enough time off work to make a trip to New Zealand worthwhile could be difficult. Most trips home were for special events, such as family or friends' weddings, significant birthdays or other family occasions. While returning to New Zealand might involve some holidaying, often the motives triggering these trips were complex. Craig, for example, returned to New Zealand in the mid-1990s after four and a half years away, to holiday with a Norwegian friend he had met travelling. He thought that it was 'a bonus in several ways as I got to spend time with him, and also to touch base, and see where I wanted to be if I did come back, and see what opportunities were available'. For those who had been away longer, 'checking in' with New Zealand was a common motive.

Frequently, those on OE would bring significant others home to show them New Zealand. Emma returned to New Zealand in 1994 for a holiday with her English boyfriend, who was 'quite keen to come and live here but he wanted to check it out first'. In 2004 one long-term expatriate in London joked that so far she had taken three serious boyfriends 'home' to check New Zealand out; she planned to take her latest the following year.

The experience of returning to New Zealand on holiday varied considerably, depending on how long one had been away. Caitlin returned to New Zealand for a month at Christmas in 2002, after being away for less than a year. She found it 'a bit weird because nothing had changed – everything was the same as I remembered it, which was good, but after a few days it felt like I had never left'. She enjoyed the fact that she was missing some of the British winter. For those who had been away longer, returning for holidays gave them mixed feelings. Josie returned to New Zealand four times on holiday and each time she came back found it a little bit harder to leave. She also found it hard to judge what New Zealand was like when 'you are just on holiday and your friends make a real effort'. Joshua returned for a holiday in the mid-1990s, after 18 months away:

The first time I came home on holiday it was really strange. Part of it was just a whirlwind tour of New Zealand visiting friends and I had never seen New Zealand from that angle before. Painful to come back, in that you see your friends, and then leave again – it wasn't like coming back and living here – there is a distance [that] creeps in. It was strange coming back to New Zealand and not having a home here.

These visits to New Zealand often included a stopover in the Pacific. Many Air New Zealand tickets offered free Pacific island stops in Hawaii, Tahiti, the Cook Islands, Tonga, Samoa or Fiji. Often, however, destinations in the Pacific were earmarked as holidays to take when one was settled back in New Zealand. As a winter sun destination, the Pacific (along with parts of Australia) offered places suitable for family holidays or for package holidays and cruises. As a stand-alone travel destination, Australia was also left for later, although it was frequently a quick stopover or place to work en route to Europe. Australian friends made in London could also be visited easily from a New Zealand base. With its larger population and better employment opportunities, Australia attracted many New Zealanders as a country in which to live following their OE.

MANY found it strange and unsettling to be a visitor in their home country. Angela was changing travellers' cheques (in the early 1990s this was still the most common way to carry money) at a bank in Christchurch. The cheques were in sterling. When the bank teller asked her for identification, Angela handed over her British driving licence (she was renewing her passport while in New Zealand, as it was more expensive to do in London). The teller then asked how her holiday was going, and what she thought of New Zealand! She had no idea what to reply. On the same trip she spent a lot of time around international tourists; on a number of occasions she was asked questions about New Zealand that she could not answer – she felt just as much a foreigner as they were. Other long-term expatriates reported similar experiences: Sandra recalled, 'The first time I went home I felt like a fish out of water – it was somewhere totally familiar but I had all the trappings of a British tourist. There were cultural differences – like I didn't know how to order a coffee in New Zealand.'

Chapter Six

FROM THE BAR TO THE BOARDROOM

WHILE TRAVEL was the primary motive for going on an OE, the reality was that most people had to work for much of the time they were away. Work was always core to the OE; the money earned was essential for living and it determined how much travel one could afford. Balancing travel and work could be difficult: one could afford the time to travel, but not the money, and vice versa. There was also tension between enjoying living overseas (which usually involved spending money) and saving money for travel. And by the 2000s the nature of OE work and its likely post-OE benefits became a consideration.

OE work cannot be classified – by location or type – as easily or neatly as travel. Many people did a variety of jobs while on OE. A number of factors determined what work people did: their skills, training, qualifications and experience; the state of the economy in the selected country; and their attitude and approach to these work experiences. For some, the OE offered an opportunity to try something different. Others found it sensible to stick with their usual occupation, particularly if it was one that travelled well by offering plentiful and well-paid work. OE work often had a serendipitous element to it, exemplified by

The bar job.
Chris Slane

unusual or unanticipated jobs in unexpected locations.

As a stand-alone facet of the OE, and because it impacted significantly on other aspects of the total experience, OE work is important. The shift from the long summer of travel (until the 1980s) to shorter holiday breaks or weekends away (during the 1990s and 2000s) was facilitated by changes in tourism infrastructure, but primarily it was driven by the change in the types of jobs people on OE did.

A working holiday

The key defining characteristic of the OE has been that it is a working holiday. The legal and longstanding right to work in Britain, along with a common language and easily transferable qualifications, meant that many ventured no further in their OE working lives. Within Britain, London offered more jobs and higher wages, although these advantages were offset by higher living costs. A substantial information and support network was available in London: friends and acquaintances offered informal support, and more formal assistance could be sought from the employment agencies and media serving the Antipodean population.

In the 1960s some London employment agencies catered almost exclusively to young colonials on working holidays; they also saw the value of recruiting directly from New Zealand. As the numbers going on OE grew, the number of agencies and the range of industries they served increased significantly, as did their representation and advertising in New Zealand. From the 1980s onwards the OE work scene – like OE travel – became more structured. One of the biggest changes in OE work during the last three decades, and particularly since the mid-1990s, has been an increase in the amount of pre-OE support available in or from New Zealand.

The OE employment market operated independently of the wider employment market: many jobs were passed on from one New Zealander to another, or positions were found through agencies established by New Zealanders, for New Zealanders. Being from New Zealand was a prerequisite for some jobs. In many cases, contacts for work came from acquaintances, friends, or family members who had previously been on OEs. In the early 1980s Vicki found a job at a school near Basingstoke. She heard about the job from another New Zealander who had previously worked at the school. In 1991 Shelley worked in a Scottish boarding school where her sister had worked the year before: 'the school loved Kiwis'.

In the late 1970s and 1980s most people going on OE looked for work when they arrived in London (although few remember exactly how they knew where to look). Classified advertisements for jobs and employment agencies appeared in free Australasian publications, and vacancies were posted on the noticeboards at New Zealand House and at the numerous travellers' clubs in London. Many people found jobs through friends or by door-knocking around pubs.

In 1981 *New Zealand News UK* published an eight-page pull-out supplement with employment advice for working holidaymakers. Prior to this, OE guides focused on travel, with very little space given to employment information. The 1978 edition of *Down Under in Europe*, for example, had only five pages out of 189 devoted to work (three of these covered work in London; the other two covered work on the Continent). The 1990 *Big OE Guide* had four pages out of 94 on 'working overseas', although it did carry an advertisement for the London-based Australasian Temp Company (whose slogan was 'We look after our own'). The only employment-related advertisers in the 1995 edition of the guide were Global Visas and International Exchange Programs (IEP), both of which had offices in New Zealand. Global Visas helped with working holiday visas, job registration and the preparation of CVs for London, and provided introductions to recruitment agencies. IEP organised summer camp jobs in the USA and also had a support programme for working holidaymakers in Britain.

The 1995 and 1996 editions of *Live, Work and Play in the UK* published extensive listings of agencies catering for all types of work, from finance to agriculture. The prominent agencies were Alfred Marks, Reed, Manpower, Prime Appointments and Bligh Appointments, some of which catered to a number of industries. Bligh Appointments, for example, offered agricultural and farming positions, as well as care and nanny work; the Australasian Temp Company offered general office and financial positions. Others were more specialised. Nursing agencies included Anzac Nurses, Nightingale Nursing Bureau and Strand Nurses: the latter two had both been around since the early 1970s. Specialist teaching agencies included Capstan Teachers, HMS Education Personnel and LHR. The *Big OE Companion* in 2004 also listed The Kiwi Agency (part of the Barnett Group); it had been offering medical, teaching and general commercial positions to New Zealanders in London since the early 1980s.

A major change in the 2000s was the growth of employment advertising on the internet, rather than in print media. Many individual employers switched from *New Zealand News UK* and *TNT Magazine* to using community internet sites such as Gumtree. Likewise, many agencies advertised their vacancies on sites like Gumtree as well on their own websites. The Gumtree website was launched in 2000 to serve the Australian and New Zealand market in London and became an Antipodean institution in just a few years. Initially, placing employment vacancies on the Gumtree was free; in 2004, over 12,000 jobs were listed. The Antipodean print media also had online options; in 2004 the *TNT* website (which featured a full online version of the magazine) attracted 128,000 unique users and three million page impressions per month. Internet technology made it possible to check out vacancies, sign up with agencies, send out one's CV, and to apply for jobs even before leaving New Zealand.

Arriving in London could still be intimidating, however, and organising employment involved more than merely 'getting a job'. As noted in Chapter Four, a number of recruitment companies ran New Zealand seminars and offered 'OE starter packs', which normally included an 'introduction to London' seminar. These seminars were especially valuable for those planning to work in professional jobs, as they covered CV formatting, appropriate dress for interviews and the workplace, and explained the British tax system. They also provided some practical assistance: in 2004, for example, BUNAC had a representative from the Department of Work and Pensions at its orientations to issue National Insurance numbers; at its seminar, 1st Contact had a banking representative from one of the major banks to help people set up accounts.

Many New Zealanders in London were not enamoured with a company that charged them to do things they could do for themselves. The general feeling was that Australians were more prepared to accept that a business is a business (and exists to make money), whereas New Zealanders were more community-oriented and inclined to look out for each other (with no money involved). Others described New Zealanders as being more 'parsimonious' or 'price discerning'. Companies like 1st Contact were often used in desperation, however, when it came to trying to open bank accounts.

As a result of growing international concern about money laundering and terrorism (especially since 9/11), banks tightened their compliance regulations and increasingly wanted to know their clients before opening accounts for them: an impossible ask for those who had just arrived in Britain, with no previous credit history in the country, no permanent address, no utility bills in their name and no job.

Over the six OE decades the types of work available were governed by a diverse array of factors, many of which were simply a function of timing:

- working-holiday regulations made it technically illegal to work in career jobs prior to 2003 (although there were some exemptions to this rule);

Many employment agencies catered expressly to Antipodean job seekers.
TNT Magazine

BY THE EARLY 2000s 1st Contact was one of the more prominent London agencies helping those on OE. The company initially offered tax and accounting services, before expanding to provide recruitment, visa and money transfers, and travel and shipping services. Its recruitment services were primarily for public-sector jobs – medical, social work and teaching – that were more recession-proof than jobs in IT or finance. In the mid-2000s 1st Contact was involved with one of the Antipodean sports leagues and owned The Elusive Camels, a chain of travellers' pubs. As the managing director explained:

It is a simple business model and it works: we find them jobs and pay them and hopefully they will use our services to set up a limited company or to do a tax return or they will drink in our pubs – we own four pubs … and hopefully in time they will use us to ship everything back [home]. The company provides everything we think these guys will need, apart from travel – the internet killed that.

- recessionary periods and political changes sometimes restricted employment opportunities in some industries;
- during the 1980s jobs that had previously attracted some of the OE workforce became out of reach due to increasing requirements for formal qualifications;
- the return of South Africa to the Commonwealth in the mid-1990s increased competition in the London job market, a pattern repeated when the expansion of the EU opened London to Eastern European workers in 2004;
- IT did not exist in the 1970s;
- from the mid-1990s the technology-inspired dot-com industry offered enormous employment opportunities, until the 'bubble' burst in 2000.

Evidence of change over time can be seen in the types of jobs advertised in the Antipodean media. In 1975, for example, employment was available on ships, as mothers' helps (usually for other New Zealanders), and on farms. Temporary office work was a longstanding OE occupation. The employment agency Bligh, then just four years old, advertised for office 'temps' in *LAM* magazine in 1978. Many more jobs were advertised in 1981, perhaps as a reflection of the increased numbers of Australians and New Zealanders in Britain. Apart from a couple of agency advertisements for office temps, most of the jobs were for unskilled nanny, pub and farm positions. A 1986 *TNT Magazine* 'Jobs Forum' page featured hotel and bar work, dental and private nursing, accountancy, finance and IT jobs, as well as work in the travel industry. From the mid-1980s and into the 1990s many IT and finance jobs were advertised, including computer jobs back in New Zealand. In August 2004 the 'general' work pages in *TNT Magazine* included advertisements for a veterinary nurse, a florist and a beauty therapist, tractor drivers, couriers, charity fundraisers and market researchers, cruise ship staff and medical guinea pigs. There were also several advertisements for people to work for paintball companies.

By the 2000s the employment pages in the London Australasian publications carried more agency advertisements than individual job opportunities. Agencies advertised positions in teaching, IT, accountancy, banking and finance, technical industries such as engineering and surveying, construction, secretarial, legal, retail, fashion and beauty industries, medical and social work, the care industry, bar and catering work, and travel. Many new agencies appeared at this time, reflecting the growing numbers of OE travellers wanting to work professionally, as well as the ongoing commercialisation of the OE job market.

The development of specialist agencies also reflected shortages in the British job market. The teaching profession in Britain experienced shortages from the late 1980s and New Zealanders increasingly worked as supply teachers filling the gaps. Between

1996 and 1999 the demand grew for teachers on both day-to-day supply and term-time, or yearly, contracts. Many new teaching agencies were established. Education agencies represented at the Big OE Evenings in New Zealand in 2006 included: Timeplan (established in 1989), Scholar UK (1999) Treble One Education (2002), Tradewind (a branch of 1st Contact, also placing social and health workers, 2000), ITN Teachers (late 1990s), Smart Teachers (1990s, merged with a pre-existing British-based company in 2008) and Impact Teachers (date unknown). Signing up with one of these agencies before leaving New Zealand offered employment security and often assistance opening a bank account.

The money or the bag?

The quintessential working holidaymaker is the traveller who is able to extend the time they spend 'on the road' by working as they travel. Types of working holiday experience can be differentiated along a continuum, according to whether the primary motives of travel are for work or for travel.[1] At one extreme are work-oriented travellers (expatriate workers), who are primarily motivated by career opportunities and the money they can earn; at the other extreme are travel-oriented/travelling workers, motivated purely by experience. The second type of working tourism was strongly supported by the conditions of most working holiday visas in Britain from the mid-1970s until 2003, when the 'career job' and temporal restrictions of the visa regulations were relaxed. There were always people on OE who never complied with the regulations, either working for their entire stay in Britain (two years) or working in their normal jobs, although it was debatable that this was 'career enhancing'. Nevertheless, prior to 2003 most OE guides advised against arriving in London with work clothes or equipment such as tools.

Another important change to the working holiday regulations in 2003 was the increase in upper age limit from 27 to 30 years (although for those not reliant on working holiday visas, or with job skills matching employment shortages in Britain, this age limit did not apply). These changes offered a second-chance OE to some. Julie, for example, decided against an OE in favour of working on her PhD, expecting to finish the doctorate when she

FOR MANY PEOPLE, the OE offered an opportunity to do something different, for at least some of their time away. On her OE in 1981, Vicki took a pub job in London because she really wanted a break from teaching. Grant, also a teacher, spent his first six months in 1994 doing a variety of other jobs but eventually went back to teaching, 'predominantly because of the money, but also because I wanted to get a bit of self-worth out of what I was doing'. Often there were multiple reasons for selecting a particular job. Pete, for example, had trained and worked as an aircraft engineer in New Zealand, but took a job as a motorbike courier in the mid-1990s, simply because it looked like a 'quick, fun way of making money, that promised a high income, and a chance to have a good look around London'.

was too old for a working holiday permit. The age limit extension allowed her to do both. Other graduates used the time to gain work experience at home first, which gave them better employment prospects in London. During the 1980s and 1990s the tendency to leave New Zealand immediately after graduation, often with no practical qualifications or skills, had restricted the type of work many OE travellers were able to do.

While the epitome of the working holidaymaker was someone who worked as they travelled, the reality for most people was segregated travel and work experiences. Some worked in casual jobs in pubs or as nannies; others worked at their normal occupation, but not in permanent positions. Many of the 'classic' OE jobs – such as teaching, nursing, and office work – fitted the needs of OE travellers. The goal was to earn money for travel and eventually a ticket home. If travellers decided to up-skill while on OE, the motive was often to earn more money, rather than to advance one's career. Once the regulations controlling type of work were relaxed in 2003, some OE travellers began to earn substantial sums; saving for their post-OE New Zealand lives as well as for travel then became a possibility.

For the true travelling worker, work was more of a recreational activity. These kinds of jobs were often undertaken outside Britain, involved work for which work permits were not checked, and were sometimes voluntary, with some living costs or allowances paid. Commonly employment of this sort offered the chance to work in countries, and at jobs, that would otherwise not be legally available to those on OE. Work at American holiday camps, on Israeli kibbutzim, on farm

IN A CONSCIOUS EFFORT to avoid the stereotypical OE based in London, Richard worked several summers at an American holiday camp in the early 2000s, interspersed with work at a garden centre in Japan. The first year at camp he had to pay his own flights and application fees and some of his salary went to the sponsoring agency; the following year, fees, flights and sponsorship were covered, making the work more lucrative. Five of the 120 staff at the camp were New Zealanders. There were four New Zealanders at the garden centre in Japan; it didn't concern their employers that they were working illegally as they worked hard and were a bit taller and stronger than the Japanese. Richard did not consider the holiday camp job work as he was outside in the sun; the Japanese job was menial, and quite hard work, but tolerable because he had travel to look forward to.

Teaching English in Japan was popular: providing information about lunchtime in New Zealand (left) and students learning the haka.

exchanges, or on voluntary programmes all fall within this category. Often the novelty of the surroundings was enough to cancel out the drudgery the work might entail.

Within the OE, these jobs were ranked according to status. The American holiday camp job, which had been available since the 1960s, was seen by some as a poor OE choice: it was not very adventurous and, being unpaid, those doing it were seen as having their skills 'pillaged'. Those doing holiday camp work argued that it was a useful way to extend an OE and a springboard for travel in the United States; it was also memorable for the insights it provided into American society. While some travellers still start their OE with a summer at a holiday camp, in recent years it has become more popular with those taking a gap year.

Perhaps because it combined work and travel in a very different country, employment on an Israeli kibbutz ranked more highly than holiday camp work. The volume of advertisements in *New Zealand News UK* and other publications indicates that work on a kibbutz was most popular between the late 1970s and the mid-1980s. A two-page feature on kibbutzim appeared in a 1978 edition of *LAM* magazine. Most of the work on offer was agricultural.

Work on a kibbutz declined in popularity, due to changes in kibbutz agriculture during the 1980s (a result of inflation in Israel) and the steady decline in kibbutz populations from the 1990s.[2] However, advertisements for both moshavim and kibbutzim appeared

A moshav and kibbutz advertisement, 1993.
TNT Magazine

Life on Kibbutz Karmiya, Golan Heights UN Territory, 1981 (above); volunteers on a camping trip at Sharm El-Sheikh on the Red Sea (left).

DURING their travels around southern Europe and the Middle East in the late 1970s, Hazel and her husband worked on a moshav (it differed from a kibbutz in that one earned more money) in the Gaza Strip for several weeks, before moving to a kibbutz for a month. The kibbutz employed about 500 people, who received free food and board and one day off a week to see the sights. Judy worked on a kibbutz at the end of her OE in the early 1980s. At the time, the PLO were bombing in Israel; her mother had written from New Zealand telling her not to go. While she heard bombs going off in the desert, she was not fearful in the same ways as the locals because she was not used to living under those conditions. In 1974 a 19-year-old New Zealand volunteer, Judi Sinton, was shot and killed by terrorists on Kibbutz Shamir.

in *TNT Magazine* in the mid-1990s. In the late 1990s Melissa decided to go to Israel and work on a kibbutz simply because her sister had done so several years earlier. She and a friend found it a real eye-opener, although not necessarily into Israeli life. There were a lot of Danish people on her kibbutz, for example, who didn't understand Kiwi jokes and with whom they did not get on. When a group of seven Australians arrived, life improved considerably. She ended up staying five months because she became romantically involved with an Israeli. While it is possible to work voluntarily on kibbutzim today, one of the longest-standing companies organising such work from Britain, Project 67, went into liquidation in September 2001.[3]

Some OE travellers were more spontaneous than others and were happy to go where their travels took them, with no fixed plan in mind. Eric, for example, was on his way to Israel to work on a kibbutz in 1977 when a chance meeting with another New Zealander in a Munich youth hostel sidetracked him into travelling around southern Europe instead. By the beginning of winter they were in Austria; Eric went door-knocking around hotels until he found a job for the winter. The place was an enclave of expatriates; a lot of the bar staff were from New Zealand and Australia. Eric didn't count his winter at the skifield as work, as he worked at night and skied all day.

Many New Zealand women found winter work in French ski resorts in the 1980s (although the 1978 edition of *Down Under in Europe* suggested that Austria and Germany offered more winter work opportunities). Some agencies insisted on Cordon Bleu qualifications for those seeking work as chalet cooks. Winter work in Canadian skifields was legally available, initially under student exchange schemes and from 1994 under the official working holidaymaker visa scheme. Whistler-Blackcomb was very popular with New Zealanders.

Summer work was available in the tourism and outdoor recreation industries

Working the bar in Austria. Note the Oktoberfest T-shirt.

across Europe; as noted earlier, the legalities of such work were often circumvented by many employers being British-registered. Having a European passport was an advantage, although the number of countries offering working holiday visas increased over time. While language was sometimes a problem, it mattered less in the tourism industry; even in Europe, the *lingua franca* was usually English.

Despite being low-skilled, poorly paid and monotonous, some tourism jobs appealed because they offered a chance to experience other languages or cultures, albeit usually in the company of other like-minded expatriates. In the mid-1980s Gail and her husband worked in a Greek bar during the summer tourist season, a job she would never have done at home, or even in London, but it appealed because she 'could try and speak my little bit of Greek'. They were working illegally: if anyone came into the bar who looked as if they might question their right to be there, they would pour themselves a coffee or a beer, sit down at the bar and look like tourists. The locals were happy to warn them when this was necessary.

Working for the travel companies catering to the OE population was always popular. These jobs were often picked up through word of mouth, or were advertised in the London media and occasionally in New Zealand newspapers. The tradition of passengers becoming staff was well documented in Bill James' history of Top Deck.[4] One travel company, which employed mostly New Zealanders as 'crew' on tours such as to Pamplona in the 2000s, explained its (somewhat alarming) rationale for doing so:

We have good relationships with our suppliers at these places … they trust our ability to manage it. We have good tour leaders that are able to deal with stuff … but you can't expect an English person to tell a bunch of Waikato farmers to pull their heads in. As much as the passengers can be 'dumb-arse dickheads' – because we are Kiwis we can

Sailing Holidays Ltd
Greek & Dalmatian Islands

Fun Flotillas

We require young, enthusiastic team players to work for our Flotilla programme in the following positions

Boat Builders, Diesel Engineers, Fibreglassers, Skippers and Floatilla sailing hostesses

Send your CV with photo to:
105 Mount Pleasant Road, London NW10 3EH
or phone: Kelvin 020 8438 1128 for a chat
or email: kelvin@sailingholidays.com
agents for Tehno Yachts & Ionian Marine Holidays

SAI38854

NZ News UK

QUALIFIED OUTDOOR ENTHUSIASTS found year-round employment by moving between hemispheres. New Zealanders on OE could be found all over the world, working as rafting, kayaking and outdoor activity guides. In the late 1980s Wayne worked in Austria, Nepal and Turkey as a rafting guide: he decided to take on this type of work, and the itinerant lifestyle involved, partly because at 30 he was too old for a working holiday permit: he would be working illegally anywhere he went. During his OE, he also worked on sailing boats in the Mediterranean, taught dinghy sailing at a resort, and had several jobs delivering yachts: one from France to Turkey, another from Europe to the Caribbean. Some saw crewing on yachts crossing the Atlantic as a 'dream' OE job, but the benefits varied according to whether it was paid work or simply a free ride in exchange for work. *Christella's Odyssey* is an often hilarious story of a New Zealander 'crewing' his way across the Atlantic to the Caribbean in the early 1970s.[5]

In 1986 travellers could work as drivers, guides, mechanics, cooks or back-up crew. *TNT Magazine*

read a situation and know how to deal with it. We always have a security team with us as well and, again, they are Kiwis – they know how to control them [the passengers].

In the 1970s and early 1980s many companies operating European camping tours employed drivers who were unable to drive until they got to the Continent, because they did not have valid bus licences for Britain (often the vehicles were also illegal in Britain). Travellers who had never been to Europe found themselves employed as couriers and tour guides. As customer expectations rose, standards of service and safety were raised, effectively reducing these opportunities. Although the motive for taking jobs in the tourism industry was to earn money while having fun – and finding them a matter of chance – in many cases they led to lifelong careers in tourism.

Some people on OE travel were forced to work because they had run out of money while travelling. There are stories of people working as film extras (Hazel worked in Egypt on a film called *The Sphinx*, for which she was paid $25 and a free lunch); as extras in police line-ups; as buskers; as temporary staff in travellers' hostels; as touts selling time-share apartments around the Mediterranean; as door-to-door salespeople (of aerial photographs and massage cushions); as fruit pickers, turnip pickers, potato graders, flower pickers, in vineyards and so on. Articles featuring New Zealanders in these unusual OE jobs occasionally appear in the New Zealand press.

Some jobs have a longstanding relationship with the OE. On her trip in 2008 Bridget planned to pick flowers in the Scilly Islands, following in the footsteps of New Zealanders since the 1950s. One of the stories in Nigel McCarter's *The Big OE* was of two New Zealanders working on a farming estate in the Scilly Islands in 1962. Finding July too cold in mainland Britain, they were told that the Scilly Islands were 'more tropical'. The first person they met when they arrived in Tresco was another New Zealander. In both the 1991 and 2001 censuses, four New Zealand-born people were living in the Scilly Islands.[6]

Farming jobs usually required some experience, especially if formally organised as farm exchanges. The success of farm work varied, as Donal found on a farm exchange in the early 1980s, during which he worked on two different Danish farms. He preferred the second of these, primarily because the farmers spoke some English; the first farmers were an older couple who spoke no English and viewed the exchange as a source of cheap labour. Shearing was a better option for earning money; by the 1970s New Zealand shearers were well known in Britain and could find jobs easily. By the 1980s New Zealanders were shearing in Italy and Norway. It is difficult to know how many New Zealanders worked in shearing jobs while on OE: by the 1990s and 2000s many New Zealand shearers and wool handlers regularly travelled to Britain and Europe to work that part of a global shearing season.[7]

For most of those on OE, volunteer or casual agricultural jobs did not offer enough financial security and eventually they returned to Britain, or to London, to make some 'proper money'. Another drawback was the seasonal nature of these jobs. Rebecca, for example, spent her first summer in Britain, in 2004, working her way around England and Wales as a volunteer on the WWOOF programme. While she enjoyed it immensely, WWOOFing opportunities were limited over the winter months; she also recognised that she needed properly paid employment in order to survive.

IN THE EARLY 1980s Alan took a job as an onboard shepherd delivering a cargo of live sheep to the Falkland Islands. Part of the deal was that he was provided with onward transport to Britain (a troopship to Ascension Island, and then air force transport to RAF Brize Norton in Oxfordshire) in order to continue his OE. He then spent time working as a shepherd in Britain and with a New Zealand shearing gang in Italy, where they encountered some animosity from local shearers unfamiliar with Kiwi shearing methods. For him, 'getting in amongst the locals was more important to him than seeing the cultural sites' in Italy; in Britain he enjoyed living in country areas, away from all the Kiwis in London. He also returned to the Falklands for a full shearing season, and on his return to Britain found a job (through a shearing contact) driving exhibition trucks around Eastern Europe.

Classic OE work

Even before the visa regulations changed in 2003 to permit professional work, most OE travellers had a clear division between travel and work episodes, returning to a British base (usually London) to work. In many ways their working lives on OE were not dissimilar to what they had experienced in New Zealand immediately prior to going on OE: working and saving hard in order to travel. Work on the OE, however, offered a break from career considerations and a normal job, or an altered approach to work. Classic OE work was exemplified by women doing office work and nannying and men working in the trades. The epitome of 'classic' was the pub job: fish factories and oil rigs were simply legendary.

Opportunities for temporary office work remained steady during the OE decades. In recessionary times, 'temps' were used to fill staff shortages and handle short-term work overloads, but over time employers realised they could reduce overheads by employing contract and qualified temporary staff. The number of agencies and the range of industries and specialist fields they catered to grew. Office work also evolved, offering everything from low-skilled general clerical work to highly skilled, technical positions.

While many office jobs could not be characterised as 'career enhancing', they could be memorable if they involved interesting projects or work for large international or multinational companies. Often, the nature of the work meant that OE travellers 'accidentally' enhanced their careers. In the mid-1990s Melanie worked for Price Waterhouse, gaining unexpectedly valuable experience. Jessie commented that the companies she worked for on her OE in

2000 – the BBC and British Telecom – looked good on her CV. What she remembered most clearly, however, was that at the BBC they had 'a pub inside the building so you could drink at work!'.

Often the only real contact those on OE had with British people was through the workplace. Many found office work more social than in New Zealand. A common earlier experience was going to the pub at lunchtime with workmates, although this practice had all but disappeared by the 2000s. Office protocol was usually more formal than in New Zealand, as was office dress (hence the time spent in employment orientation sessions describing the dress standards required). The tendency for New Zealanders to live in inner London, and for the British to live in outer London or beyond meant that few people socialised with their British workmates outside work hours. Most also found that their lifestyles were quite different from those of the people they worked with. The major difference was the New Zealanders' focus on travel, rather than on furthering their careers or raising their standard of living.

Even when they were working at their normal occupations, those on OE often found that they could take work less seriously than in New Zealand. Others found themselves being lazier at work, simply because their employers did not expect much from them. It was also possible to walk out of a job one did not like, with 'no comebacks'.

Being over-skilled for jobs was common, much to the delight of prospective employers. Nurses took employment as nannies, their training an important qualification for securing such jobs. Experiences of nannying varied widely, from those poorly paid and treated as 'slaves', to those in the employ of wealthy families (still poorly paid) with the chance to accompany them on vacations all over the world as part of the job. Nannying also offered insights into other cultures and ways of life, and to life in the middle and upper classes of Britain.

Career skills could be picked up accidentally. Simon managed a sports club

The nanny job.
Chris Slane

GAIL experienced quite different cultures when she worked for an American family, a Bengali family and a Scottish family in the mid-1980s. Also in the mid-1980s, Sally looked after two 'obnoxious little toads' whose parents treated her like a slave. Bronwyn described her 1997 nannying experience as 'dire … the hours, the brats … and they had three nannies and three children', although eight years later she was still in touch with the people she had worked for.

ON HER OE in the late 1990s, Melissa was a trained hairdresser and after a month of working in London decided that she had travelled too far to work for hardly any money. One day she phoned her boss and quit, something she would never have done in New Zealand. On his OE in the mid-1990s, Brent created a fictitious CV with the help of friends in London. He took a job as a financial trader, noting that he wouldn't have lied in New Zealand but it 'just wasn't your country and it was all about getting ahead'.

while on his OE in 2000. It was not a job he would have particularly chosen to do, but it paid well and offered a house on site. On his return to New Zealand, he was offered jobs in facilities management and event coordination, based on his British CV. He had not really realised how many transferable skills he had picked up. Caitlin was a microbiologist in New Zealand. Unable to work in that field because of visa restrictions when she first arrived in London in 2002, she worked in a variety of administrative jobs, gaining useful management experience. Mandy found that the experience of looking for work in London in the early 1990s gave her more confidence in herself and her skills.

In 2006 a spoof 'Extra curriculum vitae' (outlining qualifications and skills

Faking a CV was common enough to feature in an Andy Podean cartoon.
Jonathan Drapes

IN GENERAL, those who had trade skills found it easy to get jobs, although they often found that work standards and practices were quite different in the UK. A carpenter by trade, Kelly's first job was building in London with English people in 2002, but she didn't like it. She then found a position with a shop-fitting company, working mostly with New Zealanders and Australians, which she found much better. The company she worked for was based at Gatwick but they worked all over the country, which she enjoyed. In London she had not had to show her qualifications and found that she could 'bluff' her way into work, which was very different from her New Zealand experiences, where a CV was a prerequisite, especially in small towns (she was originally from Greymouth). The work was also very different; it was done at a very leisurely pace and when she first started she was always being told to slow down and 'don't work so fast'.

learned abroad), was published in *TNT Magazine*. The qualifications included: Event Management (organising Friday drinks), Human Resources (shared responsibility for recruiting, and dismissing, housemates in an Acton share house) and Mass Communication (emailing mates at home and random people met on Contiki tours). Skills picked up included: being able to walk into any job, put in minimal effort while still earning praise from English colleagues and bosses, and strong hospitality skills (the ability to mix drinks and not throw up). The Past Employment record listed: a 14-day research venture (with 10 colleagues) studying the effects of illicit drug use on revellers in Ibiza; the study of ocean currents off the coasts of Spain, Portugal, Italy, Greece and Croatia; and work 'behind a bar serving customers, my mates and, when the "gaffer" wasn't looking, myself'.[8]

Some New Zealand men found their OE working life (and life overall) not very different from being at home in New Zealand. Barry's friend Robert was a slaughterman by trade; in 1979, when Barry found a job in an Aylesbury pub, Robert worked in a meatworks in the nearby village of Banbury. From there, he moved to Arbroath in Scotland, where he stayed for the entire two years of his OE. He even dropped out of their planned van tour of Europe, the original reason for going overseas; the only trip he did was to Oktoberfest. Before and after his OE, Robert lived in his Glenavy bach, worked at the freezing works and

Too good for the job.
Jonathan Drapes

spent all his time fishing and whitebaiting. In Arbroath he did exactly the same things, simply transferring his Glenavy life to a spot 13,000 miles distant.

New Zealanders had good reputations in the service industries and the trades, as well as with many agency employers; they were considered to have a good work ethic and to be willing and friendly workers, with a good attitude to the job. According to *The Big OE Companion*, New Zealanders were perceived to be hard-working, flexible and reliable. A rather unusual consequence of employing Kiwis was reported in a 2002 New Zealand newspaper article on medical trial guinea pigs; the article noted that the mix of nationalities used in these British trials could distort the results. The test subjects, for example, had to report every side effect they experienced, no matter how small; however, New Zealanders were more stoic than other nationalities. One New Zealander was reported as saying, 'Between us [New Zealanders] in the month we had no complaints. Between the four South Africans they had 10 complaints. The Australian boys, two of them, had 30 complaints between them.'[9]

According to *Working in London and the UK* there were an estimated 55 clinical research units in the UK in 1999, many of which advertised for paid volunteers

Medical testing featured in several of Jonathan Drapes' Andy Podean cartoons.

ANGELA was a typical OE pub worker. Arriving in the UK in 1980 'without a clue', she had no idea there was a recession and that unemployment was high. It hadn't even occurred to her to think about these things. She planned to work in a pub (somehow knowing that was what one did on OE), despite never having worked behind a bar before. Most people she knew worked in pubs, as nannies or 'blagged' their way into jobs as office temps (unfortunately, Angela could not even type). Those who could, taught. A few people worked in professional jobs, but they often worked part time in a pub as well.

in *TNT Magazine* and other Antipodean publications. Drug testing promised a good, fast and 'safe' way to earn extra money for travelling. In 2006, however, a New Zealander was one of six men who suffered multiple organ failure after taking part in a drug test in London.

New Zealanders were also in demand as rugby players, a skill that could sometimes be used to bypass the need for a legal work permit, although, ironically, it was illegal to work as a professional sportsperson on a working holiday visa. Before the Irish Working Holiday Visa Scheme was established in 1996, signing up for a local rugby club there often came with the promise of help in getting a job, and was a popular way of gaining entry to Ireland. In the UK in the early 1980s, Barry and his friends discovered that people found them jobs if they agreed to play rugby for the local club. Simon played rugby in London in the early 2000s; the club he played for found him a job and paid him cash in hand as he didn't have a visa.

While being a New Zealander was an advantage when looking for work, in some jobs it was crucial. Few of those who subsequently worked within the OE support network went to London planning to do so: in most cases they did not even know it existed. Nor had those who set up OE support businesses travelled to London with plans to do so. In 2004 both the information officer at the New Zealand High Commission and the editor of *New Zealand News UK* were New Zealanders, but these were jobs they found while on their OEs. Such jobs were unlikely to be given to non-New Zealanders; a good background knowledge of New Zealand was a prerequisite, and usually a formal qualification was necessary for bending the British employment laws.

The quintessential OE job was working in a pub. The sheer number of pubs and relatively recession-proof nature of the industry meant that pub jobs were widely available, even to those with no previous experience and training. The provision of accommodation was a distinct bonus.

Work in pubs offered a wide range of opportunities. Some people found really good positions that they returned to after each travel episode; others worked their way into management positions or forged completely new careers through contacts they made with customers. In the early 1980s Judy worked in a central London pub for several months before getting an office job through customers. On the down side, some pub managers exploited staff and treated them badly, or workers had to deal with challenging pub clientele.

While pub work was not as well paid as many other jobs, it was good if one was intent on saving hard for travel. Working at nights reduced the temptation to spend money on entertainment, and living in saved money and time. Pub jobs could also offer a great social life. Jackie, for example, recalled partying a lot at the pub she worked at in 2000, with 'lock-ins and not having to pay for anything'. Many people recalled how pub work gave them an insight into British culture that they might not otherwise have experienced.

Working in pubs became less popular over time, due to a number of factors. One was increasing competition from other migrant groups for this type of work. Large global cities like London have always attracted migrants looking for work and opportunities. With little or no immigration restrictions placed on them, the Irish were long-established labour migrants in the UK, particularly London.[10] The Australasians came next: between the 1981 and 1991 British censuses, the numbers of Australian and New Zealand-born people resident in London increased by 42 and 74 per cent, respectively.[11] Another wave of young temporary workers arrived in 1994 when, with the end of apartheid, South Africa rejoined the Commonwealth: its citizens became eligible for the same range of entry visas as New Zealanders and Australians. Then in May 2004 the expansion of the EU opened London to migrant groups from Eastern Europe. (The same progression – the Irish, the colonials, the Eastern Europeans – occurred in other industries. In 2004, for example, competition for jobs on London building sites increased as the new EU migrants joined the job market, bringing the price of labour down.)

Cathy Coyne, who set up her pub job agency in London in 1971, experienced the effects of this migrant evolution. As she recalled, in the 1970s and 1980s it was 'Aussies and Kiwis and Irish looking for pub work, but they seem to get other jobs now – my bank is full of them. The Kiwis just don't do pub jobs much any more.' She also talked about the way the migrant groups move up through the job market, getting better jobs as time goes by: 'The South Africans are already starting to do better jobs and I expect that the Eastern Europeans are well educated but start in pubs, just to get a foot in.' In a time of recession, however, these unskilled jobs were often all that was available.

Before these changes, a prominent feature of the pub employment market was the summer exodus from London for the Grand Tour of Europe; many publicans accepted that there was no point advertising for bar staff until after Oktoberfest. There were also changes in the way those on OE looked for

SIGNIFICANT NUMBERS of New Zealanders and Australians could be found working in some London (and UK) companies. Gary worked for a company building stages and doing stage lighting all over the UK in the early 2000s. While the company was British-owned, most of the staff were South Africans, Australians and New Zealanders. He had been a butcher in New Zealand, but got the job from a chance meeting at a pub with someone he knew from his home town, Greymouth. In 2004 the company employed 14 people from Greymouth alone.

Also in 2004, Hannah worked at a central London school with three other New Zealanders; she was from Waimate, the others were from Kurow, Timaru and just north of Dunedin. Madeleine found work as a housekeeper on an estate and part time in a pub in Petersfield, a small town outside London. Few other New Zealanders were in the town, but the people she worked for on the estate had employed a New Zealander before her, and in the pub she worked at she also replaced another New Zealander.

pub work. When Cathy Coyne started her business, numerous other agencies were offering pub and cooking jobs, but by 2004 she was one of only a few left. By then most of her business was conducted by telephone and email; most job seekers she dealt with searched for jobs in *TNT Magazine* or on the internet: she advertised in both media. In her opinion, the internet had brought major change, as many big companies were able to bypass agencies by listing vacancies on their own websites. She regretted some of the effects, especially the loss of personal contact: 'People remember you ... you are not just a voice on the other end of the phone – but things change and you have to go along with it.'

Another development in the 1990s was the establishment of London pub job companies in New Zealand and Australia. One of these was the Original London Pub Company, which started in association with STA Travel in 1998. New Zealanders, Australians and Canadians could arrange London pub jobs before leaving home, and go straight from the airport to a job (usually with the first two days off to get over jet-lag). In 2012 the cost of this service was NZ$795 (not including the cost of the visa). An Australian-based company, Overseas Working Holidays (OWH), operated a similar service – Pubs UK – which was advertised through travel agents in New Zealand. OWH, part of the Flight Centre Group, started in 1994.

Pre-arranging a job in this fashion was generally not viewed positively: on the one hand, there was the danger of not liking London; on the other, there was a far greater choice of jobs to pick from once one got to London. Many of the Kiwi London publicans thought it was a 'rip-off'. Some agencies in New Zealand also offered bar training courses to those heading for Britain on their OEs, but most publicans preferred to employ staff with no experience so that they could train them the way they wanted. Also, much of what was taught in New Zealand courses – like mixing cocktails – was not useful in a London pub, where one was more likely to be asked for a 'light and bitter', a 'lager top' or a 'snakebite' than a pina colada.

One advantage of the Original London Pub Company was that it offered live-in positions, all with cooking facilities and sometimes free meals. The pub job lost its appeal over time as accommodation and/or meals as part of the job became less common. While pubs usually had plenty of room for staff accommodation, stricter health and safety regulations – such as having to put in fire escapes – severely reduced the number of live-in jobs available in central London. In contrast, in the 1970s and 1980s most pub jobs included accommodation and all meals; although Angela recalled one manager she worked for expecting six live-in staff to get by on only one pint of milk a day and whatever bar food was left over at the end of each session. She quit the job after three weeks (staying that long only because she was totally broke and had to wait two weeks to get her first pay), by which stage she was the longest-serving staff member!

Left: The author celebrating St Patrick's Day in the 1990s at the Pakenham Arms (above).

Behind the bar at the 'Duke' in the 1980s (note the Oktoberfest sweat shirt)

ANGELA considered herself lucky as her first pub job was at the Duke of Buckingham, a busy central London pub. The 'Duke' was in Villiers Street, next to Charing Cross Station (sadly, it was pulled down to make way for station development in the late 1980s), but most of the staff lived in the company's other pub just outside Leicester Square. Most of the Duke's clientele were London businessmen, along with a substantial number of friends of the manager and staff. The large staff consisted of Irish, Australians and Kiwis, with a couple of English, a Pole and a Brazilian thrown in for good measure. She learned to pour beer, to construct a 'Ploughman's Lunch', to understand unfathomable Irish (and some English) accents, and made some lifelong friends. Her lasting memories are of parties in the Bierkeller (the basement bar whose location below street level meant that they couldn't be caught trading after hours) with staff and friends (and the occasional customer), and of parties in the accommodation at the other pub. She had one Christmas at the Duke, in the company of about 20 other colonial expats (the Irish staff went home), during which they partied hard for the full three days the pub was shut.

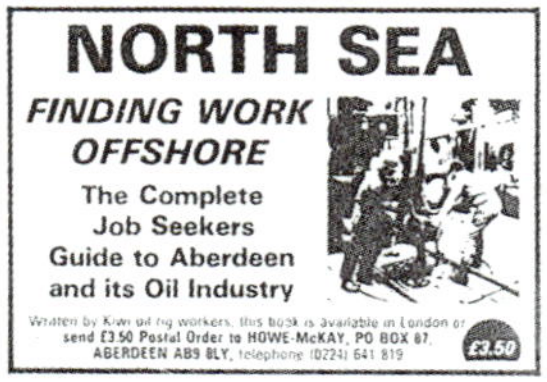

In the mid-1980s a guide to finding work offshore in the North Sea oil industry – written by Kiwi oil rig workers – was advertised in *TNT Magazine*.

TNT Magazine

ON HIS OE in the late 1970s, Eric had heard about people working on the North Sea oil rigs, so he took a train up to Aberdeen and knocked on doors until he found a job. He had no experience or practical skills applicable to oil rig employment. He worked on the rigs for about a year, living in Cologne in Germany, where he had a girlfriend, and commuting to Scotland, although technically he still had an address in London. Also in the late 1970s, Alex found an accountancy job with an American drilling and oil company that had a major office in London: 'The guy doing the hiring was an Australian and was looking for people like Australians and New Zealanders who could adapt.' He was hired as one of 15 overseas accountants and was posted to Tripoli for several years where he earned 'fabulous money, a tax-free package, had three weeks on and three weeks off and got a lot more accounting experience'. After that he was posted to Damascus for two years, a very demanding job as the rig was near the Iraqi border and there were bomb explosions in Syria at the time. He then spent several years in Malta, Saudi Arabia, Dubai and Bahrain, working for the same oil company.

Working on a North Sea oil rig.

IN THE EARLY 1980s the Australians living in the flat above Judy in London were going for interviews to work in Iceland. Judy had heard about these jobs, so went along as well. To her, Iceland was an 'out-there place'; she had no idea what to expect in a fish factory (although she had done potato grading so had some experience of manual work). The fishing company paid for the tickets to Iceland and they worked long hours, but the pay was reasonable. She became a fish trimmer – one could be either a packer or a trimmer – mostly working with cod. The workers received basic pay and were paid on fish weight once they learned to save as much of the fish as possible. At the factory where Judy worked, there were six or seven other Australians and New Zealanders. They made fun out of a really boring job and lived together in a residence called Aussie House, where they turned one area of the house into a bar and started brewing their own beer, making it a real party place. The local Lions club also ran dances; Judy recalled there being a bit of tension as the local Icelandic guys paid a lot of attention to the foreigners, and the local girls missed out. She signed up originally for eight months (the minimum period) but ended up staying slightly longer.

The Iceland experience: Clockwise from top: the first barbecue; waiting at Thingeyri Airport for a weekend in Reyjavik; Christmas with the gang in Aussie House; tobogganing in a fish bin; and fish packing.

In the 1970s and 1980s two travellers' jobs achieved almost legendary status within the OE: one of these was working on oil rigs, the other in Icelandic fish factories. During the boom period of oil exploration in the 1970s and 1980s, workers with little or no experience were employed on North Sea oil rigs; work on rigs was also available throughout the Middle East. By the mid-1990s the North Sea oil fields had reached middle age and production was slowing down, reducing the number of jobs available. Also, only skilled workers were likely to be employed.

Working over the winter in Iceland processing fish was a popular OE job in the 1980s; *New Zealand News UK* published a feature article about such work in 1986. The principal attractions were the pay and the ease of saving money in a place with few distractions and minimal daylight hours. One story in *The Big OE* described the experiences of two New Zealand women who worked in Iceland in the 1960s. They were the first New Zealanders where they worked; most of the other workers were from Iceland and the Faroe Islands. They found the job smelly (rather than onerous) and had a lot of fun playing pranks on each other with fish parts. They lived in a hostel across the road from their factory and socialised with local single men at weekend dances and parties.

The expatriate worker

The fundamental purpose of work on an OE had always been to support oneself and one's travel while away from New Zealand. In the 1960s some people trained as nurses or secretaries in order to get jobs on their OE. Many of the baby boomers going on OEs in the late 1970s and early 1980s had just finished a university education and had only the skills they had picked up from summer jobs in New Zealand. The introduction of student fees and student loans in the 1990s had a significant impact on OE travellers' objectives: increasingly they sought post-OE benefits from their employment, in terms of work experience or money. An ex-London publican from New Zealand, who employed colonials throughout the 1980s and 1990s, recalled that in the early days 'you would employ staff from all walks of life … but in the last few years they were going over there [London] to get proper jobs and to earn really good money. Their whole attitude and way of thinking had changed.'

There have always been some OE travellers working in 'proper' jobs. How appropriate this was – as judged by the authorities, and sometimes by others on their OE – depended on what the job was: continuing to work as a doctor or a dentist, for example, was acceptable; teaching and nursing were acceptable; accountancy was less so. Working as an accountant was considered by many to be not doing an OE properly; those who did were often defensive about their decision. Alex was an accountant. After seven months of extensive travelling in the late 1970s he 'got to London, borrowed some money, went and bought a suit and got a job. My whole idea for going overseas was to get some work experience *and* to see the world. I would have felt I was wasting my time on my OE unless I got a really good job.' His approach and attitude to work impacted on other aspects of his OE; his twin brother's OE was quite different as it primarily comprised a van tour and drinking trips.

Kate was unusual in that once she was on her OE she decided that she wouldn't work. She had saved enough money to travel for almost a year; after staying with friends in London who were working, she realised that she could earn much more money in her career job back in New Zealand (from which she had a year's unpaid leave) than she could being a 'temp' in London: 'All those I knew in London were doing OE jobs, except for my cousin who was an accountant.' One long-term London expatriate noted disparagingly that 'there have always been the accountants'. For those on a working holiday visa, working full time as an accountant was technically illegal, but advertisements for accountancy positions appeared in *New Zealand News UK* and *TNT Magazine* from the 1960s into the 2000s because of recurrent skill shortages in Britain.

To practise professionally in Britain, New Zealand workers often needed to register with the relevant professional bodies, some of which also offered support to new arrivals. The British branch of the Institute of Chartered Accountants New Zealand (ICANZ), established in 1970, was one of the earliest of these. Today the branch runs professional training days and some social events for members but, according to a long-term member, it started out as a 'let's go to New Zealand House and get completely pissed for next-to-nothing organisation'. In the 2000s the most popular ICANZ events were their annual wine tastings, held in conjunction with their AGM.

The London accountants had the best and most active branch of any New Zealand-linked professional body in London in the 2000s, according to their branch secretary. In 2004 the British branch of ICANZ had 1920 members, most of whom (at least 1700) were in London. However, this total did not include those who were still using a New Zealand address. Initially membership was almost entirely OE travellers, but over the previous six years this had changed to about one-third OE people, one-third expatriates staying up to 10 years, and one-third expatriates who would never leave. Many people in the two expatriate groups had started off as OE travellers.

MANY OF THOSE on OE did work in their normal occupations, often noting that it was 'a shame to waste my training' and the 'money was so good'. Prior to going on his OE in 2003, for example, Kevin (a landscape architect) 'didn't have a problem with doing something different' and thought it a good idea to do so; on the other hand, he did have the 'skills in the field' and thought it 'a shame not to use them'. As it happened, he found it difficult to get a job in landscape architecture as he didn't have CAD (computer aided design) skills. He ended up doing contracting work landscaping movie sets, including one of the Harry Potter sets. After a few months he managed to get a landscape architecture job, but as a project manager working on site, which was totally different from the office-based work he had done at home. He described his job as 'brilliant'.

For accountants, work experience in London was valuable and offered opportunities that were not available in New Zealand. As the branch secretary commented: 'In New Zealand they have a young accountant of the year and in the last two years we [London-based New Zealand accountants] have been allowed entry and they have told us that their biggest worry is that someone from here will win it every year.'

Other professional organisations serving New Zealanders in London in 2012 included the Institute of Professional Engineers of New Zealand United Kingdom Association (IPENZUK, established around 1970); the New Zealand Dental Society in London (NZDSL); and the New Zealand Lawyers' Society (established in March 1993). The ANZO Property Group, established in 1999 for Australian and New Zealand property professionals publishes comprehensive employment advice for new arrivals to London on its website, as well as a quarterly newsletter with employment advice. It also holds social events, including an annual ball.

While working in career jobs became common, taking a photo of what one was doing was less so: working for a structural engineering firm, 2005.

While at times the working holiday visa regulations, the economic situation and their own lack of useful work skills kept many of those on OE in traditional travellers' jobs, labour shortages in some industries offered career work and financial opportunities that were hard to resist. Teaching in particular paid well, and suited the OE lifestyle. Taking on temporary teaching supply positions, for example, enabled people to take travel time off whenever they wished, although supply teachers did not get paid for holidays. Permanent teaching positions offered a lot of paid holiday time; teachers were a significant portion of the OE travellers touring Europe for the whole summer in the 2000s. Severe teaching shortages in Britain made it possible for New Zealanders who did not qualify for working holiday visas or other permits to work legally in Britain, and many people who had missed out on their OE when younger took advantage of this.

A common language, as well as educational and training systems based on British models, gave New Zealanders an advantage over many other migrant groups in Britain. This was especially so when competing for more highly skilled jobs, as no extra training or certification was required for most skilled occupations. However, it was not as easy to get into a job as many expected. Ana, for example, arrived in London in 1989 expecting to 'set the world on fire with her incredible career skills'. Instead, it took three times as long as planned to get a decent job; even then, she found herself struggling to 'make it'. With what she described as 'naïve arrogance', she had overestimated her employment worth, and was unprepared for the difficulty of succeeding in London.

Sometimes people had to wait until the right job came up. In 2004, after working as a temp for two months through an agency who told her that she wouldn't get an IT job,

Tara finally succeeded in getting what she wanted: 'I was naïve when I first got there, but at least I wasn't naïve enough to believe them.' Once her foot was in the door, she was able to get a permanent IT job. Damien also struggled to get a permanent job in London in 2001. He had worked in television in New Zealand and managed to pick up some agency work, but also worked behind a bar and as an extra in police line-ups. After about six months he got a phone call with the offer of a three-week job: 'Did it matter that it was with Playboy TV?' Eventually he was offered a full-time job with them and whenever he told people where he worked 'the guys loved it, but the girls tended to not know how to deal with it'.

Often it was difficult to get professional jobs with *only* New Zealand experience. Good accountancy jobs, for example, usually required at least three months' experience in Britain. The relatively young age of New Zealanders on OE (even allowing for increases in base age over time) means that, even if they have worked in their profession in New Zealand, they are too inexperienced for many British employers, who have a large pool of candidates to choose from. Anna, an engineer, found that many recruiters were looking for people with more experience when she tried to find a permanent engineering job in London in the early 2000s. It took three months to find a job (luckily she had an aunt and uncle to stay with while she waited). Her British passport was a definite help. However, it was sometimes difficult for New Zealanders with British passports to get skilled work because employers thought they would not stay around for long. For those with only a working holiday visa, this was more of a problem.

Most people on OE thought that working illegally – outside the conditions of the working holiday visa or with no permit at all – was acceptable. It could have unfortunate consequences, as Eric found when he worked

A tough school to teach at: Morpeth School in the late 1980s.

NEIL was 57 when he finally went on his OE in 2002, taking advantage of the teacher shortage in Britain to get a work permit. New Zealand teachers were good and filled a gap, he felt, but because they wanted to travel they tended to take their money and run: what they brought to the job was not quite the full measure. Other older New Zealanders wanting to take a late OE were able to take advantage of shortages of social workers in Britain. Like teaching, social work gave people many insights into life in Britain and was more challenging than the same work at home. Janette taught in some really tough schools in London in the late 1990s, including one on a housing estate where she was 'scared most of the time'. This was not the type of school she would have chosen to teach in at home, but she found that it was normal for London. She was paid a lot: 'All I could see was pounds in front of my eyes.'

Figure 6.1 Australian and New Zealand workers in the UK by socio-economic group 1992–2000.

** Figures not available

Socio-economic group	1992	1993	1994	1995	1996	1997	1998	1999	2000
Professionals (%)	29.5	33.7	36.4	33.8	40.8	42.0	41.1	44.3	41.8
Other non-manual (%)	30.2	39.2	42.5	44.0	35.2	35.8	42.7	37.1	41.8
Manual (%)	38.4	26.3	**	22.2	24.0	22.2	**	18.6	16.5

in London for an Irish company doing demolition work in the late 1970s. He was electrocuted and ended up in hospital for several days with burns all over his face and the surface of both his eyes seared, luckily with no permanent damage, but he couldn't see for several days. He was unable to sue the company he worked for (despite its appalling safety practices) because he was working illegally.

Being far from home could be challenging when things went wrong. In the mid-1990s Pete was in an accident when he was working as a motorcycle courier. It left him with a badly broken leg, unable to work, or even to get around easily, as he had a full-length plaster cast. Fortunately, the courier company found him an office dispatch position to cover the period he was incapacitated. Not to work was not really an option, as New Zealanders were not entitled to public funds such as the dole.

According to British Labour Force surveys conducted between 2000 and 2004, 93.6 per cent of New Zealand-born new immigrants (those who arrived in 1990 or later) in the UK were employed. This represented the highest percentage among new immigrant nationalities. For settled immigrants (those who arrived before 1990), New Zealand-born people represented the fourth-highest group in employment, with 81.5 per cent employed. Just over 25 per cent of New Zealand-born new immigrants were high earners (earning more than £750 a week), the fifth-highest percentage (after the US, Sweden, the Netherlands and Australia). Of settled immigrants, New Zealand-born had the highest percentage of high earners (27.40 per cent).[12] These figures indicate the growing numbers of OE travellers doing professional jobs. Table 6.1 shows this shift for New Zealand and Australian workers in the UK as an aggregated group (they are generally considered to have similar employment profiles).[13]

Working outside London

While London was the most popular location for OE work, many people worked outside London for at least some of their OE. Many felt it was best to start in London before looking for work elsewhere. Alex began his OE in London in 1978 because he could get a visa, his brother was there so he had somewhere to crash, and London was a 'safe, easy place to start'; he subsequently worked in Europe but felt he 'could not have gone into Europe cold'.

Sometimes work was located outside London or even Britain because of one's job. Joshua was a radio engineer in New Zealand; his OE in 1994 coincided with the huge growth in the cellphone industry. People with his skills were in 'hot demand'. He took a job with Nokia, at first working near Reading and then at Nokia headquarters in Finland for several years. Because he worked for the English office in Finland, he didn't need a work permit.

There has been a recent trend among OE travellers to work outside London. This may be a result of changes in technology that facilitate access to employment information and jobs. Employment advertising on the internet, for example, has enabled OE travellers to search for work in other cities without having to physically go there. New hubs and nodes of expatriate workers have emerged as a result; having a friend in a city outside London makes work there more appealing. In 2004 Gumtree had websites targeting London, Edinburgh and Dublin, and by 2005 there were 29 other Gumtree locations listed in Britain and Ireland, 20 of which were marked as 'new sites'. In 2013 Gumtree spanned 48 cities in Britain and Ireland.

Moving outside London to work was seen by many to be 'brave' and to offer a 'better' OE than one based entirely in London, primarily because of the increased contact with British people and the greater insights into British culture that it gave. By the same token, working outside Britain was even better. It also offered an OE experience that was not cocooned within the expatriate New Zealand community. Some enjoyed being different – and therefore noteworthy – in communities where there were no other New Zealanders. Jackie and her partner worked in Brighton in 2000 and enjoyed being the only Kiwis, whereas 'in London we weren't so special'. However, some people found life outside London less appealing when they realised that their friends and acquaintances in London were having a more exciting social life.

JANE stayed with a British friend in the north of England in 1999 and found her first job through an employment agency there. It was in a Scunthorpe clothing factory, which she described as being 'just like Coronation Street'. As her first experience of England, she described working there as 'both really educational and terrible'. She found it interesting to learn about industrial culture, but could only tolerate it because it was short term. The people she was working with told her about their lives; she was 'gob-smacked' that their expectations were so limited.

Emma lived and worked in Manchester in the early 1990s, and gained an appreciation of working-class life there from her British boyfriend's family. She especially enjoyed the fact that they had stayed close to the places they were born, and had strong connections to their homes and families.

By the 2000s both Dublin and Edinburgh were established smaller hubs for young expatriate workers from Australasia. Publications similar to *TNT Magazine* in London were distributed there.
Go West magazine

Chapter Seven
A SMALL WORLD

Opposite: Yeldham Road, Hammersmith, 1981.

CHANGES IN OE TRAVEL and work impacted on the OE lifestyle. Working for longer stretches resulted in more time spent living in one place, and the desire to live more comfortably than in the past. Better jobs and longer periods of work brought higher earnings, which had a direct effect on lifestyle affordability. The increase in age of OE travellers increased the likelihood of their having work experience and financial independence in New Zealand prior to going on OE, and also created raised expectations. Many were simply not prepared to revert to the New Zealand student lifestyle they had grown out of. By the mid-1990s the living standards of the OE had improved considerably.

While London was still the most popular OE location, there was a shift away from the classic two-bedroom Earls Court flat housing 15 New Zealanders; Earls Court was replaced by Shepherds Bush and Acton in the 1990s, and the flats increased in size. Their occupants were still mostly New Zealanders, however. Changes in work and travel patterns also had a significant impact on the social lives of OE travellers. Many traditional OE jobs had involved working nights and weekends, whereas working in more professional jobs freed up time for entertainment and social activities. A significant social support network and calendar of social events evolved, providing OE travellers with a degree of cultural cushioning and, increasingly, opportunities to celebrate New Zealand culture. And for the OE travellers of the new millennium, the internet made it easier to stay connected to 'home' in New Zealand.

Identity matters

The OE population was unusual for its homogeneity. Most of those on OE were of a similar age and shared similar lifestyles and goals. The OE represented time out from normal life; extended family networks were missing and people's lives back in New Zealand were not relevant to their lives in London. No one aged (as parents did), almost no one had babies and almost everyone was young. Personal interactions and relationships were approached with more urgency, but less depth, than at home: a 'quantity not quality approach'. The two-year visa restriction contributed to the feeling that one had to 'go a million miles an hour because the clock was ticking'.

Living overseas was quite different from

visiting places temporarily as a tourist. New Zealanders had to grapple with unfamiliar transport systems, deal with many more people than they were used to, engage with new banking and commerce systems, adjust to different living arrangements and shops, and so on. Even if they lived only in London, they still had to get to grips with life in a foreign country. An outcome of this for a significant number of OE travellers was a newfound awareness of their identity as New Zealanders. In London particularly, where social venues and many aspects of social life were shared with Australians and to a lesser extent South Africans, making one's mark or expressing one's identity as a New Zealander was of paramount importance.

What's in a name?

The British often collectively grouped New Zealanders in London with other expatriates, particularly Australians, but sometimes also South Africans. The most common labels applied to these migrant populations were 'Antipodean' (by others) and 'Australasian' (by themselves). Numerous other labels appear in London expatriate literature and advertising aimed at these populations: the Tri Nations (since the advent of the rugby competition in 1996); the 'colonies' (this and 'the colonials' were terms used mainly by the British and were considered derogatory by New Zealanders); or from 'down under'. Acronyms were also employed to describe these expatriate groups, each of which had a

ACCORDING TO historian Keith Sinclair, the term 'Australasia' was invented in the eighteenth century by a Frenchman, Charles de Brosses. Originally it described all land *au sud de l'Asie*, including New Guinea, but later was more meaningfully applied to the seven British colonies in Australia and New Zealand. Its use became problematic for New Zealand. In a 1922 parliamentary debate an MP suggested that schools stop using it as its effect on business negotiations with Britain were detrimental: people gained the impression that New Zealand was part of Australia.[1]

slightly different membership. As Bronwyn Sell pointed out in *The Big OE Companion*:

***ANZSAC/ANZSAF/SANZA* explained**

You'll probably come across these terms in London. It's a way of including South Africans and Canadians in the Kiwi and Australian club. ANZSAC means Australian, New Zealand, South African and Canadian. ANZSAF is Australian, New Zealand and South African. SANZA is South African, New Zealand and Australian. Antipodean tends to encompass everyone from the Southern Hemisphere.[2]

Technically, 'Antipodean' should not include South Africans. It is also a word that is rarely used in New Zealand; many of those on OE had to ask others what it meant when they first arrived in London. In 2005–06 *TNT Magazine* published Jonathan Drapes' weekly cartoon strip about the life of 'Andy Podean', an Australian expatriate in London whose experiences were similar to those of his New Zealand compatriots in London. Also, while 'down under' could correctly apply to all three of these Southern Hemisphere nationalities, within these populations it was normally used only in association with Australians. Because of their cultural similarities and similar lifestyles and circumstances in London, New Zealanders and Australians were most commonly grouped as 'Australasian'.

In the London of the 1960s and 1970s, New Zealanders were part of a collective Antipodean identity that was more Australian – Earls Court as Kangaroo Valley, for instance – than a blend of cultures. Movies such as *Crocodile Dundee* and advertising campaigns for Fosters beer showcased Australian culture in Britain. However, New Zealand was catching up. Several significant marketing campaigns followed Steinlager winning the championship trophy at the Brewing Industry Awards in England in 1985. In the arts, Kiri Te Kanawa's home country was noticed when she sang at the 1981 wedding of Prince Charles and Princess Diana. New Zealand culture really began to register on Britain's radar with Keri Hulme's *The Bone People* winning the prestigious Booker Prize for Fiction in 1985; then the film *The Piano* won the Palme d'Or at Cannes in 1993 and the films *Heavenly Creatures* and *Once Were Warriors* attracted big audiences in 1994. Many OE travellers found that British friends and co-workers struggled to understand the New Zealand portrayed in these works, as they were more familiar with the images and messages presented by Tourism New Zealand. Films from New Zealand, such as *Whale Rider* and the *Lord of the Rings* trilogy, continued to reach global audiences, although only *Whale Rider* was a New Zealand story. As New Zealand culture became more prominent in the 2000s, Tourism New Zealand used it in advertising, raising awareness further.

Despite the inroads made by New Zealand culture, many British people still

struggled to differentiate New Zealanders from Australians. However, being confused with Australians made New Zealanders more aware of how they were different. While Anzac Day has a shared significance for each country, as Tara Brabazon pointed out in *Tracking the Jack*, the Anzac forces were not unified and the events at Gallipoli divided Australia and New Zealand as nations.[3] While Australians and New Zealanders travel together to Gallipoli for Anzac Day commemorations, once there each group has its own national agenda.

In London, New Zealanders were often perceived as a 'little brother' to the Australians, who continued to be more visible and more numerous. On the whole, the support and company of their fellow Antipodeans was welcomed by New Zealanders; being 'Australasian' was not a problem, although the widespread use of 'Antipodean' perhaps indicates a preference. The ongoing challenge for many New Zealanders was how to find a way to signify to outsiders that they were *not* Australian, and that Australians and New Zealanders *were* different.

Looking like a Kiwi

Commonly, what most clearly characterised New Zealanders were displays of Māori culture; the best-known expression of this was the haka, performed by all and sundry in London. Greenstone jewellery and Māori designs on clothing were also unmistakably 'Kiwi'. As it became increasingly fashionable throughout the 1980s and 1990s to wear 'branded' clothing, identifying oneself as a New Zealander through one's dress became easier. Obvious (and longstanding) New Zealand brands included Lane Walker Rudkin's Canterbury Clothing (worn

Left: In 1990 Steinlager launched a new billboard advertising campaign in Britain which London-based New Zealanders particularly liked.
STEINLAGER is a registered trademark of Lion Nathan Brands Company

Right: When the 100% Pure New Zealand Garden won a Silver-Gilt Flora Award for Best Show Garden at the Chelsea Flower Show in 2006, Tourism New Zealand advertised on London buses.

Jonathan Drapes captured not only the differences between Antipodeans and the British in their cold-weather clothing, but also the additional Dunedinite layer to the joke that only a New Zealander would get. Jonathan Drapes

by the All Blacks until their lucrative – and somewhat controversial – Adidas sponsorship deal in 1999) and Swanndri; these brands were joined by Icebreaker in the-mid 1990s.

The commercialisation of sport in New Zealand and, in particular, the advent of professional rugby with the establishment of the Super 12 rugby competition provided the opportunity to display national and provincial imagery that was recognisable to other New Zealanders and sometimes outsiders. International sports leagues involving New Zealand teams, such as the Warriors' participation in the Australian National Rugby League (NRL), also offered brands that had some international recognition. One of the most recognisable brands to emerge from New Zealand sport was the Beige Brigade, whose devotees wear 1980s retro Black Caps cricket clothing. It became common to display New Zealand flags (either the national flag or the silver fern) on the walls of flats, hanging from windows, or draped around oneself at public events.

It was common to display a flag on one's backpack while travelling.

More intangible clues denoting national identity were associated with dress and general demeanour. In the 1990s and 2000s many people found that wearing Kathmandu clothing was equivalent to wearing the flag. Likewise, anyone carrying a Macpac backpack was usually a New Zealander. On his OE in 2002, Neil remembered being in a pub full of 'pasty-looking English guys', then the Super 12 would come on and 'The pub would fill up with Kiwis – athletic, stronger, healthier-looking guys, more casually dressed, more sitting back – and it was definitely a different feel.'

Gearing up

A range of specialist shops sold New Zealand goods in London. Whitcoulls was the earliest, operating a bookstore in premises in the Royal Opera Arcade behind New Zealand House. Kiwifruits followed in 1983, selling mainly Canterbury clothing, New Zealand gifts, All Black essentials, flags, sew-on patches with New Zealand motifs, stickers and so on. Originally located in Covent Garden, it took over the Whitcoulls premises in 1993, where its product range grew to include New Zealand music, books and magazines. The premises expanded further in 2002. Kiwifruits was the only specialist New Zealand bookshop in Britain and also supplied a wide range of food products including Pineapple Lumps, Jaffas, Peanut Slabs, Bluebird Chips, L&P softdrink, Wattie's Tomato Sauce and New Zealand-made breakfast cereals.

New Zealand products were also sold by the New Zealand Shop in Covent Garden, part of the Anglo-Australian Trading Company which had been operating an Australia Shop since the 1960s. The New Zealand Shop opened in 2001 and shared premises with the Australia, South Africa and Canada shops: market research established that since New Zealanders and Australians lived together, they could be expected to shop together. During the 2000s the shop was involved with many New Zealand community groups in London, supporting social and corporate events and home-grown product launches. Kiwifruits and the New Zealand Shop faced similar challenges. The unusual nature of the OE population, with new cohorts arriving continually, meant that the popularity of products changed quite quickly. This made regular buying trips to New Zealand necessary, to see what was in fashion. The range of products on sale increased markedly over the years, as new products became popular in New Zealand. According to the owners of Kiwifruits, having their products

MANY ENJOYED standing out as New Zealanders, especially as Kiwis were highly regarded in the UK. Linda recalls being particularly proud of New Zealand's nuclear-free stance, and the international coverage it was given, on her OE in the mid-1980s. Sally, on her OE at the same time, always wore her koru pendant and recalled being stopped on the street by other New Zealanders who recognised it: 'It made me a lot more conscious of my identity and it made me quite proud actually – initially I was quite anxious to throw off the Kiwi bit, but as time went on, it mattered a lot and I was very proud of being a Kiwi.'

Wearing a 'Nuke-busters' sweatshirt with pride in London, 1987.

Kiwifruits, in the Royal Opera Arcade.
Belinda Kitchin

Despite their shared premises, each national shop was marketed separately, with colour-coded flyers.
Anglo Australian Trading Company

The range of New Zealand products on sale at the New Zealand Shop.
Anglo Australian Trading Company

In the 1990s some mainstream London supermarkets started selling Vegemite (perhaps indicative of the large numbers of Australasians in London). Chris Slane

for sale in London was confirmation for New Zealand producers that their brand had become a New Zealand icon.

Kiwifruits closed in February 2012, its demise the result of a number of factors: the ever-increasing cost of new stock (a result of the high New Zealand dollar); the increase in VAT to 20 per cent; the dwindling number of New Zealanders going to London because of the financial situation in Britain; competition from internet shopping; and changes the last owner of the business, Belinda Kitchin, attributed to 'globalisation in all its forms'. In particular, she noted that Kiwifruits' 'home away from home' concept was becoming less relevant, given the increased confidence of New Zealanders in their place in the world, and the fact that many New Zealanders were identifying with the Pacific.

For OE travellers in the 1980s and 1990s, Kiwifruits and the New Zealand Shop were a godsend, as one no longer had to rely on friends and family in New Zealand to send missed items from home. It was still a bonus, however, to receive care packages with Peanut Slabs for Christmas and birthdays, and marshmallow eggs at Easter. Before Kiwifruits opened, a special trip to Harrods' Food Hall – for many, the only time they went to Harrods – was necessary to get Vegemite.

The New Zealand Shop was still operating in early 2013 but was about to be restructured. From the late 1990s a number of London-based internet sites began to offer products from home to the expatriate colonial populations. SANZA (www.sanza.co.uk), for example, started in 1997 and provided community services (sports clubs, employment and accommodation noticeboards, sports competitions) to South Africans, Australians and New Zealanders in London. It also sold specialised products from each of the three countries. In 2001 a New Zealand-based internet company began

selling 'Kiwi Homesick Packs' containing Milo, Marmite, New Zealand lollies, Wattie's Tomato Sauce and Bell Tea bags. In the internet shopping era, maintaining a physical retail store for New Zealand goods in London may simply be too difficult.

Sounding like a Kiwi

Significant numbers of OE travellers had immediate family connections in the UK through British parents or were born there. It came as a surprise to many to discover that they were 'Kiwis', having spent many years in New Zealand thinking of themselves as being, at least partially, British. One's accent was a strong indicator of nationality, although often only those in the expatriate communities could clearly differentiate individual accents. Australians and New Zealanders usually picked (and sometimes ridiculed) each other's accent. European bus tour leader Brian Thacker, the Australian author of *Rule No. 5: No sex on the bus,* described how the accents (and commentary) of his New Zealand passengers sounded to the Australians on board: 'Oh yeah, but the Southern Elps in Nu Zulund are *shutloads* bitter' (than the Swiss Alps) and, 'Oh gee, the fjords are *heaps* more bitter un Mulford Sound' (than in Norway).[4] For the British and other nationalities, however, these distinctions were less discernible: the speaker was simply from somewhere 'down under'.

Nicky went on her OE in the early 1980s and felt quite connected with England: 'My father was English, and I was a bit of an Anglophile. But I was a Kiwi and I guess it took me by surprise … I particularly didn't like being teased about my accent. But it made me feel like a Kiwi – in the difference from the Poms. They [the Poms] have no get up and go … I didn't go there to go Pommie bashing but they were different.' Crystal

The New Zealand accent was seen as advantageous overseas as it engendered an automatic affinity (and usually conversation) with other New Zealanders.

Chris Slane

FOR THOSE who worked and lived outside London, or who had minimal contact with other New Zealanders, it was easy to forget how strong one's accent was. Jane, who was on her OE in the late 1990s, recalled that: 'I hadn't been around many other New Zealanders at all and when I got on the plane after Singapore – on Air New Zealand – and I heard all the voices … I thought "Oh my god, that's why people have been hassling me all the time – listen to those accents."' In the early 1980s – when phone calls home were relatively rare – it could also be a shock to hear how strong one's parents' accents were. In London it was generally quite easy to identify newly arrived New Zealanders by the strength of their accent.

Keeping his accent (and not speaking 'British') was also important to Andy Podean. Jonathan Drapes

had British parents and was born in Britain, although she grew up in New Zealand. She explained her cultural and ethnic identity in light of her OE experience in 2000: 'I always feel more British when I am here [in New Zealand] but with an accent like mine in England, you are not British, you are a Kiwi. My accent and my lifestyle are Kiwi, but my blood is British.'

A New Zealand accent could 'cut through' class boundaries and social barriers in Britain. Elsewhere, the accent could give someone considerable novelty value and facilitate social engagement. Some travellers reported that people of other nationalities sometimes talked to them simply because of their accent. Richard, who worked for several seasons in American summer camps in the early 2000s, enjoyed being a novelty because of his accent, while Andrea, on her OE in the late 1970s, was determined not to return home sounding English. Some OE travellers were very aware of their 'foreign accent' when they were first away, and wanted to sound British at work, rather than always being asked where they were from. Many found that their accents faded the longer they were away from home. Eventually, however, most were happy to reclaim their New Zealand identity.

Culture shock

A more distinct New Zealand national identity was emerging, but well into the 1990s OE travellers expected to find Britain similar in culture to New Zealand. This was in part fostered by the large percentage of television shows from Britain that were screened on New Zealand television. Most New Zealanders did not anticipate the degree of culture shock they experienced on arrival in Britain, blaming it on their small-country and often small-town origins. In 2005 the

Top: For all New Zealanders, London could be overwhelming. Frequently OE travellers made a point of stating which small New Zealand towns they were from, as a measure of just how different they were finding London from 'home'. Chris Slane

Bottom: London was also full of tourists, of course. Chris Slane

New Zealand comedian Ben Hurley was interviewed about his appearances in *Four Kiwis Walk into a Bar* (a London comedy collective). He spoke of tailoring his London show to suit his new audience: 'You poke fun at yourself a little bit for being from a funny little country. It's a whole new angle – you're a fish out of water, discovering things for the first time that people take for granted here.'[5]

London was full of people with origins in other countries, both tourists and residents. The multicultural nature of the city amplified a sense in New Zealanders of cultural difference. Pete described the area he lived in London in 1994 (Tooting) as 'foreign', but 'not English foreign, more sort of Indian and Pakistani foreign'. Teaching in London, in particular, exposed many people to a multitude of cultures. In 1999 Janette taught in a school on a housing estate at which 132 languages were spoken: she did not even know there were so many languages.

There was an expectation that life in a large city like London would be more challenging and, by association, more dangerous than living in New Zealand. A witness to the 2005 bombings in London wrote (in a New Zealand newspaper) about how it had affected her:

The bombings have not made me suddenly wish I was living back in South Canterbury,

JUDI moved into a London flat in 1980 only two days before a murder took place in the adjoining property. She remembered making a conscious decision not to write home about it immediately, in order not to upset her parents, but commented that, '[It was] nothing to do with us, really, but it was exciting – like being in a big city where it was all happening.' Vicki remembered seeing the aftermath of one of the Irish Republican Army (IRA) bombs in London in the 1980s, but did not consider herself to be in any particular danger: the positives of living in London overcame the shock of bombings. When Angela lived in London in the 1980s and 1990s she heard one IRA bomb explode and experienced countless instances of not being able to take the tube, or get to places because of bomb scares. Her usual reaction was one of annoyance at not being able to do what she wanted, when she wanted.

The spirit of London Christmas. Chris Slane

nor do I suddenly wish to move out of the city, or stop taking public transport. Mum and Dad will probably feel a lot happier when I have moved, but they realise that I live where my job takes me. If that means I am living in London, then terrorists will not stop me from making this my home and leading a normal life.[6]

Many other stories in New Zealand media echoed the same sentiments. After a second incident of attempted bombings in London in 2005, Joanna Davis interviewed several London-based New Zealanders and got similar responses: 'I always knew that, compared with New Zealand, London was a lot riskier' and 'London was a stressful city to live in anyway, and the bombings only added to that.'[7]

Most long-term expatriates in London argued that normal life there could be just as dangerous as these more dramatic events; over the years, numerous New Zealanders on OE have died or been injured in traffic accidents, workplace accidents, train crashes and the like. In 1999 two New Zealanders were killed in a Paddington rail crash; in 2001 a man died after a late-night fight in Finchley Road; in 2003 a New Zealander went missing from his London workplace (the 2011 inquest into his disappearance gave an accidental death verdict, surmising that he died from asphyxiation in an industrial accident); and in 2006 a New Zealander died after falling from a tree during a birthday picnic in a London park. In 2007 a woman was murdered when she disturbed a burglar at her London workplace; in 2009 another young New Zealander died after being hit by a bus in Shepherds Bush Road; a New Zealander's body was recovered from the River Thames in 2010; and in 2012 a woman was killed by a falling tree branch as she walked in Kew Gardens.

There was often a difference between expectations and the reality of the OE experience. On his OE in 2002, Neil expected to get involved with all sorts of people from all over the world; instead, he felt well outside his comfort zone during his first few months in London. On arrival he struggled to find a flat (he was in his fifties and many prospective flatmates saw him as a 'dirty old man'); he found himself teaching a really bad class (having deliberately looked for a teaching challenge); and he encountered terrible weather (having arrived in Britain in December). He quickly retreated into the protective custody of a group of other New Zealanders who were 'in the same boat', although he gradually relaxed, relying on this group support less and less. Eventually he found a flat with some older New Zealanders who were also in London on late-life OEs. Twenty years before Neil, in the early 1980s, Vicki found 'something special about the Kiwi community in London. It was a transition place – in another country, but we could still speak our own language.'

Some made a concerted attempt to broaden their horizons by living only with English people, although it was more

Speaking the language.
Chris Slane

common to 'have at least one [English person] in the flat'. After initial attempts to live with English people, others found that their lifestyle was too different and it was 'easier to flat with other Kiwis', as Janette found on her 1999 OE. The British tended to live less communally than New Zealanders: exemplified by each person having their own shelf in the fridge. Being able to 'relax' with other New Zealanders made stressful travel and work situations easier to deal with.

Bedding down

For many years, 'doing the Kiwi thing' meant living in Earls Court. It is common for immigrant groups to congregate together; in the 1960s and 1970s Earls Court attained legendary status as a 'home away from home' for Australians and New Zealanders in London. Its 'Kangaroo Valley' moniker persisted for several decades and is still mentioned in some guidebooks, although few of those on OE in the 2000s were conversant with it. Throughout the 1980s and 1990s, as Earls Court became more expensive, the colonial population moved further west to Shepherds Bush, Hammersmith, Acton and Ealing, areas that were more affordable, but still with good transport links. These areas also became home to an increasing number of travellers' pubs and travel agencies catering to the Australasian population. Acton supermarkets began stocking imported Australasian food items. By the 1990s Acton had become the new 'Kiwi London'. In 2004 an article in the *London Evening Standard* reported that Queens Park Rangers had won the right to stage the opening match of rugby league's Tri Nations tournament. The club – which was chosen because of the high population of Antipodeans in Shepherds Bush – stood to

Following the sheep to Shepherds Bush. Chris Slane

earn a five-figure sum for hosting Australia's game with New Zealand.[8]

According to the 1991 and 2001 UK censuses, the 10 most popular areas for New Zealand-born residents in the UK were in London (Figure 7.1). Six of the 10 most popular areas for Australia-born residents in 2001 coincided with those in the New Zealanders' top 10. New Zealand-born made up the fifth-largest group of immigrants in Acton and the fourth-largest group in both Hammersmith and Brondesbury in 2001. In Putney East, which featured only in the Australia-born top 10, the New Zealand-born population was the third-largest immigrant group recorded.[9]

According to *The Big OE Companion*, published in 2004, the most popular areas for New Zealanders were northwest London (taking in Willesden, Dollis Hill, Kilburn, Kensal Green, Queens Park, Neasden,

Figure 7.1 Ten most popular areas for New Zealand- and Australia-born populations in the UK.

	New Zealand-born Population in London				**Australia-born** Population in London	
	AREA	1991	2001	+/-%	AREA	2001
1	Acton	514	1045	103	Hyde Park	1583
2	Hammersmith	600	943	57	Hammersmith	1478
3	Brondesbury	391	786	101	Kensington	1427
4	Hyde Park	572	725	27	Fulham	1365
5	Cricklewood	255	714	180	Chelsea	1176
6	Fulham	365	697	91	Acton	1013
7	Poplar	94	691	635	Regents Park	962
8	Kilburn	478	609	27	Richmond N	920
9	Regents Park	391	575	47	Highgate	842
10	Richmond N	451	558	24	Putney E	830

Cricklewood and Finchley Road) and the west (taking in Hammersmith, Shepherds Bush, Acton and Ealing). For young professionals, slightly more upmarket areas included Camden, Angel and Islington in the northeast, and West Kensington, Barons Court, Fulham, Parsons Green, Putney and Wimbledon in the southwest.

In 2005 *TNT Magazine* surveyed almost 5400 of its London-based readers (aged between 18 and 35) about their lives in London: 24 per cent (1296) of those surveyed were New Zealanders. Figure 7.2 shows the eight most popular locations (by postcode) for the New Zealanders and Australians surveyed.[10] While the geographical boundaries used for the *TNT* and census data sets differed slightly, the areas identified were very similar. It is reasonable to assume that the *TNT* survey figures were more likely to be OE participants (because this is the target market of the magazine), while the census figures included many long-term expatriates as well as OE migrants.

Figure 7.2 Eight most popular areas for New Zealanders and Australians (2005).

	New Zealand-born		Australia-born	
	AREA	%	AREA	%
1	W3: Acton	8.2	SW6: Fulham	7.8
2	NW2: Cricklewood/ Neasdon	5.6	W3: Acton	5.9
3	SW11 & SW4: Clapham/ Battersea	5.0	SW11 & SW4: Clapham/ Battersea	5.7
4	W12: Shepherds Bush	4.7	NW2: Cricklewood/ Neasdon	4.6
5	SW6: Fulham	4.7	W12: Shepherds Bush	4.5
6	NW6: W Hampstead/ Kilburn/Queens Park	4.4	W6: Hammersmith	4.3
7	W6: Hammersmith	4.1	SW13 & SW15: Barnes/ Putney	4.2
8	SW19: Wimbledon	4.0	NW6: W Hampstead/ Kilburn/Queens Park	3.7

These figures and the 'where to live' advice given in guidebooks suggest that the New Zealand-London population has become more dispersed over time. The British census figures, for example, showed a more than 600 per cent increase in the number of New Zealand-born living in Poplar. The *TNT* survey findings suggested that although Acton has remained a popular area, the increasing popularity of the Clapham–Battersea areas (for both New Zealanders and Australians) signified a move away from the more traditional west London areas, such as Shepherds Bush. The shift towards more expensive areas such as Fulham, Bayswater and Paddington indicated that living standards were also increasing. However, the propensity of newly arrived New Zealanders to stay with those already resident ensured the continuing popularity of some parts of London.

London is an expensive city. Many of those going on OE relied on friends or family members already there to accommodate them when they first arrived. The definition of a 'friend', or even 'family', was often loose: a 'friend' could be an acquaintance or a

Distant acquaintances.
Jonathan Drapes

friend of a friend, while 'family' could be distant and previously unknown relatives. In his 1986 political thriller based on New Zealanders on their OEs, Keith Ovenden caught this well in the observations of one of his characters, Tom:

Tom moved into this cramped little flat at the end of August. New Zealanders began arriving to stay with him a few days later. He had no real idea how this happened since he had not then even had time to send his new address to his mother, and there was no prospect of his name appearing in the London telephone directory until long after he would have left. Somehow his whereabouts just seemed to spread, like gossip. The unwritten New Zealand code of spontaneous hospitality-taking stretches from the Maniototo to the northern fiords of Norway, but it is at its most ruthless in the great cities of western Europe.[11]

As noted in Chapter Four, many OE jokes describe new arrivals from New Zealand knocking on London doors looking for their 'cousin's ex-boyfriend's sister', and so on. This became a popular scene in OE films. In 1996 Jonathan Brough's short film *Permanent Wave* (based around a party in London), began and ended with such a doorstep scenario. Several films shown at the 2003 UpOverDownUnder Film Festival featured a continual stream of New Zealanders and Australians arriving on the doorsteps of London flats looking for somewhere to stay. Some arrived in London expecting to be treated as heroes (having got themselves to London) and were shocked to find they were just another arrival from New Zealand.

With growing numbers of OE travellers, the chance of knowing people already in London increased. London flats became more homogeneous; by the 1990s it was increasingly common to find flats full of teachers from Christchurch or Invercargill, accountants from Wellington, and so on. There was a 'Gore flat' in Neasden, which at any one time in the 2000s housed at least one person, but usually up to four or five people, from Gore. In contrast, flats in the 1970s and 1980s were likely to be occupied by New Zealanders and Australians who were previously strangers. For some, the opportunity this (and the OE in general) afforded them to meet people from other parts of Australasia was one of the highlights of their OE.

The predilection to live (and socialise) with other New Zealanders became known as 'doing the Kiwi thing'. It involved living in shared flats, usually with many more people resident than would be tolerated at home. The Gore flat mentioned above, for example, housed seven people in a semi-detached house with three double and one single bedroom, one bathroom and toilet, and a small kitchen and living room. In some ways it closely resembled student life back in New Zealand; many of the jokes used by Haydn Butler in his short film *Fresh* (about a New Zealander arriving in London looking for somewhere to stay) were student jokes transposed to London.[12]

Whatever the location, a common feature of many London flats was the 'dosser'. In common British usage, 'dosser' is a slang term used to describe a street person or a tramp: in the OE vernacular, a 'dosser' is someone staying temporarily in a London flat. Dossing was an officially recognised

The number of dosser spaces available was often oversubscribed, as Jonathan Drapes' 2006 Andy Podean cartoon shows; the second cartoon depicts the progression up the flat hierarchy.
Jonathan Drapes

position in many London flats and has been a feature of the OE for decades. In 1975, for example, Andrea flatted with 'loads of Kiwis and we would charge a pound a night for anyone who wanted to just doss down to help pay the rent and the gas meter'. Many OE travellers began their London life as dossers, before moving up in status. In 1994 Pete spent his first six weeks sleeping on his friend's floor, paying a portion of the rent, before moving into a bedroom that was too small to fit a double bed in. He lived in that room for a year. The high cost of accommodation in London meant that most flats charged dossing rates regardless of how close, or previously well known, visitors were. Even visiting parents were sometimes charged for accommodation.

Many flats offered both regular rented rooms and dosser 'spots': in a *TNT* article about life in London one expatriate described the flat she was living in as having 'six official housemates and two dossers'. In *TNT* and on the Gumtree website permanent dosser areas were advertised alongside rooms to rent. In 2005 one Gumtree advertisement offered 'a bed on the top floor landing of our place available for dossers'; another advertised a room for rent in a flat described as having 'two decent sized living areas (one is currently taken up with the pool table and the dossing quarters, though our dosser is leaving next Wednesday)'. Dossing was a good option for those who needed only temporary accommodation and was much cheaper than renting a room. The price of dossing fell in real terms, from the 1970s 'pound a night' remembered by Andrea (a 1975 pound was worth £8.45 in 2004 in terms of average earnings).[15] In 2004 Brydie's flat only charged their dossers (mattress provided) £25 per week, but they also had to buy the flat's bread and milk.

Despite the enduring dosser culture, the living standards of those on OE gradually improved over time. In 2005 the advertisements on Gumtree were for flats with 'Sky TV, nice little back yards and pool tables'. In 2008 rooms were available in houses with fitted kitchens, full appliances (dishwasher, washing machine, dryer),

DOSSING became a more formal arrangement over time. The 1st Contact *Big OE Guide* explained the 'rules' of dossing in 2003:

Dossing *– if you are staying with a friend or sleeping on their couch you will be known as a dosser. You will have to be very flexible as your bedroom is also the tv room, dining room and party room. Dossers have no rights in the flat and they usually pay around £5 per night. Make sure you do your bit to help out and try not to outstay your welcome.*[13]

In a letter to *TNT Magazine* in 2004 the writer complained about dossers 'overstaying' their time, and suggested that a possible solution for this problem would be to increase the dossing rates. Among the raft of responses penned in subsequent weeks was the following:

To the complete prat who wrote in moaning about dossers. I've lived in London for ten years and putting dossing rates up won't solve your problem. Most houses have dossing time limits to stop people taking advantage and to allow other people to join the house … Perhaps you could tell your dossers that their time is up … Remember the staple rule of dossing is that dossers have no rights.[14]

Top: Life in a dungeon, 1980s. Chris Slane

Bottom: Many of those on OE saved money by socialising at home; the barbecues are fired up over the summer months in back yards all over London. Chris Slane

central heating, power showers, free wifi and free satellite TV: a far cry from the cold, cramped and basic housing standards experienced by many New Zealanders in London in the 1960s, 1970s and 1980s. In a 2005 'room wanted' advertisement a New Zealand teacher was keen to find a flat where she could 'have fun and hang out with flatties at home', but wanted no drugs or 'crazy student-type parties'. Having seen many houses in London, she was also 'not into living in dumps or underground dugouts'. In 2008 most listings offered some outdoor living areas: 'big back garden', 'paved back yard', 'courtyard for summer BBQs', and 'large grassed back yard'.

Kiwi culture

Many OE travellers in London socialised with their compatriots as well as living with them. The number of New Zealand social and cultural clubs expanded in the 1980s, with the foundation of the Matariki Māori Cultural Group (1984) and London Connections (1985), a business and social networking forum for New Zealanders. In 1997 Ngati Ranana set up Te Kohanga Reo o Ranana to educate expatriate Māori children in te reo and tikanga. Other cultural clubs and groups in London include Manaia (2004), a company providing professional Māori performing arts services and Māori cultural knowledge, and Maramara Tōtara (2003), the London branch of Te Whare Tu Taua o Aotearoa (the National School of Ancient Weaponry of New Zealand). Since 2004 Maramara Tōtara has held an annual kapa haka competition in London; the 2012 event was hosted in the penthouse suite of New Zealand House. These social clubs spread beyond London, with the establishment of the New Zealand Ireland Association in 1987 and the New Zealand Society Scotland in 1998.

Each year organised events have been held to commemorate New Zealand holidays and special occasions; many have become annual fixtures as part of a New Zealand London 'calendar'. *TNT Magazine* hosted an annual Anzac Ball in London from 1988; in 2012 the renamed Anzac Gallipoli Legacy Ball was held at Australia House.[16] The New Zealand Society holds a formal Waitangi Day Dinner each year, along with wine tastings and other social events. Performances by members of the London Māori clubs are longstanding; an annual Toast Life festival, celebrating New Zealand wine, food and culture, began in 2000; an annual UpOverDownUnder Film Festival (showcasing films by young London-based New Zealand, Australia and South African filmmakers) ran for a number of years in the 2000s; and in 2004 the weekly comedy show entitled *Four Kiwis Walk into a Bar* was launched.

New Zealand culture was also celebrated with performances by visiting New Zealand musicians and artists over the decades of the

Mobile barbecue, 2000s.

OFTEN OE travellers made more effort to see New Zealand musicians in London than they did in New Zealand. In the early 2000s Ruth saw Anika Moa, Dave Dobbyn, The Feelers and Stellar* perform in London. Playing to the OE population presented special challenges for these New Zealand musicians: at the concert Ruth went to, Stellar* played their new album and she noticed that people who had been in London for more than two years didn't know the songs and got a bit restless.

New Zealand in concert.

OE. In the 1960s New Zealanders in London were entertained by Prince Tui Teka, the Maori Volcanics, John Rowles and Human Instinct. In the 1970s Frankie Stevens, Shona Laing, and Max Merritt and the Meteors all performed in London. Split Enz played at the Apollo Victoria in the early 1980s and the Mutton Birds played London in the 1990s. In the 2000s countless New Zealand artists performed in London, including Nathan Haines, the Finn Brothers, Shihad, Salmonella Dub, Fat Freddy's Drop, the Black Seeds, Bic Runga, Breaks Co-op, Katchafire and the Datsuns. Flight of the Conchords were regular performers at *Four Kiwis Walk into a Bar*, and Dave Dobbyn and Hayley Westenra performed at the 2006 Toast Festival.

Periodically, OE life also featured in film and theatre. In August 1981 the play *Leaving Home* by Barbara Ewing was performed at New Zealand House in London before going to Edinburgh Festival Fringe. It explored the reasons why New Zealanders left home and their thoughts about New Zealand while away. The London performance of the play generated a month's worth of readers' responses in *New Zealand News UK*. In 2003 Melanie Tait's *The Vegemite Tales* (a comedy about expatriate life in London) was performed at the Edinburgh Fringe and went on to debut in London's West End in 2006. Jonathan Brough's (1996) short film *Permanent Wave* took a satirical look at a group of New Zealanders at a London party in 1983. Life overseas was the predominant theme of the UpOverDownUnder Film Festival.

Travellers' pubs

A social life based around 'the pub' was an integral part of London life. During the 1990s a number of travellers' pubs that catered specifically to expatriate Antipodeans emerged. The names of some of these bars – the Walkabout, the Redback and the Captain Cook – clearly link them to their Australian and New Zealand patrons.

Although described as 'legends' in many OE guides, the Redback and the first pub in the Walkabout chain were established only in 1993 and 1994, respectively.

In the 1980s the various travel clubs offering accommodation also had their own bars where they held 'new arrivals' nights and other social events. In 1983 *New Zealand News UK* reported on an Anzac weekend seven-a-side rugby tournament that was followed by a hangi and barbecue: the tournament was won by the Maori Wanderers–Golden Lion team; the Duke of Buckingham team was second. In the 1980s and 1990s the Polar Bear in Soho was popular with Antipodeans, but the most enduring of the 'informal' Australasian pubs was the Prince of Teck in Earls Court, a popular pub since the Kangaroo Valley days of the 1960s and 1970s. In 2005 the London Fancyapint website still listed it as a pub in which one's 'Antipodean cousins' might be found and described it as: 'A haunt of Antipodeans when Walkabouts were still on the design board. It's the big screen and the Aussie social club atmosphere that pulls in the punters though.'[17] In 2012 the website noted that the pub was 'no longer solely the province of Antipodeans' and asked 'where have they all gone?' Many travellers' pubs were established in the west London areas of Acton and Shepherds Bush that were becoming home to expatriate Australasians.

The decor of the Redback beer garden reinforced its 'Australasian' character. This flavour of home was completed with a free barbecue, popular with their ('more parsimonious') New Zealand clientele on Sunday afternoons.
Below: These pubs were preceded by less formally designated, but strongly Antipodean-focused pubs.
Chris Slane

A GOOD NUMBER of mainstream London pubs had New Zealand owners and managers. Brian, for example, had the Red Lion at Waterloo for 16 years; while most of the pub's clientele were British Londoners it also had a reputation as a Kiwi pub, simply because he was a New Zealander. Sophie worked there in the late 1990s and remembered Brian flying the All Black flag from the roof at half-mast if they lost a game. In 2000 Jackie and her boyfriend worked for a New Zealand manager in a Wimbledon pub. She described it as 'a Kiwi-focused one – not like the Walkabout, but we had Kiwi wines and sold food like New Zealand-style burgers and Steinlager.'

Patronage of these travellers' pubs varied considerably: there were those who went every week; others shunned them completely, although it was common to go at least once, to 'see what it was like' (if only to reinforce one's negative preconceptions). For others, these pubs were important at the start of their OEs, becoming less important as they became more settled in London. Tara and James enjoyed living in Acton in 2003, with 'the Redback pub about 400 yards away … when we first got here it was pretty good because there was a free barbecue on a Sunday and £1 New Zealand beers, and it was a similar atmosphere to New Zealand pubs … but we only go down there about once a month or so now.'

The pubs themselves were firmly anchored in the Australasian expatriate community as venues for watching television broadcasts of rugby games from the Southern Hemisphere, such as the Super 12(14) or Tri Nations competitions, or of other major sporting events involving New Zealand teams. The pubs secured the continuing patronage of New Zealanders and Australians with specials nights offering cheap New Zealand and Australian beer, by hosting special events celebrating New Zealand and Australian holidays, and by providing popular venues for New Zealand musicians and bands. As well, they hosted numerous post-tour parties and reunions held by London travel companies. In the mid-1990s pre-tour parties were common: *TNT Magazine* carried advertisements for a Pamplona warm-up party, a pre-Europe Combi party, a van tour leaving party and a pre-Europe beach party.

Although originally catering to the Australasian market, the pubs began to attract increasing numbers of British patrons; however, the Shepherds Bush Walkabout remained more Australian than other pubs in the Walkabout's British-wide chain,[18] hosting many expatriate events and advertising widely in expatriate publications. One of the owners of the Redback in 2004 explained some of these changes:

It was very Australian and New Zealand initially, every night of the week. Now Sunday is the real day when it is very Aussie and Kiwi – Friday and Saturday are lots of English people. You get a bar that is very busy and has a good reputation – people tell their friends about it – they tell their English colleagues – it is a real party pub. You get this English component coming in and then it sort of loses the Aussie/Kiwi feel that is the reason they all go there in the first place.

These pubs also became tourist attractions for other tourists in London. The independent website Itchy Guide described the Redback and the Shepherds Bush Walkabout:

Redback: The red-painted den of iniquity hides away in murky Acton. No dress code, no funny door policy, no posing, no looking cool, no sitting around the side of the bar. But you can be certain of huge queues, ridiculous tribute bands – Clouded House anyone? – and that the Antipodean crowd is completely up for a raging night out. Brilliant and shocking in equal measures.

Shepherds Bush Walkabout: Aussie tucker, booze aplenty and intensive live sport action. Yes, it is a theme pub. Yes, you'd have to be drunk and desperate to even consider going here. But at 1am when you're gagging for a pint – who's arguing?[19]

Some other Australasian-focused events were held at clubs, pubs and other venues around London. In 1994 *TNT Magazine* carried advertisements for a weekly Wednesday 'Backpackers Night' at the Kings Head Pub in Earls Court, and for 'The Sunday Session' of the Ultimate Australasian Club ('Poms welcome'), an event to be held at the Shepherds Bush Empire. In 2004 advertisements in *TNT Magazine* included a new Antipodean promotion for a Sunday indoor swimming and pool party at Old Street; the Puzzle chain (with pubs in Fulham, Acton and Earlsfield) offering '2-4-1 Speights' on Mondays; the Slug at Fulham advertising Tri Nations rugby, Antipodean DJs and 'Antipodean speed-dating'; and the four Elusive Camel pubs were showing the Tri Nations and offering cheap drinks.

The Church

One of the longest-standing Antipodean social events and one of the most (in)famous symbols of Antipodean London was, without doubt, The Church:

This is like no other place you've ever seen. If you've come to London to party hard this is a place to get going on a Sunday afternoon … Don't expect traditional pub decor, the management of The Church believe in interior decoration with alcohol – that is, the more you drink the better it looks. Typical church decor consists of knee-deep beer cans complemented by pallets of beer next to the bar. Nothing will prepare you for The Church experience.[20]

Named because the peal of bells from a nearby church coincided with its Sunday lunchtime session, The Church began in 1979 at the Golden Lion pub in Fulham Broadway. The pub was owned by an English-New Zealand couple. Initially it attracted the patronage of a group of New Zealanders and Australians who happened to live nearby; by the time the owners sold the premises several years later the session had become well established within the wider Australasian community. According to The Church website, it became 'an institution among fun-loving Antipodeans, providing a haven for its disciples who were wanting to have fun and get pissed in a country far removed from the sun-drenched shores of home'.[21]

For a decade The Church moved from pub to pub around west London – the Greyhound Pub in Fulham Road, the Fox in West Kensington, and the White Hart in Willesden – before relocating to a more central London venue. The original owners

Entry card, 2000s. The Church

THE 'DISCIPLES' at The Church varied: sometimes 'freshies' turned up with their backpacks on, having arrived in London only that day; some went only once – often at the end of their OE (and often just to buy their 'been-there done-that' T-shirt). Janette recalled going to The Church in 1999 'just twice. My brother had told me about it from when he'd been eight years earlier and I thought "I've got to go, because he went there."' Many were Church regulars, often embarrassed to admit how many times they went.

of the Golden Lion continued to host the party. Eventually, larger premises were required and in 1990 The Church spent a year at Busby's in Tottenham Court Road before moving (this time for less than a year) to the Dome in Tufnell Park. The next move was to Bagleys Nightclub in Kings Cross, where it remained until early 2004, when it moved to the Forum in Kentish Town. Free transport was provided from the old premises at Kings Cross to Kentish Town for the first three months. In 2010 The Church moved to the Clapham Grand in St John's Hill. The Church has been a family business for over 30 years and in 2012 was still owned by the original founder's wife and two daughters.

Despite the relaxation of British licensing laws in 1990 (to allow all-day opening on Sundays), The Church still operated only from noon until 3.30 pm each Sunday; according to one of the owners, 'The format has not changed in any form since I can remember – the idea is "if it is not broken don't fix it" – there is a bit of music, a bit of comedy, a stripper, a special act which might be a male stripper, then some games and some more music.' The 'games' consist of drinking contests between 'representative' teams of participating countries: Australia, New Zealand and South Africa prevail. The religious theme continues with an 'order of service' and the security team are known as Church Wardens.

Go to The Church, buy the T-shirt.

The Church regularly attracted 2000 revellers, an impressive statistic for an event that was rarely advertised. Traditionally, bank holiday weekends (offering an extra day to recover) and pay days were especially busy, as were sessions that celebrated special events. The Church became popular with both the British and with tourists of other nationalities, similar to the travellers' pubs. Some people perceived this to be a threat to The Church's 'colonial' cultural flavour. The Church owners, however, were of the opinion that with growing numbers of Aussies and Kiwis in London 'you don't feel as isolated, or away from home, in quite the same way as you did 20 years ago – so they don't need us so much now anyway'.

Despite some cultural dilution, The Church is still seen as an Aussie–Kiwi venue, its Australasian 'flavour' enhanced and reinforced (again, similar to the Redback) by the sale of imported Australian and New Zealand beers and hamburgers served 'New Zealand-style' (with beetroot). Also, despite the fact that the owners were themselves English, they recognised the importance of staffing The Church with 'colonials' who understood the crowds and could talk to them. Many of the staff had worked there for a long time by OE standards; four of the 2004 staff had been 'Church Wardens' for more than five years.

Most OE travellers in the 1990s and 2000s had heard of The Church, even if they had not personally been to a session. Mention of The Church provoked strong reactions from many people; in relation to 'Kiwi London', it was almost universally regarded as the epitome of 'ghastly', although that did not always stop people from going for at least one look. Peter Moore, the Australian author of *The Wrong Way Home*, visited The Church the day before he left Britain to travel home overland in 1994 and describes the mayhem well, right down to a drunk girl throwing up on his shoe.[22]

In the 2000s many visiting parents were introduced to The Church, although a *TNT Magazine* article in 2006 included it in a list of 'five things NOT to do with your parents if they visit you in London': 'No matter how appealing this sounds to mum, drinking from a plastic bag of bottles tied to her waist won't.'[23] However, those parents who did get taken along are reported to have 'had a ball'. There was also a second generation of Church-goers coming through: the mother of one of the The Church staff in 2004 used to go there in the early 1980s.

'Getting your Kiwi fix'

A chapter in *The Big OE Companion* entitled 'Getting your Kiwi fix' outlined the many ways in which OE travellers could connect with and celebrate home. Waitangi Day and Anzac Day were the pre-eminent New Zealand events. 'ANZAC Day starts off fittingly sombre in the UK, with dawn and lunchtime services in many towns and cities, and ends in a mess of high-spirited young New Zealanders and Australians in the Antipodean pubs.'[24]

Waitangi Day

The two best-known London Waitangi Day events were the New Zealand Society Waitangi Day Dinner and the Circle Line Pub Crawl. While the former generally catered for older, long-term expatriates, some OE travellers attended: in fact, the New Zealand Society was attracting younger members during the 2000s. The pub crawl – starting on the Circle Line at Paddington Station, and then moving clockwise with a drink stop at the nearest pub to each station (which represented a New Zealand city or town) – was 100 per cent patronised by OE travellers.

In 2004 *New Zealand News UK* covered both Waitangi Day events with a multi-page pictorial report. At the New Zealand

Australasians also celebrated each other's national days.

Jonathan Drapes

Top: Kiwiana on display in London at the Waitangi Day pub crawl.

Clint Heine

Above: The haka: the highlight of the day.

Scottie T Photography

Society dinner, people gathered 'amid a sea of sequins, diamantes, and bow ties' at the prestigious Dorchester Hotel for an event showcasing New Zealand wine and food. Prince Edward was welcomed with a 'somewhat spine-tingling Maori haka'.[25] In contrast, the pub crawl (noted as the best way to really appreciate how many New Zealanders are in Britain) involved 'thousands of people wearing all forms of Kiwiana – Tui/Speights/DB Shirts, All Black jerseys, beige cricket outfits, inflatable sheep, provincial rugby jerseys, and even a New Zealand police officer's uniform, in fact anything that had a connection with their place of birth'. Painted faces and New Zealand flags were popular and 'those who couldn't find anything symbolic wore the next best thing – black'.[26]

The Waitangi Day pub crawl was usually held on the Saturday closest to Waitangi Day. According to a *TNT* article, its origins are debated: 'This might all be urban legend but definitely at some point, maybe as early as 1983, someone started doing a haka at Westminster.'[27] The same article reported that T-shirts commemorating the crawl first appeared in 1997. Richard experienced the crawl when he first arrived in London in 2001:

It was February the 6th when we got to London because the next day was the Waitangi Day pub crawl. It was weird because I bumped into two people I hadn't seen since graduation. There were thousands doing the Circle Line – it was just a blackout. Everywhere there were All Black jerseys and at Westminster we went out at five o'clock and stopped the traffic for a good 10 minutes doing the haka – it was pretty awesome.

In 2005 engineering works on the Circle Line meant that it would not be open on the designated day. Alternative options were advertised by two different event organisers, and for a short time it appeared that there could be competing events. Eventually the confusion was sorted, and it was announced that the event would go ahead one week early (on 29 January), continuing the tradition of using the Circle Line. The *New Zealand News UK* article reporting the event details stressed that: 'Both organisers have reminded those taking part that they will be representing their country and therefore to behave in a responsible manner to ensure the event continues for years to come.'[28]

In 2006 the Readers' Letters in *TNT Magazine* included a Waitangi Day message from the New Zealand High Commissioner, asking that the 'tens of thousands of New Zealanders in the United Kingdom and Ireland will spare a moment on Waitangi Day to reflect upon their heritage and to continue proudly representing our country while living, working and travelling overseas.'[29] In contrast, an advertisement on Gumtree instructed New Zealanders in London to 'Giddy up and sort yourselves out. Break out those sheep costumes, DUST OFF YOUR WORDS TO TU TERA MAI NA IWI, TEN GUITARS and KIWI UP!' [sic]. The author of this advertisement noted the disruption caused by the event, and commented, 'How we get away with it every year is a mystery.'

The crawl attracts large crowds of both participants and spectators. An estimated crowd of 4000 watched the Waitangi Day pub crawl in Parliament Square in 2005. Good weather in 2008 saw the numbers on the crawl peak at about 12,000, bringing parts of London to a standstill: there were road closures around Westminster and the Circle Line had trouble coping with the volumes of people. Numbers have dropped slightly in the years since, to 8000–9000 in 2009, 7000 in 2010 and 6000 in 2012. Clint Heine, the unofficial organiser, meets with the Metropolitan Police before the event each year to discuss potential problems: one issue is a street drinking ban for the Borough of Westminster, which is the location of the final hour/s of the event (including the haka). According to Clint, the rules are slightly bent for the crawl, as long as people don't bring glass into the area. Also, the police exercise leniency on the day, as long as the crowds behave.

Given its controversial history in New Zealand, it was an unusual experience for many to celebrate Waitangi Day (beyond its obvious value as a public holiday), as the following letter to the editor of *TNT Magazine* in 2004 illustrated:

I didn't really want to go on the Circle Line pub crawl. To me, Waitangi Day is all about protests and people trying to make the headlines. But my housemates dragged me out and for that I am truly grateful because it showed me Kiwis can come together to celebrate their special way of life … Sure, alcohol helped lubricate the socialness of the occasion but everyone was in high spirits and keen to show the world that they were Kiwi. It truly made me proud to be a Kiwi.[30]

In *The Big OE Companion*, Bronwyn Sell also noted that the Antipodean pubs celebrated Waitangi Day and that 'Kiwi bands and singers will often cash in on the nationalistic fervour by timing a tour to coincide with Waitangi Day'. She quoted from a *New Zealand News UK* interview with Dave Dobbyn, after his performance at a Waitangi Day concert in Brixton: 'Everyone was so homesick, they loved everything we did. There were some magic moments there. I got all glassy-eyed when the local iwi gave it heaps at the start. When you see that kind of patriotism offshore it kind of moves you to understand your New Zealandness on another level.'[31]

Taste of New Zealand

During the six decades of OE travel, New Zealand food and cuisine gained international attention and from the 1980s and 1990s offered travellers a point of cultural distinction. New Zealand-style food, beer and wine were provided at many sporting and social events and were also on the menus of the travellers' pubs. The Toast Life Festival showcased New Zealand food and drink for a number of years. The festival usually attracted 6000–10,000 people, depending on venue capacity. Most years about 2000 tickets were sold in the first week alone. The 2009 festival, held at Clapham Common, featured former international rugby player Zinzan Brooke (offering tips to wannabe stars), the Beige Brigade (giving visitors the chance to test their batting skills), and performances by Ngati Ranana, Dave Dobbyn and singer songwriter Jason Norris. According to the pre-festival press release, the barbecues would be loaded with New Zealand lamb burgers and piles of fresh green-lip mussels, with pavlova and hokey-pokey ice cream to follow. Over 100 varieties of New Zealand wines were also available.

A group of expatriate Kiwis started a new annual event, Homelanz, in 2011, after the demise of Toast. Their goal was to 'have a community day to celebrate good food, wine/beer and music – pretty much backyard BBQ, hence our phrase "your place and mine" and meet up with old friends and hopefully make some new ones!' In 2013 its official media partners included *TNT Magazine,* the New Zealand Society and a new online Kiwi community group (www.facebook.com/LondonKiwis). Blue King Brown, Desmond and the Tutus, Glenn Aitken and Ngati Ranana performed. Food offerings included gourmet pies and pavlova.

A number of London restaurants have showcased New Zealand food. Suze in Mayfair, owned by New Zealanders Tom and Susan Glynn, has been a London Australasian fixture since the late 1980s. World-renowned New Zealand chef Peter Gordon made his reputation at the London restaurant The Sugar Club (based on the Wellington restaurant of the same name). In 2001 he opened The Providores and Tapa Room, offering a blend of New Zealand casual dining and an upmarket British restaurant. Among the incongruous choices on the breakfast and brunch menu at the Tapa Room in 2009 were 'soft-boiled eggs with Vegemite soldiers' and 'paprika roast potato, caramelised onion, feta and edamame tortilla with tomato and piquillo pepper salsa, Greek yoghurt and rocket'.

Peter Gordon also had input into the burgers offered by the Gourmet Burger Kitchen (GBK) chain. Started in 2001 by a trio of New Zealanders with a single restaurant in Battersea, there were five GBK branches scattered around London by 2004. By 2009 there were 29 GBKs in Greater London, and another 20 in other parts of Britain; by 2012 54 GBK branches were operating in Britain. Another New Zealand-inspired restaurant – the Kiwi Kitchen – opened in Ealing in 2004. HELL Pizza opened its first London branch in 2007, and in 2010 four Wellingtonians opened Caravan in Exmouth Market.

For many Australasians, the most important thing missing in London was a decent cup of coffee. In 2005 an Australian (with the help of two New Zealanders) opened Flat White in Soho. This award-winning coffee bar not only sold flat whites (unheard of in London), but also featured Antipodean treats such as Anzac biscuits, ginger crunch and afghans. Physically setting up the café was made easier by employing Kiwi Constructions, a company that employed only New Zealanders and Australians; when it came time to source coffee, they chose Monmouth Coffee, a Covent Garden company that employed several New Zealanders. A sister café, Milkbar, was opened in 2008. Flat White heralded the advent of Antipodean coffee culture in London; by 2012 Nude Espresso, Ozone and the Roastery were also offering Kiwi coffee culture.

Sporting London

Sport – whether watched, played or celebrated – contributed greatly to OE life, with rugby, the All Blacks and the haka taking centre stage. Some people were avid rugby fans and players, and followed rugby just as they had at home in New Zealand. Clubs all over London, Britain and Europe have New Zealanders playing in their ranks:

Tickets to rugby games were distributed by New Zealand House to New Zealand passport-holders and were also available as travel 'packages' through many of the Antipodean travel agencies in London.

New Zealand News UK, Scottie T Photography (below)

MANY wore rugby clothing or New Zealand team shirts, some noting that it made them feel patriotic for the first time. Ben recalled that he 'became pretty patriotic, no flag on the backpack, but I had an All Black shirt and my league top' on his OE in the late 1990s. Some travellers found themselves going to a rugby game for the first time in their lives. Recalling her OE in the late 1970s, Barbara commented, 'In New Zealand I would be bored stiff to go to one, but over there if it was a game involving a Kiwi team you would be there.' In 1982 Donal went to Cardiff to see New Zealand Maori play Wales, which he would never have done in New Zealand, but he had been working in Europe for a few months and liked the idea of being with a bunch of other New Zealanders.

Simon found that as a Kiwi he was expected to play rugby on his OE in 2000. All Black games were an important part of the OE travel and social calendar; some, like seeing the All Blacks play at Twickenham or Cardiff Arms Park, were imbued with more cachet than others.

For those wishing to play sport, there were many choices from a long list of New Zealand sports clubs in London. Throughout the 1980s, 1990s and 2000s the London New Zealand Rugby Football Club (established in 1926) entered teams in London rugby competition leagues and played in invitation Sevens tournaments. The club colours for competition games were black jerseys, shorts and socks; as Bronwyn Sell noted in *The Big OE Companion*: 'Here's your chance to wear the silver fern: the London New Zealand club is said to be the only team permitted to wear the fern aside from New Zealand national sides.'[32] They also contested the 'Battle of the Aotearoa Challenge Shield', an annual fixture played against an invitation Maori Wanderers team.

The Maori Wanderers – started in 1980 by 'three Maori boys who were working in London' – played in a Sunday league, formed to allow those who worked on Saturdays to play rugby. The Wanderers never train and have two rules – no kicking is allowed (during the game) and if a player scores three tries they must shout the bar afterwards. For the challenge match noted above, they try to get a New Zealand referee who will allow the game to flow for both spectators' and players' benefit. Initially the team was based at the Battersea Ironsides Rugby Club in southwest London, but they have made their headquarters at a variety of clubs during the years since. Players do not have to be Māori, or even from New Zealand (although most are). Bruce Matheson (the New Zealander who 'organised' the team from 1992 to 2000) recalled many 'anxious Sundays spent outside Acton Town tube waiting for our "team" to turn up from all over London. Any known flat nearby was raided and anyone able to play rugby was dragged out.' The team had a bag full of spare boots in all sizes and someone always had a spare pair of shorts and socks. He estimated that more than 800 people had played for the Wanderers in the years he was in charge.

The club also went 'on tour' (along with wives, girlfriends and supporters) and, over the years, played matches in a variety of European destinations, as well as in the

United States. For their 1994 US tour the team fundraised by cooking hangi in a pit at a west London pub called the Lord Nelson. The pub was owned by a New Zealander and they delivered food by the van-load to other New Zealand pubs on occasions like Anzac Day and Waitangi Day. Evidence of broader changes in the OE can also be seen through changes in the club: in 1983 the team was sponsored by the Golden Lion, the west London pub where The Church started; in 2006 it was sponsored by London 1st, an accounting services company.

Over the years *TNT Magazine* and other businesses involved with the expatriate Australasian community hosted Sevens tournaments and other sporting events. These games became more regular and more formal with the establishment, in the early 1990s, of dedicated New Zealand, Australian and South African sports leagues for touch rugby and netball. To suit those who were in London for only a few years – and who wanted to be out doing things at weekends – competitions were held on regular week nights (unlike traditional sporting competition models with mid-week training and weekend games). The number of these sports leagues increased from the late 1990s, although much of the change resulted from a rearrangement of existing structures, organisers and sponsorship. From the 2000s the range of sports on offer increased. In the mid-2000s the touch and netball leagues operating included Commonwealth Netball UK (CNUK), in2touch, Social Sports, London Touch Rugby and the West London Sports Club. In 2004 there was a SANZA soccer league. Since 2000 the ANZSAC Basketball Association (ABA) has run weekly competitions, although access to indoor facilities is limited in London. The Last Man Stands Cricket Competition – a laidback version of the game – has been held since 2005: in 2008, 170 teams played in the London league. For those wishing to play the more traditional form of the game, the London New Zealand Cricket Club (established in 1951) was still around.

These sports leagues attracted sponsorship from businesses involved with the Antipodean community. London Touch Rugby and Netball have been running since the early 1990s with the support of, among others, First Festival Travel, On the Go Tours, TNT, Anglo Pacific World Movers and the Redback Tavern. The competition on Tuesday and Wednesday evenings is held at a sportsground in Acton and play is followed by drinks and a barbecue with their 'Famous burgers! – beetroot, pineapple and cheese'.[33]

Most of the leagues ran year round, although the spring and autumn seasons were the busiest as the lack of indoor facilities made winter sport more difficult; summer was traditionally quiet because many people were away travelling. The operators of CNUK, however, found their summer season was increasing in popularity in the mid-2000s. Started by an Australian couple in 2002, CNUK was run as a business with four full-time people employed to

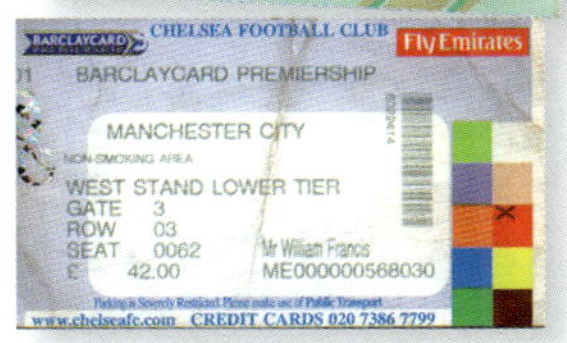

New Zealand cricket tests and sporting events such as Wimbledon were always popular; by the 2000s attendance at a least one Premier League football game became *de rigueur*.

A New Zealand team at a One Netball UK sports day. One Netball UK

organise the competitions and secure sponsorship. At the 2004 CNUK Netball World Cup, an all-day competition that brought all the players together, the origins of the teams playing were clearly identifiable by their national colours. The ubiquitous barbecue provided New Zealand-style burgers; other stalls sold New Zealand and Australian products. In 2008 Social Sports and CNUK merged to form One Netball UK.

In *The Big OE Companion*, Bronwyn Sell suggested travellers join one of these sports leagues as a way to 'avoid the Heathrow injection'. This descriptive phrase was commonly used to describe the tendency for New Zealanders to gain weight on their OE (primarily because of a more sedentary lifestyle and increased beer-drinking. The leagues were also a good way to meet people and organisers often saw themselves as providing more than just the opportunity to play sport. CNUK, for example, had a lot of individuals registered: the organisers made an effort to match players on a combination of ability, where they were from, where they lived in London, and so on.

The sports leagues hold their award ceremonies and parties in the travellers' pubs; in the mid-2000s *In London* organised an annual awards ceremony for all the leagues. The ceremony imitated the annual sports awards held in New Zealand, and the outstanding (London) sportspeople of the year were recognised. This institutionalisation of sports in London was also a formal acknowledgment of the strength of the London expatriate community. There were signs that this community had progressed well beyond the poor backpacker image: in 2004 the sports awards was a black tie event.

Playing up

Taken together, these depictions of New Zealand culture in London paint a somewhat stereotypical picture of London life, which – even if they went out of their way to avoid it – was recognised by most of those on OE. It was described perfectly by the New Zealand film maker Haydn Butler, whose short film *Fresh* won both the top prize and audience award at the UpOverDownUnder Film Festival in 2003. As he explained, the film 'was the whole [Aussie-themed booze barns] Redback, Walkabout thing; shagging everybody, coming home trashed as, sleeping on the floor, sleeping in the cupboard'. According to the festival organiser, *Fresh* stormed the field because 'it was so recognisable to the cinema full of Antipodeans'.[34]

The social aspects of this stereotypical New Zealand lifestyle in London were not always seen in a positive light. Many accounts suggest that expatriate behaviour degenerated over time, but given generational changes in what is deemed socially acceptable (and openly talked about), it is difficult to judge if this is the case. One constant was that many OE travellers took advantage of being far away from home to 'play up', because Mum and Dad weren't watching. One story from the 1960s, reported in the *New Zealand News UK* 75th anniversary supplement, was of a New Zealander who got pregnant to a Scottish waiter on the *Northern Star*. Apparently she could not find the father again and eventually arrived home from her OE with – to her mother's surprise – a baby.

The Big OE Companion described The Church as 'fun but not pretty' and recommended that if you 'find yourself there for the fourth weekend in a row, head out the door immediately, take a tube to Heathrow and catch the first flight home. For your poor mother's sake.'[35]

The perception that one was beyond the reach of one's normal social controls – and within reach of the opportunities offered by cosmopolitan London – facilitated the development of a heavy drinking and drug

IN THE LATE 1960s David McGill took full advantage of what London had to offer a repressed and oversexed (his words) New Zealander: his exploits were recorded in *The Dolly Lolly Diaries*.[36] The author of the *Down Under in Europe* guidebooks in the 1970s wrote that 'Australasian girls in London don't have the kind of reputation Great Aunt Martha would hope for and it is generally rumoured that girls who don't at home, do abroad.'[37] The health section in the guidebook gave information on waiting times and prices for abortions in Britain. An interesting account of OE work and life in the 1970s can be found in *Dancing Naked: An exhibitionist revealed*, which is the story of a New Zealand Sunday school teacher who worked as an exotic dancer in Amsterdam and then spent two years in the chorus line at the Folies Bergère while on her OE.[38] Another candid OE account from the same era was Diane Brown's memoir *Liars and Lovers*.[39]

British drinking culture and pub social life were unlike New Zealand's and there were many traditional English pubs to explore, in addition to the travellers' pubs. Chris Slane

culture. While some saw this as merely an exaggeration of the worst of New Zealand culture, drugs had always been readily available in London (and were often much cheaper than in New Zealand). Over time, the types of drugs changed considerably: in the early 1980s Moroccan and Lebanese hashish were common; in the 1990s ecstasy was more popular, associated with the clubbing lifestyle. In the 2000s long-term expatriates talked of a large New Zealand underground culture in London, with New Zealanders dealing drugs door-to-door at their compatriots' flats on Friday nights. Duncan Sarkies' first book, *Stray Thoughts and Nose Bleeds*, included a fictitious account of an OE traveller's drug experiences.[40] Drugs were also prominent in Craig Marriner's 2006 OE novel *Southern Style*.[41] The plot follows the rootless lives of three young post-colonials in London – a New Zealander, an Australian and a South African – and describes a counter-cultural milieu of 'crap' jobs, hedonism and brushes with criminal lowlife.

LIFE IN LONDON was usually a lot busier than it had been in New Zealand. In 2004 James and Tara played netball on Monday nights, touch rugby on Tuesdays, tried to get out of London at least once a month, and did things in London the other weekends. The biggest difference from home was how long it took to get places; they soon learnt that it took at least an hour to get anywhere. That also meant getting up earlier to get to work. They found themselves re-learning life skills. When they first arrived in London they didn't appreciate how tired they would be and how useful the convenience food (pre-prepared in plastic bags) on sale at supermarkets could be. Other differences they noticed were that when going out in New Zealand they just took their eftpos card, whereas in London they had to have their cellphone, driver's licence and credit cards with them at all times. Others talked about just accepting after a while that you will spend much of your life on transport, and that one should always take a book.

A proper OE

Doing of lot of different things in London was seen as 'doing the OE properly'; staying within the New Zealand expatriate community was referred to as the 'London trap'. Making the most of life in London was paramount for some and they took full advantage of what was on offer, embracing both expatriate and British entertainments and activities. The live music scene was enjoyed by many, as were the multitude of clubbing options. Films, theatrical and dance performances, and art exhibitions catered to a huge diversity of interests. London parks offered respite from the city and were a favourite place for picnics and informal sporting competitions. There was also a wealth of museums and tourist sites to visit. The London markets were popular, as were the many events and festivals held in the city, such as the Oxford–Cambridge boat race, the Notting Hill Carnival and the Chinese New Year celebrations in Soho.

Each year, a number of balloted tickets to the Royal Garden Party at Buckingham Palace, Royal Ascot and the Trooping of the Colour were available to colonials. These were popular in the 1980s. Vicki and her flatmates, who went to the Garden Party in the early 1980s, were typical; far from being ardent royalists, they simply went for the experience.

For some, the only way to avoid the London trap was to stay out of London completely; others stayed in London, but attempted to stay away from other New Zealanders as much as possible. On his OE with his girlfriend in the mid-1990s, Brent noted that 'we did lots of stuff that probably wasn't very Kiwi – like we went to markets a lot, went out into the countryside with bikes and that, and to a lot of music venues – we would see the odd Kiwi, but they weren't Kiwi haunts. In fact it was a bit heinous when we were around Kiwis.'

While those who lived outside London had more contact with the local British population and culture, in many cases they still gravitated towards other New Zealanders; often the original attraction was that they knew New Zealanders already living there. Likewise, those who lived outside Britain usually found themselves socialising in expatriate communities; the only difference from Britain was that the expatriates represented a more diverse set of nationalities. Sally, for example, found in Japan that her social circle in the late 1980s included *any* westerner, rather than just the New Zealanders and Australians she had mixed with in London. Mike worked in Japan

Above: Royal Ascot offered a chance to really dress up, the girls wearing frocks and hats and the boys top hats and tails: somewhat incongruous dress for those travelling by Combi van in the 1980s.

Enjoying British culture, 1980s, 1990s and 2000s.

for a year in 2000 and found himself mostly 'hanging out' with the other English teachers: it was 'like a whole culture – every bar you go to it was English teachers'. Also, he found that conversation was focused on the expatriate life, rather than on things Japanese. He never made it to London and considered his OE a failure for having missed that experience.

Those on OEs in earlier decades seemed to have had more of a problem with the London trap. More recent OE travellers reported combining the New Zealand aspects of their London life with their British experiences more easily, possibly as people moved into careers and professional work. While many still abhorred the worst excesses of 'doing the Kiwi thing', the development of the sports leagues, restaurants and New Zealand cultural events in London gave New Zealand a stronger cultural presence than in the past. Each successive OE population cohort became more confident of their national identity as a result and any sense of connection to an ancestral British homeland was fading. The OE experience became less about the meeting of the two cultures and more about experiencing the hybrid culture of 'London, New Zealand'.

By the 1990s and 2000s, OE travellers were doing things on OE that had their roots in OE history. This change was advanced by the nature of the OE population: a self-replacing cohort of travellers who continually reinforced established patterns of behaviour. The end result was that it became more acceptable to engage with, and to celebrate, one's New Zealand culture in London. Increasingly, OE travellers returned home able to admit that they were 'gutted to have missed The Church', or that what they had enjoyed most about London was their expatriate lifestyle and the chance it gave them to show themselves off to the world as New Zealanders. The gap between New Zealand and the world had shrunk.

IRONICALLY, it was often easier to avoid the London trap if one did a typical OE travellers' job, especially if it was live-in. Those with live-in jobs tended to be more widely dispersed around London; working nights and weekends restricted social time available and removed the social temptations that came with shared house life. A live-in job could also situate one in more heterogeneous communities. Allison, for example, really enjoyed the job she had at a small pub just outside London in the early 1980s because it was in a community-oriented place; she got to know locals of her own age and also their parents and grandparents. Also, she 'didn't hang out with other Kiwis in London – I was determined I wasn't going all that way to hang out with other Kiwis.' Hazel avoided working in London for the entire three years of her OE in the late 1970s, purely because 'London was full of Kiwis as far as we were concerned, and that was what put us off really because we wanted to meet people from other countries.'

The shrinking world

Changing technology, and the internet in particular, had a significant impact on the everyday practices of the OE. The sense of isolation felt by OE travellers in the 1950s, 1960s and 1970s diminished, as staying in touch with home became both easier and cheaper. The first issue of *TNT Magazine* (1983) published the 'current' cost of phone calls to New Zealand and Australia: 50p per half minute or 99p a minute, discounted to £9.89 for 10 minutes. There were ways around these high costs: periodically, word travelled around London about a certain public phone that was 'broken' (not charging the caller to make calls).

A British Telecom advertisement in *TNT Magazine* in 1994 announced a permanent reduction in the cost of calls to Australia and New Zealand: at the new rates, a five-minute cheap-rate call was just £2.92, down from the old price of £3.36. A standard-rate call was reduced from £4.05 to £3.41. In 2004 calling cards were available that charged only 3p a minute to New Zealand, and in 2006 one telecommunications company offered a package that included free calls to New Zealand on Fridays. In 2008 a room in an Acton house advertised on Gumtree came with free calls to Australian and New Zealand landlines.

OE travellers usually felt the distance between New Zealand and Britain most keenly when something went wrong at home, although those on OE were/are selective about how much they share with their loved ones at home. Pete, for example, was working as a motorbike courier in London when he broke his leg in 1995. He lost his job and struggled for weeks both financially and physically, but never told his mother in New Zealand because she would have worried too much. Telecom looked after its customers in 2005 when it announced that it would credit all home-phone customers who called landlines in Britain after the London bombing. It wanted New Zealanders and visitors to New Zealand, phoning to check on the safety of friends and family, to know that Telecom was thinking of them.

A significant change brought about by internet technology was that family and friends back in New Zealand were able to keep track of one's OE in 'real time'. Photographs could be emailed home, or posted on social network sites alongside travel blogs describing exactly what one was doing. Mobile phone technology also made it possible to call and text from wherever one was. New Zealanders watching the All Blacks

In 1981 Angela worked in a pub opposite a London telephone exchange. For the price of a few drinks, the guys working in the exchange would patch calls through to both the New Zealand number she wanted and her London number so that no one was actually making the call.

play live on television at London travellers' pubs, for example, can (and do) phone their families in New Zealand at half-time and again at full time to dissect the game.

Texting and emailing involved two-way communication, of course. Some found that getting emails from friends at home – who were busy child-rearing, wallpapering and gardening – when they were in London just living for the next trip, was a good way to stay focused on their different priorities. Alice went to Britain on her OE in 2008 and could not wait to get the internet set up. She stayed in touch with her parents (from the 'letters and postcards' generation) via text and email, and 'loved having Skype and webcam'. She wrote home that she didn't know what she would have done if she didn't have her laptop with her: it was the most important thing she had in London (along with her passport, cellphone and camera). She didn't miss getting mail as it would take up weight and space.

In the early days of the OE, the mail services provided by New Zealand House and the travel clubs were a vital link home for travellers; their demise was directly related to the rise of the internet. In contrast, much of the network of social entertainment and activities that developed from the 1990s was dependent on the internet. For the people running the various sports leagues, it would have been impossible to reach the OE population – who were relatively mobile in London (and often didn't bother with landlines) – without the internet and mobile phones.

The internet and mobile phones also kept OE travellers in touch with each other, although this was possible by other means in earlier times: using the noticeboard in New Zealand House, writing home to Mum to get her to phone the mother of the friend you were looking for. However, being able to contact people easily in London (and even knowing they were there), took away an element of surprise that was a special feature of the OE. Early travellers all have stories of the surprise of unexpectedly bumping into people they knew from home: in German youth hostels and European camping grounds, walking down Oxford Street or on the tube.

MOBILE PHONE and internet technology brought the expectation that OE travellers would stay in touch on a regular (and frequent) basis. By the 2000s, parents in New Zealand panicked if they had not heard from their offspring for more than a few days, in stark contrast to the earlier decades when OE travellers could be missing, or out of touch, for months at a time. When Barry went on OE in 1979 one of the first things he had to do was find his younger sister, who had not communicated in six months. She had left New Zealand when she was only 16 and their parents had to sign consent forms for her to go. He found her quite easily and she was fine; the only reason she had not contacted her family was that she had been busy! In contrast, Crystal emailed home every night when she went away for a year in 2000, while Caitlin, who first arrived in Britain in 2002, emailed home frequently; this practice had dropped off by 2004, but she still spoke to her family in New Zealand every weekend and texted them regularly.

PART III

A CULTURAL ICON

Chapter Eight

COMING HOME

GOING ON AN OE was a relatively straightforward undertaking, particularly given its social acceptability in New Zealand. Setting off into the unknown for an unspecified period of time, simply to satisfy long-held ambitions to travel, was an adventure. Returning home was a different matter altogether. The logistics were easy, although saving the money required took some effort. Making the decision to return was more difficult, particularly if one did not have to leave: for those in the UK on two-year working holiday permits, the decision was usually made for them, although some stayed on illegally.

The working holiday visa was a popular topic of conversation in London, as it was not only the key determinant of how long one could stay in Britain, but also influenced how one's OE was approached. A British passport or Ancestry Visa put people in 'a different frame of mind to their friends simply because they didn't *have* to leave'. Often those with no restrictions felt sorry for their compatriots on the two-year visas because 'they were so pressured – having to sit down and work out the best use of their two years'. Some were happy they had this restriction: Jessie was ready to come home in 2002 after her two years, admitting, 'It was hard leaving London, but I was kind of glad I only had a two-year visa, because I never got homesick. I knew I would have to go home in two years and I never had to make the decision to come home.'

No matter how long one stayed away, New Zealand was still home. While most people recognised that they had been changed by their OE experiences, they did not usually anticipate having trouble fitting back into life in New Zealand. They expected New Zealand to have remained the same and they expected to be able to slot back into their previous lives, but the reality for many was that they no longer fitted in at home.

Time to go home

Most people on OE had a rough idea how long they would be away when they left New Zealand. In some cases they had taken a year's leave from their job – which was possible with many government jobs in the earlier decades of the OE – or had purchased a return air ticket, valid for only a year (in the passenger shipping era, return tickets were open for two years). Some of those who bought return tickets were merely being cautious, not wanting to commit to a

The expectation and the reality.
Chris Slane

longer OE until they knew what it was like. Cashing in the unused half of a ticket was a fairly common practice, as was phoning the boss in New Zealand to say one wouldn't be back as promised. On occasion, family or personal crises brought OE travellers home earlier than originally planned. A few were so determined to go on their OEs that they went leaving significant others behind in New Zealand; finding out how much they missed them sometimes curtailed OE plans.

Most OE travellers, however, found their experience enjoyable and commonly stayed away longer than initially planned. This was driven by a combination of factors: a developing addiction to travel (with an ever-expanding list of new places to travel to); reluctance to leave interesting (and sometimes well-paying) jobs; a lively social life in London; serious relationships with non-New Zealand significant others; and wanting to delay the inevitable decision on what to do next in life.

Pre-1993 – when it was still possible to stop and start the visa clock every time one

SOME PEOPLE returned earlier than planned because they didn't like being on OE, although it is surprisingly difficult to find people who admit to this. Jane was away for 11 months in 1999; although she hated the whole experience, she didn't feel that she could have come home any earlier. 'I would have felt ashamed of myself if I'd come home after five months or something – and hadn't done it properly.' Vicki did several OEs and admitted that she would have felt like a failure if she had not stayed away for at least a year the first time; the second time she didn't feel the same pressure, although she ended up marrying an Englishman and it was eight years before she returned permanently to New Zealand. Lisa was away for only four months in 1988 – she had left a partner behind in New Zealand (whom she was missing) – but felt like a failure when she returned because she didn't particularly like being overseas, and 'you are supposed to like overseas'.

left the UK – the two years of the working holiday permit could be substantially extended: a long summer of travel could add months to the permit; even adding weekends away gave one a surprising amount of extra time. When the regulations changed so that the two years ran continuously from one's date of first entry into the UK (regardless of any time spent travelling), not only were OEs shortened, but travel episodes within the OE were also curtailed, although it was possible to travel at the start of an OE before activating one's working holiday permit. The problem with this option was that one had to save even more money before leaving New Zealand. This was made more difficult when a 'valid from' date had to be specified on one's application for a visa.

Overstaying the visa was possible – and many did – although this was less advantageous as one was then 'stuck' in the UK, unable to travel abroad. A popular way of getting around the visa restrictions was to apply for extensions that did not exist: one was able to stay in the UK while the application was in the system. There were companies that helped with these visa extension applications, for a fee.

For some, the visa system proved too hard to beat. After a six-month trip to South America and New Zealand in 1996, Pete returned to the UK with his South African girlfriend. They had both used up their two-year visas. He was planning to work illegally for a couple of months in the UK, before leaving for good. He had some funds in the form of travellers' cheques and a credit card, as well as his ticket to leave for South Africa in two months' time, but the immigration authorities made him bring his departure forward. They didn't believe him when he said he was just going to 'see some friends and pick up his stuff'; he was told that if he wasn't out of the country within six weeks, he would be 'blacklisted'. His girlfriend was leaving for home in South Africa within the week; they let her stay that long, but gave her 'a really hard time'.

For those without the two-year restriction, making the decision to come home was more difficult. According to many long-term expatriates, the natural length of an OE was about four years: the first year was spent settling in, during the second year one got quite comfortable and by the third year one was completely settled, but already had an eye on leaving. There was, however, a fine line between the third and fourth year;

GAIL worked with an Australian woman in the late 1980s who desperately wanted to stay after her working holiday visa had run out (she was in a relationship with a British woman). She advertised in *Time Out* magazine for a husband and received about half a dozen offers, which her workmates found entertaining reading. The going rate for a husband at the time was about £1000. Eventually she took up an offer of marriage at no charge from one of the customers (a gay man) at the pub she worked in. Their wedding reception was at the pub, much to the bemusement of the other customers! Several months later they were interviewed separately by the Home Office; they were asked about each other's habits, their preferred underwear styles and so on. They both passed.

Another way to stay was to marry a Brit.
Jonathan Drapes

once one got past the four-year mark, there was a good chance one would stay for 10–15 years. The shipping companies in London found that if expatriates didn't go home by the time 10 years was up, then they wouldn't consider moving until 15 had gone by; if they were still there after 15 years, there was only a one in five chance that they would *ever* return home. Ultimately, what brought many longer-term OE travellers back to New Zealand was either having children or planning to have them, and wanting them to have the childhood one had experienced oneself: a pattern described by some as using New Zealand like 'a breeding colony'.

If one stayed away for more than a few years it also became questionable as to whether one was still on OE. Some defined the end of an OE as when one married and had children, or when one was living with just one other person, rather than five. A common answer to this conundrum was that the OE ended when one bought a couch (or anything that was too big to fit into a tea chest). For others, it was a mental state: Barry and William, for example, were both in Britain for over 20 years; they both married British women, bought houses and had children; to all intents, they made new lives for themselves in Britain. Barry thought that he was still on his OE (after 20-plus years) because over all those years he always planned to return to New Zealand 'one day'; William considered himself to be an expatriate New Zealander.

ON HER OE in the late 1990s Sophie had already used up her two years (as well as a six-month tourist visa) when she flew into Heathrow after a holiday in the Middle East. She had tried, unsuccessfully, to get a flight back to Britain through Ireland, from where it was sometimes easier to get back in. The immigration officials at Heathrow were suspicious of her motives, and she was not allowed in. After being detained for three hours, during which they phoned her old employers to ask about her, she was escor ted onto a depar ting flight. She took some comfort in the fact that they didn't say she could never go back; the only evidence of being thrown out of the country was a black cross through the last Heathrow stamp in her passport.

STAYING AWAY for a long time took one outside the parameters of the standard OE. Steve was away for seven years in the 1990s. While he enjoyed all his years in London, as he moved into his late twenties he found increasingly that he wanted more space and a more settled life. He also found that it was difficult to maintain friendships when everyone else was on the two-year cycle: he had been involved with a really good group of friends who had all moved on, so life just wasn't the same.

After staying for four years in the 1980s, Sally found herself an old hand. She grew tired of making new friends all the time and seeing them move on; the pool of people who had been there for longer got smaller and smaller; and she found herself not wanting to mix with the new people. By the late 1980s she was thinking of starting a family and about where she wanted to spend the rest of her life: New Zealand was it.

There has been considerable interest in New Zealand in the reasons why expatriate New Zealanders return home. One study interviewed 50 travellers, who had returned during the 1990s and early 2000s, about their OEs: why they went, where they went, their priorities, their experiences overseas, what they learnt, how they built their expertise and careers while away, their reason for returning to New Zealand, and how they re-adjusted to life and employment once home. The study found that the main reasons for returning from OE were family-related (such as family illness, worries about ageing parents, seeking to resume or develop a relationship with a partner in New Zealand or a desire for more family contact). Some felt they had simply been away too long or needed a break, while a few were forced to return because their visas had expired.[1]

A 2006 study of 18,000 expatriate New Zealanders undertaken by the Kiwi Expatriate Association (KEA) examined differences between those who planned to return to New Zealand and those who didn't, and the degree to which lifestyle was bringing them back.[2] Of the 13,123 expatriates in the sample who were located outside Australia (i.e. potentially the OE population), more than half selected 'New Zealand lifestyle and culture', and 39 per cent selected family/marital connections, as the responses that best described their reason for returning to New Zealand. However, these survey results are problematic in that 'expiry of visa' was not one of the listed reasons for return.[3]

Another study from 2000 found that the key motives of 2608 highly educated New Zealand emigrants in choosing where to live were, in order of priority: culture and travel opportunities, career, economics, relationships, quality of life and political environment. Half of the respondents were living in Britain and a third planned to be back in New Zealand within five years, with children's education, retirement or anticipation of having sufficient financial savings being the main reasons for returning.[4] In 2008 recruitment consultants Global Career Link surveyed more than 800 New Zealanders living in Britain and found that 32 per cent of those who planned to return to New Zealand in the following three months were doing so in order to be closer to friends and family.[5]

One of the English owners of The Church, who had a lifetime of involvement in the London Australasian community, thought the choice – between living in Britain and New Zealand – was difficult, particularly as the same things were not being measured: 'You are balancing lots of people, access to Europe, money – against quality of life, barbecues … it is hard to decide between such different things.'

Some travellers were like Vicki who, after two years away at the end of 1982, was ready to live in a normal community with a mixture of ages again. The attraction of this did not last, however, and she returned to Britain after 18 months in New Zealand. She was only able to do this because she had a British passport. In contrast, Wendy had had enough after two winters in Britain in the mid-1980s. She found that the crowds were getting to her, especially as she struggled to get to and from work on the tube. Mostly, though, it was the pull of New Zealand that brought her back – it was home, where she had been raised, and she wanted the outdoor life it offered.

A substantial number of those who stayed away for longer periods made scouting trips back to New Zealand before returning permanently. Also, with higher incomes and cheaper airfares, it became more common for even short-term OE travellers to return to New Zealand mid-OE for special events and holidays: such trips made the expatriate experience more tolerable.

Aaron, who returned to New Zealand in 2004 after three and a half years away, said, 'I was always going to anyway and I wanted some more of my other life – the New Zealand outdoor one. That was the big attraction.' In 1993 Kylie returned to New Zealand after five years in London because she 'wanted the house and the New Zealand life' (although she later regretted not staying in London). Shelley got homesick for 'tussock grass and things like that' in the mid-1990s. Craig had always said 'five years' when asked how long he was going away for (but only because people wanted a number); his plan was just to let things take their course. As it happened, he did stay away for five years, after which he was happy to come home to stay in 2000. Ruth was happy in London in the 2000s but planned, ultimately, to return to New Zealand because she had a better chance of being able to buy her own

MANY OE TRAVELLERS could not articulate their reasons for returning home much beyond it being 'time' to do so. Heather, for example, returned to New Zealand at the end of 1985 after travelling on and off for 10 years and just thought it was 'time'. Judy came back at the end of 1981, after two and a half years, because she was 'starting to get a bit tired from travelling'. After six years away in the early 1980s, during which he worked mainly in the Middle East, Alex had 'had enough' and returned to New Zealand. Vicki, who returned after two years (but didn't stay), did so without really thinking it through. 'I was sick of living in pubs and my money was quite tight – I should have applied to teach over there, but I had a great travel plan to get home and I needed a bit of a break – what I should have done was just go home on holiday.'

house: she wanted to 'be able to have a house with a garden and a garage and not have to commute for an hour to get anywhere'.

The Big OE Companion listed 18 indicators that showed one had been in London too long. These included: thinking Hyde Park is nature; your idea of personal space is no one actually standing on you; calling soccer football and supporting a team that is not Manchester United; believing that every night is a good night for drinking (and that drinking during the day on Sunday is entirely reasonable); and regarding a tube jumper as not so much a tragedy, as an inconvenience.

Getting home

At some point during the OE one had to save the fare home. Many managed to do only this, with no spare money to enable travel en route. In the 1950s and 1960s it was difficult to get passage on New Zealand-bound ships as they were generally full of new migrants. Ian and Gill made enquiries after they had been away for two years in the early 1960s and found that many shipping companies had reduced their sailings to New Zealand, putting pressure on the spaces available. They had to wait a few months before passage on the *Arkadia*, one of the Greek ships, became available. Likewise Lynette, who didn't have the money to fly back in 1964, had to go on a waiting list for a ship passage.

Many people returned home broke; some were in debt to their parents, others (in later years) to credit card companies. In 1977 *New Zealand News UK* reported on a scheme started by a travel agent by which destitute New Zealanders stuck in London who were desperate to get home could 'fly now, pay later'. In their three years away in the early 2000s Jackie and her boyfriend never once had the money for a ticket home (they also overstayed their visas, and were lucky not to get caught), but they always had their mothers to bail them out if necessary and they had their credit cards (which they usually had charged to the max). A *Sunday Star-Times* article on the OE in 1996 told the story of a New Zealand woman who paid off her student debt and left New Zealand with a healthy bank balance, vowing to return with a huge Italian leather bag filled with French designer clothes, rather than in debt like some of her friends. She arrived home 18 months later with a Turkish leather bag full of English ashtrays and an over-the-limit credit card.[6]

Those who could afford to do so made at least one stopover on the way home, although often it was not because of any great desire to add to their travel experiences. On her way back to New Zealand in 1988 Kate stopped for four days in Hawaii, purely because 'the place was warm and the plane went past'. Gail and her husband, also returning home in the late 1980s, knew people who had done the 'Asia and Thailand thing' but they weren't that interested themselves. However, they did stop for a week each in Turkey, India and Singapore on their way home because their ticket gave them free stopovers.

Relatively few travelled home overland in recent decades of the OE. In a rare Asian overland story from the modern OE era, Tim Mulliner set off to cycle home from London in 2001. The story of his 24,000-kilometre, 428-day journey, crossing 22 countries, was told in *Long Ride for a Pie*: the idea for the journey came to him in London when he was yearning for a good Kiwi pie.[7] Another unusual homecoming story was that of Justin Brown who, having lost a bet with an Australian friend in London (over the result of an All Black versus Wallabies rugby match), was forced to busk his way around Britain to raise the money for his flight back to New Zealand. His story was told in *UK on a G-String.*[8] As noted in Chapter Five, it became common in the late 1990s to return to New Zealand via Africa, usually on an overland truck from Nairobi to South Africa and on an onward flight from there. Steve and Melanie, who met in London in the early 1990s, travelled back to New Zealand overland in the late 1990s. They were looking forward to leaving Britain and their big trip, but after nine months by motorbike through Africa they were pleased to finally get home.

In the earlier decades of the OE, part of the attraction of an overland trip was using it to transport vehicles purchased in Europe to New Zealand. In the 1960s and 1970s New Zealand customs duty on new or luxury cars could be avoided if one had been absent from New Zealand for at least 21 months, and could prove one had owned the vehicle for at least 12 months. With careful timing, one could avoid British purchase tax on 'export' vehicles by leaving Britain with the car within 12 months of its purchase (as the travellers did in *For Love and a Beetle*). Also, owners of export and foreign-registered vehicles did not have to pay English road tax. Of course, driving a new car overland through Asia was not the best way to keep it in good condition for later use in New Zealand. Commonly, OE travellers purchased cars while on OE and used them to travel around Europe before shipping them back to New Zealand; some sold these cars once they returned to New Zealand in order to recoup the cost of their trip.

MANY OF THOSE who left by boat flew home. Mary, who departed on her OE in 1962 on the *Orcades*, returned home by air 18 months later. She had left a romance behind in New Zealand and he didn't want to stay the distance. She was heartbroken, so her parents paid for her to fly home. Flights between Britain and New Zealand in the 1960s were an endurance experience, involving multiple flight legs. Mary recalled flying from London to Athens on a flight leaving at four in the morning because it was cheaper. After a day in Athens, she flew on to Beirut, where she spent another day, and then to Bangkok, where she picked up some money her parents had sent and stayed with a friend for several days before flying on to Hong Kong, Sydney and home. She had to pay her parents back as soon as she got a job. Diane, who went by boat in 1973 and flew home two years later, recalled that on the ship she felt the journey was a long way – 'you could see how fast you were going' – whereas on the plane it was an anticlimax to get back so quickly.

Bringing home an MG: the car being lowered onto the wharf at Port Chalmers, 1969.

IT TOOK CAROL and an English girlfriend 14 months to travel overland from London to New Zealand in 1970. Carrying suitcases, they travelled on local buses and trains via the Middle East, Afghanistan, Pakistan, India, Thailand, Malaysia, Indonesia and Australia. They went deck class on boats in Indonesia and flew only between Calcutta and Bangkok, and from Bali to Portuguese Timor and on to Darwin. They didn't have a guidebook, but exchanged information on hotel addresses and cheap deals on boat or bus tickets with other travellers along the way. Quite a few other young people were travelling the same way: mostly Germans, Australians, Canadians and Americans. (Many of the latter group were military personnel on R&R from Vietnam.)

A lot of travellers had developed a drug habit: 'In Afghanistan every five minutes you were offered a smoke of something – we came across a lot of people who were totally out of their trees – they were lost souls.' Broke when they arrived in Darwin, they took jobs as chambermaids for a few weeks to get enough money for onward bus tickets; they then did 'a bit of travelling around the Barrier Reef' before hitchhiking to Sydney where, once again, they had to get jobs in order to buy onward tickets.

Carol remembered meeting some German travellers (whom they had met previously in Kabul) in Mazar e Sharif, in the north of Afghanistan. The Germans were going on to see the Bamiyan Buddhas (which were dynamited and destroyed by the Taliban in 2001) but, because it would cost them another £5, she and her friend decided not to go: 'I know you can't do everything but you could kick yourself now.'

Excess baggage

Those leaving Britain by ship in earlier decades travelled with trunks and suitcases. Early air returnees sent a trunk by sea and flew with suitcases. From the late 1970s the young traveller on OE used a backpack: luggage which, a decade or so later, became the defining feature of youth travel, with the emergence of the 'backpacker' market. How did they get the stuff they had accumulated home?

Even if one did not buy any large souvenir items, over two or three years the little stuff could add up. Houses all over New Zealand are adorned with trinkets picked up in the Plaka in Athens, at the Grand Bazaar in Istanbul or from some historic house in Britain. There was also the miscellaneous memorabilia – the concert tickets, theatre programmes, bus and train tickets, tourist brochures, old pay slips – evidence of the accomplishment of an OE. In the days before digital photography, one's

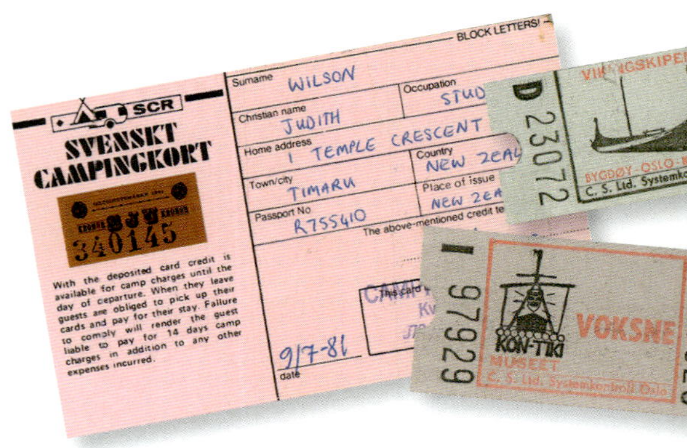

Most OE travellers collected at least some souvenirs on their travels, although some were fiercely determined not to buy that carpet or leather jacket in Turkey.
Jonathan Drapes

photographs alone could fill a tea chest.

Most departed from New Zealand with a single backpack; the return home often required the services of a shipping company. The advantage of shipping belongings home was that freight was charged by volume, rather than weight. There was no size restriction: the shipping companies shipped anything, from suitcases, cardboard cartons, tea chests, crates, bicycles, skis and part-containers, to cars. The price usually included pick-up and drop-off, shipping cost and insurance. Door-to-door services offered delivery in New Zealand, although often there were additional port clearance and customs charges to pay. There were also charges for having camping and outdoor equipment fumigated. For those who had been away from New Zealand for more than 21 months, all household goods and personal effects were duty free, provided they had been used. Liz bought a stereo in Hong Kong on her way home to New Zealand in 1982; not

The miscellany of an OE.

unexpectedly, since it was still pristine in its original packaging, she had some difficulty convincing New Zealand Customs that she had used it.

The amount of space devoted to the topic of 'Getting home' in the OE guidebooks varied considerably over time. Neither edition of the 1970s *Down Under in Europe* gave practical advice on shipping (although they did give advice on how to behave once one was home). In the 1990s the YHA's *Big OE Guide* included a section on how to ship excess belongings home. In 2004 *The Big OE Companion* included several pages of practical departure advice, including how to get rid of stuff you did not want to take home, shopping around for shipping quotes and a full page of tips for choosing a shipping company. The main things to consider were where they delivered to in New Zealand, their time frames for delivery, pricing structures, and what insurance deals they offered. The price could add up, but it was worth getting one's treasured belongings home intact. Even with comprehensive insurance, some people did not want to surrender precious photographs to shipping companies. *The Big OE Companion* recommended sending photographs and negatives separately.

In the 1980s the usual 'trunk' was a tea chest: plywood chests that had once transported tea (one's clothes smelt of tea for a long time after); in later years, these were replaced by cardboard versions of the same. Usually the goods did not leave Britain until a container was full: getting goods to New Zealand could take up to 10 weeks. If one didn't expect to arrive home for some months, and wanted to be there to receive belongings in person, it was possible to request that the goods did not leave Britain until after a certain date.

Although passenger shipping services had ceased by the mid-1970s, container shipping services between New Zealand and Britain were frequent. The number of New Zealanders returning home post-OE, along with ongoing British emigration to New Zealand, contributed to a competitive shipping market. A large portion of the advertising space in London's Australasian publications was taken by the baggage-shipping companies. During the OE peak of the early 1980s, advertisers in *TNT Magazine* included Anglo Pacific, which had started in 1978 as a 'specialist shipper of personal effects for London's young Antipodean community'. Among those advertising in 1993 were SBS Freight, Interpack, Budget Shipping, Cargo Forwarding, Australasian Forwarding Agency (established in 1959), Austpac International, Personal Shipping Services (PSS, established in 1982) and Excess Baggage Company (established in the mid-1980s). While many of these companies were still operating in the 2000s, there were newer advertisers including Freedom Shipping (in 2006, '12 years' advertising to *TNT* readers'), Allfreight Excess Baggage and Removals, and Global Moves.

Connections across the Antipodean community: Backpacker Co., 2004.

Many of these businesses were divisions of pre-existing companies: in 2002 The Baggage Company and Interpack Worldwide were part of Excess Baggage; in 2004 SANZ International Shipping was a division of Anglo Pacific (whose website content was identical to the Australasian Forwarding Agency in 2009). In 2002 *LAM* magazine carried an advertisement for Seven Seas Baggage Worldwide (established in 1996), a company which also advertised in *New Zealand News UK* and in *LAM*'s 2004 *London Directory*; it was the only shipping company that did not advertise in *TNT*.

Most shipping advertisements were full- or double-page spreads and, as most did not give prices, could be published each week, year after year, with little change. Shipping to New Zealand was relatively cheap, given the distance travelled; it could cost more to move one's belongings around New Zealand than from Britain. Seven Seas was one of the few companies to quote prices in its advertisements: in 2002 it cost about £80 to send one carton door-to-door to New Zealand; for two to eight cartons the price dropped to £40 each (in 2004 this had increased to £45). Most companies offered discounted prices for bulk shipping. In 2006

PSS International Removals advertised two tea cartons for £120, with each extra one costing £35; Freedom Shipping advertised four boxes from only £129, while Allfreight had a summer special of four cartons door-to-door from £130.

Some of the shipping companies were directly affiliated with travel companies and provide evidence of the somewhat incestuous nature of the Antipodean business community in London. In the 2000s Anglo Pacific displayed the Contiki logo in its advertisements, while the Australasian Forwarding Agency was the Top Deck baggage agent. In 2006 SANZ International Shipping was aligned with Backpacker Co.: its advertisements included a map pointing to the travel company's office. The New Zealanders who bought Backpacker Co. in the late 1990s had previously worked for a shipping company that went broke; they then started their own shipping company, selling travel on the side. 1st Contact also offered shipping services throughout the 2000s. Anglo Pacific offered tax services as well and was one of the sponsors of London Touch Rugby's finals day in 2003 (the other sponsors were Backpacker Co., Downunder Worldwide Travel Insurance, Stray Travel and the Redback Tavern). Anglo Pacific also sponsored Commonwealth Netball UK in 2004 and was a partner for the 2012 Homelanz festival. In 2009 First Festival Travel (which had been Backpacker Co.) was teamed up with Anglo Pacific.

ADJUSTMENT to New Zealand was usually reckoned to take at least two years. Ben and his partner thought they were ready to come home in 2002 when 'the weather got to us', but even after two years back they were still unsettled. For Aaron, who also returned to New Zealand in 2002, it was hard coming back after three years away. Two years later he still hadn't settled down and admitted that he had expected it to be easier to get a job and a place to live: 'I was a lot more proactive about those things in London.' Mandy, who returned in 1994 after three years away, had heard from friends that it would take two years to settle back into New Zealand life. She thought 'How could it? This is home!' What most surprised her and her partner were other people's reactions to their return:

People that hadn't done it themselves couldn't care less – it just sounded like bragging to them. They were still where we had been three years previously, but luckily we knew enough people who had travelled. I thought that with my friends I'd worked with I would slot back into where I was before and it would be great to see everybody again but it wasn't like that. I had changed and been and seen so much and experienced the world. They had just stayed in Christchurch.

Culture shock (again)

Getting one's belongings home was considerably easier than transporting oneself. In *The Big OE Companion*, Bronwyn Sell described two types of returnee: those who appreciate New Zealand a lot more than when they left, and those who find it claustrophobic and spookily familiar. In fact she was describing extremes, as most people found the return experience a mixture of the two. Hazel had a sense of unreality when she returned to New Zealand in 1981 after three years on OE: 'We lived in a bit of a glass bubble when we got back, like we didn't really belong here – it didn't feel real and it was like I was in this room full of all my own life, but I wasn't really a part of it any more.'

The final section in *Down Under in Europe* addressed being 'Back home' and advised the following: drop your Pommie accent fast (because no one will like it); when people ask about your trip, don't make the mistake of telling them, as even doting mothers will have limited interest; the only time to take out your slides [this was written in the 1970s] is when you are at home alone; don't be disparaging about things back home; and keep it a big secret that you are now worldly wise, cultured and sophisticated,

While Chris Slane's cartoons from the early 1980s still have an element of truth, the advent of Facebook and travel blogs means that many have now shared their OEs (and their photographs) before they get home.
Chris Slane

except when you are with kindred souls.

While it was usually easier to talk to others who had been on OE, even they needed to have had experiences similar to one's own. Often returnees were surprised at how many people they met who had done an OE, and who had been to all the same places and had the same types of experiences as they had, particularly in Britain and Europe. People were usually happy to talk about those experiences, but not ones that were slightly different. Mike, for example, returned to New Zealand after several years in Japan and found that he could never join in when his friends talked about their OEs, because his experiences were so different from theirs. He also felt that they considered his Japanese experience to be a 'soft OE'; to counteract this, he often found himself pulling out stories of travelling in the United States, including hearing gunshots outside the Los Angeles backpackers he stayed at.

WHEN she first got back to New Zealand in 1988, Kate found that she still behaved as she had overseas. She continued going to museums and art galleries, which she hadn't done very often in New Zealand pre-OE: 'I was still in the travel lifestyle so I was actually moulding the two together, but it didn't last very long.' Paul recalled looking at photos of New Zealand when he was away and thinking, 'What a beautiful country.' He flew back and thought 'Look at those mountains,' but 12 years later he was still waiting to get out there. 'You make the most of things like that when you are away, and you take it for granted when you are here.'

The Big OE Companion had a more practical approach to the return 'to do' list than that of *Down Under in Europe*, in part reflecting social changes over 30 years: take a deep breath and smell the clean air; tell the Inland Revenue you are back; exchange your British driver's licence for a New Zealand one; and get your mobile phone unlocked and, if necessary, a new connection. Several accent-related items featured in a 'things to expect' section: accents would sound cartoonish ('Wulcum to Niew Zillind. Please keep all your buggage with you ut all toimes')[9] and you would be teased for 'speaking like a Pom' (having spent the last three years being teased about your Kiwi accent). Also, New Zealand would probably seem small, friendly, deserted, and very far away from the rest of the world. Relationships with friends would have changed and would have to be re-established, and there would be a change in personal priorities, especially as one no longer had to save for travel.

Although many people struggled to adjust to being back in New Zealand, they also noticed things about home that had previously been of little account. Ian and Gill found that their view of New Zealand had changed enormously in the three years they were away in the early 1960s. On their return they thought it all looked a bit 'makeshift', as if the locals had made everything themselves. It took them a good six months to settle down. Gill's overwhelming impression was that there were so many things New

Jonathan Drapes' cartoon shows what one might miss when leaving the UK in the 2000s.
Jonathan Drapes

Zealand didn't have, like big buildings, old churches, museums and theatres (although they acknowledged that returning to live in New Plymouth was a factor in this). They eventually moved to Christchurch; what Ian noticed most was that Manchester Street looked like the wild west: it was very wide and the buildings were low. He also found his mother's accent extraordinary – 'She'd talk about "eppells"' (apples) – and he had no idea she sounded like that. Lynette still remembers standing on James Smith corner in Wellington in 1965, thinking what a funny little antiquated place it was, having previously thought that it was a great big, busy intersection. She also disliked the accents ('they sounded dreadful'), but particularly noticed the little houses, with their brightly painted roofs, as she sailed into Wellington Harbour.

The New Zealand that people were returning to in the earlier decades of the OE *was* very different from where they had been while away. Eric returned in the late 1970s: 'Coming back from Europe in those days was hard, because even in Christchurch you couldn't buy a decent cappuccino, or anything like that, and everything shut at 10 o'clock at night, whereas in Europe you were just going out then.' When she returned in the early 1970s Diane noticed how monocultural New Zealand society was and struggled to settle back in: 'Most of my peers had married and moved away – I didn't know what I wanted to do with the rest of my life. It took me a long time to find a niche. My mother's theory was that the OE almost ruins you because it unsettles you so much – because you have glimpsed things.' For those returning in more recent decades, in the age of globalised culture, the difference between New Zealand and the rest of the world has not been so marked.

Returnees experienced significant pressure to conform, mostly to the social ideals of settling down and getting careers on track. Some found themselves doing repeat OEs because they didn't have clear post-OE goals. Donal, for example, went away three times in the 1980s and had trouble settling back into New Zealand each time; he thought the main reason was that he didn't have a job or a career in mind. Grant, who went away for two years in the mid-1990s, had a life plan that did not extend past his OE: 'It was always going to be – study at university, work for a year and then go overseas. That was about six years planned for. There wasn't anything after that and I thought that during that time something would come up and nothing did. It made coming home hard because I had to make a decision and face up to a sense of responsibility.'

Some found that on returning to New Zealand they could not settle and subsequently moved either to Australia or, if they had the right passport or visa, back to Britain. The advice in *The Big OE Companion* for dealing with reverse culture shock was to spend time in one of your favourite places, give it some time, try living in a different place in New Zealand, and finally, if things get really bad, go back to Britain.

A new life in New Zealand

Adjustment to New Zealand was made easier with a proactive approach to this new phase of one's life. Many OE travellers returned at a time when they were ready to marry, have children, buy houses or resume their careers. These post-OE expectations could be disappointed, however, as returning to New Zealand often brought a drop in income. Also, British work experience, especially in finance, accountancy and banking, was often too specialised for the New Zealand employment market. Although many OE travellers gained valuable experience working for large organisations, they were usually involved in only a small part of the operation, whereas New Zealand businesses tended to require more generalist skills. Some people developed skill sets overseas that were simply not applicable to the New Zealand situation. For many returnees, doing a less interesting job, or one with less responsibility, added to the difficulties they were encountering in adjusting to life back in New Zealand. Usually, the longer they had been away, the worse it was; those whose returns were most successful moved back for lifestyle rather than career reasons.

Over the years there has been much discussion in the media about New Zealand's 'brain drain' and the work prospects and valuable skills of those who return. In 2003 1st Contact conducted a survey of 105 New Zealanders living in Britain: 82 per cent felt they had learned skills working in London that they could not have learnt at home; 69 per cent thought New Zealand should offer incentives to get them to return. The survey also found that 68 per cent of New Zealanders planned to start their own business post-OE. While this figure seems high there are numerous New Zealand entrepreneurial success stories that have followed close on the heels of an OE. A considerable number of OE travellers returned to New Zealand planning to completely change their careers; many have become involved in the tourism industry as a result of their OE experiences.

In the 2000s many advertisements for jobs in New Zealand appeared in London's Australasian publications. Businesses preferred to employ New Zealanders rather than new migrants, as it removed the need to engage with costly and time-consuming immigration procedures. Also, the experience of businesses was that once New Zealanders had decided to come home, they were more committed to staying. In a curious irony, however, those who brought foreign partners to New Zealand often found that their partners adjusted much better than they did.

Even well into the 2000s, when the internet enabled people to stay more in touch with home, returning New Zealanders often needed advice on 'migrating' to New Zealand. An article in *TNT Magazine* in 2006 gave five tips for 'Settling in – New Zealand':

1. *Don't say a bad word about Trade Me (which according to most New Zealanders could solve everything, including the Israel–Palestine conflict);*
2. *Don't bother excitedly telling people about your OE (as most other Kiwis have either been, or were about to go, or else they were never going to go);*
3. *Don't leave the UK with credit card debt in pounds sterling;*
4. *Don't leave the UK in summer to return home in winter;*
5. *A New Zealand five dollar bill is no fiver.*

The author also noted that what was most noticeable when they returned to New Zealand was the smell: with smoking banned in pubs and bars, nothing remained to mask the body odour of customers. Other notable differences were that parents had a few more wrinkles (and slightly more intransigent socio-political views) and that the seemingly incessant London conversations, about working holiday visas and weekend trips away, had been replaced by repetitive New Zealand conversations about house prices.[10]

A New Zealand newspaper article from a 2005 returnee also noted that home ownership was a national obsession.[11] The author reflected on several issues: New Zealanders were hopeless romantics about their past; New Zealand was a wonderful place to live, but one paid for it through taxes; the choice of beer at the supermarket was both impressive *and* a health hazard; one's friends all had children and were broke; compared to the rest of the world, New Zealanders had relatively little to worry about; New Zealanders were impervious to the cold; and they did not think that money is everything. Most noticeable, however, was that Kiwis were more comfortable being Kiwis and that New Zealand was no longer a mini-England.

Chapter Nine
THE OE STORY

IN JANUARY 2009 the *Dominion Post* reported the sighting of a Hector's dolphin in Wellington Harbour. As this endangered dolphin is usually found only in South Island waters and there was no way of knowing why it had strayed so far from home, Department of Conservation staff thought it may have just been 'doing something different, doing its OE'.[1] Today, the acronym for Overseas Experience has become a label to attach to a multitude of human and non-human travel experiences; in another report, All Black Dan Carter, having been to France on his 'rugby sabbatical OE' in 2008, was described as going on his 'honeymoon OE' in 2012. We confuse foreigners travelling in New Zealand by asking them if they are on their OEs. While these are undoubtedly overseas experiences, calling them 'OEs' almost always introduces an ironic undertone as they simply do not encapsulate either the magnitude nor the true essence of *the* OE.

Chris Slane captured this in his cartoons drawn while on his own OE in the 1980s, introducing us to 'The Great Overseas Experience'. By the 1990s it had been christened the 'Big OE'. Whatever its title, the OE began as a response to New Zealand's geographical

'I'm just going overseas and may be some time!'
Chris Slane

and cultural isolation, developed into a travel phenomenon in its own right – so that 'doing an OE' became the goal – and matured into a cultural practice that sits alongside and is enshrined in the myriad myths that celebrate kiwiana. We New Zealanders have an intrinsic understanding of what an OE is *and* of what it represents for individuals and for New Zealand. The OE brings out the New Zealanders' penchant for understatement: as Kev notes in the cartoon opposite, 'I'm just going overseas and may be some time!'

A long journey

The OE has definitely been a matter of 'some time'. For more than six decades young New Zealanders have been working, travelling and – in the words of the YHA poster in Chapter Four – 'sleeping their way around the world!' Although OE travellers leave home to see the world, for most, the world inhabited by the OE is centred on Europe and London; the classic OE remains firmly tied to these locations. Historically, London is the home of the OE.

The overseas experience over time.

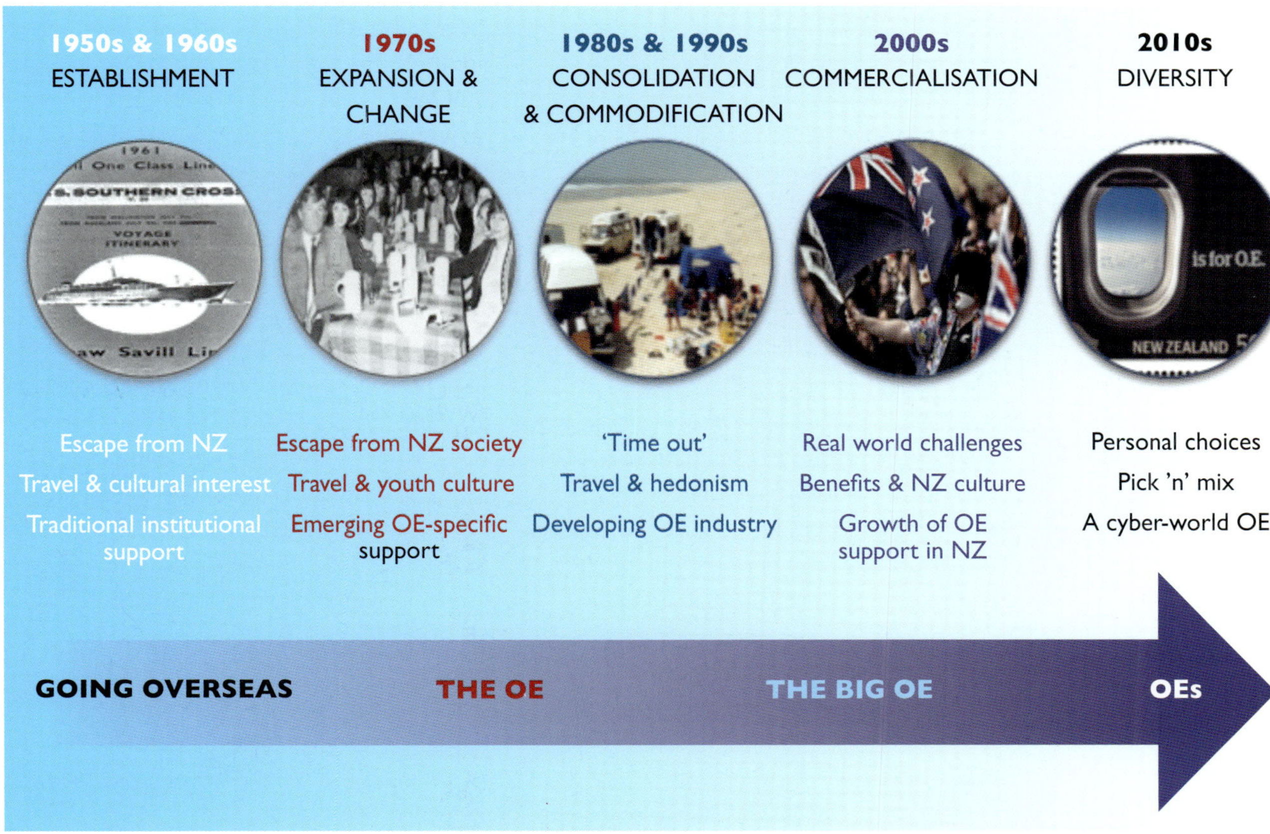

Since the first OE travellers left in the 1950s there have been substantial social, political, economic and technological changes in New Zealand and globally. Some of these changes made the OE harder, some made it easier, others just made it different. The outer form of the OE – a two- to three-year working holiday – is recognisable across all six decades, but the nature of OE experience, and the support network that surrounds it, have changed significantly over time.

The first trickle of OE travellers had support from the New Zealand establishment in London. Increases in the numbers travelling and changes in the services required by young travellers put pressure on this traditional support network; by the 1970s considerable OE-specific support was becoming evident. During the 1980s an OE support 'industry' developed, as both the expatriate New Zealand population and its (often specialised) support network of employment agencies, travel companies, social clubs, sports clubs, retail and media outlets grew exponentially. This OE support network consolidated throughout the 1990s, with informal community support becoming increasingly commodified; by the 2000s many OE support services had become commercial business ventures. The support network, helped by technology (and the internet in particular) and informed by OE returnees, had also spread to New Zealand; for OE travellers, going overseas was no longer such an adventure into the unknown.

The OE had always been driven by a mix of the need to escape (from home) and a desire for the challenge of survival (overseas). However, the New Zealand each successive generation of OE travellers was escaping from was different, as was the overseas they were going to. There were also some subtle variations in the nature of the escape. That of the early decades was primarily from the isolation and social constraints of New Zealand. In contrast, the middle years of the OE offered a more personal life-cycle stage of escape from career advancement and serious adult life; crucially, this 'time out' continued while overseas.

Travel was a fundamental part (and challenge) of the OE experience. The motives and travel practices of many OE travellers changed over the years, however, as travel increasingly incorporated celebrations of youth culture and hedonism, and – some would argue – diluted interest in the cultural exploration that had been a feature of early OE travel. The result was that OE life and travel became as much about New Zealand culture as it was about other cultures. The emergence of mass tourism, especially budget and youth tourism, changed the backdrop to the OE; more tourists, and fewer opportunities for genuine exploration, robbed travel of some of its challenge. If the traveller was based in London, increasing OE community support eased the challenges of OE life more generally.

A notable change occurred towards the end of the 1990s, as OE travellers began to place greater emphasis on the work portion of the experience and to consider potential post-OE career and financial benefits. The balance in the OE shifted as a number of key (and interrelated) changes occurred: leaving New Zealand when slightly older (as a result of the extension of the visa age limits) gave travellers more pre-OE work experience, which facilitated better OE jobs; better jobs had to be taken more seriously, with less time off for travel and a stronger focus on living a comfortable life in London. This generation of travellers might have known more about the world they were going to, and had more help to get there than their predecessors, but they also faced different challenges. By the 2000s for many travellers the challenge of the OE was the real-world one of survival in the global employment market.

Despite these not insignificant changes, some stable aspects of the OE are evident across the decades. The OE travellers of the twenty-first century might be looking out of an aeroplane window (rather than a porthole) when they travel overseas, but new arrivals in London are still referred to as being 'fresh off the boat'. Oktoberfest offered an enjoyable (albeit alcohol-fuelled) cultural experience, whatever the decade. The van tour, which epitomised the travel ideals of independence and self-exploration, quickly became (and remained) a cultural icon of the OE. OE travellers have always celebrated (and displayed) their New Zealand culture: in the earlier decades the props were home made and the celebrations were circumspect; by the 2000s there was a social calendar of New Zealand events in London. These features underpin the stereotypical (or, to be more complimentary, 'classic') OE and are recognised, regurgitated, revered and reviled in equal measure.

While the stereotype holds the core values of the OE – independence and competence, self-testing and survival, being a New Zealander and celebrating New Zealand culture – the ways in which these manifested in the OE changed with circumstances, and with each new generation of travellers. The stereotype itself also changed over time. Those going on OE in the boom days of the early 1980s, for example, had already missed the ship voyage, the Hippie Trail and Kangaroo Valley, and were too early for Anzac Day in Gallipoli and the Waitangi Day Pub Crawl. The classic OE for this generation was the pub job, Oktoberfest, ski trips in Europe and travel on a Eurail Pass, but a lot of the things these travellers did – like Sunday sessions at The Church and visiting Pamplona for the Running of the Bulls – would be elevated to classic status a few years later.

In the second decade of the twenty-first century the OE is exemplified by diversity: of destinations; in the length of time spent away; in the types of work and travel styles undertaken; of the ages of the OE travellers; and in the way the OE is approached.

Travellers appear to be taking an increasingly 'pick 'n' mix' approach to the OE (and to travel more generally), but many of the classic OE elements are still evident. OEs have become more personalised, a change fostered and facilitated by technology and the internet. Cyber-world support for the OE has also changed the perception of distance for travellers. Faster transport and the increasing affordability of travel went some way towards reducing the distance between New Zealand and overseas during the first few OE decades; in the later decades, developments in communications technology – broadband and wireless internet, Skype, mobile phones, texting – have made contact with home easier, cheaper and more immediate.

Distance lies at the heart of the OE. New Zealand is physically distant from the rest of the world, a geographical circumstance that not only had to be overcome in a practical sense, but which has traditionally been perceived to impact on our national psyche. The OE involves travelling a great distance: going to Australia is not an OE. Credit for the development of a confident New Zealand national identity has been attributed to the national propensity for going overseas and the perspective of distance this has consistently offered. By highlighting the ways in which New Zealanders differed from others, OE experiences helped many to understand and define themselves. Distance also helped them to define 'home'.

The view from New Zealand

The setting for the OE might be overseas, but its home is in New Zealand, where the OE story is presented and judged from a variety of perspectives. The value of the OE – for both New Zealand society and for the individuals who go – is constantly assessed and reassessed. Linked to this is an ongoing examination of the motives for and purpose of the OE. Regular updates to working holiday or visa regulations are reported in print, radio and television media; the OE is front-page news if changes to visa regulations are perceived to be in any way detrimental to the plans of those on OE or planning to go. There is a peculiar tension, however, between complaints that more restrictive visa conditions constitute a threat to people's opportunities and right to experience an OE, and the recognition that such conditions might actually be beneficial to New Zealand as they could halt a perceived 'brain drain'.

The brain drain

The OE became a political issue in the 1990s and 2000s amid reports of a significant and increasing brain drain. The student loan system, in particular, was blamed for driving many young New Zealanders overseas, either as a way to escape their debt, or to earn higher wages to pay loans back. This triggered a flurry of government-funded research into the relationship between student loans and OE departures, including attempts to quantify the extent of the brain drain. The majority of these studies returned inconclusive results, however. One Ministry of Education study found that those with higher student debt were more likely to be overseas five years after completing their studies, and that those overseas repaid their loans at a slower rate in the first three years after study than did those who stayed in New Zealand. This suggested that people were going overseas to avoid their loans, rather than to earn more money in order to pay them back more quickly.[2] Another study found that, given the diversity of factors that influence people's decisions to go overseas, it was impossible to say with any certainty why they went.[3]

The student loan issue also featured in some of the more anecdotal human-interest OE stories published regularly in magazines and newspapers. The *Timaru Herald*'s 'Class of 90', for example, traced the travels and lives of a cohort of 20 Timaru high school students over a 10-year period. Altogether, 10 of the students had experienced some form of OE while four others still planned to. Five of the 20 students were based overseas in 2000: one was in London, two were in Australia and one in Ireland (another classmate could not be contacted, but was thought to be living in the United States). Eight of the classmates' 41 siblings were also living overseas. These students went to university the first year that student fees were introduced (the student loan system was introduced two years later in 1992). Ten years on, seven of them still had student loans: four owed $30,000, one had $20,000 outstanding, while the other two owed smaller amounts. None of the four with the largest loans was living overseas.[4]

In the mid-2000s brain-drain concerns centred on the continuing loss (and potential non-return) of young, highly qualified New Zealanders. The government initiated a number of campaigns to attract New Zealanders home from their OE (and from overseas more generally). One involved posters in London asking New Zealanders to 'remember what it was like at home'. From 2007 student loans became interest-free as long as one stayed in New Zealand, but the IRD accommodated the OE by offering a three-year repayment holiday for those who went overseas. At the time, this repayment

In the media, the exodus of young New Zealanders – referred to emotively in 2000 by Richard Poole as the 'lost generation' – attracted the attentions of political cartoonists such as Garrick Tremain.

Garrick Tremain. Alexander Turnbull Library, New Zealand Cartoon Archive Collection, Paintings and Prints (DX-022-270)

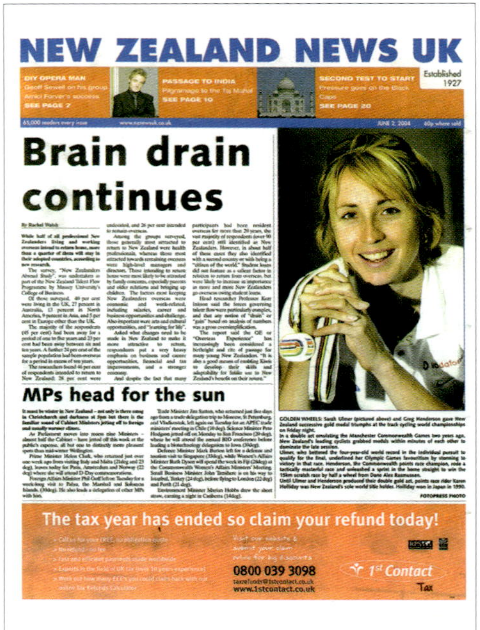
NEW ZEALAND NEWS UK

Established 1927

DIY OPERA MAN — SEE PAGE 7

PASSAGE TO INDIA — SEE PAGE 10

SECOND TEST TO START — SEE PAGE 20

Brain drain continues

MPs head for the sun

The tax year has ended so claim your refund today!

0800 039 3098

www.1stcontact.co.uk

1st Contact Tax

The brain drain was also of interest in the Antipodean London media.
New Zealand News UK

holiday was seen as a 'pragmatic way to deal with the problem of the tradition of the OE'.[5] In 2012 the student loan repayment holiday for those overseas was shortened to only one year.

In the late 2000s debate surrounding the brain drain re-emerged in the context of the global economic recession. Some reports noted that the recession was potentially favourable for New Zealand as it could reduce OE population losses. Others argued that although the loss of thousands of productive people impacts on the New Zealand economy and society, in most years those leaving are replaced by migrants to New Zealand. This argument was followed by some acceptance that really nothing could be done about either OE departures or the New Zealand expatriate population more generally, and that – even if they are living overseas – these New Zealanders constitute a valuable economic resource.

A cultural icon

The media and other popular culture also reinforce the importance and strength of the OE as a cultural icon and its value for individuals who go. Periodically (and again often corresponding with changes in the visa regulations), OE stories appear in the media. These descriptive pieces usually include some OE history, give an estimate of the numbers going, and explain the rationale for the OE. Common underlying themes are that the OE is still driven by New Zealand's geographical isolation, and that it is a New Zealand institution through which New Zealanders can 'pit themselves against the real world'.[6] For individuals, the OE is perceived to be beneficial and is seen as a rite of passage, the successful completion of which bestows a certain degree of status at home.

Having OE experiences neatly packaged into a stereotype facilitates its dissemination in popular culture in New Zealand and its continued acceptance in local society. There are, however, some differences between the media reports on the OE and those that appear in advertising. The latter, for example, encapsulates the OE into its stereotypical form, enabling the less salubrious details to be glossed over and the OE sanitised.

The high incidence of hedonistic behaviour in both travel episodes and London life is rarely articulated in OE representations in New Zealand culture. This allows the OE to maintain its position as a socially accepted norm. The constant media attention afforded the OE reinforces for many New Zealanders how 'ordinary' the OE is.

The media take a more pragmatic approach in reporting 'warts and all' OE stories, often emphasising the negative features of the stereotype. There are occasional articles that deride the benefits of the OE, instead of lauding the positives of overseas travel experience. They highlight the degradation at Gallipoli caused by the badly behaved crowds who attend each year, and the tick-it-off mentality of OE travellers who have no appreciation of culture. They also point out that the OE has changed from what it was – at some undefined point in time – and is somehow not as good as it used to be.

Some of the blame for this is attributed to the fact that because so many people have done an OE, the experience is somehow cheapened. Yet it is only because the OE has a long history that such comparisons can be made. For those going on an OE, there is often some tension as they try to resist following the stereotype; it is common to introduce the negative stereotypical features as justification for *not* going on an OE. Collectively, however, the stereotype provides new travellers with an accessible OE template, even if it is one they go out of their way to avoid.

In the early 2000s a STA Travel campaign focused on the 'UKOE'; Go Holidays and the House of Travel also used the OE and London for their campaigns.

STA Travel; GO Holidays, Auckland, New Zealand; House of Travel

An OE template

Advertising reinforces the idea of what the OE should be (where one should go, what one should do, and so on). Travel advertising, in particular, reinforces London as the primary OE destination, with numerous companies basing their campaigns on the OE. Travel advertising is also a useful indicator of changes in travel behaviour and preferences. A 2007 STA Travel advertising campaign proposed a more diverse range of destinations, suggesting that the OE could be more individualistic, and was based around the slogan 'Define your own OE'; few of

Diversity in the OE. STA Travel

the options they suggested were new to the OE, however. In their view, 'Work your way around the world' offered – in addition to Overseas Experience – Obscure Encounters, Offbeat Exploits, and with Open Eyes there were Opportunities Everywhere. The 'Offbeat Encounters-Experiences-Exploits' included travelling around South Africa on the Baz Bus, sipping champagne before taking a helicopter flight over Las Vegas, and learning to surf in Brazil. With 'Open Eyes' one could see the sights of London on a River Thames cruise, visit the sites of ancient Rome or 'career' through Korea with a rail pass. 'Opportunities Everywhere' were available to those with a British Ancestry Visa, or for those who wanted to travel around Canada on the hop-on hop-off Moose Travel Network. No examples were given for Obscure Encounters.

In 2012 the STA Travel website noted the importance of flexibility when planning an OE and suggested a range of flight options allowing OEs from between six and 18 months or longer. The longest option was for those 'planning to stretch it out as long as possible', for which STA Travel had 'excellent one-way fares to London'. Photos in the 2012 STA brochure, however, were shot in Thailand and showed a traveller with an array of destination badges on their backpack. It was more generically entitled coming 'face to face with your overseas experience' – rather than with an OE. In the last few years New Zealanders have begun to adopt the post-school 'gap year' (which

We can also laugh at Roger Hall's *Taking Off*, in which four women set off for the UK and Europe on belated OEs; or at the two couples on 'The Big OE when you're pasta your prime ...' in *Four Flat Whites in Italy*. Court Theatre, Christchurch

started in Britain) as a mini travel 'rite of passage'; the plan, however, is usually for 'a gap year now and do the OE later'.

The success of the OE in popular culture and advertising is possible only because there is an understood version of the OE. We can easily imagine the backdrop of novels set around the OE, whether they are in the context of 1980s political intrigue (Keith Ovenden's *O.E.*) or in the drug-riddled experiences of an OE in the 2000s (as in Craig Marriner's *Southern Style* and Steven Gannaway's *Seraphim Blues*).[7] Thousands of New Zealanders of all ages can identify (at least in part) with the van tour story told in Grant Lahood's 2003 movie *Kombi Nation*.

It is often those who went on their OEs in the earlier decades who bemoan the changes it has undergone. More recent OE travellers in London are perceived as merely reproducing their social life from home and spending their time down at the pub watching the big match, having gone on OE because their friends are there. Older travellers see the younger generation as travelling in a more arrogant way than in the past; instead of experiencing other cultures, they simply go off and 'do' the Running of the Bulls, Oktoberfest and Gallipoli as part of an OE checklist. They question whether today's OE travellers gain any respect for other cultures, if they really want to celebrate diversity, and whether all their travel does is cement certain prejudices about foreigners.

A review of *Kombi Nation* bemoaned the fact that the characters' lack of interaction with the locals made it more a 'transplanting of Kiwi culture than a compelling overseas experience'.[8] Another reviewer noted that 'when my daughter is packing up for Europe in about 20 years I'm going to plonk her down in front of *Kombi Nation* and say, in true old-fart fashion, "You look out for guys like Scott" [the "louche, conniving and ferrety" male character].'[9]

Despite these changes in attitude towards it, many aspects of the OE have been surprisingly stable. Two generations of one family may have done OEs – 30 years apart – that included trips to an All Blacks game,

Chris Slane questioned the impact of OE on travellers back in the early 1980s.
Chris Slane

Oktoberfest, Scandinavia, North Africa and so on. Perhaps travel in the 1950s, 1960s and 1970s felt more special because fewer people were travelling (generally, not just on OE). While it is perhaps impossible for the modern OE traveller to find new and previously undiscovered travel destinations, after six decades of the OE it is also not feasible to expect to do a wholly original OE. Most of what is now done is done because it *is* the OE: the proponents are on their OE and they do the things they *know* an OE involves. Despite the apparent lack of interest that greets travellers returning to New Zealand, the cumulative effect of six decades of OE travel has been much wider exposure of family members, friends and acquaintances to travel role models.

In the first half of the twentieth century, when the parents of many subsequent OE travellers migrated to New Zealand, most thought they were leaving home for ever. They had no expectation of ever returning to their homeland, even for a holiday. Most probably never imagined that a few decades later their children and grandchildren would be visiting their families back home on a relatively regular basis. Many of the early OE travellers have now seen their own children, grandchildren, nieces or nephews depart on OEs. Being the parent left at home prompts some interesting reflection on one's own OE, and on how times have changed. In particular, the easy and cheap contact with their children overseas by email and regular phone calls reminds many just how isolated from home and family they were in the 1950s, 1960s and 1970s.

Going on OE with a partner often made it more special; many couples treasured their shared memories in later life. Some families have evolved particular OE traditions. When Bob went on his OE in 1972, for example, he bought a small silver camel figurine – a ship of the desert – in Bahrain, and travelled with it 'round my neck alongside a tiki'. The camel became a family talisman and in 2012 – 40 years after Bob bought it – the camel was on another OE with one of his daughters.

By the 2000s there were many more parents who had gone on OEs themselves and who often did not understand why their offspring would not want to go. Some were concerned that their children were doing the 'right' kind of OE. In 2009 Wendy's daughter Bridget left New Zealand on her second OE, a possibility provided by the luxury of an Ancestry Visa. She flew to Scotland, where she had worked previously as a housemaid and a nanny (and where, incidentally, her mother had also worked while on her OE in the early 1980s). She was a qualified early childhood teacher and before she left New Zealand a friend put her in touch with the head of an Edinburgh preschool where she had worked; a maternity-leave position was

ALTHOUGH the ready acceptance of the OE in New Zealand society makes the OE easier, personal motives and circumstances for going varied considerably. When Barbara left in 1977 she recalled, 'It wasn't really a considered kind of decision to go to the UK. I was just thinking there's a plane going.' In 1988 Kylie decided to go only a few weeks before leaving, unlike friends and others she knew who had saved up for months. As she recalled, 'It wasn't even my dream. I was paranoid about my CV not looking good and I had gone back to uni and not stayed, and because I had this disaster I thought the only way to fix it was to go overseas – going overseas was acceptable – you were allowed to do that.' Shelley was also struggling at university, but had no career or work plans in mind either. She used her OE in 1991 as a means to get away from a situation in which she had lost all motivation, thinking that getting away from home and having to stand on her own two feet – and realising what the world was about – would be a cure. The fact that her sister had already gone and her family were glad to see her go – plus she had a few friends who had gone as well – made it seem as if it was a fairly normal thing to do: 'the way was paved'.

According to Chris Slane, even in the early 1980s there were few untouched places left to discover. Chris Slane

DAWN AND MARK decided to go on their OE together in 1988, but Dawn recalled thinking that Mark 'had more to live up to' than she did, because his family had travelled extensively and he had more people to follow, while she, on the other hand, had only one brother who had done an OE. Emma's OE in 1992 was also driven in part by family expectations: 'I just thought I had to go – I was very conscious that in my family everyone's travelled an awful lot. My mum and dad both lived overseas for ages and it's kind of a family culture.'

available and after a quick interview Bridget had the job. She had time to take a tour to Gallipoli (for Anzac Day) before starting work. While Wendy was pleased that Bridget had found a job so quickly, she was especially pleased that it was only a temporary position, as it meant that she would be less likely to succumb to a longer-term (and possibly mundane) working life in Scotland, but would, instead, be in a good position to take off and travel.

Although their own travels provided the impetus for their children's subsequent OEs, often these parents were reluctant to ruin their children's OE experiences by telling them too much about their own. For most of those on OE, knowing what their mothers (or fathers) had done was not always welcome information. Hannah, for example, told her mother about the amount of drinking she and her friends did on a Hogmanay trip to Scotland. Her mother (who went on her OE at the same age) said she had done that as well. Hannah's response was, 'Oh god, Mum.' When Hannah had left New Zealand on her OE, her mother was distressed to see her oldest child off to the other side of the world, but admitted that having been there herself, and knowing how excited and apprehensive her daughter must have been made it easier to deal with.

From the 1990s the probability of one's parents visiting London increased: some to relive their own OE, some to take holidays or do later-life OE and many to use their overseas-based children as an excuse for travel. By the mid-2000s summer time in London had become 'parent season'; the featured topic in a 2006 edition of *TNT Magazine* was 'Entertaining the olds in London'. The author of one article entitled 'Bed time' suggested not having them stay at your flat, unless you really wanted your mum bumping into your flatmate's one-night-stand coming out of the shower, or your dad making polite conversation in the kitchen about careers while your dosser's stubbed-out spliff was sitting in the ashtray.[10]

Hannah's mother went back to London in 2004 (her own OE was in 1974). Initially, she and her husband wanted to put off going *because* Hannah was there; they thought they should leave her alone to experience her OE. Then they realised that they might have to wait two or three years, at which point their next child would be over there, so they decided to go anyway. When they asked their daughter, she had no problem with them visiting: many of her friends' parents were going over. Many OE travellers take advantage of being treated to a free holiday in Europe courtesy of their parents (one of the changes described in the new form of the classic OE in Chapter One).

An OE pilgrimage

For many New Zealanders, their travels in later life incorporate an element of OE pilgrimage as they return to see the places where they had once worked or lived. For most, the trip to their OE destinations and locations was markedly different in style from their earlier experiences, primarily as a result of having a lot more money. In general, London was surprisingly unchanged: the pubs they had worked in were still there, although for some it felt a little surreal to think that they had once stood behind the bar. For many, the most noticeable change in London was that the tube was a lot busier (although most noted that it still smelled the same).

Some older New Zealand travellers repeat their original OEs, like the couple in *For Love and a Beetle: A tale of two journeys*. Later-life OE travellers may have been overseas previously, but were now venturing on their first extended trip; one that would involve work and experience of life overseas, rather than just a holiday, a 'proper OE'. These later-life OEs are more like those of the 1950s and 1960s, despite occurring in the 2000s. While these travellers might still enjoy time at the pub, it is unlikely to be the Redback or a Walkabout. Most accounts suggest that older OE travellers are more interested in history and in tracing their genealogy than their younger compatriots. They are also more likely to take on unusual jobs and jobs outside London, as they are motivated more by novelty than by a concern for their future careers. The stories of these 'greypackers' add increasing diversity to the OE experiences that are regularly reported in the New Zealand media. They also reinforce nostalgia for the OE of old.

The OE successes

The media treatment of the OE covers the full gamut of experiences, from OE and post-OE successes, to failures and disasters. Some people do well on OEs – setting up their own businesses or finding international acclaim while they are away. Many New Zealand artists and musicians still seek success on the international stage; doing so while on an OE – rather than having international success as one's sole motive – offers a more relaxed experience than that encountered by New Zealanders struggling to make it overseas in the cultural-cringe days of the early- to mid-twentieth century. Back then, life overseas was a much more isolated and isolating experience.

Another type of OE success regularly reported in the New Zealand media relates to the achievements of New Zealanders in business and other fields. Among the New Zealand 'occupational successes' listed in a 2003 newspaper article, for example, were: the vice-chancellor of Oxford University, the head of Railtrack (England's railway infrastructure company), the first foreign-born headmaster of Eton College, Britain's National Statistician, and Preacher of the Year in Britain in 2000. While these people would usually be classified as long-term expatriates, they often started their expatriate lives as OE travellers, as was the case with the other two New Zealanders featured in the article in question. Malcolm Grant and Dame Judith Mayhew left New Zealand on their OEs in 1972, both with law degrees: in 2003 Grant was appointed as provost and president (the top job) at London University, while Mayhew was appointed provost of King's College, Cambridge. She had been a key figure in British government and London Corporation finance and policy circles, and chair of the Royal Opera House.[11]

There are also those who have made their names or found business success because of the OE. Numerous OE ventures grew from their founders' own OE experiences, with enterprises and business ideas transplanted from overseas to New Zealand (and sometimes back again). Some of the recruitment companies that serve the OE community – like 1st Contact and KiwiOz Nannies[12] – were started in London by New Zealanders on their OEs, and subsequently opened offices in New Zealand and Australia. Others, having developed new business ideas overseas, returned to New Zealand to put their ideas into practice. Neil Geddes, for example, co-founded Kiwi Experience (the first hop-on hop-off backpacker bus network in the world) in the 1980s, and Oz Experience in the 1990s. He wrote the business plan for Kiwi Experience while on his OE; his co-founder was a Contiki driver in Europe. After developing a similar network in the UK (Stray Travel), he founded Spaceships – at the time a new type of campervan for the more adventurous and independent traveller – which Neil described as 'the VW Combie of the twenty-first century'. In 2009 the company launched Spaceships in the UK.[13]

A diverse range of other businesses have emerged from the OE. John Managh (the founder and managing director of Wilderness Motorhomes in New Zealand), for example, built his first campervan while on OE in California and another for an overland trip from London to Cape Town. The ideas behind a furniture design company and an orange juice company were hatched on OEs;[14] Ray Barker (of Barkers menswear) attributed his love for fashion to his two-year OE in Britain and a job at Burton Tailoring during the early 1970s.[15] The OE also crops up incidentally in numerous 'life story' or career accounts, in which the first successful business or career steps were taken 'when I got back from my OE'.

The OE failures

The OE failures are what are *not* supposed to happen on an OE, but often do, simply because it *is* the real world out there. Sometimes OE travellers simply find themselves in the wrong place at the wrong time. They encounter natural disasters, or criminal or terrorist activity that causes significant personal trauma. They are involved in accidents and incidents that cause serious injury or have fatal consequences. They take part in medical trials that go horribly wrong. The normality of the OE makes it easy to forget that the world can be a dangerous place, and that life does not always go according to plan. In this regard the concept of the OE is protected in the New Zealand media to some extent: when the deaths of travellers are reported in the New Zealand press, the victim has commonly been 'living in London for two years'; if they have survived an accident, they are 'on their OE'. The OE is a positive experience that one is supposed to return from.

The reality of the OE experience can be a shock for many, especially as the amount of pre-OE information available, along with the easy treatment of it in the New Zealand media, suggests that it is a simple undertaking. The wealth of OE information circulating is not always correct; in fact many OE media releases are designed to correct misinformation – the Big OE Evenings were originally designed with this purpose in mind. The internet provides a window into the OE. One can see YouTube clips of London social events, other people's travel adventures and the Waitangi Day Pub Crawl, for example, before even leaving New Zealand, but it is impossible to appreciate what it is like to actually be there. Likewise, modern communications allow friends to text, email and make phone calls cheaply; they are much more likely to say 'get over here – the social life is great' than to admit to having a really bad day at the office, or on the tube, or to communicate their misery when they are midway through a depressing British winter, unable to afford a holiday.

Being an expatriate *is* difficult. Life in London *is* more challenging than life at home in New Zealand. The OE almost always comes loaded with the promise of more travel and adventures than one can afford. Life on the OE is often reduced to a matter of doing one's laundry, joining the local library and spending time with friends from home. Yet, coming home is often no easier: it is hard to settle back, so far away from the world one has seen and experienced. Time does help, and priorities change. Returnees get used to the wind and the cold houses.

Winter in England.
Chris Slane

They bring things back to New Zealand, not least their own reappraisal of the country, of what it means to be a New Zealander and of how they fit in the world.

The legacy of the OE

Compared with the 1950s and the 1960s when the OE began, young people on working holidays can now be found in many countries, including New Zealand. As the number of countries with which New Zealand established working holiday visa schemes grew, so did the number of working holiday-makers spending time in New Zealand. In 1997–98 New Zealand issued working holiday visas to 6897 young people from six countries. In 2010–11 there were 45,000 working holiday visas issued to young people from 32 countries. The opportunity to work temporarily in New Zealand enables these young travellers to extend the length of time they can afford to travel. One key difference between a working holiday experience in New Zealand and the OE, however, is that New Zealand is the primary destination – rather than simply being a useful work and home base – for these travellers. New Zealand is on a well-established and popular 'round-the-world' circuit, but there is no Europe next door.

The ready availability of working holiday permits and the opportunity to live temporarily in an English-speaking country (with a reputation for adventure and nature tourism) offers undoubted appeal to many working holidaymakers. Most have no affiliation to New Zealand although, arguably, those from Britain may feel some connection to the colony that was once part of their empire. While the regulations for working holidaymakers from the UK are now on par with New Zealanders going the other way, the colonial legacy noted in Chapter One allows many thousands more New Zealanders entry to the UK as a result of their ancestry. The 9878 British working holidaymakers in New Zealand in 2007–08, however, represented an almost equal trade, with 10,600 New Zealanders entering the UK in 2007 in an 'others given leave to enter' category.[16] This category included working holidaymakers and British Ancestry Visa holders, but not visitors, students or work permit holders, and so was reasonably representative of the OE population. What these records still do not account for are the number of New Zealanders eligible for British passports, about 20,000 of which are issued each year in New Zealand.

Figures from the British Home Office also suggest a number of alternative endings to the classic two- to three-year New Zealand OE. Each year since 1997, for example, between 1000 and 3000 New Zealanders have been given 'grants of settlement' to remain permanently in the UK: the numbers increased annually from 1155 in 1997 to a peak of 2920 in 2003, and then declined each year, with a fall to 1280 in 2007. In 2007, 215 of these New Zealanders were admitted to the UK as a husband or fiancé, and 240 as a wife or fiancée. The number of New Zealanders removed from the UK has also been consistent over the last few years, with 205 removed in 2005, 220 in 2006, and 225 in 2007.[17] In 2008 there were 260 removals, and 270 in 2009; also in 2009, of the 1405 people given grants of settlement, 260 were as husbands and 305 were as wives.[18] Although these represent small percentages of the grand totals – in 2007, for example, a total of 124,855 people were given grants of settlement and 63,365 were removed from the UK – the long history of the OE and the nature of the migration it has engendered has bestowed the New Zealand population in Britain with a significance that belies both its size and its visibility as a migrant population.

Invisible migrants?

As noted, the true size of the New Zealand population in London is difficult to determine as one must add to the official figures those with British or European passports, those who remain illegally, and those who just don't fill in the census. New Zealanders on OE do not fit any of the four categories used to classify migrants in Britain, nor are they normally counted in the international passenger survey data, except when they first arrive. The ongoing nature of the OE also adds incrementally to the total number of New Zealanders in Britain, particularly as in most years more are added than leave. Also, just as is the case with New Zealand migration figures, it is difficult to differentiate the OE population from the larger expatriate New Zealand population.

The expatriate New Zealand population in London is not a highly visible migrant group. Londoners may encounter New Zealanders in the workplace, or when they are going about their daily lives, but they don't register as a collective group. Often it is only when the topic of 'New Zealanders in the UK' is deliberately introduced into conversation that British people reflect on the New Zealanders they know and realise they work with three New Zealanders, have one working in their bank or serving them in their local pub, have another working at their doctor's surgery, the guy who fixed their leaking roof was from New Zealand, and so on.

The substantial OE support network and infrastructure that has developed in London also flies under the local radar; often it is recognisable only to those for whom it is relevant. Apart from a few select areas, the New Zealand population is reasonably well dispersed around the city (even if the Earls Court–Kangaroo Valley association still lingers).

Some New Zealand (and OE) 'events' – sessions at The Church, the Waitangi Day Pub Crawl – have become London tourist attractions. London guidebooks and backpacker websites also commonly list Antipodean attractions such as the travellers' pubs and sporting events (although Antipodeans probably make up a large proportion of their target audience anyway). The struggle by many of these venues to

The Waitangi Day Pub Crawl is one of the few occasions when New Zealanders stand out.

Chris Heine

remain 'Australasian' is an indication of their broader popularity; in the early 1990s, for example, there was a popular fallacy that British people were not allowed at The Church. The Antipodean sporting leagues attract many Britons who hear of them through working with New Zealanders and Australians, and who simply like the idea of playing social sport midweek. Antipodean co-workers might also take them to events like the annual Toast Festival and introduce them to travel destinations such as Oktoberfest and Pamplona.

Going global

It is in the travel and tourism industry that the OE has probably had the most impact on a global scale. Several global travel companies have strong associations with New Zealand and Australian travellers. STA Travel, for example, had its joint origin as Student Travel Australia and STA Travel in Britain. The company was formed to meet the travel needs of adventurous students in the 1970s and expanded to cater to the broader youth travel market in the 1980s. Now Swiss owned (by Diethelm Keller Ltd), STA Travel had a worldwide network of more than 400 branches in 2008 and had more than 100 branches in Australia and New Zealand. In 2012 the company employed more than 3000 people.

TrailFinders, one of the largest travel operators in Britain, started business as an overland tour operator in 1970, with a staff of four. Over time, the company expanded to provide air and other travel services; in 2012 it employed over 1100 people.[19] In the early days of the company, the thousands of young Antipodean travellers in Europe, doing overland tours on the Hippie Trail or needing air tickets to travel between New Zealand and Australia and Britain/Europe made up an important segment of their clientele.

Many other travel companies were started by OE travellers, either while they were on their OEs or after they returned to New Zealand. Contiki and Top Deck grew out of the OE: the founders of Top Deck went on to start Flight Centre. Many of the tourism business models these OE travellers introduced have subsequently been copied the world over and many of the people involved in the tourism industry both in New Zealand and overseas appear to have 'cut their teeth' on a European camping tour.

The numerous OE support businesses have also made significant economic contributions in Britain and in New Zealand. Publications like *TNT Magazine* are long-standing and significant for the number of jobs they create, their distribution figures and the advertising revenues they generate, even if most of it is within the community they serve. The New Zealand shops operated as informal tourist information points in London, as well as test outlets for New Zealand products. In many cases these products subsequently became significant and mainstream exports to Britain. The travellers' pubs offered outlets for New

Zealand beers and wines that were invaluable for New Zealand producers wanting to 'crack' British and European markets.

Bringing the world to New Zealand

The OE has also left an ongoing legacy in New Zealand. The majority of OE travellers eventually return to New Zealand and it is reasonable to assume that, after living, working and travelling overseas for some years, they come back to New Zealand with new ideas and expectations. For example, returning OE travellers are often credited with bringing decent coffee to New Zealand (and, ironically, taking it back to Britain), with introducing a diet more exotic than the traditional meat and three vegetables, and with the development of a wine palate. However, it is difficult to quantify the contribution the OE has made to New Zealand society and culture. It would be a fascinating area for research. What is undeniable is that the OE changes people's attitudes to their own country: it increases awareness of one's national identity which, coupled with the continuing reassessment of New Zealand by successive generations of OE travellers, has given us a more realistic view of both the world and ourselves.

Another legacy of the OE has been the introduction of many new migrants to New Zealand, a result of many OE travellers being of an age when they were likely to meet significant others. An early 2000s OE joke was that one could go all the way to London to 'end up' with someone from one's home town. Quite a number of OE travellers left New Zealand with one partner and returned with another.

Many of the OE travellers whose stories enhance this book met and married foreigners with whom they subsequently shared life in New Zealand; one of the 1960s OE travellers brought an Italian home to New Zealand, another married a Jordanian. Of those who were away in the 1980s, one returned with an American wife (whom he met in Switzerland); another returned with an Irish husband (whom she met in Japan); another met her English husband in China, married him in the Channel Islands, and after a few years in London brought him to New Zealand; yet another married an Australian she shared a squat with in London, before bringing him to New Zealand to live; another, having spent several years in Britain, moved to Los Angeles where she met and married – back on the farm in New Zealand – an Israeli.

One consequence of the OE is that many New Zealanders now have family and friends scattered all over the world. The offspring of the various OE unions noted above, for example, have grandparents and cousins in Italy, Ireland, America, Israel, Jordan and countless other countries. The downside to this is the expense in later years of taking one's children to visit grandparents and in-laws. One solution to this problem was to bring them back to New Zealand with you: after 20 years in Britain, Brian and his British

In the late 1960s Beverley's workmates (at a natural history publishing company) presented her with a hand-drawn farewell card: they waved goodbye to their Kiwi (flying with the aid of a parachute), as she headed – via a stop in New Orleans – back to her natural habitat, carrying the two books that signified her London achievements.

wife Sue and their children finally moved to New Zealand (Brian had always planned to return 'one day'); Sue's parents came to visit and decided to buy a house in New Zealand. They now spend seven months of each year near their New Zealand family, as they qualify for permanent residence.

Flying Kiwis

The OE has indisputably changed over time from being a response to a set of circumstances to being an entity in its own right. Economic crises have changed or threatened it, as have visa regulation changes and technological developments. New generations and cohorts of travellers want and expect different things from their OE experiences, but what they do while on OE remains essentially the same, as do the perceived benefits of the experience for the individuals who go. The phenomenon of the OE experienced two boom periods: the first, in the early 1980s, was driven by the commercial opportunities surrounding a burgeoning market of young travellers; the second, in the early 2000s, was a more fleeting flurry of OE activity facilitated by internet technology. Little enduring evidence of these survives.

The OE is an important element of New Zealand's cultural history, however, and is closely entwined with other recognisable symbols of national identity. A 2010 'Guide to being a New Zealander', published in the *Listener*, noted: 'You're probably not a proper New Zealander unless you … kidded to people during your OE that you spoke fluent Māori by reciting *Pokarekare Ana* and stringing a few places names together (accompanied by haka actions) … (and) … worked in a bar or restaurant, preferably overseas.'[20] The same article suggested that independence and the high value we place on freedom are defining characteristics of the New Zealand identity, albeit with the caveat: 'We're like the teenager of the world. We want to do our own thing, and we're doing it

– but we still really want that pat on the back from overseas.'[21]

Somehow, no matter whenever or wherever we went, we can still identify with today's OE. Two postage stamps illustrated Chapter One of this book. One, from 1997, depicts the flightless kiwi (the bird) leaving New Zealand on the back of a Buzzy Bee; the kiwi wears a black and white scarf and carries a suitcase that says 'OE'. The other, from 2008, has a black background, a silver fern, and shows a view of the horizon and of clouds framed by the 'O' of an airplane window: the 'O' is for O.E. We Kiwis have always found a way to fly.

We know everything and nothing about the OE. If the numbers are to be believed, most New Zealanders have never actually been on an OE. It is understood in a somewhat mythical and stereotypical form that never existed. Thousands of OE travellers never went to London, never went to Oktoberfest and never went on a Contiki tour; but many thousands did. With our newfound cultural confidence we no longer need to do an OE in the ways that we once did: we grew up and so did the OE. What started as simply *going overseas* became *the OE*, was elevated to *The Big OE*, and has now dissipated into innumerable and increasingly diverse *OEs*. There are signs pointing to the eventual demise of the (classic) OE experience, but we shouldn't mourn its passing: it was a very real and culturally important New Zealand travel practice for more than 60 years. The OE served its purpose. The OE is and was significant, not least for those who went.

'Oh … it was nothing, reelly!' Chris Slane

NOTES

Chapter 1

1 Sell, B. *The Big OE Companion: A guide for New Zealanders in the UK* (Auckland: Random House, 2004), 10.
2 According to Max Cryer in *The Godzone Dictionary* (2006), the term 'OE' was actually coined by the father of Massey University lecturer John Muirhead, who used it in the 1960s. Tom Scott heard the term when he was a student at Massey.
3 Mulgan, J. *Report on Experience* (Auckland: Oxford University Press, 1984), 3–4.
4 'New Zealand overseas travel trends and statistics by Asmal': www.asmal.com/
5 Stead, C.K. For the hulk of the world's between. In K. Sinclair (ed.), *Distance Looks Our Way: The effects of remoteness on New Zealand* (Auckland: Paul's Book Arcade, University of Auckland, 1961), 79–96.
6 Brasch, C. The Islands. In J. Bornholdt, G. O'Brien & M. Williams (eds), *An Anthology of New Zealand Poetry in English* (Auckland: Oxford University Press, 1998), 372.
7 Clark, M. (ed.), *Godwits Return* (Wellington: Bridget Williams Books, 1992).
8 Graham, S. *The Tender Traveller: A New Zealander abroad* (Wellington: A.H. & A.W. Reed, 1963), 13.
9 Focamp, P. 'Maud Island', Christchurch *Press*, 26 February 2005, D9.
10 'New Zealand Post, 40c – Garrick Tremain', *Stamp Archive – 1997 Cartoonists*: www.secure.nzpost.co.nz/cgi-bin/nzstamps/web_store/web_store.cgi?cart_id=&page=archive/nzstamp_archive.htm
11 Helyer Donaldson, R. 'Overseas – and experienced', *New Zealand Listener*, 14–19 June 2004, 17.
12 Salmond, A. *Between Worlds: Early exchanges between Maori and Europeans 1773–1815* (Auckland: Viking, 1997), 345.
13 Savage, J. *Some Account of New Zealand; Particularly the Bay of Islands and surrounding country* (Christchurch: Capper Press, 1807), 39–40, 110.
14 Salmond, A. *Between Worlds: Early exchanges between Maori and Europeans 1773–1815.*
15 McLintock, A.H., 'Hongi Hika', *Te Ara – the Encyclopaedia of New Zealand*: www.TeAra.govt.nz/1966/H/HongiHika/en
16 Scherzer. In H. Hogan, *Bravo, Neu Zeeland: Two Maori in Vienna 1859–1860* (Christchurch: Clerestory Press, 2003), 5.
17 Ibid., for a full translation of this journey.
18 Ibid.
19 Ibid.
20 Phillips, J. 'The New Zealanders: Maorilanders', *Te Ara – the Encyclopedia of New Zealand:* www.teara.govt.nz/NewZealanders/NewZealandPeoples/TheNewZealanders/5/en
21 King, M. *The Penguin History of New Zealand* (Auckland: Penguin Books, 2003).
22 Gould, B. Does our history matter? In R.G. Patman (ed.), *New Zealand and Britain: A special relationship in transition* (Palmerston North: Dunmore Press, 1997), 67–79.
23 King, *The Penguin History of New Zealand.*
24 Phillips, 'The New Zealanders: Maorilanders'.
25 Phillips, J. 'The New Zealanders: Empire's loyal sons', *Te Ara – the Encyclopedia of New Zealand:* www.teara.govt.nz/NewZealanders/NewZealandPeoples/TheNewZealanders/7/en
26 Sinclair, K. *A Destiny Apart: New Zealand's search for national identity* (Wellington: Unwin Paperbacks, 1986).
27 McLean, D. *The Prickly Pair: Making nationalism in Australia and New Zealand* (Dunedin: University of Otago Press, 2003), 227.
28 Brabazon, T. *Tracking the Jack: A retracing of the Antipodes* (Sydney: University of New South Wales Press, 2000).
29 Sinclair, *A Destiny Apart.*
30 Ell, G. *New Zealand Traditions and Folklore* (Auckland: Bush Press, 1994).
31 Woods, N. Converging challenges and diverging identities. In R.G. Patman, *New Zealand and Britain*, 27–39.
32 King, *The Penguin History of New Zealand.*
33 Ibid., 381.
34 Sumpter, H.K. *Travelling Light: To Europe and back on £200* (Invercargill: Southland Times Print, 1934), 5.
35 www.rbnz.govt.nz/statistics/0135595.html
36 High Commissioner for New Zealand, *New Zealand Handbook, 1929* (London: Helen Ferguson, 1929).
37 Donnelly, I. *The Joyous Pilgrimage: A record of months that realised a dream* (Letchworth: Temple, 1935).
38 Ibid., 221–22.

39 See, for example: McGibbon, I., & Goldstone, P. Anzac Day. In *Oxford Companion to New Zealand Military History* (Oxford: Oxford University Press, 2000); Mulgan, *Report on Experience*; and Pugsley, C. *Gallipoli: The New Zealand story* (Auckland: Hodder and Stoughton, 1984).
40 Tullet, J.S. *Nairn Bus to Baghdad* (Wellington: A.H. & A.W. Reed, 1968); and www.fuchs-online.com/overlandmail/articles/The_Nairn_Way.htm
41 Sutherland, L. *I Follow the Wind* (London: Southern Cross Press, c. 1960).
42 www.nzhistory.net.nz/war/second-world-war/counting-the-cost
43 Wolfe, R. *Looking Back: New Zealand 1900–2005* (Auckland: Whitcoulls, 2007).
44 Brewer, Gunner N.H. (Joe). *The Soldier Tourist: A personal account of World War II* (Auckland: Reed, 1999).
45 Allison, E.S. *Kiwi at Large* (London: Robert Hale, 1961); and Allison, E.S. *Kiwi Vagabond* (London: The Travel Book Club, 1969).
46 Mason, M.J. *The Water Flows Uphill* (Auckland: Blackwood and Janet Paul, 1964).
47 Mulgan, *Report on Experience*, 17.
48 Easthope, J. Home away from home: The recent history of overseas travel by New Zealanders to Britain, c. 1960–1975 (Unpublished Honours research paper, Victoria University, Wellington, New Zealand, 1993).
49 Ibid.
50 Sutherland, R. *Land of the Bog-cotton* (London: Hodder and Stoughton, 1960), 14.
51 Easthope, Home Away from Home.
52 Calder, P. *Travels with my Mother* (Auckland: Tandem Press, 2003).
53 'Change in form of NZ passport', Christchurch *Press*, 18 February 1964, 14.
54 Patman, *New Zealand and Britain.*
55 'New immigration rules explained', Christchurch *Press*, 31 January 1973, 18.
56 'Entry to Britain', Christchurch *Press*, 31 January 1973, 16.
57 'Bitter reaction to British immigration rules', Christchurch *Press*, 1 November 1972, 3.
58 'Peer's plea on immigration', Christchurch *Press*, 8 December 1972, 2.
59 Patman, *New Zealand and Britain.*
60 King, *The Penguin History of New Zealand*, 418.
61 'Whim Wham' was the pseudonym under which the poet Allen Curnow wrote topical satirical verses in the *Press* and the *New Zealand Herald*, in the 1940s and 1950s; Sinclair, K. (ed.), *Distance Looks Our Way: The effects of remoteness on New Zealand* (Auckland: Paul's Book Arcade, 1961), 40.
62 Grayland, E. *More Famous New Zealanders* (Christchurch: Whitcombe and Tombs, 1972).
63 Harris, N. *The Fly Away People* (London: Baynard-Hillier, 1971).
64 Clark, *Godwits Return.*
65 Ibid., 79.
66 Patman, *New Zealand and Britain.*
67 Bluck, J. *Waking Up in Strange Places: Where do New Zealanders belong?* (Christchurch: Hazard Press, 1999).
68 Reeves, P. Issues of identity. In Clark, *Godwits Return*, 104.
69 Clark, *Godwits Return*, 83.
70 Ibid., 96.
71 There has been a strong focus in the literature on the search for a New Zealand national identity and on the identity issues that have beset the non-Māori population. These are explored in collections such as: Sinclair, *A Destiny Apart*; King, M. (ed.), *Pakeha: The quest for identity in New Zealand* (Auckland: Penguin, 1991); King, M. *Being Pakeha Now: Reflections and recollections of a white native* (Auckland: Penguin Books, 1999).
72 Sinclair, *A Destiny Apart*, 7.
73 Frame, J. *The Envoy From Mirror City* (Auckland: Century Hutchinson, 1986), vol. 3, 5.
74 Heenan, B. 'Population', *Pacific Viewpoint* vol. 2, no. 2, 1979, 95–102.
75 McGill, D. *Kiwi Baby Boomers: Growing up in New Zealand in the 40s, 50s and 60s* (Lower Hutt: Mills Publications, 1989), 171.
76 Scott, T. *Overseizure* (Christchurch: Whitcoulls, 1978).

Chapter 2

1 Hodge, I., & McGovern, P. *For Love and a Beetle: A tale of two journeys* (Sydney: New Holland, 1999).
2 Miles, S., & Bolot, P. *Down Under in Europe: A survival kit for Australians and New Zealanders in London and thereabouts* (London: Pan Books, 1973), 10.
3 These and all subsequent New Zealand currency calculations were made using the Reserve Bank CPI Inflation Calculator: www.rbnz.govt.nz/statistics/0135595.html
4 'Ships Nostalgia' is an online discussion forum for people with an interest in ships and shipping: www.shipsnostalgia.com/showthread.php?t=9858
5 This is calculated using the Reserve Bank of Australia Inflation Calculator: www.rba.gov.au/calculator/annualDecimal.html
6 Thomas, G., & Forbes Smith, C. *Flightpaths: Exposing the myths about airlines and airfares* (Perth: Aerospace Technical Publications International, 2003).
7 Union Travel Service advertisement, Christchurch *Star*, 8 February 1963, 3.
8 The largest and most northern of the Phoenix Group, Kiribati – now known as Kanton Island or Abariringa Island. Originally a stopping point for flying boat services, a 6000-foot airstrip was constructed on the island during World War II. After the war, the island became

a stopping point for commercial flights across the Pacific. Following the withdrawal of a NASA tracking station in 1965, the airfield was used only for emergencies and was finally abandoned in 1975.
9 Graham, S. *The Tender Traveller: A New Zealander abroad* (Wellington: A.H. & A.W. Reed, 1963).
10 'New low fare to London due soon', Christchurch *Star*, 6 October 1979, 17.
11 Thomas & Forbes Smith, *Flightpaths.*
12 Rennie, N. *Conquering Isolation: The first 50 years of Air New Zealand* (Auckland: Heinemann Reed, 1990).
13 Theroux, P. *The Great Railway Bazaar* (London: Hamish Hamilton, 1975).
Several detailed accounts of the hippie trail have been published in recent years: Alderson, F. *The New 'Grand Tour': Travelling today through Europe, Asia Minor, India and Nepal* (Newton Abbot: David & Charles, 1971); MacLean, R. *Magic Bus: On the hippie trail from Istanbul to India* (London: Viking, 2006); Marnham, P. *Road to Kathmandu* (London: Macmillan, 1971); Neville, R. *Play Power* (London: Jonathan Cape, 1970); and Tomory, D. *A Season in Heaven: True tales from the road to Kathmandu* (Melbourne: Lonely Planet Publications, 1998).
14 A limited amount of information on this guide can be found at: hqinfo.blogspot.com/2006/08/alternative-society-1970s-bit-travel.html
15 Jenkins, D. *Student Guide to Asia* (Melbourne: Australia Union of Students, 1973).
16 Gage, M. *The Overlander's Handbook: A guide for the overland adventurer to India and beyond* (Perth: Id Publications, 1976), 18.
17 Jenkins, *Student Guide to Asia*, 12.
18 Wheeler, T. *Across ASIA on the Cheap* (Sydney: Lonely Planet Publications, 1973), 14.
19 Wheeler, T. & Wheeler, M. *Once While Travelling: The Lonely Planet story* (Melbourne: Penguin, 2005).
20 James, B. *Top Deck Daze: Adventures on the frog and toad* (Avalon Beach, NSW: Halbooks, 1999), 77.
21 These calculations are based on the Retail Price Index (figures were available only to 2011): www.measuringworth.com/ukcompare/
22 US$ calculations were made using: www.usinflationcalculator.com/
23 An overland website, constructed by ex-Asian Greyhound driver Derek Amey, has accounts of many of the overland companies along with photos, brochures and a forum to reconnect people who travelled overland: www.indiaoverland.biz/
24 Wheeler, *Across ASIA on the Cheap*, 55.
25 Sutherland, L. *I Follow the Wind* (London: Southern Cross Press, c. 1960), 1.
26 McCarter, N. *The Big OE: Tales from New Zealand travellers* (Auckland: Tandem Press, 2001), 72.
27 James, *Top Deck Daze,* 235.
28 www.indiaoverland.biz/overland/asiangreyhound.html
29 The Anglo Australian Comfortable Coach Company, history, reunion and memorial site: nickw.worldonline.co.uk/timh.html
30 'Stranded overseas through a tour operator going bust?' *Consumer, 157,* December 1978, 338–39.

Chapter 3

1 A number of references to the Overseas Visitors Club can be found on the internet, although there appears to be some debate as to the accuracy of the information reported: theoldbluetruck.wordpress.com/about/d-then-came-keith/the-overseas-visitors-club/. See also de Souza, F.H. *No. 3, Templeton Place* (London: Minerva Press, 1998); and de Souza, F.H. *Earls Court, the OVC and Me* (South Africa: Kiaat Creations, 2008).
2 Parr, C.J. 'A foreword', *New Zealand News,* 29 November 1927, 1.
3 Sumpter, H.K. *Travelling Light: To Europe and back on £200* (Invercargill: Southland Times Print, 1934), 48.
4 Graham, S. *The Tender Traveller: A New Zealander abroad* (Wellington: A.H. & A.W. Reed, 1963), 78–79.
5 Harrop, A. 'Twelve thousand reasons', *New Zealand News,* 29 November 1927, 1.
6 Dunbar, J. *Travelling Abroad* (London: English Universities Press, 1957), 86.
7 Elliott, M. 'Time to travel', *Weekly News,* 26 April 1962, 15.
8 'Hope and glory fades for young adventurers when money runs out', *New Zealand News,* 13 August 1975, 3.
9 Andrew, P. *Life with Louise* (Dunedin: Southern Cross Press, (1964).
10 McGill, D. *The Dolly Lolly Diaries: Tales of a tame Kiwi lad transformed by tempting London lasses* (Wellington: Silver Owl Press, 1998), 6.
11 Graham, *The Tender Traveller*, 77.
12 Miles, S., & Bolot, P. *Down Under in Europe: A survival kit for Australians and New Zealanders in London and thereabouts* (London: Pan Books, 1973), 47.
13 Ibid., 21–22.
14 The club history can be found at: www.lnzrugby.co.uk/history.html
15 For a history of the club see: Gaffikin, Paddy, *Kiwis on the Common: 50 years of the London New Zealand Cricket Club* (Brighton, East Sussex: Tasman Publications, c. 2002), or: www.lnzcc.org/kiwis_on_the_common.htm
16 All that remains of the New Zealand connection are the Aorangi Picnic Terrace, the Aorangi Food Court and Aorangi Café. The Aorangi Picnic Terrace is now popularly known as Henman Hill.
17 Dudson, M. *Oamaru to Europe: 'What do you want to go there for?'* (Christchurch: Kitchen Table Top Publishing, 1995).

18 Ibid., 199. The Tivoli Pub was attached to the cinema of the same name.
19 Ibid.
20 'Travelling on the Continent', *New Zealand News,* 26 October 1965, 5.
21 Ibid.
22 'Reputation rocked by young Kiwis abroad', *New Zealand News,* 23 September 1970, 6.
23 Eurail backgrounder 2004/2005: www.eurail.lwb-online.info/index.php?view=cms_2707
24 History of Inter Rail: www.interrailnet.com/history.dhtml
25 www.topdecktravel.co.uk/about
26 Miles & Bolot, *Down Under in Europe*, 72.
27 Anderson, J. *Only Two Seats Left: The incredible Contiki story* (Australia: The Great Gathering Company, 2010). Some information on the history of the company can also be found at: www.contiki.com/en-NZ/About.Us/; and *North & South,* February 2005, 48–56.
28 Miles & Bolot, *Down Under in Europe*, 73.
29 These calculations are based on the Retail Price Index (figures were only available to 2010) and were calculated from: www.measuringworth.com/ukcompare/
30 Immunisation stopped in many countries, such as the US, in 1972. New Zealand and Australia were the only countries who had never vaccinated widely, instead relying on protection by distance and strict quarantines. All intending international travellers were, however, required to have smallpox vaccinations. The 1975 edition of *Down Under in Europe* listed a smallpox certificate as compulsory documentation for getting into Britain. In 1979, WHO recommended that vaccination against smallpox be stopped in all countries, the only exception being special groups, such as researchers working with smallpox and related viruses.
31 Dudson, *Oamaru to Europe.*
32 Reserve Bank of New Zealand, Exchange Control: Travel and fares, June 1968.
33 Graham, *The Tender Traveller,* 22.
34 Miles & Bolot, *Down Under in Europe*, 55.
35 Graham, *The Tender Traveller,* 35.
36 'Christmas telephone calls', *New Zealand News,* 16 December 1970, 1.

Chapter 4

1 Miles, S., & Bolot, P. *Down Under in Europe: A survival kit for Australians and New Zealanders in London and thereabouts* (London: Pan Books, 1973), 5.
2 'A plea for antipodeans', *Christchurch Star,* 22 January 1980, 7.
3 'UK places limits on young NZ visitors', Christchurch *Star,* 19 January 1980, 16.
4 Dekker, D. 'End of the Big OE?' Christchurch *Press,* 12 February 2002, 21–22.
5 'Big OE rules', Christchurch *Press,* 26 August 2003, B7.
6 'Kiwis to flock to UK', Christchurch *Press,* 12 August 2003, A6.
7 There has been a Working Holiday Scheme allowing British citizens into New Zealand since May 1993.
8 Bleakley, L. 'Britain tightens rules on work visas', Christchurch *Press,* 9 February 2005, A10.
9 The accuracy of these statistics is reliant on the validity of the stated intentions of travellers when they fill in arrival and departure cards. People may jump categories (for example, recording that they are leaving for more than a year, but returning sooner and vice versa).
10 In New Zealand the baby boom generally describes the population born between 1946 and 1965, although the end date is often left unspecified as the post-1965 generation was not significantly smaller than the baby boom.
11 *New Zealand Now: Baby boomers* (Wellington: Statistics New Zealand, 1995).
12 Statistics New Zealand, 'Demographic trends 2003': www.stats.govt.nz/analytical-reports/dem-trends-2003/default.htm
13 Data available from International Labour Organization: www.abetech.org/ilm/english/ilmstat/table06.asp
14 Population Monitoring Group, *On the Move: Migration and population – trends and policies (PMG Report No. 6)* (Wellington: New Zealand Planning Council, 1991).
15 Bryant, J. & Law, D. *New Zealand's Diaspora and Overseas-born Population,* (New Zealand Treasury Working Paper WP04/13, 2004).
16 Rogers, S. 'The UK's foreign-born population: See where people live and where they are from': www.guardian.co.uk/news/datablog/2011/may/26/foreign-born-uk-population
17 *The Big O.E.: A do-it-yourself world travel guide for Kiwis* (Christchurch: Youth Hostels Association of New Zealand, 1990).
18 McCullum, S. *Live, Work and Play in London and the UK: For young New Zealanders* (2nd ed.), (Auckland: Viking, 1996).
19 *Big OE Guide: Essential reading for all New Zealanders travelling overseas* (Christchurch: YHA New Zealand, 1997).
20 McCullum, S. *Live, Work and Play in London and the UK: For young New Zealanders* (revised ed.), (Auckland: Penguin Books, 2000).
21 Sell, B. *The Big OE Companion: A guide for New Zealanders in the UK* (Auckland: Random House, 2004).
22 *New Zealand News UK, Directory* (2nd ed.), (London: New Zealand News Ltd, 2004); and 1st Contact, 'The Big OE Guide 2004': www.1stcontact.co.uk/nz
23 Sell, *The Big OE Companion.*
24 Miles & Bolot, *Down Under in Europe.*
25 Those attending each evening were invited to enter a prize draw; the entry forms collected some demographic data on attendees as well as information on their OE and travel plans.

26 When South Africa rejoined the Commonwealth in 1994, young South Africans became eligible for UK working holiday permits. A dedicated South African news and sport section first appeared in *TNT* in April 1996.
27 '*NZ News UK* calls it a day', Christchurch *Press*, 5 August 2006, A12.
28 Sell, *The Big OE Companion*, 14.

Chapter 5

1 Hindley, G. *Tourists, Travellers and Pilgrims* (London: Hutchinson, 1983).
2 Odin, M., & Odin, L. *Europe: By camper van* (Sydney: Emma Books, 1979).
3 Rowe, C. *Europe by Campervan* (Garradunga: Garradunga Press, 1991), 2.
4 In an 'apology to Kiwis who read this book', the author noted that 'references to Australia throughout the book generally mean Australia and New Zealand, however it was too unwieldy to mention both all the time'. At the time, the term 'Australasia' was not in common usage.
5 Hibbert, C. *The Grand Tour* (London: Hamlyn, 1969); and Towner, J. *An Historical Geography of Recreation and Tourism in the Western World 1540–1940* (Chichester: John Wiley & Sons, 1996).
6 Urry, J. *The Tourist Gaze* (London: Sage, 1990).
7 Urry, J. *The Tourist Gaze* (2nd ed.), (London: Sage, 2002).
8 Dickman, S. *Tourism: An introductory text* (3rd ed.), (Rydalmere, NSW: Hodder Education, 1998), 4.
9 Pepperell, S. 'The Big OE – garbage TV', Waikato *Times*, 19 June 2000.
10 Quigan, A., & Gumbley, R. *The Big O.E.* (Christchurch: Court Theatre, 17 April 2002).
11 Hay, C., & Strykert, R. 'Down under'. On *Business as Usual*: Men at Work, 1982), CBS.
12 Lahood, G. *Kombi Nation*, Arkles Entertainment, 2003.
13 Gumtree (www.gumtree.co.uk) was launched in 2000 as a local London classified advertisement and community site serving Australian and New Zealand expatriates. In 2005, Gumtree became part of the Kijiji family within eBay.
14 'Van tour survey', *TNT Magazine,* 1 April 1996, 61.
15 Ferns, S. 'Home and away', *Evening Standard,* 21 April 1995, 20-21.
16 'Van tour survey', *TNT Magazine,* 1 April 1996, 61.
17 Glanfield, T. 'Campervan Kiwis at risk of becoming endangered', *New Zealand Herald,* 20 June 2005.
18 'Van tour: What's it all about?': vantour.co.uk/index.html
19 www.tntmagazine.com/travel/big-trip/the-ultimate-european-summer-road-trip---get-your-camper-van-and-come-along/page/4
20 According to some sources the current Sundowners has no connection to the original company of the same name.
21 'About us': www.contiki.com/en-NZ/About.Us/
22 White, M. 'On the road: John Anderson's Contiki journey', *North & South,* 21 February 2005, 48–56.
23 *The Big OE*, MF Films, 2000.
24 Henger, K. 'The big OE', *New Zealand Woman's Weekly,* 12 June 2000, 24–25.
25 'Top Deck Travel – All about us': www.topdecktravel.co.uk/about
26 'Eurail backgrounder 2004/2005': www.eurail.lwb-online.info/index.php?view=cms_2707; and 'History of Inter Rail': www.interrailnet.com/history.dhtml
27 Hand, J. *Let's Go: Europe* (USA: Harvard Student Agencies, 1981).
28 Ibid; Michener, J. *The Drifters* (New York: Random House, 1971); 'The Rough Guide to Europe: 2004 edition': www.roughguides.com
29 James, B. *Top Deck Daze: Adventures on the frog and toad* (Avalon, Australia: Halbooks, 1999); and James, B. *Top Deck Daze: Adventures on the frog and toad* (revised ed.), (Australia: Kokoda, 2010).
30 'A brief history': www.pptravel.com/pphistory.asp
31 www.firstfestivaltravel.com/
32 Henderson, K. '100 Club at Beerfest in Munich', www.travoholic.com/euro/articles/2100club.htm
33 Bradbury, F. 'American man paralysed by Pamplona bull', *Independent,* 8 July 2006, 28.
34 O'Connor, M. *The New Zealand European Connection* (Wellington: Grantham House, 1989), 48.
35 MacDonald, F. 'Pamplona, check. Beerfest, check. Gallipoli, check', *Sunday Star Times,* 1 May 2005, C10.
36 Pepperell, S. 'Sacred pilgrimage for Kiwis who flock to "ANZAC season"', *Daily News*, 17 June 2005.
37 Hanna, C. 'The results are in', *TNT Magazine,* 1145, 8 August 2005, 25.
38 Nowicki, D. 'Pilgrims urged to take rubbish with them', *TNT Magazine,* 1176, 13 March 2006, 39.
39 O'Connor, *The New Zealand European Connection.*
40 'PP Travel – The Party Professionals website': www.pptravel.com/default.asp
41 van Geldermalsen, M. *Married to a Bedouin* (London: Virago, 2006).
42 Woodward Swinburn, A. *The Scent of Rosewater: A New Zealand bride in Iran* (Christchurch: Shoal Bay, 1998).
43 A website called Spirit of Encounter has been set up for past passengers and crew to connect to: www.spiritofencounter.co.uk/
44 Crowther, G. *Africa on the Cheap* (Melbourne: Lonely Planet Publications, 1977).
45 Antweiler, W. 'Foreign currency units per 1 British Pound, 1948-2004': www.fx.sauder.ubc.ca/etc/GBPpages.pdf.
46 Officer, L.H., 'Five ways to compute the relative value of a UK Pound amount, 1830 to present': www.measuringworth.com/ukcompare/
47 Else, D. 'The complete guide to: Africa overland', *Independent*, 8 October 2005: www.independent.co.uk/travel/africa/the-complete-guide-to-africa-overland-509994.html

48 Sutherland, L. *The Impossible Ride: The first bicycle ride across the Amazon jungle* (London: Southern Cross, 1982).
49 'A brief history of Goway': www.goway.com/glance/goway_hist.html
50 Officer, 'Five ways to compute the relative value of a UK Pound amount'.

Chapter 6

1 A number of typologies of working holidaymakers have been proposed, some of them specifically based on the New Zealand OE experience: Uriely, N. '"Travelling workers" and "working tourists"': Variations across the interaction between work and tourism, *International Journal of Tourism Research*, no. 3, 2001, 1–8; Myers, B., & Inkson, K. 'The Big OE: How it works and what it can do for New Zealand', *University of Auckland Business Review*, vol. 5, no. 1, 2003, 1–11; and Conradson, D., & Latham, A. 'Escalator London? A case study of New Zealand tertiary educated migrants in a global city', *Journal of Contemporary European Studies*, vol. 12, no. 2, 2005, 159–72.
2 Fidler, J. Kibbutz: 'What, why, when, where': www.jewishvirtuallibrary.org/jsource/Society_&_Culture/kibbutz2001.html
3 Civil Aviation Authority, 'Israel and Hungary specialist ceases trading': www.caa.co.uk/application.aspx?categoryid=2027&pagetype=2065&applcationid=2009&mode=detail&nid=2228
4 James, B. *Top Deck Daze: Adventures on the frog and toad* (Avalon Beach, NSW: Halbooks, 1999).
5 Scott, J. McK. *Christella's Odyssey* (Christchurch: Caxton, 1999).
6 Dorling, D., & Thomas, B. *People and Places: A 2001 census atlas of the UK* (Bristol: Policy Press, 2004).
7 The history of New Zealanders shearing overseas can be found in Riseborough, H. *Shear Hard Work: A history of New Zealand shearing* (Auckland: Auckland University Press, 2010).
8 'Extra curriculum vitae', *TNT Magazine,* 1201, 4 September 2006, 10.
9 Manhire, T. 'Travelling guinea pigs', *Sunday Star Times,* 22 December 2002, C4.
10 Chance, J. The Irish in London: An exploration of ethnic boundary maintenance. In P. Jackson (ed.), *Race and Racism: Essays in social geography* (London: Allen and Unwin, 1987).
11 White, P. 'The settlement patterns of developed world migrants in London', *Urban Studies*, vol. 35, no. 10, 1998, 1725–44.
12 'Born abroad: An immigration map of Britain. Economic: How different immigrant groups perform': www.news.bbc.co.uk/2001/shared/spl/hi/uk/2005/born_abroad/economics/html/overview.stm
13 Dobson, J., Koser, K., McLaughlan, G., & Salt, J. 'International migration and the United Kingdom: Recent patterns and trends', *RDS Occasional Paper No 75* (London: Home Office, 2001), 175–76.

Chapter 7

1 Sinclair, K. *A Destiny Apart: New Zealand's search for national identity* (Wellington: Unwin Paperbacks, 1986).
2 Sell, B. *The Big OE Companion: A guide for New Zealanders in the UK* (Auckland: Random House, 2004), 182.
3 Brabazon, T. *Tracking the Jack: A retracing of the Antipodes* (Sydney: University of New South Wales Press, 2000).
4 Thacker, B. *Rule No. 5: No sex on the bus (Confessions of a tour leader)* (Crows Nest, NSW: Allen and Unwin, 2001), 138.
5 Power, G. 'Far from an orphan', *New Zealand News UK,* 21 December 2005: www.newzealandnews.co.uk/story.cfm?NewsID=2109.
6 Gilkison, K. 'Life must go on', Timaru *Herald,* 20 August 2005, 25.
7 Davis, J. 'Kiwis in London not changing plans', Christchurch *Press,* 23 July 2005, A2.
8 'QPR pocket cash as rugby host', *Evening Standard,* 12 May 2004, 61.
9 These figures were based on research by the Institute for Public Policy Research and Sheffield University Social and Spatial Inequalities Research Group, and presented combined census data (from the 1991 and 2001 censuses) with data collected from quarterly Labour Force Surveys taken between 2000 and 2004; 'Born abroad: An immigration map of Britain. Countries of birth: New Zealand': www.news.bbc.co.uk/2001/shared/spl/hi/uk/2005/born_abroad/countries/html/new_zealand.stm; and 'Born abroad: An immigration map of Britain. Countries of birth: Australia': www.news.bbc.co.uk/2001/shared/spl/hi/uk/2005/born_abroad/countries/html/australia.stm
10 Estreich, J. 'Where we live', *TNT Magazine,* 1158, 7 November 2005, 12–17.
11 Ovenden, K. *O.E.* (Auckland: Benton Ross, 1986), 19.
12 Butler, H. *Fresh London*: UpOverDownUnder Film Festival, 2003.
13 1st Contact, *Kickstart London: The big OE guide 2003* (2nd ed.), 2003, 27: www.1stcontact.co.uk/nz
14 Morris, L. 'Dossers take the piss', *TNT Magazine,* 1086, 21 June 2004, 5.
15 Officer, L.H. 'Five ways to compute the relative value of a UK Pound amount, 1830 to present': www.measuringworth.com/ukcompare/
16 The Legacy organisation has assisted the families of Australia servicemen from World War I until the present day. **Unique to London Legacy, New Zealand widows are allowed eligibility in Europe:** www.legacy.com.au/Assets/1409/1/Legacy_in_Europe.pdf
17 'Prince of Teck': www.fancyapint.com/main_site/thepubs/pub1562.htm
18 In 2008 the Walkabout Chain had 50 pubs located all over the UK; in 2012 there were 36.
19 'Itchy London: Redback': www.itchylondon.co.uk/venues/2385.html
20 'London: Drinking': www.bugeurope.com/london/eatdrink.html
21 A brief history of The Church': www.thechurch.co.uk/beginning.htm

22 Moore, P. *The Wrong Way Home* (Sydney: Bantam, 1999).
23 'Greet the parents', *TNT Magazine*, 1181, 18 April 2006, 12–17.
24 Sell, *The Big OE Companion*, 168.
25 Walsh, R. 'Dancing the night away', *New Zealand News UK*, 11 February 2004, 4.
26 Hotton, M. 'Celebrating our day – our way', *New Zealand News UK*, 11 February 2004, 4.
27 Gower, P. 'Circle work', *TNT Magazine*, 1170, 30 January 2006, 12–15.
28 Hotton, M. 'Pub crawl confusion sorted', *New Zealand News UK*, 19 January 2005: www.newzealandnews.co.uk/register.cfm?ref=story&NewsID=2958
29 Rt Hon Jonathan Hunt ONZ, 'NZ High Commissioner's message for Waitangi Day', *TNT Magazine*, 2006: www.tntmagazine.com/uk/regulars/displayPage.asp?ID=letters
30 'Jonno', *New Zealand News UK*, 11 February 2004, 2.
31 Sell, *The Big OE Companion*, 168.
32 Ibid., 175.
33 www.londontouchrugby.com/index.htm
34 Manhire, T. 'Cupboard love', *Sunday Star Times*, 7 December 2003, 20–21.
35 Sell, *The Big OE Companion*, 173.
36 McGill, D. *The Dolly Lolly Diaries: Tales of a tame Kiwi lad transformed by tempting London lasses* (Wellington: Silver Owl Press, 1998).
37 Miles, S., & Bolot, P. *Down Under in Europe: A survival kit for Australians and New Zealanders in London and thereabouts* (London: Pan Books, 1973), 10.
38 Austin, M. *Dancing Naked: An exhibitionist revealed* (Auckland: Random House, 1998).
39 Brown, D. *Liars and Lovers: A travel memoir* (Auckland: Vintage, 2004).
40 Sarkies, D. *Stray Thoughts and Nose Bleeds* (Wellington: Victoria University Press, 1999).
41 Marriner, C. *Southern Style* (Auckland: Vintage, 2006).

Chapter 8

1 Myers, B., & Inkson, K. 'The Big OE: How it works and what it can do for New Zealand', *University of Auckland Business Review*, vol. 5, no. 1, 2003, 1–11.
2 Fursman, L. 'Living the good life? New Zealand expatriates, intentions to return, and the importance of lifestyle', Institute of Policy Studies Working Paper 10/06, (Wellington: Victoria University, 2010).
3 'Every one counts': www.keanewzealand.com/news/eoc-summary.html
4 Thorn, K. *Flight of the Kiwi: An exploration of motives and behaviours of self-initiated mobility* (Massey University, 2008).
5 Hartevelt, J. 'New Zealanders abroad', Christchurch *Press*, 24 December 2008, A6.
6 Thomson, J. 'Lure of foreign parts still strong', *Sunday Star Times*, 14 July 1996, 6.
7 Mulliner, T. *Long Ride for a Pie: From London to New Zealand on two wheels and an appetite* (Auckland: New Holland, 2006).
8 Brown, J. *UK on a G-string: A stranded Kiwi busks home* (Auckland: Random House, 2002).
9 Sell, B. *The Big OE Companion: A guide for New Zealanders in the UK* (Auckland: Random House, 2004), 230.
10 Gower, P. 'Settling in: New Zealand', *TNT Magazine*, 1201, 4 September 2006, 80.
11 Herrick, S. 'Expat Kiwi's culture shock', Christchurch *Press*, June 18 2005, D9.

Chapter 9

1 McDonald, G. 'Straying dolphin may be on its OE', *Dominion Post*, 31 January 2009.
2 Griffin, F., Scott, D., & Smyth, R. 'Living with a Student Loan: A profile of student loan debt and repayment, post-study income and going overseas' (Wellington, New Zealand: Ministry of Education, March 2005): www.educationcounts.govt.nz/__data/assets/pdf_file/0003/7446/debt-report.pdf
3 Smart, W. 'Do student loans drive people overseas – what is the evidence?' (Wellington, New Zealand: Ministry of Education, April 2006): www.educationcounts.edcentre.govt.nz/
4 'Class of 90 – where are they now?' Timaru *Herald*, 4 December 2000.
5 Trevett, C. 'Students on OE to start repaying loans earlier', *New Zealand Herald*, 4 April 2012, A6.
6 See, for example, Dekker, D. 'End of the Big OE?', Christchurch *Press*, 12 February 2002, 21–22.
7 Ovenden, K. *O.E.*, (Auckland: Benton Ross, 1986); Marriner, C. *Southern Style* (Auckland: Vintage, 2006); and Gannaway, S. *Seraphim Blues* (Auckland: Reed, 2003).
8 Croot, J. 'Successful Kombi Nation', Christchurch *Press*, 20 September 2003, E4.
9 Lamb, M. 'Rough diamond on the road', *Sunday Star Times*, 8 December 2002, A10.
10 Maher, S. 'Bed time', *TNT Magazine*, 1181, 18 April 2006, 17.
11 Crean, M. 'Academics top the bill in England', Christchurch *Press*, 6 June 2003, A5.
12 'Kiwi Mary Poppins up and away', *New Zealand Herald*, 2 December 2005.
13 www.spaceshipsrentals.co.nz/contact-information/spaceship-story/
14 See, for example: Sheeran, G. 'Driving force for a bright future', *Sunday Star Times*, 18 January 2009, 22; 'Innovation beats the importers', *New Zealand Herald*, 21 January 2005; 'The juice man',

New Zealand Herald, 2 February 2005: www.nzherald.co.nz/index.cfm?ObjectID=10112705

15 Mead, K. 'Cotton tales', Sunday Magazine, *Sunday Star Times*, 15 April 2012, 16.

16 'Control of Immigration: Statistics United Kingdom 2007': www.homeoffice.gov.uk/rds/pdfs08/hosb1008.pdf

17 Ibid.

18 'Control of Immigration: Statistics United Kingdom 2009': www.gov.uk/government/publications/control-of-immigration-statistics-united-kingdom-2009

19 www.trailfinders.com/media.nsf/aboutus?readform

20 Clifton, J. 'The 2010 guide to being a New Zealander: Choice, bro', *Listener*, 3–9 July 2010, 17.

21 Ibid., 16.

SELECT BIBLIOGRAPHY

Early travel accounts by New Zealanders

Allison, E.S. (1961). *Kiwi at Large*. London: Robert Hale.

Allison, E.S. (1969). *Kiwi Vagabond*. London: Travel Book Club.

Brewer, G.N.H.J. (1999). *The Soldier Tourist: A personal account of World War II*. Auckland: Reed Books.

Donnelly, I. (1935). *The Joyous Pilgrimage: A record of months that realised a dream*. Letchworth: Temple Press.

Graham, S. (1963). *The Tender Traveller: A New Zealander abroad*. Wellington: A.H. & A.W. Reed.

Hogan, H. (1997). *Hikurangi Ki Homburg: Henare Kohere and Terei Ngatai with the Maori Coronation Contingent 1902*. Christchurch: Clerestory Press.

Hogan, H. (2003). *Bravo, Neu Zeeland: Two Maori in Vienna 1859–1860*. Christchurch: Clerestory Press.

Mason, M.J. (1964). *The Water Flows Uphill: A Kiwi returns to Italy*. London: Allen & Unwin.

Mulgan, J. (1967). *Report on Experience*. Auckland: Blackwood and Janet Paul.

Quinn, W. (1920). *Through the Coral Seas to Java*. Invercargill: Southland Times Print.

Sumpter, H.K. (1934). *Travelling Light: To Europe and back on £200*. Invercargill: Southland Times Print.

Simpson, C. (1959). *Wake Up in Europe: A book of travel for Australians and New Zealanders*. Sydney: Angus & Robertson.

Travel novels

OE

Farrell, F. (2004). *Book Book*. Auckland: Random House.

Marriner, C. (2006). *Southern Style*. Auckland: Random House.

Gannaway, S. (2003) *Seraphim Blues*. Auckland: Reed.

Ovenden, K. (1986). *OE*. Auckland: Benton Ross.

Other

Garland, A. (1997). *The Beach*. London: Penguin.

Michener, J. (1971). *The Drifters*. New York: Random House.

Sarkies, D. (1999). *Stray Thoughts and Nose Bleeds*. Wellington: Victoria University Press.

Sutcliffe, W. (1998). *Are You Experienced?* London: Penguin.

Expatriate stories (and the search for national identity)

Bluck, J. (1999). *Waking Up in Strange Places: Where do New Zealanders belong?* Christchurch: Hazard Press.

Clark, M. (ed.). (1992). *Godwits Return*. Wellington: Bridget Williams Books.

Grayland, E. (1972). *More Famous New Zealanders*. Christchurch: Whitcombe and Tombs.

Harris, N. (1971). *The Fly Away People*. London: Baynard-Hillier.

King, M. (ed.). (1991). *Pakeha: The quest for identity in New Zealand*. Auckland: Penguin.

King, M. (1999). *Being Pakeha Now: Reflections and recollections of a white native*. Auckland: Penguin.

Morgan, J. (2008). *Speaking for Themselves: Ex-pats have their say*. Auckland: Cape Catley.

Patman, R.G. (ed.). (1997). *New Zealand and Britain: A special relationship in transition*. Palmerston North: Dunmore Press.

Shaw, T. (ed.). (1998). *A Passion for Travel: New Zealand writers and their adventures overseas*. Auckland: Tandem Press.

Sinclair, K. (1986). *A Destiny Apart: New Zealand's search for national identity*. Wellington: Unwin Paperbacks.

Sinclair K. (ed.). *Distance Looks Our Way: The effects of remoteness on New Zealand*. Auckland: Paul's Book Arcade, University of Auckland.

Travel histories

Anderson, J. (2010). *Only Two Seats Left*. Sydney: Great Gathering Company.

Gaffikin, P. (2002). *Kiwis on the Common: 50 years of the London New Zealand Cricket Club*. Brighton: Tasman Publications.

de Souza, F.H. (1998). *No. 3, Templeton Place*. London: Minerva Press.

de Souza, F.H. (2008). *Earls Court, The OVC and Me*. South Africa: Kiaat Creations.

James, B. (1999). *Top Deck Daze: Adventures on the frog and toad*. Avalon Beach, NSW: Halbooks Publishing.

James, B. (2010). *Top Deck Daze: Adventures on the frog and toad* (revised ed.). Lane Cove, Australia: Kokoda Press.

Rennie, N. (1990). *Conquering Isolation: The first 50 years of Air New Zealand*. Auckland: Heinemann Reed.

Tullet, J.S. (1968). *Nairn Bus to Bagdad*. Wellington: A.H. & A.W. Reed.

Wheeler, T. & Wheeler, M. (2005). *Once*

While Travelling: The Lonely Planet story. Melbourne: Penguin.

Hippie Trail

Alderson, F. (1971). *The New 'Grand Tour': Travelling today through Europe, Asia Minor, India and Nepal.* Newton Abbot: David & Charles.

MacLean, R. (2006). *Magic Bus: On the hippie trail from Istanbul to India.* London: Viking.

Marnham, P. (1971). *Road to Katmandu.* London: Macmillan.

Tomory, D. (1998). *A Season in Heaven: True tales from the road to Kathmandu.* Melbourne: Lonely Planet.

Armchair travel stories (by New Zealanders and some Australians)

Andrew, P. (1964). *Life with Louise.* Dunedin: Southern Cross Press.

Austin, M. (1998). *Dancing Naked: An exhibitionist revealed.* Auckland: Random House.

Brown, D. (2004). *Liars and Lovers: A travel memoir.* Auckland: Random House.

Brown, J. (2002). *UK on a G-string: A stranded Kiwi busks home.* Auckland: Random House.

Brown, J. (2009). *Bowling Through India: Five Kiwi blokes take on India at cricket.* Auckland: Random House.

Burgess, L. (2000). *Allons Enfants: A New Zealand family in France.* Dunedin: Longacre Press.

Calder, P. (2003). *Travels with my Mother.* Auckland: Tandem Press.

Cawley, N. (2005). *Divorced and Gone to Europe: A travel memoir.* Auckland: New Holland.

Dudson, M. (1995). *Oamaru to Europe: 'What do you want to go there for?'* Christchurch: Kitchen Table Top Publishing.

Farrell, F. (1993). OE. In M. Gifkins (ed.), *The Good Tourist and the Laughing Cadaver: Travel stories from Australian and New Zealand writers.* Auckland: Random House.

Geraghty, D. (2001). *A Snake in the Shrine: Journeys with Nobby through Middle Japan.* Dunedin: Otago University Press.

Gilkison, J. & Pether, R. (eds.) (2009). *Jandal Prints on the Globe: Capturing the overseas experience.* Whanganui: Stead & Daughters.

Harford, D. (1970). *4 Kiwis and a Falcon.* London: Robert Hale.

Hodge, I., & McGovern, P. (1999). *For Love and a Beetle: A tale of two journeys.* Sydney: New Holland.

Lay, G. (2007). *Inside the Cannibal Pot: Different ways to travel the world.* Auckland: New Holland.

McCarter, N. (2001). *The Big OE: Tales from New Zealand travellers.* Auckland: Tandem Press.

McGill, D. (1998). *The Dolly Lolly Diaries: Tales of a tame Kiwi lad transformed by tempting London lasses.* Wellington: Silver Owl Press.

Moore, P. (1999). *The Wrong Way Home.* Sydney: Bantam.

Mulliner, T. (2006). *Long Ride for a Pie: From London to New Zealand on two wheels and an appetite.* Auckland: New Holland.

Rowling, D. & Rowling, R. (2008). *Campervan Odyssey.* Wellington: D & R Rowling.

Scott, J. McK. (1999). *Christella's Odyssey.* Christchurch: Caxton Press.

Scott, T. (1978). *Overseizure: The saga of a New Zealand family abroad.* Christchurch: Whitcoulls.

Sutherland, L. (c. 1960). *I Follow the Wind.* London: Southern Cross Press.

Sutherland, L. (1982). *The Impossible Ride: The first bicycle ride across the Amazon jungle.* Waihola: Southern Cross Press.

Sutherland, R. (1960). *Land of the Bog-cotton.* London: Hodder and Stoughton.

Thacker, B. (2001). *Rule No. 5: No sex on the bus (Confessions of a tour leader).* Crows Nest, NSW: Allen and Unwin.

van Geldermalsen, M. (2006). *Married to a Bedouin.* London: Virago Press.

Woodward Swinburn, A. (1998). *The Scent of Rosewater: A New Zealand bride in Iran.* Christchurch: Shoal Bay Press.

Wright, T. (2003). *Turn Right at Istanbul: A walk on the Gallipoli Peninsula.* Crows Nest, NSW: Allen and Unwin.

OE poems, plays and films

Antony, R. (27 December 2004). Summer Camp USA [Television Documentary]. New Zealand: Cream TV, TV2.

Brough, J. (1996). *Permanent Wave* [Short Film]. New Zealand: New Zealand Film Commission.

Butler, H. (2003). Fresh [Short Film]. London: UpOverDownUnder Film Festival.

Butler, H. (2004). Stale [Short Film]. London: UpOverDownUnder Film Festival.

Christie, D. (26 July 2011). The Big OE. On *Hindsight* [Series 2, Episode 4]. New Zealand: TVNZ7.

Collins, I. (2010). *pOEms: Verse from an Overseas Experience.* Lincoln: Ian Collins.

Ewing, B. (1981, August 26–27: September 1–5). *Leaving Home* [Play]. London & Edinburgh: Te Wahapu Company

Flightmate Films. (1994). The Big O.E. On *Inside New Zealand* [Television Documentary]. New Zealand: TV3.

Hall, R. (2004, November). *Taking Off* [Play]. Wellington: Circa Theatre.

Hall, R., (2005, November). *Four Flat Whites in Italy* [Play], Wellington, Circa Theatre.

Johnstone, I. (2007). *Geriatric OE.* Replay Radio: Radio New Zealand.

Lahood, G. (2003). *Kombi Nation* [Movie]. Arkles Entertainment.

MF Films. (2000). *The Big OE* [Television Series]. New Zealand: TV 3.

Quigan, A., & Gumbley, R. (17 April 2002). *The Big OE* [Play]. Christchurch: Court Theatre.

Tait, M. (31 July–25 August 2003). *The Vegemite Tales* [Play]. Edinburgh Fringe: Itchy Feet Theatre Company.

Travel and OE guides

Gage, M. (1976). *The Overlander's Handbook: A guide for the overland adventurer to India and beyond.* Perth: Id Publications.

Havenhand, B. et al (1999). *Working in London and the UK, plus Ireland, the Netherlands and Malta: For Australians and New Zealanders.* Newcastle: Global Exchange.

Jenkins, D. (1973). *Student Guide to Asia*. Melbourne: Australia Union of Students on behalf of the International Student Travel Conference.
Lonely Planet (1977). *Europe: A traveller's survival kit*. Melbourne: Lonely Planet (originally published in Britain by Vacation-Work).
McCullum, S. (1996). *Live, Work and Play in London and the UK: For young New Zealanders* (2nd ed.). Auckland: Viking.
McCullum, S. (2000). *Live, Work and Play in London and the UK: For young New Zealanders* (Revised ed.). Auckland: Penguin.
McCullum, S. (2000). *Live, Work and Play Around the World*. Auckland: Penguin.
McLean, J. (2002). *Guide for the New Zealand Traveller in Britain*. London: Winter Productions.
Miles, S., & Bolot, P. (1973). *Down Under in Europe: A survival kit for Australians and New Zealanders in London and thereabouts*. London: Pan Books.
Miles, S., & Bolot, P. (1978). *Down Under in Europe: A survival kit for Australians and New Zealanders in London and thereabouts* (Revised ed.). London & Sydney: Pan Books.
New Zealand High Commission (1929). *New Zealand Handbook 1929: For New Zealand visitors to London*. London: Helen Ferguson.
O'Connor, M. (1989). *The New Zealand European Connection*. Wellington: Grantham House Publishing.
Odin, M., & Odin, L. (1979). *Europe: By camper van*. Sydney: Emma Books.
Rowe, C. (1991). *Europe by Campervan*. Garradunga: Garradunga Press.
Sell, B. (2004). *The Big OE Companion: A guide for New Zealanders in the UK*. Auckland: Random House.
Smith, P. (1975). *Overland Club Travel Handbook*. Wellington: Overland Club.
Southerden, L. (1997). *Japan: A working holiday guide for Australians and New Zealanders*. Newcastle, NSW: Global Exchange.
Wheeler, T. (1973). *Across ASIA on the Cheap*. Sydney: Lonely Planet.
Williamson, L. & Williamson, K. (2008). *Family OE: A really useful Kiwi guide to travelling overseas with your children*. Auckland: New Holland.
YHA. (1990). *The Big OE: A do-it-yourself world travel guide for Kiwis*. Christchurch: Youth Hostels Association of New Zealand.
YHA. (1997). *Big OE Guide: Essential reading for all New Zealanders travelling overseas*. Christchurch: Youth Hostels Association of New Zealand.

INDEX

Page numbers in **bold** refer to illustrations.